JOURNAL FOR THE STUDY OF THE NEW TESTAMENT SUPPLEMENT SERIES
2

Editors
Ernst Bammel
Anthony Hanson
David Hill
Max Wilcox

Editorial Secretary
Bruce D Chilton

Department of Biblical Studies
The University of Sheffield
Sheffield S10 2TN
England

STUDIA BIBLICA 1978

II. Papers on The Gospels

SIXTH INTERNATIONAL CONGRESS ON BIBLICAL STUDIES (6th : 1978 ; Oxford).

Oxford 3-7 April 1978

Edited by E. A. Livingstone

**Journal for the Study of the New Testament
Supplement Series, 2**

**Sheffield
1980**

Copyright © 1980 JSOT Press

ISSN 0143-5108
ISBN O 905774 22 1

Published by
JSOT Press
Department of Biblical Studies
The University of Sheffield
Sheffield S10 2TN
England

Artwork by University of Sheffield
Printing Unit
Printed in Great Britain by
Redwood Burn Limited Trowbridge and Esher

1980

Contents

Prefaces

EDITOR'S PREFACE

    The Sixth International Congress on Biblical Studies met in
Oxford from 3 to 7 April 1978, under the direction of the Rev. Dr
H.F.D. Sparks and the Rev. Dr G.B. Caird. After the invitations
to the Congress had been sent out, the publishers of the *Journal
for the Study of the Old Testament* kindly offered to issue the
proceedings, and these volumes contain the majority of the papers
which speakers were willing to have included. It is my pleasant
duty to thank those who spoke at the Congress, and especially
those whose papers were offered for publication, since it is upon
the speakers that the value of any such congress primarily
depends.

15 St. Giles,   E.A. Livingstone
Oxford

GENERAL EDITORS' PREFACE

    Studia Biblica 1978: II is the second of three volumes
devoted to the proceedings of the Sixth International Congress on
Biblical Studies held in the Examinations Schools of the University
of Oxford from April 3rd to 7th, 1978. The previous volume, on
Old Testament and related subjects, was published by JSOT Press
in June, 1979 as volume 11 in the Supplement Series of the *Journal
for the Study of the Old Testament*. The remaining papers, on Paul
and other New Testament authors, will be published as volume 3
in the Supplement Series of the *Journal for the Study of the New
Testament*. This collection of the three volumes of *Studia Biblica
1978* forms the sequel to *Studia Evangelica,* the successive volumes
of which have presented papers from previous Congresses, and have
been published by the Berlin Academy in their series *Texte und
Untersuchungen zur Geschichte der altchristlichen Literatur*. The
change of title from *Studia Evangelica to Studia Biblica* reflects
the broadened scope of the papers read.

At the 1978 Congress more than 470 participants from many countries gathered to hear and discuss the 170 lectures, papers and communications scheduled and skilfully organised by Miss Elizabeth Livingstone. The General Editors of the Supplement Series of the *Journal for the Study of the New Testament* are pleased to be able to make available to a wider audience, as well as to participants themselves, the greater part of the proceedings. One report of the Congress, in the *Catholic Biblical Quarterly* for July, 1978, commented: "Since the only disappointment of the Congress was that it was humanly impossible to hear all the major papers, not to mention the countless *deliciae* of the short reports, the published proceedings will be eagerly anticipated".

A word about the format of the published papers is in order. Readers of papers were asked to take the responsibility of preparing their papers according to the conventions of the *Journal of Theological Studies,* with the exception of the use of Arabic rather than Roman numerals for reference to Biblical chapters. In the case of those papers which were prepared according to some other system of conventions no endeavour has been made to enforce a rigid adherence to the *JTS* style. The General Editors are, however, deeply grateful to the Editors of the *Journal for the Study of the Old Testament,* David J.A. Clines, Philip R. Davies, and David M. Gunn, for their labour in preparing authors' type-scripts for reproduction in a format that is in each case internally consistent and intelligible. Any minor blemishes remain the authors responsibility.

Ernst Bammel
Anthony Hanson
David Hill
Max Wilcox

March 1980

Gehenna — According to J. Jeremias

W.J.P. Boyd,
Falmouth.

The *Theologisches Wörterbuch zum Neuen Testament*, edited by
G. Kittel, and now translated and edited in English by G.W. Bromiley,
has deservedly acquired a new and widespread influence in the
English speaking world, It is all the more important, therefore,
that the views expounded in it should be subjected to careful
critical scrutiny. That doyen of NT scholarship, Professor Joachim
Jeremias, in his eleven contributions to the first volume alone,
wrote two articles, one on ᾅδης (I. 146-9) and the other on γέεννα
(I, 657-8). It is a puzzling feature that they seem to have been
written independently of each other, and do not reflect the same
point of view.

On Gehenna, he begins by giving a useful account of the
linguistic, historical and geographical background to the name /1/,
and then, in paragraph 2 he expounds its eschatological significance:

'Fundamental for an understanding of the γέεννα passages in
the NT, which occur only in the Synoptists and John, is the sharp
distinction made by the NT between → ᾅδης and γέεννα. This
distinction is a. that Hades receives the ungodly only for the
intervening period between death and resurrection, whereas Gehenna
is their place of punishment in the last judgment; the judgment of
the former is thus provisional but the torment of the latter eternal
(Mk 9:43 and par.; 9:48). It is then b. that the souls of the
ungodly are outside the body in Hades, whereas in Gehenna both body
and soul, reunited at the resurrection, are destroyed by eternal
fire (Mk 9:43 and par., 45,47 and par., 48; Mt 10:28 and par.)'.

This paragraph is an example of theological synthesis, but
once one looks at the NT data, using precisely those tools of Gospel
analysis at which Jeremias has shown himself to be so adept, this
neat picture he has sketched, falls apart at the seams. It is my
contention that virtually every point made in his a. and b. is
wrong when applied to the Gospel dicta. Firstly we must note the
distribution of the terms *Gehenna* and *Hades* in the NT.

Gehenna occurs in the NT in seven logia, if we discount the
parallels: Matt. 5:22. He who calls another a fool will be in
   danger of the Gehenna of fire.
Matt. 5:29 advises us to cut out the offending eye lest the whole
   body be cast into Gehenna.
Matt. 5:30 repeats the advice for the offending right hand.
Matt. 18:8 'to be cast into eternal fire' = Mk. 9:43,45: the
   offending hand and foot are best cut off, rather than that
   the whole body should enter into Gehenna's unquenchable fire.
Matt. 10:28 = Lk. 12:5 (Q) 'fear him who is able to destroy the
   whole person in Gehenna'.
Matt. 23:15 is figurative, 'a son of Gehenna'; cf. Jn. 17:12, 'the
   son of perdition'. Matt. 23:33 speaks of 'the judgment of
   Gehenna'.
Jas. 3:6 claims that the fiery tongue of malice is lit by the
   flames of Gehenna.

Hades occurs nine times in the NT, if we discount a parallel:
Matt. 11:23 = Lk. 10:15 (Q); cf. Isa. 14:13,14: Capernaum will be
   demoted from Heaven to Hades. This is a striking figure of
   speech for a catastrophic fall like the original fall of
   Lucifer.
Matt. 16:18 is again figurative: 'the gates of Hades' will not
   prevail against Peter, the Rock.
Lk. 16:23 concerns Dives in Hades.
Ac. 2:27 = Ps. 16.10: 'Thou wilt not leave my soul in Hades'.
Ac. 2:31 comments on the quotation from the Psalm.
Rev. 1:18 Alpha and Omega has the keys of death and Hades.
Rev. 6:8 Hades rides hard after Death.
Rev. 20:13 Hades yields up its dead for judgment.
Rev. 20:14 Death and Hades are flung into the lake of fire.

Immediately we can see that it is very precarious to generalise
about a NT view on *Hades* and *Gehenna*, in that neither of these terms
is found in the Gospel of John, the Pauline epistles, the general
epistles of Peter and John and the epistle to the Hebrews; that is,
say, about half the NT. Further, Mark knows only *Gehenna* and never
mentions *Hades*. Matthew has most instances of Gehenna, whereas
Luke has only one instance, derived from Q (Lk. 12:25). Further
Matthew uses the term *Hades* solely in a metaphorical and figurative
way. Clearly, Jeremias has used the eschatological scheme found in
Revelation as normative for the NT. This is a major assumption,
however, and the data hardly support it. He sees the use of
ἐμβαλεῖν εἰς τὴν γέενναν in Matt. 10:28 = Lk. 12:5(Q) as reflecting
the same eschatological concept as found in Rev. 20:14: 'Then Death
and Hades were flung into the lake of fire'. Whilst this may be so,

yet the lake of fire is not identified with Gehenna and, indeed, the term does not occur in the whole of Johannine literature. The logia which prescribe the cutting off of an offending part of the body lest the whole body enter Gehenna clearly have not Hades in mind at all - that concept would be a complicating and confusing factor and considerably diminish the force of the evangelical advice!

Unfortunately, Jeremias's views are fraught with exceptional difficulties. These misgivings are particularly acute when we compare the 'sharp distinction made by the NT' between Hades and Gehenna with actual Gospel dicta. For in the parable of Dives and Lazarus every statement Jeremias makes about Hades is contradicted: in Lk. 16, Dives is tormented in Hades, not Gehenna (καὶ ἐν τῷ ἅδη...ὑπάρχων ἐν βασάνοις). Hades is no mere ante-room where discarnate spirits of the ungodly await reunion with their former bodies at the resurrection of the wicked for the final verdict of the Last Judgment. We note that Dives, by contrast, is very much in the body he has always had: for he can lift up his eyes and see Abraham afar off and Lazarus close by him (23) and he can bawl loudly enough for Abraham to hear him (φωνήσας, 24), and implore that Lazarus should cool his tongue (24), 'because I am in great pain in this flame'. We may well ask whether the mention of flames in Hades makes it equivalent with Gehenna. Did Jeremias think that Dives was in Gehenna? There is no suggestion of anything provisional about Dives' punishment; but, on the contrary, nobody, not even Father Abraham himself, can traverse the gulf between Paradise and Hades to help poor Dives. Hades is characterised quite bluntly as 'this place of torment' (28). Abraham's rebuff to Dives' request to warn his brothers makes it quite clear that there is no necessity for Dives' brothers to go to Hades, provided that they believe and obey Moses and the prophets (29); so Hades cannot be thought of as the inevitable place or destination for the dead. The eschatological scheme in Revelation concerning the relation between Hades and Gehenna does not fit the Gospel dicta. The Synoptics know of a resurrection of the just (Lk. 14:14; the parallels of Mk. 12:23 and Mt. 22:28, Lk. 20:36 imply the resurrection of the just). Only the Fourth Gospel speaks of a resurrection to judgment (Jn. 5:29) without mentioning either Hades or Gehenna. As far as the Gospels are concerned, it is precisely in Matthew and Luke where both Hades and Gehenna occur that the distinction between them is least obvious, for two of the references to Hades are concerned with punishment as the result of judgment already passed, and the figurative Q passage is unequivocally concerned with judgment on Capernaum. It is interesting that W.F. Albright and C.S. Mann are very hesitant about

the right way to translate Gehenna in Matthew: 'It is possible that
Gehenna (The Greek word here employed) was considered equivalent to
hell in NT times, but there is no evidence for this, and the
equation Gehenna = Hades is never made' /3/. Therefore they prefer
to translate Gehenna, not as referring to an eschatological destiny,
but simply as 'fiery death'. Though these scholars hesitate to
regard Gehenna and Hades as synonyms, yet the similarity between the
the two terms is far greater than their difference in the Gospels.

Gospel usage, then, suggests that Gehenna and Hades are
synonymous terms, for unless clear distinctions emerge in books
where both terms occur, then any alleged sharp distinctions between
them must always remain highly speculative and problematical.
Interestingly enough, in his article on *Hades*, Jeremias fully
allows for varying views held by NT writers, in a way that he does
not in his article on *Gehenna*. Were they written at different
times, or did he farm one of them out to a pupil to write for him?
One may ask, which article represents his later views?

NOTES

/1/   The Venerable C. Witton-Davies reports that the Valley of
Hinnom, or to give it its modern name, Wadi er rababi in south
Jerusalem, has been re-developed most attractively by the Israeli
government, and there is nothing in its present pleasant features
to suggest even remotely its former malign associations.
/2/   Note that the word *Gehenna* does not occur in the Johannine
writings. Was Jeremias working from W.F. Moulton and A.S. Geden's
Concordance to the Greek Testament (Edinburgh, 1926)? If so, he
may have misread Ja 3:6 as Jo 3:6; alternatively, the abbreviation
in German, *Js*, could have served for both John and James.
/3/   Cf. W.F. Albright and C.S. Mann, *Matthew, Introduction,
translation and notes,* Anchor Bible, New York, 1971, p. 61.

The Greek Manuscripts connected by their Lection Systems with the Palestinian Syriac Gospel Lectionaries

Dr. Y. Burns,
Longridge, Claremont Road,
Claygate, Surrey.

The distinguished scholar F.C. Burkitt, in a paper read at the Oriental Congress of 1899 in Rome, affirmed that the three Palestinian Syriac Gospel Lectionaries /1/ "agree in attesting some very curious readings of an ancient type... But", he continued, "the whole matter still awaits thorough investigation, and I fear the origin of the rarer readings will never be quite cleared up until we know more of the range of variation found in Byzantine Greek Lectionaries" /2/.

This opinion stemmed from the fact that the lections given in the Palestinian Syriac Gospel codices follow the general Byzantine order, unlike those in the earlier Syriac codices that Burkitt had studied /3/, and comparatively little attention had been paid to Greek lectionaries. This neglect continued, especially with respect to the range of variation found in them /4/, and it was because published works did not contain sufficient data concerning the differences between lectionary MSS that it became necessary for me to undertake the research myself, since my work on the Slavonic version required it.

My method of work in the field of Greek Gospel Lectionaries is able to shed light on many problems of this type. It consists of grouping manuscripts according to their rubrics and lection systems /5/, and then considering various hypotheses that would explain how the systems developed. Other scholars have concentrated largely upon the text /6/, but it is the purpose of this paper to describe certain characteristics of the lection system and the rubrics of the Palestinian Syriac Gospel lectionaries, and to distinguish the particular Greek manuscripts that exhibit similar characteristics. This provides manuscripts that have a greater chance of possessing linguistic affinities with the Syriac lectionaries than manuscripts chosen at random.

All information concerning the Greek manuscripts /7/ has been

obtained from first-hand study of the manuscripts themselves, or of
microfilms /8/, but that concerning the Syriac lectionaries could
be obtained only by studying Miniscalchi Erizzo's edition of the
Vatican manuscript /9/, and Lewis and Gibson's 1899 edition of the
Sinai manuscript /10/ with its critical apparatus utilizing the
Vatican manuscript and the second Sinai manuscript. These three
lectionaries were written in 1030, 1104 and 1118 A.D., and are
referred to as A, B and C, respectively, a notation chosen by
Mrs Lewis, the discoverer of B. In addition, Paul de Lagarde's
1892 edition of A /11/ has been consulted.

     Byzantine lectionaries, in general, consist of two annual
cycles, usually referred to as the Synaxarion and the Menologion,
which are based respectively upon the lunar and the solar
calendars. The Synaxarion commences with the lection for Easter
Sunday, whilst the Menologion gives lections for festivals month by
month, from September to the following August.

     In the Synaxarion, most Greek lectionaries contain a lection
for every day from Easter Sunday until Whit Monday. Of these, the
majority continue with lections for Saturdays and Sundays only
/12/, while about two-fifths of the total have lections for every
day except the weekdays of Lent /13/.

     Research on the Greek weekday lectionaries /14/ led me to the
conclusion that the differences between two of the three Byzantine
systems I had distinguished could best be explained on the
assumption that lectionaries had existed with only one week of
weekday lections after Pentecost, thereafter lections being given
for Saturdays and Sundays only. In order to obtain confirmation of
this hypothesis, I searched for such lectionaries amongst those
designated Saturday-Sunday lectionaries in the Aland list /15/.
To date I have found fifteen Greek lectionaries of this type, and
the same variations in the lection boundaries that exist in the
weekday lectionaries for the first week after Pentecost are also
to be found in these fifteen Greek lectionaries. However, it is of
special interest in the present context that the largest sub-group
contains a combination of pericopae which, although rarely
occurring together in the Greek weekday lectionaries, are the very
ones we find in the Palestinian Syriac lectionaries under
discussion.

     Here, then, is the first group of Greek lectionaries to which
we may turn as exhibiting one particular characteristic of these
Syriac lectionaries, namely lects 1608, 29, 77, 91, 767 and 90
/16/. Nevertheless, it does not seem likely that the archetype of

the Syriac lectionaries had been translated from a predecessor of
these Greek lectionaries, since a number of the lection boundary
variants from the Greek Byzantine system found in all three
Syriac MSS are not to be found in those of them that it has been
possible to study in some detail /17/. The particular types of
variants are, as we shall see, entirely consistent with the
archetypal Syriac lectionary having been compiled by means of
lection rubrics in a continuous text.

In the Byzantine lection system as found in the Greek
lectionaries there are a number of places in the gospels where a
verse or two, or part of a verse, are not read in any pericope,
and yet others where two lections overlap by part of a verse, or
more, presumably to make a satisfactory introduction and
conclusion.

Although some continuous text gospel codices, such as E /18/,
were carefully rubricated for church use, in others the required
ἀρχή or τέλος (indicating the beginning and the end of a lection)
were sometimes accidentally omitted. In fact, so common is it in
codices later than E to find τέλος omitted, when the next pericope
follows immediately without gap or overlap, that it may have
become the accepted practice in such cases. In other cases, the
absence of one or other of the rubrics would lead the reader to
make a mistake in the lection boundary: the absence of ἀρχή would
cause the lection to begin after the previous pericope had been
concluded, while the absence of τέλος would cause the lection to
end immediately before the commencement of the next pericope.

When such a characteristic is found in a lectionary, we may
conclude that its archetype had been obtained by a fresh
compilation from a continuous text by means of rubrics. If a
number of lectionaries contain the same boundary variants from the
standard, we may conclude that they form a sub-group which has a
common archetype. This common archetype would normally be a
lectionary that had been compiled in the manner described, but
certain kinds of variants within the group could imply that more
than one lectionary had been independently compiled from the same
rubricated codex /19/.

The three Palestinian Syriac lectionaries contain a number of
examples of lection boundary variants /20/ from the Greek
Byzantine system which fall into this category, but as in general
all three codices /21/ contain the same lection boundary variants
in the Easter cycle we must conclude that they have a common
archetype which was a Syriac lectionary compiled from a continuous

text containing lection rubrics. This is, of course, entirely
consistent with the fact that the earlier Palestinian Syriac
manuscripts extant are continuous texts containing lection rubrics.

Probably the most striking lection boundary variant found in
the three Syriac lectionaries is that of the pericope for Easter
Monday which ends with verse 34 instead of 28 /22/. The pericope
for Wednesday is, correctly, verses 35 to 52. When the Johannine
Bahnlesung /23/ was chosen for the weekdays between Easter and
Pentecost, the portion 29 to 34 was omitted because it was already
in use for the Commemoration of John the Baptist (given on
January 7th in these Syriac codices). This suggests that the
archetype may have been compiled from a continuous text which did
not have τέλος after verse 28, and did not contain the menological
rubric for John the Baptist, so that the scribe continued straight
on until he reached the pericope for Wednesday /24/.

Another significant lection boundary variant involves the
exhortation "He that hath ears to hear, let him hear!", which is
the explicit of a number of lections in the standard Greek
Byzantine lectionary. In some cases it is also part of the
continuous text, and in others it is not (except on rare occasions
under the influence of lection rubrics in the predecessors of the
codices concerned). Luke 8 normally contains this exhortation at
the end of verse 8 in continuous texts, but in Byzantine
lectionaries the pericope for the fourth Sunday of the New Year
does not normally contain it at this place, but after verse 15, as
the explicit. The Syriac lectionaries, however, end this lection
with verse 8 and this explicit. This could have happened under
the influence of a list of incipits and explicits, such as are to
be found at the beginning or the end of many continuous texts.
Although most give a word or two before the stereotyped explicit,
some do not give any, in which case the pericope would appear to
end wherever the exhortation happened to be written in the text,
namely in this case at the end of verse 8. Since the kind of
variants already considered suggest the compilation of a lectionary
from a rubricated continuous text, it would appear that the list
has been used to rubricate a continuous codex, rather than in the
production of the archetype itself. The omitted verses were
added to codex A by an early corrector, but the fact that all three
Syriac lectionaries originally had this variant confirms their
common origin.

Although some Greek lectionaries omit certain verses that are
included in others for the fourth /25/, fifteenth /26/, and
sixteenth /27/ Saturdays of Matthew and for the sixth /28/ Sunday

of Luke, all three Palestinian Syriac lectionaries give all the
verses. In origin these variants, even in the Greek codices, are
more likely to have arisen from the use of rubricated continuous
texts, but at least two are very early variants, since the eighth
century Greek lectionaries lect 563* /29/ and lect 627 contain
them, and therefore this particular characteristic does not give
us conclusive evidence, one way or the other, of the language in
which the archetypal lectionary was written. Nevertheless, it does
confirm the use of a rubricated text in its compilation.

We must conclude from the evidence of the lection boundary
variants that it is unlikely that the archetypal lectionary had
been obtained by translating a Greek lectionary, but, on the
contrary, it is consistent with this lectionary having been
compiled by means of lection rubrics in a continuous Syriac text.
Confirmation of this is given by the word *shelem* /30/ at the end
of many of the lections. This means, "It has come to an end", and
is the normal word to place at the end of a Syriac book. It
corresponds to the word τέλος which is not normally found in Greek
Byzantine lectionaries /31/, but which, as we have already seen,
is correct practice in a rubricated text. According to the Lewis
and Gibson edition, 75% of the Johannine lections have *shelem* at
the end in one or more of the codices, A having the greatest number
and C the least. This leads one to the supposition that the
compiler of the archetypal lectionary, under the influence of the
continuous text from which he was copying, considered it customary
to write *shelem* at the end of every lection, but this tended to be
omitted on occasions by subsequent copyists, perhaps because they
did not see it in Greek codices, or perhaps because it seemed
superfluous.

Let us now consider the introduction, the rubrics and the
colophon for the period from Easter to Pentecost.

In early times, before the Byzantine system had evolved /32/,
the fifty days of Pentecost represented a period of rejoicing,
during which there was neither fasting nor kneeling, the earliest
reference being the Acts of Paul, written about 180 A.D. After a
while greater emphasis came to be placed upon the fiftieth day, and
it began to take on the form of a separate festivel, which
eventually resulted in the Byzantine lectionaries containing a
lection for the morrow of Pentecost, that is to say, Whit Monday,
and, later, lections for the remaining days of the octave, such as
we find in the Palestinian Syriac lectionaries and some Slavonic
lectionaries, as well as the Greek manuscripts already mentioned.

It seems, therefore, that the numbering of the fifty days of Pentecost that I have discovered in some Greek lectionaries and rubricated codices was a relic of old usage, which we also find in all three Palestinian Syriac lectionaries.

If we study the introductory rubrics in the Syriac lectionaries, we find that all three mention that fifty lections follow, and further investigation shows that these lections are, in fact, numbered for every day except two /33/ in B and for every day except three /34/ in C, while A numbers only twelve /35/.

These numbers must not be confused with the Roman numerals used in the Lewis and Gibson edition to number the pericopae found in the lectionaries, since the latter were provided by the editors to facilitate reference, and were not intended to translate the rubrics.

An important Greek manuscript with this feature of numbering the Johannine pericopae is one already mentioned, the eighth century Saturday-Sunday lectionary lect 563*, which has other archaic features. It also contains Arabic translations added above some of the Greek rubrics. A second is lect 514* /36/, of the ninth century, an example of a proto-αβ weekday lectionary /37/ and another is lect 519 /38/, an α lectionary of the twelfth centruy /39/.

In addition to these three examples, similar rubrics have been found in Acts (which was also read during the fifty days of Pentecost), in the fourth century codex Vaticanus (O3) /40/, written, of course, by a later hand, as well as in the cursive continuous text 461, written in 835 A.D., and 230, a Ferrar MS written in 1013 A.D., while another, 788, uses the same form of words in one rubric /41/.

In the Syriac lectionaries a colophon is to be found at the end of the fifty days, that is to say, after the Sunday of Pentecost, to the effect that this is the end of the gospel of John (written) in Greek at Ephesus. This puzzled Mrs Lewis /42/, who was given what she described as an ingenious explanation by Dr Rendel Harris, namely, "that the section *de adultera*, John 7:53 to 8:11, was at one time appended to St. John's Gospel after the final colophon, and that in the Greek or Syriac MS. from which the lessons of the Palestinian Lectionary were taken, the section was removed to the place (between chap. 7 and chap. 8) which it now usually occupies; but that this being done by scribes who were not highly endowed with intelligence, the colophon was transported with it".

   Such a complicated explanation is, however, not required,
because such colophons are in fact not unknown in Greek
lectionaries. They have arisen because each of the four gospels
has become associated with a particular period of the year, which
has in consequence taken on the name of that gospel. These four
periods of the year are from Easter to Pentecost, when the lections
are taken from John's gospel, from Pentecost to the New Year at the
Autumn equinox, when the lections are taken from Matthew's gospel,
from the New Year to Lent, when the lections are from Luke, and
finally Lent, when the lections are taken from Mark. Thus the
tenth century Greek uncial lect 47 /43/ and all three Palestinian
Syriac lectionaries state after the lection for Pentecost that the
end of the gospel of John has been reached, and similarly for
Matthew before the start of the New Year, and so on.

   As is natural in a lectionary emphasising the fifty days of
Pentecost, the archetype clearly wrote the rubric for John after
the fiftieth day, the Sunday. In the Greek field, however, so
closely did this period of the year become associated with the
gospel of John, that when a lection was written down for the morrow
of Pentecost the colophon was placed after it, in spite of the
fact that the additional lection was actually taken from Matthew.
An example of such a lectionary is lect 16 /44/ but it is of
particular interest to us that one of the Greek lectionaries
containing the same full week of lections as the Syriac, lect 77,
actually places this colophon at the end of the weekdays, in spite
of the fact that all the five preceding lections are from Matthew.
This shows that the week was thought of as the octave of Pentecost,
and thus the extension of the Pentecostal period, which was
considered the Johannine period. We therefore have examples of
the three stages in the use of a colophon stating the end of the
gospel of John, firstly lect 47 and the Palestinian Syriac writing
it after Sunday, where it undoubtedly was originally written, then
lect 16, which put it after Monday, and finally lect 77, which put
it after the extra weekday lections. We therefore find that the
Syriac codices exhibit an earlier form.

   Continuing to the end of the Matthean period, we find that the
Matthean colophon in A adds that the Matthean period consists of
sixteen Saturdays and Sundays. This represents an early state of
affairs still preserved in some Greek lectionaries /45/, including
lect 47. On the other hand, B and C have a lection for the
seventeenth Saturday, and the pericope given is the usual one. In
A this particular pericope is given, under the title "For Holy
Christian Women", as the first of three written at the end of the
codex. Some Greek manuscripts also have it in a similar position,

while it is to be found in a pre-Byzantine Greek lectionary lect
846 of the seventh or eighth century /46/, preserved on Mount
Sinai, showing that originally this pericope was used as part of
a Commune Sanctorum; but the menologion, as it began to take on its
present form, gradually took over the function of the Commune
Sanctorum, writing each pericope for a particular day, and
referring to that day on all future occasions. Some lectionaries
still added useful pericopae at the end, but the need for this
dwindled as the menologion increased in size.

The final pericope in A, under the heading "For the eleventh
Sunday" /47/, is the pericope Matt. 15:21-28, which is known as the
"the Canaanitess" /48/. It is not given at all in B and C. In
later Greek lectionaries it is given as the seventeenth Sunday of
Matthew, and is read at the end of the Lucan period if the date of
the following Easter necessitates an extra Sunday at that time. It
was obviously a later addition to the Byzantine lectionary, and
once again the Syriac lectionaries show earlier forms. If extra
lections were required it would be natural to use those written as
extra lections at the end of the codex.

Another relic of early use is the pericope, Luke 19:29-48,
written in B and C after the Resurrection lections used at morning
service, and before the beginning of the menologion. It is an
extra lection for Palm Sunday, which is found in only a very few
Greek lectionaries /49/. In spite of its rarity in the extant
codices, it must have been in use at the time and in the place
where the earliest weekday lection system, the proto-$\alpha\beta$ system, was
compiled, since this pericope was not utilised in the $\alpha\beta$ Lucan
Bahnlesung. It is also found for this day in the lists of lections
in the MSS of the Ferrar Group.

If we consider the lections for Holy Week, we find that no
two of the three Palestinian Syriac lectionaries have precisely
the same combination of pericopae for Tuesday. Since the earlier
forms of the Greek Saturday-Sunday lectionary (e.g. eighth century
lect 563*) did not contain lections for the first part of the Holy
Week, and wrote the Gospels of the Passion at the end, instead of
in their proper place, it seems probable that the Palestinian
Syriac archetypal lectionary did not contain as many lections for
this week as we see in the extant codices. When extra lections
were added during copying they must have been added in different
ways to different copies, just as occurred when the Greek
lectionaries first had the additional lections incorporated in
them.

A similar phenomenon may be observed in the menologion.

Mrs Lewis considered that "the lessons in all three codices follow the same order till the end of lesson CLII. After that the divergence is considerable" /50/. However, the apparent divergence after lesson CLIII in her numbering, where the menologion begins, largely disappears when the Carshuni /51/ rubrics are read and the complete picture of the menologia of the three manuscripts becomes clear. There is a basic core of days for which lections are given in all three manuscripts, either by means of reference to the synaxarion, or to another day in the menologion when it is possible, or, if the pericope has been given nowhere else, by writing the lesson in full. For the majority of these days the pericope concerned is the same in each codex. From this we can deduce a possible archetype of the menologion. The similarity between the rubrics in all three codices in these cases is too great to think it likely that they did not come form a common archetype.

There are, however, references in A for days not mentioned in B and C, and references in B, although fewer, for days not mentioned in A, and some for which the references are different from those in A. There are also some in C that are not in B. This picture is entirely consistent with a common archetype that has been copied and recopied at various times, new references being added whenever the copyist desired to include a day not mentioned in his exemplar.

Considering in detail the lections that are given in full in the menologia of the three codices, the differences in order and content are minimal. They are as follows:

1.   The pericope Luke 10:16-21 is given for 18th October in A, but for 6th September in B and C. However, A refers 6th September to 18th October, while B and C refer 18th October to 6th September, so that the final results are the same.

2.   The pericope Matt. 11:27-30 is placed at the end of the volume in A, and in B and C it is written for 18th September. In A, the reader is referred on that day to 25th September, which in turn is referred to 17th Sunday of Matthew, a day which is not explicitly given in A.

The scribe of a common ancestor of B and C must have decided to write the pericope in full for 18th September (perhaps not finding a pericope for 17th Sunday of Matthew), instead of referring to another day, and used the pericope he found at the end of a predecessor of A.

3. The lections given in A for 21st September, 3rd October,
8th October, 26th October and 29th July /52/, are not given
here in B and C, nor are they given in any other part of the
codices. This indicates that the scribe of A (or a predecessor
of A) added these to the system he found in his exemplar.
Confirmation of this is given for 29th July by the fact it is
written after 6th August, instead of in its correct place.
This may also indicate that the exemplar had no more lections
in the menologion after 6th August, the subsequent entries
in the extant codices being later additions to the system.
Some early Greek lectionaries do in fact end the menologion
with 6th August.

The addition of new lections at various times during the
copying and re-copying of lectionaries is a well-known phenomenon,
and has been accepted in the case of Greek lectionaries as the
reason why the nature of the text of a lectionary differs in its
various parts /53/. It is to be expected, therefore, that the
Palestinian Syriac lectionaries should exhibit a similar
difference.

Eberhard Nestle /54/ and, more recently, Bruce M. Metzger /55/
have made comparisons of a number of verses that occur in duplicate
(or triplicate) passages in the Palestinian Syriac Lectionary, and
have discovered that textual variation does exist.

In each of the examples quoted, one passage is to be found in
the synaxarion (exluding Holy Week), and would be expected to have
existed in the archetype, while the other passage is either in the
menologion or in Holy Week, the very parts of the lectionary where
lections from another source might be expected. In the case of
triplicate passages, the two from the synaxarion contain the same
text, as opposed to that in Holy Week.

Nestle's example is to be found in John 17:7. Although C
gives the plural meaning of the Greek ἔγνων consistently on both
days for which it is written, A and B use the singular form of
the verb in the lection read on the Sunday before Pentecost.

In the first place, as mentioned above, it is not impossible
that the First Gospel of the Passion, in which this verse is to
be found, was obtained from a different source. It has been in
use from time immemorial, before the first lectionaries had been
written, and it would have been customary to read it from a
continuous text, expecially since it is a very long pericope. In
the second place, it may be significant that the difference between

the two forms in Syriac consists only in the omission of one stroke,
which could arise from a misreading in an old MS. Finally, the
fact that Greek continuous texts give three other variants at this
place makes it possible that one form could have been changed to
another during copying, under the influence of Greek codices which
did not give the ambiguous ἔγνων.

Bruce M. Metzger has pointed out /56/ that the Palestinian
Syriac version exhibits many Graecisms, even transliterating such
words as ὄχλος, "crowd", by *oklos* instead of the customary *kensa*,
and mechanically re-translating the Greek translations of Semitic
words retained in the Greek text, producing pleonasms. There is
every reason to suppose that the copyists continued to depend on
Greek manuscripts, since the additions to the lection system of
the archetype follow the lead set by the developing Greek
lectionaries. It is therefore not surprising that variants exist
in the added lections since variants exist in similar circumstances
in the Greek lectionaries.

The final piece of evidence /57/ that indicates conclusively
that the archetype of the Palestinian Syriac lectionaries was not
obtained by translating a Greek lectionary, but by using a
rubricated continuous text, is the fact that the stereotyped
incipits are followed by the passage as it would appear in a
continuous text, without the omission of those words for which the
Greek lectionaries have substituted the incipit. Greek continuous
texts exist in which the day followed by the incipit is given in
the margin, without the extra words which would indicate the change
to be made in the text. There seems to be no reason to doubt that
such a continuous text in Palestinian Syriac must have been used to
compile the archetype of the lectionaries, since it is known that
the MSS of this version from the earlier epoch were, in fact,
continuous texts /58/. If the compiler of the lectionary had been
translating a Greek lectionary he would not have had those
particular superfluous words in front of him.

This brief survey has linked the Palestinian Syriac gospel
lectionaries with five groups of Greek MSS, namely, those containing
the same extra week from Matthew /59/, those that number the days of
Pentecost /60/, those with particular colophons /61/, those with a
Lucan lection for Palm Sunday /62/, those with sixteen Saturdays
and Sundays in Matthew /63/, as well as a lectionary differing in
type from the usual Byzantine lectionary /64/. It is interesting
that some manuscripts appear in more than one category, while
detailed investigation reveals yet more characteristics in common
/65/.

It is clear that a thorough investigation of these manuscripts
would shed more light, not only upon the origin of the Syriac
lectionaries, but also upon the transmission of the Greek text.
We should expect the results to be interesting since the Greek MSS
concerned include Codex Vaticanus, the earliest Saturday-Sunday
lectionary, the earliest proto-αβ weekday lectionary and the
Ferrar Group.

The validity of this kind of selection of manuscripts is
confirmed by the fact that it has distinguished Codex Vaticanus
(03), which, according to Adler has the nearest text to that
represented by the Palestinian Syriac lectionaries; as well as the
Ferrar Group which Lake, Blake and New have shown joins them as
witnesses to the Caesarean Text /66/. Since these methods and the
arguments presented in this paper indicate a continuous Syriac
text (which must itself depend upon a continuous Greek text) as
the source of the Palestinian Syriac lectionaries, an investigation
of the other continuous gospel, 461, may prove fruitful.

The present investigation has certainly confirmed Mrs. Lewis's
opinion that "it is a matter of regret that [the Syriac] has not
been rendered into Greek" /67/, since the Latin translation of
Miniscalchi Erizzo proves at times misleading. The manuscripts
that have been distinguished would make a good foundation for
such a rendering, and there is certainly a need to have a new
edition incorporating all the rubrics in the correct places,
together with the Greek forms from which they were translated.

NOTES

/1/ For a survey of publications and research concerning these
MSS, see Bruce M. Metzger's essay, A Comparison of the Palestinian
Syriac Lectionary and the Greek Gospel Lectionary, in
Neotestamentica et Semitica: Studies in Honour of Matthew Black,
ed. E. Earle Ellis and Max Wilcox, Edinburgh, 1969.
/2/ F.C. Burkitt, Christian Palestinian Literature, Journal of
Tehological Studies, II, Oxford, 1901, p. 181.
/3/ F.C. Burkitt, The Early Syriac Lectionary System, Proceedings
of the British Academy, X, London, 1921-3.
/4/ In 1932 work began in Chicago to determine what E.C. Colwell
called "The Lectionary Text" (see Harvard Theological Review, 25,
1932, pp. 73-84) and continued for more than thirty years. It was
not the purpose of that work to consider those lectionaries that
had an unusual text, although some were mentioned in passing in
the series Studies in the Lectionary Text of the Greek New
Testament, Chicago, 1937-66. However, Merrill M. Parvis carried

out some unpublished research on the relationships between MSS, and
K.W.Rutz wrote an unpublished doctoral thesis which succeeded in
showing that all lectionaries were not identical, a copy of which
I saw after my own doctoral thesis had been completed.
/5/ Yvonne Burns, A Comparative Study of the Weekday Lection
Systems found in some Greek and Early Slavonic Gospel Lectionaries,
Doctoral thesis, University of London, 1975. This will be
published, with some additional material, under the title, The
Byzantine Weekday Lectionaries, New Testament Tools and Studies,
Leiden.
/6/ See Bruce M. Metzger, op. cit.
/7/ Except lect 767. See Jacob Geerlings, Family E and its allies
in Mark, Studies and Documents, XXXI, Salt Lake City, 1968, pp.
70-87.
/8/ Thanks to the magnificent microfilm collection of the
Institute for New Testament Textual Research in Münster, Westphalia.
The writer wishes to acknowledge her indebtedness to the Director,
Professor Kurt Aland, and to his staff, for the facilities extended
to her.
/9/ Comes Franciscus Miniscalchi Erizzo, Evangeliarium
Hierosolymanum ex codice Vaticano Palaestino, Verona, 1861.
/10/ A.S. Lewis and M.D. Gibson, The Palestinian Syriac Lectionary
of the Gospels, London, 1899.
/11/ Paul de Lagarde, Bibliotheca Syriaca, Göttingen, 1892.
/12/ These are known as Saturday-Sunday lectionaries, abbreviated
to lesk.
/13/ These are known as weekday lectionaries, abbreviated to le.
/14/ Yvonne Burns, op. cit., pp.27-46.
/15/ Kurt Aland, Kurzgefasste Liste der Griechischen Handschriften
des Neuen Testaments, Berlin, 1963.
/16/   lect 1608, XI century, Istanbul, Serai, 114
        "   29, XII century, Oxford, Bodleian Library, Auct. D.
                                                    infr. 2.15
        "   77, XII century, Paris, Bibliothèque Nationale, Gr.
                                                    296
        "   91, XIV century, Paris, Bibliothèque Nationale, Gr.
                                                    318
        "   767, XIV century, Alexandria, Patriarchate, 73
        "   90, 1533 A.D., Paris, Bibliothèque Nationale, Gr. 317
/17/ It would be a different matter if another example of this type
of Greek lectionary were to be discovered to contain these
particular boundary variants.
/18/ E (07), VIII century, Basel, University Library, AN III 12.
/19/ Yvonne Burns, op. cit., sect. 02-03 (Thesis, pp.15-20).
/20/ The system of numbering the verses in the three editions of
the Syriac lectionaries is that of the Vulgate, which in some
places differs from the Greek system, so that some apparent lection
boundary variants are not, in fact, differences in content.

An example of a lection ending immediately before the
commencement of the next is that for 5th Saturday of Matthew (Matt.
9:9-17, instead of the usual Matt. 9:9-13, the 6th Saturday
commencing with verse 18). On the other hand the lection for 13
John (Friday of 2nd week) is properly John 5:30b-47, 6:1,2, but
that for 32 John begins immediately afterwards, instead at verse 5.
/21/ Occasionally A has corrected the lection boundary to the
Byzantine norm.
/22/ The pericopae for Easter Sunday and Monday are normally John
1:1-17 and John 1:18 respectively.
/23/ I.e., pericopae read in the order in which they are to be
found in a continuous text codex.
/24/ The pericope for Tuesday is taken from Luke.
/25/ Matt 8:14-23 (omits 19-22).
/26/ Matt 24:1b-13 (omits 10-12).
/27/ Matt 24:37-44 (omits 38-41).
/28/ Luke 8:27-39 (omits 36-37).
/29/ An asterisk after the number of a Greek lectionary denotes
that the lectionary contains chapter numbers. See Yvonne Burns,
Chapter Numbers in Greek and Slavonic gospel codices, New Testament
Studies, XXIII (3), Cambridge, 1977.
/30/ My grateful thanks are due to Professor J.B. Segal for his
very generous help in checking the accuracy of the Latin
translations of some of the Carshuni rubrics given by Miniscalchi
Erizzo, and for the translation and pronunciation of this word.
/31/ I have seen it in a Slavonic lectionary, however (Library of
the Romanian Academy of Sciences and Political Sciences, MS Sl.
176, 1503 A.D.), which appears to have been compiled from a
rubricated Slavonic continuous text of the period in a similar
manner to that suggested in this paper.
/32/ Yvonne Burns, The Numbering of the Johannine Saturdays and
Sundays in early Greek and Slavonic Gospel Lectionaries,
Paleobulgarica, I (2), Sofia, 1977, pp.46-47.
/33/ 8th and 49th.
/34/ 8th, 24th and 49th.
/35/ 9th, 10th, 25th, 32nd and 47th, in addition to the first week.
/36/ lect 514* IX century, Messina University Library, 96.
/37/ Yvonne Burns, op. cit. (Thesis), sect. 4. This is the
earliest type of weekday lectionary.
/38/ lect 519, XII century, Messina University Library, 96.
/39/ Yvonne Burns, op. cit. (Thesis), sect. 4.
/40/ Greek gospel B (03), IV century, Rome, Vatican Library, Gr.
1209.

/41/ 461, 835 A.D. Leningrad, Gosudarstvennaja Publitschnaja
Biblioteka im. M.E. Saltykova Schtschedrina, Gr. 219.
     230, 1013 A.D., Escorial, y.III.5.
     788, XI century, Athens National Library, 74.
/42/ A.S. Lewis and M.D. Gibson, op. cit., p. xv.
/43/ lect 47, X century, Moscow, Historical Museum, V.11, s.42.
/44/ lect 16, XII century, Paris, Bibliothèque Nationale, Gr. 297.
/45/ Yvonne Burns, op. cit.(Thesis), pp.227, 233.
/46/ lect 846, VII/VIII century, Sinai, St. Catherine's Monastery,
MS. 212.
/47/ According to Miniscalchi Erizzo. If this title is not a
mistake, it raises interesting questions.
/48/ Yvonne Burns, 'The Canaanitess' and other additional lections
in early Slavonic lectionaries, Revue des études sud-est européennes,
XIII, Bucharest, 1975.
/49/ lect 767, XIV century, Alexandria, Patriarchate, 73.
lect 547*, XIII century, Rome, Vatican Library, Gr. 1217 (the
Ferrar Saturday-Sunday Lectionary). See Jacob Geerlings, Studies
and Documents, XVIII, Salt Lake City, 1959, p.34.
/50/ A.S. Lewis and M.D. Gibson, op. cit., p.xiv.
/51/ Arabic written in Syriac letters。
/52/ Luke 11:29-33, Matt. 13:44-54, John 8:1-11, Matt. 8:23-27,
Matt. 17:10-22.
/53/ See Ernest Cadman Colwell and Donald W. Riddle, Prolegomena to
the study of the Lectionary Text of the Gospels, Studies in the
Lectionary Text of the Greek New Testament, vol 1, Chicago, 1933.
/54/ A.S. Lewis and M.D. Gibson, op. cit., p. xvi.
/55/ Bruce M. Metzger, op. cit., pp.217-220.
/56/ Op. cit., p.213. See also Friedrich Schwally, Idioticon des
christlich palästinischen Aramäisch, Giessen, 1893; Die
griechischen und lateinischen Lehnwörter, pp.103-113; Anton Schall,
Studien über Fremdwörter in Syrischen, Darmstadt, 1960; S.P. Brock,
Greek Words in the Syriac Gospels (Vet and Pe), Muséon 80, 1967,
pp.389-426.
/57/ See Bruce M. Metzger, op. cit., p. 216.
/58/ F.C. Burkitt, op. cit. (Christian Palestinian Literature), p.
180.
/59/ lects 1608, 29, 77, 91, 767, 90.
/60/ lects 563*, 514*, 519, B (03), 461, 230, 788.
/61/ lects 47, 16, 77.
/62/ Luke 19:29-48; lect 767, lect 547* (the Ferrar Saturday-Sunday
Lectionary), lect 1627, lect 574*, lists of 124,346,543,788,826,983.
/63/ lects 640, 47, 704, 455, 373, 337, 939, 941, 464, 638, 854,
876, 1074, 930, etc.

/64/ lect 846.
/65/ Several have Arabic translations beside some of the rubrics.
Like the Palestinian Syriac and the earlier Syriac lectionaries,
e230 and lects 547*, 574* call the Sunday after Easter "New
Sunday".   The menologia of the lectionaries studied exhibit
certain features in common.
/66/ Novi Testamenti versiones Syriacae Simplex, Philoxeniana et
Hierosolymitana, J.G.C. Adler, Hafniae, 1789.
Kirsopp Lake, Robert P. Blake, Silva New, The Caesarean Text of
the Gospel of Mark, Harvard Theological Review, XXI,4, October
1928, p.320.
/67/ Op. cit., p.x.

"Not to Taste Death": A Jewish, Christian and Gnostic Usage

Bruce D. Chilton,
Department of Biblical Studies
University of Sheffield.

James Robinson and Helmut Koester have introduced the term "trajectory" into the vocabulary of New Testament exegetes, and have thereby offered a paradigm for understanding early Christianity /1/. The great strength of their model is that it would place the New Testament in the context of both its literary origins and its impact upon subsequent literature. The principal weakness is that the trajectory paradigm may lead the investigator to posit a development from one document to another without first establishing a literary connection between the two. Such empirical grounding is essential if trajectories are to be taken seriously as historical explanations /2/. The use of some form of the construction "not to taste death" in Jewish, Christian and Gnostic circles is sufficiently prevalent to merit attention, and the phrase is so striking as to suggest, *ab initio,* that there is a relationship between the three spheres of usage. In this brief discussion, I will consider the development in the application of this construction by way of testing the trajectory paradigm.

From the first century, Jewish usage understands "those who do not taste death" as immortal figures. In IV Ezra 6:26 "the men who were taken up, who have not tasted death since their birth" make their appearance, and the apparent reference is to those like Enoch and Elijah /3/. The pseudo-Jonathan Targum has Moses swear by witnesses who do not taste death at Deuteronomy 32:1, where the Masoretic Text refers to heaven and earth /4/. Aloysius Ambrozic has taken Norman Perrin to task for asserting on the basis of this evidence that the construction is a "stock phrase from apocalyptic" /5/. It is true that Perrin's characterization was exaggerated, and yet our sources use the phrase as if it would be understood as a matter of course, and this does suggest that the usage was established by the time of writing.

Rabbinic diction, evidenced in documents representing Amoraic

discussion, takes a systematic turn. R. Ḥama b. Ḥanina, in
Genesis Rabbah 9.5, explained why Adam, who should not have tasted
death, in fact did so: "Because the Holy One, blessed is He,
foresaw that Nebuchadnezzar and Hiram would declare themselves
gods". In R. Ḥanina's name, R. Berekiah compared Adam to Elijah,
who did not taste death (cf. IV Ezra 6:26), but of course he
recognized that Adam in fact died (*Genesis Rabbah* 21.5) /6/.
Adam's death becomes prototypical, because, as R. Simeon b. Halafta
put it, "all experience the taste of death" (*Leviticus Rabbah* 18.1
/7/; cf. *Qohelet Rabbah* 12.5 /8/ in the name of R. Simeon b.
Lakish). Nonetheless, he goes on to say, "every righteous man has
an eternity of his own". Theologically, an important distinction
is expressed here between not tasting death, a quasi-angelic trait
/9/, and tasting death, which is endemically human even if it is
not the last word on the fate of the righteous.

At first sight, it might appear that the only two uses of the
construction in the New Testament (Mark 9:1; John 8:52) altogether
part company with Jewish diction in that they promise immortality
to disciples rather than refer to deathless, quasi-angelic figures.
But closer inspection shows that this is not the case. Jesus'
assertion that there are some standing who will not taste death
until they see the kingdom in power may be compared to Moses' oath
by witnesses who will not taste death /10/. There are two possible
objections to such a reading of Mark 9:1, but they dissolve on
analysis. First, the placement of the logion contexts it in a
discussion of discipleship, so that it is natural to take "the
ones standing" as referring to Jesus's followers. In fact, of
course, this placement is Markan, as the redactional introduction
(καὶ ἔλεγεν αυτοῖς) clearly shows (cf. 2:27 especially), and in any
case the wording of the logion suggests that those who are standing
(τινες ὧδε τῶν ἐστηκότων) are distinct from those who are addressed
(αμὴν λέγω ὑμῖν). Second, the use of "until" might be taken to
indicate that the group referred to will die after seeing the
kingdom. But this seems to be an unduly literalistic reading of the
Semitic לא-עד (= οὐ μὴ-ἕως) idiom: after all, when God promises
Jacob in Genesis 28:15, "I will not leave you until I have done all
that I have promised", it is not a pledge to depart at a certain
time, but an undertaking to act in the way indicated /11/. By
analogy, Jesus at Mark 9:1 is promising the kingdom in power; those
who do not taste death, like Moses and Elijah in the Transfiguration
scene which follows, are sureties of the promise, and their eventual
death is not in view /12/. This is to say that Jesus stands in line
with Jewish diction, and that Mark applies the saying to disciples.
Why should Mark have done this? Presumably, by his time the phrase
was used in this connection, as it appears in John 8:52, where Jesus

is quoted as saying, "If anyone keeps my word he will never taste death". It must be stressed, however, that this is not actually presented as a dominical logion in John, but as a parody of Jesus' position in the mouths of his opponents /13/. In 8:51, Jesus asserts that his follower will not see death (cf. 5:24; 11:26), and this is caricatured into the absurd claim that such a follower will not taste death, i.e. that he will be like Enoch and Elijah. But any writer or community which failed to discern that John 8:52 is an expression of offense might well use such language as if it authentically represented Jesus' position about his disciples. Such a misunderstanding lies behind the present placement of Mark 9:1.

The development of the "trajectory" is so far quite clear. The Jewish and dominical usage is substantively the same, and refers to special, immortal figures. But in a Hellenistic compass, the construction is used to articulate Jesus' assertion, at first expressed in different words, that his disciple(s) would not in some sense die. At this point already, the "trajectory" has changed lanes (if I may stretch the metaphor) in a surprising way: the meaning of the usage has altered. This is due more to a switch in the language of communication, it would seem, than to any unfolding of the proper meaning of the phrase we are considering.

By the time the Gospel according to Thomas came to be written, this at first inadvertent change was pressed to its logical extreme /14/. "Whoever finds the interpretation of these words will not taste death" /15/ - the opening logion of the "Secret Sayings" puts into Jesus' mouth the outrageous assertion which in John is a parody of his promise, and 11.18,19 also apply the construction to the gnostic's quest. Such usage might be said merely to make explicit what Mark presupposed, but in Thomas the claim is made in the full knowledge of its Jewish background /16/. Saying 85 parallels the Jewish theology expressed in *Genesis Rabbah* 9.5:

"Adam existed from great power and great wealth, and he was not worthy of you. For if he had been worthy, he would not have tasted death".

It is therefore apparent that "not to taste death" is applied in Thomas to promise the gnostic a different sort of existence from Adam's. There is no question here of an inadvertently scandalous claim: Jewish diction is being used against itself to present the words of Jesus in as stark a manner as possible.

We are now in a position to evaluate the trajectory paradigm

in respect of the present investigation. It seems to me that
the model is deficient in three ways, and my reservations accord
with those voiced by reviewers of the Robinson-Koester volume.
Writing in *The Journal of Theological Studies*, Robert Wilson
observed:

> "It is, however, questionable whether 'trajectories' is the
> *mot juste*. The projectile on a trajectory, be it a rocket or a
> golf ball, is a self-contained unit which does not add to its
> load in flight" /17/.

In the present case, it is apparent that (quantitatively) the
weight of the payload changed, and that (qualitatively) the
direction of flight altered. What began as a Jewish oath
theologoumenon was taken by Christians to promise immortality to
disciples, and their gnostic colleagues self-consciously
incorporated the new meaning into their anti-Jewish *Tendenz*.
Indeed, this line of development is so erratic that one might
wonder with F.H. Agnew whether the "recognizable continuity"
which Koester and Robinson posit is "real or only paradigmatic"
/18/, and the dictional similarity between Jewish, Christian and
Gnostic sources in their "not taste death" usage makes their
conceptual divergence all the more striking. Nonetheless, I would
readily admit that the trajectory approach stimulates necessary
historical inquiry into the causes of such dictional similarity,
and this is an important contribution of the hypothesis. Lastly,
one is bound to note that the development of this particular
usage was largely a matter of first removing the locution from
its native Jewish milieu and then using it as a weapon against
Judaism. Does a ping-pong ball have a trajectory? If not, the
paradigm does not suit the present purpose because it would tend
to obfuscate the role of conditional historical factors in the
development of the usage. As Norman Perrin put it:

> "Another question I would want to raise for discussion is
> that of whether this plotting of trajectories does justice to the
> concrete historical circumstances which surround and indeed call
> for the creation of a given work" /19/.

In practice, and without refinement, the trajectory model may
straightjacket the exegete as much as the orthodoxy-heresy
polarity which it is in part designed to replace /20/.

NOTES

/1/   J.M. Robinson and H. Koester, *Trajectories through Early Christianity* (Philadelphia, 1971).
/2/   See Norman Perrin's review, *Interpretation* 26 (1972) 212-215 (quoted below).
/3/   See the Charles (G.H. Box) and Kautzsch (H. Gunkel) editions *ad loc*.
/4/   The antiquity of the locution is also suggested by the possibility that the more fully developed Targumic expression, "not to taste the cup of death" (Neophyti at Deuteronomy 32:1) is reflected in the Gospels (Mark 10:38-39 par.; 14:24 parr.; 14:36 parr.). See R. Le Déaut, "Goûter le calice de la mort", *Biblica* 43 (1962) 83-86.
/5/   A.M. Ambrozic, *The Hidden Kingdom: A Redaction Critical Study of the References to the Kingdom of God in Mark's Gospel (C.B.Q.* Monograph Series, 1972) 209; cf. N. Perrin, *Rediscovering the Teaching of Jesus* (New York, 1967) 201.
/6/   H. Freedman, *Midrash Rabbah* (Genesis) (London, 1939).
/7/   J. Israelstrom and J.J. Slotki, *Midrash Rabbah* (Leviticus) (London, 1939).
/8/   A. Cohen, *Midrash Rabbah* (Ecclesiasticus) (London, 1939).
/9/   As cited by Adolf Schlatter (*Der Evangelist Matthäus* [Calwer, 1957] 524), *Midrash Tanḥuma* actually refers to "ministering angels who do not taste death". Alongside this systematic diction, the Rabbis could apply the usage in an untheological way, e.g., "Let him who would experience a taste of death put on shoes and sleep in them" (Yoma 78b, cited from L. Jung, *The Babylonian Talmud: Seder Moʿed* (Yoma) (London, 1938).
/10/ Detailed discussion will be found in my 1976 Cambridge Ph.D. thesis, *God in Strength: Jesus' announcement of the Kingdom*, now published in the monograph series of *Studien zum Neuen Testament und seiner Umwelt* (Vienna, 1979). A simplified version of the chapter on Mark 9:1 appears in *Themelios*, 3 (1978) 78-85.
/11/ This is not to deny that such constructions occur in passages which do carry a temporal emphasis (e.g., Matthew 10:23; Mark 13:30 parr.; Luke 2:26; John 13:38 parr.), or which admit of a temporal aspect which they do not emphasize (e.g., Matthew 5:26 par.; 23:39 par.; Mark 13:19 par.; 14:25 parr.; Acts 23:12,14,21). In John 8:52, on the other hand, the form οὐ μὴ...εἰς τὸν αἰῶνα clearly does not mean that he who keeps Jesus' word will die "in the age"; the whole force of the statement is that he does not die and never will (cf. Matthew 5:18; John 4:14; 10:28; 11:26; 13:8; I Corinthians 8:13). According to Barnabas Lindars's analysis (*The Gospel of John* [London, 1972] 332-333), John 8:52 is actually a version of Mark 9:1, and the replacement of the ἕως phrase with

the εἰς phrase is part of "John's regular practice of making
eternal life the equivalent of the kingdom of God in the tradition"
(and he cites 3:3,5,15). On this reconstruction John understood
the Synoptic logion as referring to those who endure until the
kingdom and beyond, not to people who die after the kingdom.
/12/ See "The Transfiguration: Dominical Assurance and Apostolic
Vision", forthcoming in *New Testament Studies*.
/13/ As Rudolf Schnackenburg observes (*Das Johannesevangelium* II
[Freiburg-Basel-Wien, 1971] 296 note 1), this is an obstacle to
the view that the passage is dependent on Mark 9:1 parr. (replying
to the analysis of H. Leroy). Schnackenburg's incisive reading
of the passage, which is so sensitive at the levels of redaction
and of tradition, should be quoted in full:

"Sie nehmen - wie stets in joh. Missverständnissen (vgl. 3,4;
4,11.33; 6,52; 7,35 usw.) - die Worte Jesu in einen buchstäblichen,
ausserlichen Sinn, als spräche er von einem unvergänglichen
irdischen Leben. Der Gedanke, ein Mensch konne vom Tod verschont
bleiben, lag nicht gänzlich ausserhalb des jüdischen Denkens
(Entrückung des Henoch und des Elias)".

Schnackenburg's reading is supported by the observation that there
are "a great number of Old Testament and Jewish themes in the
gospel particularly at the points where puzzling statements are
made and misunderstanding results" (Robert Kysar, *The Fourth
Evangelist and His Gospel: An examination of contemporary scholarship* [Minneapolis, 1975] 151). For possible OT allusions in 8:51:
52, see Günther Reim, *Studien zum alttestamentlichen Hintergrund
des Johannesevangeliums: S.N.T.S.* Monograph Series [Cambridge,
1974] 98, 142, 194, 201).

At a less specialist level, B.F. Westcott precisely caught the
change in meaning between v. 51 and v. 52:

"The inaccuracy of quotation is significant. The believer,
even as Christ (Heb. II.9), does 'taste of death' though he does
not 'see' it in the full sense of v. 51" (*The Gospel according to
Saint John* [London, 1958] 139).

John Marsh's reading is along the same lines, if a bit
anachronistic in its reference to "soul" and "body" (*The Gospel
of St. John* [Harmondsworth, 1968] 369). On the other hand,
Lagrange saw here merely "une nuance légèrement plus accusée"
(*Évangile selon Saint Jean* [Paris 1948] 252), and Bultmann
condemned Odeberg's argument that a change of meaning takes place
between v. 51 and v. 52 as "oversubtle" (tr. G.R. Beasley-Murray,
The Gospel of John [Oxford 1971] 325 note 2). Among recent
commentators, this point of view is represented by Leon Morris

(*The Gospel according to John:* New International Commentary [Grand
Rapids, 1971] 469 note 104). I hope already to have shown that
the Jewish understanding of the phrase can not be excluded from
view when its meaning for John is under consideration.
/14/ One can take this document, as part of the Nag Hammadi find,
as representative of Gnostic diction without thereby implying
that it is Gnostic in provenience. That it is gnostic, without
necessarily being dualistic, is evident from *l. 1.* I have used
the Coptic text of A. Guillaumont *et al., The Gospel according to
Thomas* (Leiden, 1976).
/15/ Following Wolfgang Schrage (*Das Verhältnis des Thomas-
Evangeliums zur synoptischen Tradition und zu den koptischen
Evangelien, B.Z.N.W.* [Berlin, 1964] 28f.), Jacques-É. Ménard
observes that Thomas may be dependent on the "Western" text in
omitting εἰς τὸν αἰῶνα (*L'Evangile selon Thomas:* Nag Hammadi
Studies [Leiden, 1975] 77). But, remembering Lindars's analysis
(see note 11), one is attracted to Ménard's speculation that "il
pourrait représenter un stade antérieur du texte johannique, car
εἰς τὸν αἰῶνα semble secondaire..." (*ibid*). If this was the case,
then Thomas better represents the sort of diction which influenced
the Markan placement of 9:1 than does John, which is in turn
partially dependent on Mark:

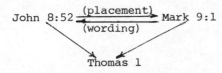

          Thomas 1

        / (placement)
Mark 9:1 ⟶ John 8:52
         (wording)

Alternatively, Schrage (28, followed again by Ménard 77) points
out that Thomas might have been influenced by Mark 9:1 in the
omission of εἰς τὸν αἰῶνα, in which case we would have:

                    (placement)
    John 8:52 ⟶ Mark 9:1
                    (wording)

               ↘   ↙
               Thomas 1

In short, the evidence of Thomas does not permit us to settle the
source cirtical question, and we must recall that Lindars'
analysis of εἰς τὸν αἰῶνα is not conclusive (cf. note 13).
Further, Thomas *ll. 1,* 18, 19 use "not to taste death" as an
unqualified locution and it might have been that an εἰς or ἕως
phrase was dropped lest the emphatic addition be taken as a
temporal limitation.
/16/ The anti-Jewish tendency of Thomas is manifest in *ll.* 6, 14

(cf. 27), 43 (cf. 39, 102), 52, 53, 71, 72. For other forms of
immortality diction see *11*. 11, 46. This is not to deny that
there is Semitic tradition in Thomas (see Ménard 9-13), and even
traces of rabbinic influence (see below).
/17/   *J.T.S.* 23 (1972) 476.
/18/   *C.B.Q.* 34 (1972) 534; see also Robinson-Koester 14.
/19/   Page 214 (work cited in note 2).
/20/   Robinson-Koester 270f.

The Messianic Secret and the Enemies of Jesus

John Coutts,
Bridge Cottage, Pangbourne, Berks,
RG8 7DN England.

In *The Teaching of Jesus* T.W. Manson maintains that "... a careful study of the Synoptic record reveals: that there is not one uniform strain of teaching delivered to all and sundry alike, but that there are three distinct and readily distinguishable streams. Jesus has one way of dealing with the Scribes and Pharisees, another for the multitudes and yet another for his intimate disciples. This fact stands out clearly in Mark. That it is obscured in Matthew and, in a lesser degree, in Luke is due to the manner of composition of these two Gospels".

When we, with Manson's words in mind, turn back to read once more William Wrede's *Das Messiasgeheimnis in den Evangelien*, we realise that he has much to say of the Secret in relation to the teaching of the disciples and the crowd, and is able to point to characteristics which give a unity to each kind of material, but that he does not give the same degree of attention to the encounter of Jesus with his enemies, though he refers at some point to all of the relevant passages. In this paper I shall try to make a preliminary examination of this material.

Let us begin with Mark's account of the trial before the High Priest. This is shown as the supreme encounter between the representatives of the old Israel, with the High Priest at their head, and the one who is Messiah and Son of God, deserted by his followers, and therefore in himself the new Israel. The rejection of the old Israel has been foreshadowed by the judgement of Mark 7:6, "In vain they worship me", and it will be made absolute by the rending of the veil of the Temple, 15:38.

As Mark describes it, the trial has five stages:
(a) Many witnesses bear false witness against Jesus, but their witness does not agree, 14:56.
(b) Certain men witness falsely that he said, "I will destroy this Temple made with hands and in three days I will build another not

made with hands". Their witness does not agree, 14:57-59.
(c)   The High Priest questions Jesus concerning the witness given
against him. Jesus does not reply, 14:60-61.
(d)   The High Priest puts to Jesus a direct question, "Art thou
the Christ, the Son of the Blessed One?" Jesus answers, "I am and
you shall see the Son of man seated at the right hand of the Power,
and coming with the clouds of heaven", 14:61b-62.
(e)   The High Priest rends his robes and says, "Why do we need
further witnesses? You have heard the blasphemy". The Sanhedrin
decides that he is guilty of a capital crime, 14:63-64.

        The question of the High Priest contains two titles which
Jesus unhesitatingly accepts, *Christ* and *Son of the Blessed One*;
that is, Messiah and Son of God. It is unnecessary to cite here
the passages which show that these titles have supreme significance
in this Gospel, especially if we accept the longer reading in its
first verse. Further the reply of Jesus contains the prediction
that his hearers will see the Son of man coming with the clouds of
heaven, and the effect of this for the author is to define the
term Son of man, which may hitherto in the Gospel have contained
an element of enigma, as Messiah and Son of God.

        Whatever may have been the facts of Jewish law at this time,
there is no doubt that Mark represents Jesus as having been
condemned for blasphemy, and that it was the claim of Jesus to be
Messiah and Son of God which he sees as the substance of the
alleged blasphemy.

        Two questions arise. The first is, Why does Mark suppose that
Jesus breaks his silence and gives a direct answer to the High
Priest's question? Surely the answer must be that Mark sees this
question as the one which Jesus must answer. Peter in the court,
when directly questioned, denies his master, but Jesus must
witness a good confession. His followers will be called upon to
acknowledge him before the tribunals of men, 13:9. It is
unthinkable that Jesus should not acknowledge himself.

        The second, and, for our purposes, perhaps the more important,
question is this. How did Mark suppose that the High Priest
obtained the knowledge which enabled him to ask the question which
Jesus could not avoid answering? There are several possible
answers to this. One might be that Mark cared for none of these
things. But one plausible answer is that Mark thought the High
Priest had this knowledge because there was nothing new about the
claim of Jesus to be Messiah and Son of God. It could not, of
course, have been made in the explicit form which is implied by

Jesus' answer. There would then have been no need for the High
Priest to put the question. Nor, it seems, can Mark think of it
as advanced in a form readily intelligible to the crowds or to
the disciples. It would therefore have been made in an indirect
and parabolic way which the religious leaders, because of their
training, could at once penetrate, but which would give no grounds
for a capital charge. I should like to suggest that it should be
a leading principle of exegesis in relation to the Messianic
Secret in Mark that Jesus clearly and unambiguously reveals it
to his enemies, and that they completely understand his claim.
In other words, no secret, but only the mystery of rejection.

In Mark, the first meeting of Jesus with his enemies comes
at the beginning of the second chapter. It is, I think, probable
that Mark regards this meeting as the result of a kind of
challenge issued by Jesus at the end of the first chapter, 1:44.
εἰς μαρτύριον αὐτοῖς /1/ will then have the meaning 'testimony
against' or 'sign condemning'. This is certainly the meaning at
6:11, and probably at 13:9. Whether this be so or not, Jesus and
his enemies first meet in the incident of the Healing of the
Paralytic, 2:1-12. In this pericope Jesus pronounces forgiveness
of sins, cures grave sickness, shows supernatural insight into
the reasoning of his enemies, and claims that the healing
demonstrates the authority of the Son of man to forgive sins. The
The enemies of Jesus, here described as 'certain of the scribes',
assert that to claim to forgive sins is to claim what belongs to
God alone, and that this claim amounts to blasphemy. It is of
very great significance that here, at the beginning of the
Ministry, and at Jesus' first meeting with his enemies, Mark
represents them as formulating the charge on which, according to
his account, Jesus is later condemned, and that the claim which
gives rise to this charge is not a matter of deliberate statement
but an inference from his actions and words.

We may surmise that Mark is laying down the principles on
which all the subsequent meetings of Jesus with his enemies are
to be interpreted. Hence in the series of stories of which this
is the first, 2:1-3:6, Jesus prophesies the day when he, the
bridegroom, shall be taken away, and, in order to show what
manner of 'taking away' is being thought of, Mark records, at
3:6, that the Pharisees take counsel with the Herodians 'to see
how they could make away with him' (NEB). Jesus is shown, as
Son of man, to be Lord of the Sabbath. The passing of the Old
Israel is foreshadowed in the similes of the old and new cloth,
and the old and new wine. And perhaps we are to see Jesus as
the one to whom is granted greater licence in holy things than

was granted to David, and hence as Messiah of David's line,
2:25-26.

It is important that the sayings concerning the bridegroom,
the new and old cloth and wine, the parallel with David, and the
Lordship of the Sabbath all require interpretation, though the
word 'parable' is not used.

Of equal importance is the section 11:27-12:12. After the
Cleansing of the Temple the enemies of Jesus ask him by what
authority he acts, and this question is followed by the parable of
the Wicked Husbandmen. Those who question Jesus and hear the
parable are described as 'the chief priests and the elders and
the scribes'. This exact description of the enemies of Jesus is
used by Mark elsewhere only at 14:53, where it describes the
tribunal which condemns him for blasphemy. The whole scene takes
place in the Temple.

Consider first the section 11:27-33. The enemies ask him,
'By what authority doest thou these things, and who gave thee
this authority?' Jesus replies with a counter-question, 'The
baptism of John, was it from heaven or from men?' The enemies
reason that if they say 'from heaven', Jesus will answer, 'Why,
then, did you not believe him?' But they did not dare to answer,
'From men', for fear of the people: 'for they all held John to be
a prophet'. Jesus does not say, 'Why did ye not obey him?', but,
'Why did ye not believe him?' The implication is that there was
some declaration made by John conveying a plain message which the
enemies did not believe. Not to believe that message to be true
is to deny that John was a prophet. There is in Mark only one
such declaration: 'The stronger one comes after me, whose shoe's
latchet I am not worthy to stoop down and unloose. He shall
baptise you with Holy Spirit'. The baptism of John was 'unto
remission of sins', but without Holy Spirit, Mark 1:7-8.

John's prophecy is seen to be fulfilled, and the identity of
the 'stronger One' is established when Jesus comes for baptism,
1:9-11. (Mark underlines the fact that, whereas the others who had
come to be baptised were 'all Judaea and all the people of
Jerusalem', 1:5, Jesus comes from "Nazareth in Galilee', 1:9).
When Jesus emerges from the water, the heavens open, the Spirit
descends, and the heavenly voice declares, 'Thou art my beloved
Son. In thee I am well pleased'. It is a matter of dispute
whether the signs that accompany Jesus' baptism are thought of
by Mark as public to John and to a presupposed crowd, or as a
private experience of Jesus. But certainly the phrase φωνὴ ἐγένετο

suggests that the designation of Jesus as the beloved Son is
thought of as public (Cf. Wrede, *loc.cit.*, p. 72).

We may therefore conclude that at 11:31 what the enemies of
Jesus knew of, but did not believe was: (a) John's prophecy that
he would be succeeded by the stronger one who would make remission
of sins effective through baptism in Holy Spirit, and (b) that
this stronger one was Jesus of Nazareth, designated as the beloved
Son. This makes it all the more significant that Jesus' first
encounter with his enemies should turn on the authority of the
Son of man to forgive sins, demonstrated by miracle, 2:1-12.

Now let us turn to the parable which follows, 12:1-12. Jesus
tells how a man prepared and planted a vineyard. The terms of
the description recall the Song of the Vineyard in Isaiah 5:1-7.
The key to the parable, therefore, is given at the beginning to
those who have the necessary knowledge of the Scriptures. The
vineyard is let out to husbandmen who kill or maltreat the
owner's servants when they come to claim the fruit of the vineyard.
At the last the owner sends his beloved Son, in the hope that they
will reverence him. But they kill him and cast him out of the
vineyard. The owner of the vineyard will come and destroy the
husbandmen and hand over the vineyard to others. Then Jesus
directly addresses his hearers, 'Did you not read this scripture?:
The stone which the builders rejected has become the head of the
corner. This is the Lord's doing, and it is marvellous in our
eyes', 12:10-11.

There is no doubt that the meaning of the Parable will have
been transparent to Mark's readers. The vineyard is the house of
Israel; the husbandmen are the leaders of the nation, past and
present; the servants are the prophets; the beloved Son is Jesus;
the leaders kill Jesus; God gives the vineyard to the new Israel;
the beloved Son is raised from the dead and exalted (see Acts
4:11). How much of this does Mark suppose that the enemies
understood at the time? His appended comment is, 'And they sought
to seize him and they feared the people; for they knew that he
spoke this parable against them'. Therefore, their knowledge
must include the knowledge that Jesus is claiming to be the
beloved Son sent by Jehovah; that he is prophesying that they, the
leaders of Israel, will kill him; that the result will be their
supersession and his vindication by the direct act of Jehovah.

Thus the section 11:27-12:12 presupposes that everything that
is revealed to the disciples in the prophecies of the Passion and
Resurrection, 8:31, 9:31, 10;33-34, and in the story of the

Transfiguration, 9:7, but is not understood by them, has also
been revealed to the enemies, been understood by them, and
rejected.

The fact that the enemies understand the Parable of the
Vineyard leads us to consider Mark's use of the word 'parable'.
It is used by him on only five separate occasions; once it is
used of words addressed to the four disciples, Peter, Andrew,
James and John, 13:28; twice it is used of words addressed to the
crowds, or to the disciples enquiring about what has been
addressed to the crowds, 4:1-34, 7:17; twice it is used of words
addressed to the enemies, 3:23, 12:12. The earliest use in the
Gospel is not of words to the crowds or to the disciples, but of
words addressed to the enemies, and, as at 12:12, there is no
suggestion that what is said as parable is not understood, and
every reason to suppose that Mark intends his hearers to assume
that it was understood. Thus we may formulate the principle
governing Mark's use of Parable as it relates to the audiences to
whom Jesus is speaking. The crowds do not understand and are not
meant to understand. The disciples do not understand but are
meant to understand. The enemies understand and are meant to
understand but reject what is revealed.

Now let us consider in more detail the encounter of Jesus
with his enemies which Mark describes at 3:22-30. Here Jesus'
enemies are described as 'the scribes who had come down from
Jerusalem'. They pronounce judgement on his exorcisms. These
are possible because he is possessed by Beelzebub, the prince of
devils, and it is in his power that he acts. Jesus summons them
and speaks to them in parables. His words in fact fall into three
sections. First there is the crucial question which is not itself
a parable, 'How can Satan cast out Satan?' There follow two
parables which expand the question. The compound parable of the
House and Kingdom Divided asserts that the judgement of the
enemies involves an absurdity, and the meaning of it is included
within the poetic structure of the saying: ' and if Satan has
risen up against himself and is divided, he cannot stand but has
an end'. The second parable is the Binding and Plundering of the
Strong Man.

The character of the exorcisms of Jesus has already been made
known to the readers of Mark. At 1:34 the demons are silenced
because 'they knew him'. At 1:24 he has been recognized as 'the
Holy One of God'. At 3:11 they fall down and cry out, 'Thou art
the Son of God'. It may well be that Mark thinks that the enemies
of Jesus shared this knowledge. But in any case, within the section

itself it is assumed that the exorcisms are evidence of a degree
of supernatural power that his enemies can explain only as either
by the power of the supreme demon or by the Holy Spirit.   (Mark
makes no distinction between Beelzebub, the prince of demons, and
Satan.)   They therefore assert that Jesus exorcises by the power
of Beelzebub and because he is possessed.   It would be contrary to
Mark's tenor to suppose that he regards the scribes as making a
judicial choice between alternatives, each possible on the evidence.
What we have here is pure hostility in attitude and perversity in
judgement.   The parable of the Divided House and Kingdom is
intended to demonstrate the absurdity of the assertion of Jesus'
enemies.   The parable of the binding of the strong man asserts
that Jesus exercises the power of God to bind Satan.   In the
context of the judgement which they have pronounced it is clear
that the enemies of Jesus understand his claims and reject them.
This rejection is perverse, for in some sense they know the truth
and are seeking to suppress it.

The perversity is underlined by the sayings concerning the
blasphemy against the Holy Spirit which is the sin which has no
forgiveness, for this is the climax of the section.   This saying
has given rise to much troubled discussion among Christians, but
to Mark the meaning is plain.   The scribes from Jerusalem represent
the religious leaders of Jerusalem.   Because they attribute Jesus'
exorcisms to Satanic possession, they are guilty of the eternal sin
and will not ever be forgiven.   The remission of sins which John
the Baptist foreshadowed, 1:7, which the Paralytic experienced, 2:5,
and which is implicit in the call of sinners, 2:17, will never be
theirs.   The charge of blasphemy which they level at Jesus, 2:7,
recoils on them in a more terrible form, 3:28.

Up to this point we have reviewed Mark's account of the Trial
before the Sanhedrin, and approximately two thirds of the material
from the first twelve chapters of the Gospel which deals with the
encounter of Jesus with his enemies.   The remaining one third is,
for the most part, neutral.   On the one hand, there is no
suggestion of secrecy; on the other, there is no material which
contains or implies a Christological claim, and therefore nothing
which suggests that the enemies have knowledge of such a claim.
This seems true of 7:1-13, Clean and Unclean; 10:1-9, the Question
of Divorce; 12:13-17, Paying Tribute to Caesar; 12:18-27, The
Question of the Resurrection.   There are, however, two important
passages which fit well into Mark's general view as we have
sketched it, but which may be thought to contain ambiguities or
obscurities.

The first of these is 8:11-12. The Pharisees ask Jesus for
a sign from heaven, tempting him. Jesus replies, 'Why does this
generation seek a sign? Verily I say to you, a sign shall not be
given to this generation'. This passage has sometimes been cited
as part of the 'secrecy material', under some such heading as,
'Jesus refuses the sign which would reveal to his hearers what he
knows himself to be'. This is to misunderstand how the word
'sign' is being used. σημεῖον in the LXX is the normal
translation of the hebrew אות. A sign in this sense implies a
claim or prediction already explicitly made, or a task assigned.
The hearers or observers already know the content of what is said.
The sign is what assures them of the truth of the claim or
prediction, or the help needed for the task. So, at Exodus 4:1-9
Moses argues with Yahweh that the Israelites will not believe him
when he claims to have been sent by God, 3:13, and that God has
appeared to him, 4:1. Yahveh bids him perform three signs to
convince them. So at Mark 8:11-12 the Pharisees ask for a sign,
and this implies a claim which has been made and understood. The
nature of the claim would need a special sort of sign to confirm
it, a sign 'from heaven'. We may confidently interpret the passage
in the light of Mark's general view of the relationship of Jesus
and his enemies.

The second passage is Mark 12:34-37, David's Son and David's
Lord. The enemies of Jesus have asked three hostile questions.
One of the scribes, who is not hostile, asks a fourth, and is
commended as being not far from the kingdom of God. From then on
no one dares to ask Jesus any further question. Then Mark seems
to make a new beginning. We are told that as Jesus is teaching
in the temple, where we should have assumed him already to be.
It seems that, because the questioners have been silenced, Jesus
puts the question which, perhaps through his supernatural insight,
he perceives that the scribes would have put if they dared. The
question implied would be hostile, and of the form, 'Is the
Messiah the Son of David? If so, is he not necessarily of lower
status than his ancestor, as the son is less than the father?'
To this the response is to interpret the opening of Psalm 110,
understood as a prophetic utterance of David. David in a vision
was present at a heavenly scene in which Yahweh addressed the
Messiah, and bade him take his seat at his right hand until his
enemies should become his footstool. When David sets down his
account of the vision, he introduces the Messiah as 'my Lord'
(Adonai), not as 'my son'. Therefore, David himself witnesses
that his descendant will be his master. There is much here that
is obscure, but some things are clear. Jesus has been publicly
recognised as David's son by Bartimaeus, 10:49, and the crowd who
see his entry into Jerusalem see it as the coming of 'the kingdom

of our father, David', 11:9. Therefore, in the passage before us,
the discussion of the status of the Messiah is the discussion of
the status of Jesus. There is no concealment, and at the same
time there is no open claim. Jesus does not say, 'I am David's
Lord, who will be seated at the right hand of God'. So far the
pattern which we have observed is maintained. But what of the
discussion of the status of David's son and the Messiah which is
implied in the question, 'How say the scribes that the Messiah is
the Son of David?' Does Mark suppose that it had direct reference
to the claims of Jesus, or does he think of it as part of general
speculation concerning the Messiah? In the latter case the
passage would not presuppose any specific knowledge of Jesus'
claims such as we have found elsewhere. In the former case, the
scribes would be recognising a claim of Jesus to be Messiah, in
the sense of one who was inferior in status to David, and this
claim is much less than that which is implied in 2:6 and 12:1-12.
However, it would not be out of line with Mark's thinking if we
were to put the argument like this: 'The scribes know what is
meant by the title Messiah. They, as students of the scriptures,
know the relevant texts and predictions. One of these is Psalm
110:1. This predicts the Messiah's heavenly session, and complete
victory over his enemies. In it David acknowledges that the
Messiah has a position far higher than his own. However, when
Jesus is greeted as Messiah by Bartimaeus, and when the crowd,
at his entry into Jerusalem, accept this, the scribes do not wish
the true interpretation to be the one which gains credence.
Therefore they circulate the minimising theory that the figure
of David's son is less than the figure of David'. Whether or
not this is a correct interpretation of Mark's thought, it is
clear that he sees the final claim made in public by Jesus to be
that he is the Messiah who is to be exalted to the right hand of
God, and whose enemies are to be subdued. Thus it looks forward
to the answer to the High Priest, 'I am, and you will see the Son
of man seated at the right hand of the Power, and coming with the
clouds of heaven'.

The narrative of the Passion, culminating in the news of the
Resurrection, dominates Mark. The action of the enemies of Jesus
in crucifying him is occasioned by the recognition that what he
claims spells the end of their power, and of the old ways of
worship and conduct. There must be a new garment and new wine.
A new era begins when the strong man is bound. Worship in vain
when linked with representing commandments which come from men as
eternal truths from God. The Vineyard of Israel will be handed
over to others. All this happens under the heavenly authority of

Jesus who exercises divine prerogatives and is the beloved Son.
If we begin from this point in studying the Gospel, the 'secrecy
Material' seems less important, and the difficulties of
exhibiting it as a single phenomenon increase.

NOTE

/1/   εἰς μαρτύριον αὐτοῖς is a stereotype. For this reason there
is no clash between the singular τῷ ἱερεῖ and the plural αὐτοῖς.
At Leviticus 13:49, 14:2-32 τῷ ἱερεῖ clearly means 'a member of
the priesthood'; therefore the plural is in mind. The alternative,
'as a proof to the people' (RSV; compare NEB, TEV), is less easy,
since there is no plural in the earlier part of the section.
Note the juxtaposition of singular and plural at 6:11.

Studia Biblica 1978: II, 47-61

The Tassel of his Cloak: Mark, Luke, Matthew — and Zechariah

J.T. Cummings,
Theological College,
Catholic University of America,
Washington, D.C. 20017, U.S.A.

The story of the woman healed of an issue of blood is common to all three synoptic Gospels (Mk. 5.24b-34, Mt. 9.20-22, Lk. 8.42b-48). The agreement of Mt. and Lk. in reading that she laid hold of the *tassel* of his cloak against Mk. who reads simply his cloak has caused considerable perplexity for editors of the New Testament.

Thus Bruce Metzger writing in 1971 on behalf of the editorial committee of the United Bible Societies' Greek New Testament comments on Lk. 8.44 /1/:

> The words τοῦ κρασπέδου constitute one of the so-called minor agreements of Matthew and Luke against Mark. The committee regarded this as accidental and decided to follow the overwhelming weight of the external evidence supporting the inclusion of the words.

Tim Schramm also writing in 1971 commented more negatively /2/:

> Die Übereinstimmungen sind wenig beweiskraftig and könnten - abgesehen von ἰδού v.41 and τοῦ κρασπέδου v.44 - zufällig enstanden seien.

To which he adds in a footnote:

> Wenn nicht ... τοῦ κρασπέδου bei Lk. überhaupt zu streichen ist, so Wellhausen ....

The Ms. tradition reflects the same perplexity. Scribal editors of Lk. had a tendency to omit the words, while those of Mk. had a tendency to add them /3/. Thus the Ms. history shows both awareness of the problem and a trend toward assimilation.

A survey of the scholarship on the passage from the emergence

of the Two Source Theory to the present indicates that the
majority of critics have considered it one of the more significant
of the minor agreements (e.g. Hawkins, Burton, LaGrange, Streeter,
J. Schmid, and McLaughlin /4/) with solutions varying from textual
emendation /5/, to explanation as accidental agreement /6/, to
positing a common source /7/. I would support the solution of a
common source and argue that that source is Mk. - not indeed Mk.
5 where it does not occur but Mk. 6.56 where it does. This
conclusion, although arrived at independently, is not original.
It was already proposed by E. Haenchen in 1966, incisively if
laconically /8/:

Mk. 6.56 bietet sie auch schon.

And in 1969 the same view was taken by H. Schürmann regarding
Luke /9/:

...muss Luk Mk. 6.56 (=Mt. 14.36) gelesen haben, da sie im
NT sonst nur noch Mt. 23.5 begegnet. Von Mk. 6.56 her wird
sie auch Matth. hier eingeschleppt haben, womit die
auffallende Mt-Lk-Übereinstimmung diff. Mk. erklärt wäre.
Wir hatten dann erneut (s. schon o. zu V 40) ein Indiz,
das Luk Mk. 6.53-56 gelesen hat! Beide Berührungen mit
Mk. 6.53-56 bestätigen sich gegenseitig.

I would further argue that from this common source both Mt.
and Lk. each adopted it into the pericope of the afflicted woman
for very deliberate and specific reasons of their own /10/. To
determine those reasons let us look at each of the synoptics,
beginning with Mk. himself.

Two stylistic devices characteristic of the gospel of Mark are
to be observed:
   1) The "sandwich technique" /11/ (here the insertion of this
      story into the Jairus story).
   2) Triadic structure.

The presence of triadic structure in Mark has been noted by
E. Trocmé /12/:

Le caractère ternaire de certains groupements de textes
est difficile à contester: la *triple* prophétie de la
Passion (8.31, 9.31, 10.32-34)...le ministère jérusalémite
est presenté sous trois aspects successifs (actes en 11.1-25;
discussions publiques, 11.27 à 12.40; enseignement privé de
12.41 à 13.37); l'évangéliste a choisi trois paraboles pour
montrer quel enseignement Jesus donnait à la foule (4.1-34)
et *trois* miracles pour illustrer sa puissance (4.35 à 5.43:

la guérison de la femme à la perte de sang, insérée au
milieu du récit relatif à la fille de Jairus ne fait qu'un
avec celui-ci); etc....

Likewise Vielhauer has drawn attention to a triadic structure
intensifying to a climax in the crucifixion scene within the
passion narrative /13/:

Titulus am Kreuz: ὁ βασιλεὺς τῶν 'Ιουδαίων   (15.26)
Spott der Juden: ὁ Χριστὸς ὁ βασιλεὺς 'Ισραήλ   (15.32)
Akklamation des Heiden: ἀληθῶς οὗτος ὁ ἄνθρωπος (15.39)
                        υἱὸς θεοῦ ἦν

and has extrapolated therefrom three climactic moments within the
overall structure of Mk.'s gospel /14/:

In dieser Komposition kommt der dreimaligen Prädizierung
Jesu als Gottessohn bei der Taufe, Verklärung, und
Kreuzigung hohe Bedeutung zu.

They constitute a "deutlich beabsichtigen Steigerung", that
of "Adoption 1.11, Proklamation 9.7, Akklamation 15.39".

Now the insertion of the story of the afflicted woman into
the Jairus story creates one continuous episode building by 3
ascending stages (triadic structure) to a final climax:

1) The request of Jairus that Jesus heal by *imposition of
   hands* his daughter who is *at the point of death*.
2) The story of the afflicted woman intervenes. It is an
   ascent to a higher level of faith - Jairus believed in
   the exercise of power through imposition of hands; the
   woman believes that the slightest contact suffices -
   even to touch his cloak - and her faith is corroborated
   by event and pronouncement ("Your faith...").
3) The Jairus story resumes with word of the girl's death.
   What ensues is a greater miracle than asked or expected
   and demands a greater faith. The intervening story has
   prepared for this ultimate miracle by already exemplifying
   greater faith and greater healing power than stage 1.

But our story has a wider context in Mk. It has both a
prelude and a postlude, an anticipation and a sequel - again
triadic structure building by ascending stages to a climax.

1) Mk. 3.9-10: διὰ τὸν ὄχλον, ἵνα μὴ θλίβωσιν αὐτόν·
               πολλοὺς γὰρ ἐθεράπευσεν, ὥστε ἐπιπίπτειν
               αὐτῷ ἵνα αὐτοῦ ἄψωνται ὅσοι εἶχον μάστιγας.

The passage is part of a summary (3. 7-12) and has verbal
anticipations (in the underlined words) of the central story of
the afflicted woman within the triple miracle section (4. 35 - 5. 43)

2) Mk. 5.24b-34:   ...ὄχλος πολύς, καὶ συνέθλιβον αὐτόν.
                   ...ἐν τῷ ὄχλῳ ὄπισθεν ἥψατο τοῦ ἱματίου
                   αὐτοῦ...ἴαται ἀπὸ τῆς μάστιγος...τὸν
                   ὄχλον συνθλίβοντά σε... σέσωκέν σε...ἀπὸ
                   τῆς μάστιγός σου.

There is clear ascent. She seeks to touch not him but even (κᾶν)
his cloak (from αὐτοῦ to τοῦ ἱματίου αὐτοῦ).

3) Mk. 6.56   ...ἐν ταῖς ἀγοραῖς ἐτίθεσαν τοὺς ἀσθενοῦτας,
              καὶ παρεκάλουν αὐτὸν ἵνα κᾶν τοῦ κρασπέδου
              του ἱματίου αὐτοῦ ἄψωνται. καὶ ὅσοι ἂν
              ἥψαντο αὐτοῦ ἐσῴζοντο.

Once more we have a summary, once more with verbal correspondences
with the central episode. Here is the third stage with the
climax - from touching him (αὐτοῦ) to touching even his cloak (κᾶν
τοῦ ἱματίου αὐτοῦ), to touching even the tassel of his cloak (κᾶν
τοῦ κρασπέδου τοῦ ἱματίου αὐτοῦ).

This discernment reached independently on the basis of
Trocmé's and Vielhauer's observations of triadic structure finds
corroboration in the similar conclusion of R. Pesch /15/:

Von der Berührung Jesu (3.10) über die Berührung seiner
Kleider (5.27f.) zur Berührung des "Schaufadens" an
seinem Gewand ergibt sich im Arrangement...des Mk-Ev
eine gezielte Steigerung der Illustration der "Kraft" Jesu.

But for Pesch both summaries (Mk. 3 and 6) are the work of a
pre-Marcan redactor of the miracle catena that Mk. has inserted
between chaps. 3 and 6 /16/:

Markus schliesst den ersten Abschnitt des zweiten Hauptteils
seines Evangeliums mit einem Sammelbericht, der die
vormarkanische Sammlung von Wundergeschichten abschloss
und wie das diese Sammlung einleitende Summarium (3.7-12)
seine Bildung deren Redaktor (und nicht, wie meist angenommen
wird, dem Evangelisten) verdanken wird.

Whether Marcan or pre-Marcan redaction /17/, what is
important for the synoptic question is the fact of the artistic
connection between Mk. 5 and Mk. 6 since that is what both Lk. and
Mt. must have noted and on its basis inserted into their accounts
of the afflicted woman for their own respective reasons.

For Lk. I would posit an artistic/stylistic reason. He seems
(not surprising in view of his own artistry) to have noted the
interconnection of all three Marcan passages /18/. Thus Lk. also
provides us with a prelude (Lk. 9.19 = Mk. 3.10):

καὶ πᾶς ὁ ὄχλος ἐζήτουν ἅπτεσθαι αὐτοῦ, ὅτι
δύναμις παρ' αὐτοῦ ἐξήρχετο καὶ ἰᾶτο πάντας.

The first part is a Lucan adaptation of Mk. 3.10 while the
second part (δύναμις ...ἐξήρχετο) is a deliberate and explicit
anticipation of the pericope of the afflicted in Lk. 8 (par. Mk.
5) /19/, and the Lucan prelude points far more emphatically to the
event than did the Marcan. Yet by incorporating the "tassel" from
Mk. 6 into his central episode in chap. 8 and suppressing the
sequel (Mk. 6.56 has no parallel in Lk.) he seems to have both
seen Mk.'s 3 stages and yet to have reduced them to 2 stages. But
is this actually the case? Rather it appears Lk. has postponed
the final climax even further - has made it one of his joins
between Gospel and Acts (as a combined work) - namely to Acts 5.15
(where Peter's shadow brings healing) and 19.11 (handkerchiefs
touched to the body of Paul do the same). In short Lk. has seen,
adapted, and improved creatively - gone Mk. one better.

Mt. on the other hand has suppressed the prelude, inserted
τοῦ κρασπέδου from Mk. 6 into his otherwise drastically compressed
pericope and retained the sequel (Mt. 14.36 = Mk. 6.56):

καὶ προσήνεγκαν αὐτῷ πάντας τοὺς κακῶς ἔχοντας, καὶ
παρεκάλουν αὐτὸν ἵνα μόνον ἅψωνται τοῦ κρασπέδου τοῦ
ἱματίου αὐτοῦ· καὶ ὅσοι ἥψαντο διεσώθησαν.

While following the Marcan order he has widely distanced it
from the pericope of the afflicted woman by his own inserted
material. By suppressing any prelude (if he even saw it) Mt.
presents at best only a repetition then between the faith gesture
of the central event and its sequel and only the slightest element
of climax - from a single individual to the multitude. The
artistic/stylistic considerations operative in Lk. appear lacking
in Mt. Rather a different consideration seems to have been
operative for Mt. - namely that he perceived in the touching of
the tassel of Jesus' cloak an allusion to the prophecy of Zech.
8.23:

Thus says the Lord of hosts: "In those days ten men from
the nations of every tongue shall take hold of the
tassel of a Jew saying 'Let us go with you, for we have
heard that God is with you.'"

Although originally in Zech. it referred to the exaltation
of Jerusalem with the uniting of the Gentiles in the eschatological
pilgrimage, in the first century it had come to be recognized as a
messianic prophecy /21/. Jerome in his commentary on Zech.
recognized 8.23 as messianic, referring it to Christ but
allegorizing the tassel as the apostles /22/. Aland in his listing
of scriptural parallels also adduces the Zech. passage in connection
with our pericope /23/. So too Pusey in his commentary on the
Minor Prophets already drew attention to our pericopes as
fulfillment of Zech. 8.23 /24/. That Mt. would perceive such a
connection is not surprising, in view not only of his sensivity to
Judeo-Christian thought patterns, but also of his marked
preoccupation with Zech. as a source of Messianic prophecy. Thus
Mt. alone identifies the Zech. alluded to by Christ (23.25) with
Zech. the prophet. He alone alludes to Zech. 11.12-13 and the 30
pieces of silver (Mt. 27.9). He alone of the synoptics (Mt. 21.
4-5; cf. Jn. 12.14-15) quotes Zech 9.9 in connection with the
triumphal entry into Jerusalem. And we may also note that Mt. in
the counterpart story of the Syro-Phoenician woman adds to Mk.'s
title "Kyrie" the title "Son of David" from royal messianic
prophecy (Mt. 15.22). While logically it may be objected that the
woman afflicted with an issue of blood is not a gentile and so
does not provide a fulfillment of the prophecy in a strict sense,
it can be asserted that in line with the prophecy what would hold
true of a gentile (salvation by touching the tassel of the
Messiah) would hold even truer for a daughter of Israel /25/.

This brings us to a final question. Did the reading
originate with Mk. 6.56 (our common source for Mt. and Lk.) or is
it pre-Marcan? For Pesch there is no problem since he regards
the summary of Mk. 6 as already part of the pre-Marcan miracle
collection. In terms, however, of Paul Achtemeier's *more suasive*
theory of the existence of not one but two miracle catenae, each
triadic in structure /26/, it is a real question. The summary of
Mk. 6 is very definitely Marcan. It serves not only to link the
two catenae, but also replaces the first miracle story of the
second, the healing of the blind man of Bethsaida; - which Mk. has
deliberately displaced for structural-theological reasons to
8.22-26 (i.e. after the end of the second catena) /27/. According
to the Achtemeier thesis both the insertion of the story of the
afflicted woman into the Jairus story and the two summaries of
Mk. 3 and Mk. 6 are works of Marcan redaction /28/. This would
make it probable that Mk. already found τοῦ κρασπέδου as part of
the story of the afflicted woman and deliberately shifted it for
the stylistic purpose of the tripartite ascending climax outlined
above. Therefore a further question arises: what purpose did it

serve in that story as part of the miracle catena?

While agreeing with Achtemeier that the catena is
appropriately viewed as a liturgical catechesis within a
eucharistic context (miraculous feeding of the multitude as climax
of both) /29/, I sharply disagree with his analysis of the import
of both catenae, namely that the miracle stories are "epiphanic"
in terms of a "theios aner" Christology. Rather I would insist
with Pesch /30/ that:
> In älterer wie in jüngerer (Georgi, Achtemeier, Keck, Smith,
> Weeden, Kuhn, Schenke u.a.) Forschung ist der atl. Einfluss
> auf die ntl. Wundergeschichten unterschätzt, der Einfluss
> der sog. θεῖος-ἀνήρ-Vorstellungen überschätzt.

And I would add with Raymond Brown on the gospel miracles /31/:
> ...they fulfill Old Testament prophecies... At times this
> fulfillment of Old Testament prophecy seems to become
> the prime purpose of the miracle.

And /32/:
> ...the miracle is a symbolic action prophetic of the nature
> of the kingdom.

In line with such an interpretation, the sea crossing miracle
at the start of each of the two catenae introduces the "new
exodus" and "new Moses" theme and with it deliverance through water
to newness of life (thereby suggesting a baptismal as well as
Achtemeier's eucharistic context, i.e. a paschal context). The
ensuing 3 miralces of the first catenae continue that deliverance
theme: from bondage to Satan (the Gerasene demoniac), from the
effects of sin (the scourge of uncleanliness in the afflicted
woman), from the ultimate effect of sin - death (the Jairus story).
Finally the miraculous feeding shows Israel gathered and
reconstituted, fed miraculously by its eschatological shepherd
(Ezech. 34, Zech. 10.2; cf. Mk. 6.34: "like sheep without a
shepherd"). The symbolism is both that of the kingdom and of the
paschal mystery of initiation therein through baptism and
eucharist. And Christ is presented in terms of messianic
expectation, prophetic fulfillment: the prophet like unto Moses of
Dt. 18.15, the fulfillment of Is. 65.2,4 and Ps. 68(67).6 (the
Gerasene demoniac) /33/, as the counterpart of Elijah/Elisha
(Jairus story), as the eschatological shepherd of Ezech. and Zech.
10.2, and, assuming also the presence of τοῦ κρασπέδου in the
central miracle story, as the messiah who will lead in the
eschatological pilgrimage, for he is God with us. This is all
very far from a crude "theios aner" Christology, very close to
Judeo-Christian thought patterns, very appropriate for a paschal
catechesis in preparation for baptism and eucharist. In

particular the central stories of both catenae, the afflicted
woman and its counterpart, the Syro-Phoenician woman, can be seen
as validating stories appropriate to a eucharistic celebration:
the first abrogating ritual exclusion because of the Mosaic law
of impurity (i.e. a context appropriate to a relatively early
origin in a Palestinian Jewish Christian setting when a return to
ritualism and observance of the law was a contested issue /34/,
the second resolving a dispute over Jewish-Gentile table-fellowship
including eucharistic table-fellowship.

Such a line of reasoning rules out Achtemeier's hypothesis
of an origin of the first catena in a Gentile Christian community,
possibly Corinth /36/. Both catenae would have originated in
Palestine, the first in a Jewish-Christian community, the second
in a Jewish-Gentile setting, modeled on the first but adapted to
that setting (perhaps in northern Galilee, as Pesch thinks). It
also rules out Pesch's hypothesis that the first catena was
compiled for the Gentile mission /37/, but not the possibility that
it was subsequently employed in it, circulating as a liturgical
catechesis along with the second and so ultimately reaching Mark
who redacted both into his gospel.

If the foregoing analysis and reconstruction is correct, we
have the intriguing picture of the Zech. prophecy /39/ playing
initially a key role in the pericope of the afflicted woman, then
losing that significance in Mk., only to regain it in Mt. /40/.

Epilogue

To summarize the positions taken on questions of structure in
Mk.:
Conceding the consensus since the time of J. Schmid that the
structure of Mk.'s gospel was primarily pre-determined in its
later section by the pre-Mk. passion narrative (for an alternative
view proposing greater Marcan creativity in the passion narrative
see *The Passion in Mark,* ed. W. Kelber, Philadelphia 1976, esp. p.
157 in Kelber's concluding chapter), and at least tentatively
accepting Pesch's position that that pre-Mk. passion narrative
extends over the entire second half of the gospel (8.27-16.8) we
have argued that the triadic structure, already part of that pre-
Mk. passion narrative (a structure discerned by Pesch himself),
probably occasioned and motivated Mk.'s use of it in giving
structure to his gospel as a whole (a possibility also entertained
by Pesch).

Examples of Mk.'s use have been adduced in particular in the
tripartite division of the first half of the gospel (1.1-8.26) as
postulated by Léon-Dufour & Kuby, favored by Trocmé, and employed
as a working hypothesis by Pesch. Mk.'s key positioning of the
Baptism (1.9-11) to combine for triadic structure with (the
already fixed) Transfiguration (9.2-8) and Crucifixion-
Resurrection Epiphany (15.33-16.8) (so Vielhauer) should, we have
suggested, be seen as closely connected with a further triadic
structure also with ascending climax of 8.22-6, 10.46-52, 16.1-8
(building here on Perrin's central section emphasis and Schweizer's
and Pesch's acceptance of the key position of 8).

Finally we would argue that the same dominant triadic
structure so carefully discerned by Pesch in the pre-Mk. passion
narrative is very strong corroborative evidence for Achtemeier's
discernment of *two* pre-Mk. miracle catenae, each triadic in
structure (rather than Pesch's postulate of only one, lacking such
structure). With Achtemeier we have postulated as a Sitz-im-Leben
liturgical catechesis (but pre-baptismal as well as pre-eucharist,
viz. paschal) and have adduced the analogy of lesson cycles in the
liturgy as an argument against the need for either introductory
or concluding summaries for such a catena. Rather, their insertion
into the gospel has motivated and occasioned in all probability the
redaction by Mk. of these summaries (Mk. 3 and 6), and the
insertion into the Jairus story of the central miracle of the
first catena, the pericope of the woman, has motivated the
transferral of the "tassel" from that episode to the concluding
summary (Mk. 6).

NOTES

/1/   *A Textual Commenatry on the Greek New Testament* (Stuttgart
1971) pp. 145-6.
/2/   *Der Markus Stoff bei Lukas* (Cambridge 1971) p. 126.
/3/   Omission in Lk. is characteristic of the Western tradition,
cf. K. Aland, *Synopsis Quattuor Evangeliorum* (Stuttgart 1973) p.
190. As Streeter already observed: "...it is fallacious to
suppose that every omission by the Western text is right...
omission...is quite possibly an attempt to harmonise..." (*The Four
Gospels,* London 1930, p. 130). For Lk. 8.44 he did not follow his
own dictum but classed it as a "Western non-interpolation", i.e.
an assimilating interpolation based on Mt. in those mss. of Lk.
where it occurs (see p. 313).
/4/   Such a survey is found in F. Neirynck, *The Minor Agreements
of Matthew and Luke against Mark* (Louvain 1974) pp. 11-48 (p. 102

for index on our passage).   Cited hereafter as Neirynck.

/5/   Cf. Neirynck p. 32.

/6/   In whatever way that "accident" may be explained.   Thus
Neirynck himself classifies it under his class 23 (= class 1 of
Abbott's 8 classes): "Mt. and Lk. defining the object" (Neirynck
p. 267).

/7/   Which Hawkins insisted upon (Neirynck p. 26 n. 70) and which
P. Wernle attempted to find in positing a text of Mk. similar to
the Western tradition and more original than the textus receptus
(Neirynck pp. 16-17).

/8/   *Der Weg Jesu* (Berlin 1966) p. 210.

/9/   *Das Lukas Evangelium* vol. 1 (Freiburg 1969) p. 490 n. 138.

/10/   Reasons more significant than a common desire to be more
specific about the object.

/11/   The story of the afflicted woman is distinctly different in
style from the Jairus story and from the Marcan gospel's style
in general (see particularly the commentaries of V. Taylor, *The
Gospel according to St. Mark,* London 1966, and C.E.B. Cranfield,
The Gospel according to Saint Mark, Cambridge 1963).   For the
"sandwich technique", cf. E. Trocmé's study: *La Formation de
l'Évangile selon Marc* (Paris 1963) p. 66(82).   Page references
in brackets are to the English translation of Trocmé, London 1975.

/12/   *Op. cit.* p. 65 (81).

/13/   P. Vielhauer, "Erwägungen zur Christologie des
Markusevangeliums", *Aufsätze zum Neuen Testament* (Munich 1965)
p. 209.

/14/   Vielhauer, *op. cit.* pp. 211-12.   Nor is Vielhauer alone in
positing triadic structure as a basic framework for the gospel of
Mark.   See Trocmé, *op. cit.* p. 62 (77-8) for the schemata of
Wellhausen, Klostermann, Montefiore, and pp. 63-4 (80) for the
convergence of Kuby, Léon-Dufour, and Riesenfeld on a division
into two groups of three, a schema also adopted by R. Pesch:
Das Markusevangelium vol. 1 (Freiburg 1976) pp. 32-40 (cited
hereafter as Pesch 1).   Pesch also distinguished in his
reconstruction of the pre-Marcan passion narrative a basic
triadic structure (39 episodes of Mk. 8.27-16.8 divided into 13
groups of 3.   See R. Pesch, *Das Markusevangelium* vol. 2 (Freiburg
1977) pp. 15-20 (cited hereafter as Pesch 2).   Although all of
the instances cited by Trocmé (note 12 above) are then pre-
Marcan (the passion predictions and Jerusalem ministry belonging
to the pre-Marcan passion narrative, the parables to a pre-Marcan
parable collection and the miracles to a pre-Marcan miracle
collection) this does not preclude the possibility that a
conservative redactor like Mark (as Pesch designates him) would
have imitated this stylistic pattern already established in the
tradition in order to give unity both to parts of his gospel and

to the whole; thus Pesch also notes: "Ob der dreiteilige Aufbau
der ersten Evangelienhälfte durch die Vorgabe fur die Zweite mit
inspiriert ist, kann erwogen werden" (Pesch 2 p. 20). Pesch,
while questioning Vielhauer's interpretation of adoption,
proclamation, acclamation (preferring vocation, confirmation,
confession), nonetheless writes (Pesch 2 p. 82): "Die
Verklärungserzählungen bildet so einen wichtigen Pfeiler in der
Gesamtkomposition des Evangeliums...". Likewise N. Perrin,
setting out this schema of Vielhauer, calls Mk. 15.39 the
"Christological climax of the gospel" ("The Literary Gattung
'Gospel'", *The Expository Times* 82 (1970) p. 4).
/15/   Pesch 1 p. 366.
/16/   Pesch 1 p. 364 and cf. pp. 198-202 and 207-281.
/17/   I am inclined in this instance to favor the "majority
opinion" ("wie meist angenommen wird") and to see the summaries
as Marcan redaction (reasons will be taken up when we come to the
pre-Marcan history of the pericope) and also to favor the Marcan
insertion into the Jairus story (which Pesch also denies: Pesch 1
p. 295; and cf. p. 24). Certainly the creation of a three-stage
climax by the insertion is preferable to the theory of a narrative
delay frequently postulated as the motive of the insertion (so
E. Schweizer, *The Good News According to Mark,* Atlanta 1976, p.
116; D.E. Nineham, *St. Mark*, London 1963, p. 157; R. Bultmann,
The History of the Synoptic Tradition, New York 1976, p. 215).
The appropriateness of this explanation has also been questioned
by P. Achtemeier, "Toward the Isolation of the Pre-Marcan Miracle
Catenae", *JBL* 89 (1970) p. 277, and T. Burkill, *Mysterious
Revelation* (Ithaca N.Y. 1963) p. 121. Such a delay is
inappropriate in the circumstances of the Jairus episode and seems
to have motivated Mt.'s drastic condensation of the story of the
afflicted woman - in addition to his general tendency (cf.
Haenchen, *op. cit.* p. 260) to condense Mark.
/18/   Why should Lk. be less perceptive than Pesch or myself?
/19/   Cf. Schürmann, *op. cit.* p. 322 n. 29.
/20/   See Aland, *Synopsis* p. 190 (*re* 1.20); Schürmann, *op. cit.*
p. 491 n. 139; Haenchen, *op. cit.* p. 207 n. 1a and p. 260 n. 2.
/21/   See A. Edersheim, *Life and Times of Jesus the Messiah*
vol. 2 (New York 1906) pp. 735-6. J. Bowman, *The Gospel of Mark*
(Leiden 1965) suggests the existence in the first cent. A.D. of
a Zechariah midrash or collection of testimonia (pp. 146-70 and
270-71).
/22/   *Commentarioli in Prophetas* CC 76A (Turnhout 1970) pp. 822-4.
Jerome's allegory may have been inspired by noting the connection
with Acts 5 and 19 (why should Jerome have been less perceptive
than Schürmann, Haenchen, Aland and others?).
/23/   *Synopsis* p. 190 (*re* 1.20).

/24/   Vol. 2 (New York 1889) pp. 392-3 n. 13.
/25/   Or, as an outcast because of her affliction, was she perhaps
equal in status to a gentile? On "Kyrie", see Pesch 1 p. 389.
/26/   P. Achtemeier, "Toward the Isolation of the Pre-Marcan
Miracle Catenae" *JBL* 89 (1970) pp. 265-91 (cited hereafter as
Achtemeier, 1970). P. Achtemeier, "The Origin and Function of the
Pre-Marcan Miracle Catenae", *JBL* 91 (1972) pp. 198-221 (cited
hereafter as Achtemeier 1972). For Achtemeier each catena
consisted of: 1) A sea crossing, 2) 3 miracle stories, 3) a
feeding/multiplication story (thus neatly solving the
multiplication doublet). Pesch (Pesch 1 pp. 277-81) posits only
one miracle collection, identical with Achtemeier's first catena
except that he adds the second sea crossing and the summaries of
Mk. 3 and Mk. 6. Achtemeier's first catena is found in Mk. 4.35-
6.44, and the second in Mk. 6.45-56 and 7.24-8.10 (both with
inserted material). Mt. has kept the second largely intact (14.
22-15.39) but has widely dislocated the episodes of the first
(8.23-34, 9.18-26, 14.12-21), while Lk. has virtually dissolved
the first and kept the second (8.22-9.17). Cf. also J. Konings,
"The Pre-Markan Sequence in Jn. 6: a critical re-examination",
L'Évangile selon Marc (Louvain 1974) p. 147 ff. (a sceptical view).
/27/   See Achtemeier, 1970 pp. 284-6 (linking effect not stressed
by Achtemeier). Bethsaida, as Achtemeier emphasises, is
mentioned in Mk. only in 6.45 and 8.22-6 and the two references
make the best sense only in terms of the displacement of 8.22-6
from its proper sequence. The displacement is deliberate,
creating the intended balanced frame of the blind man of
Bethsaida and the blind man of Jericho (Mk. 8.22-6 and 10.46-52),
the concluding episodes for sections 3 and 4 of Mk.'s gospel
(cf. E. Schweizer, *op. cit.* p. 163 and pp. 224-5 and 384-5). It
also inevitably sets up in terms of the over-all structure of the
Marcan gospel a triadic structure of sections 1-3 (Mk. 1.1-8.26,
i.e. the first half of the gospel), section 4 (Mk. 8.27-10.52) and
sections 5-6 (Mk. 11.1-16.8 i.e. the Jerusalem section, already
stressed by Wellhausen in his schema, see note 14 above), a
triadic structure subordinate to the dual division (passion
narrative and preceding ministry). Schematically this can be
presented as:

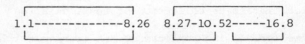

```
    ┌──────────────┐    ┌─────────────┐
    1.1─────────────8.26   8.27-10.52─────16.8
    └──────────────┘    └──────┘ └──────┘
```

This deliberate positioning of 8.22-6 as a counterpart to the
Bartimaeus story of Mk. 10 (its position already fixed in the pre-
Mk. passion narrative; see Pesch 2 p. 167 and pp. 174-5) sets up

a frame which highlights section 4 of the gospel as crucially
significant, a fact to which N. Perrin has repeatedy drawn
attention (e.g. *A Modern Pilgrimage in New Testament Christology*
[Philadelphia 1974] pp. 90, 117, 129; "The Interpretation of the
Gospel of Mark", *Interpretation* 30 [1976] pp. 122-2; "The Literary
Gattung 'Gospel'", *The Expositiory Times* 82 [1970] p. 6). It is
section 4 which also includes the Transfiguration (9.2 ff),
thereby linking this secondary triadic structure with that
discerned by Vielhauer. More important, the triadic structure
builds to an ascending climax, from the opening of the eyes of the
blind man of Bethsaida to the opening of the eyes of Bartimaeus
to the ultimate opening of the eyes of the blind in the
centurion's cry of 15 and the resurrection proclamation of 16 with
Jesus now vindicated as son of God, messiah and son of man (cf.
Pesch 2 p. 541 on 16.1-8). The deliberate positioning of 8.22-6
is not only granted but stressed by Pesch (Pesch 1 pp. 415, 420-21)
although for him it means the incorporation of a particular story
(free-floating?) which he traces originally to a local Bethsaida
tradition. (Note that in his discussion Pesch makes no reference
to Achtemeier.) According to the Achtemeier thesis this
displacement both occasions and motivates the creation of the
redaction summary of Mk. 6.
/28/ The summary of Mk. 3.7-12 is best seen as Marcan redaction
involving traditional elements. See E. Keck, "Mk. 3.7-12 and
Mark's Christology", *JBL* 84 (1965) pp. 341-358 and cf. Achtemeier,
1970. E. Schweizer has pointed out (*op. cit.* pp. 78-9) that the
summary of Mk. 3 serves as a joint introduction to both the miracle
collection and to the parable collection, and suggests that v. 9
and v. 7a may have been the original introduction to the parable
collection. This would make it certain that the summary as found
in Mk. did not take this shape until the parable collection and
the miracle collection were joined - and the obvious reason for
joining them would seem to be their incorporation into a larger
narrative structure, i.e. into the gospel. Distinguishing further,
I would suggest that v. 10 could also have originally been the
introduction to the story of the afflicted woman (note the verbal
correspondences). To "unsandwich" that story:

5. 21 & 24b: καὶ διαπεράσαντος τοῦ Ἰησοῦ ἐν τῷ πλοίῳ πάλιν
              εἰς τὸ πέραν συνήχθη ὄχλος πολὺς ἐπ' αὐτόν,
              καὶ συνέθλιβον αὐτόν·
3. 10   πολλοὺς γὰρ ἐθεράπευσεν, ὥστε ἐπιπίπτειν αὐτῷ
              ἵνα αὐτοῦ ἅψωνται ὅσοι εἶχον μάστιγας.
5. 25   καὶ γυνὴ οὖσα κτλ.

While the Jairus story would reconstruct:

5. 21b   καὶ ἦν παρὰ τὴν θάλασσαν.
5. 22-23   καὶ ἔρχεται κτλ.
5. 35-6   Ἔτι αὐτοῦ λαλοῦντος κτλ.
(insert 24a: καὶ ἀπῆλθεν μετ᾽ αὐτοῦ. καὶ ἠκολούθει αὐτῷ
             ὄχλος πολύς.
5. 37   καὶ οὐκ ἀφῆκεν κτλ.
(Note that Pesch 1 p. 299 takes 5.21b as the original introduction
to the afflicted woman story.)

Such a reconstruction would indicate that joining of the two
collections, sandwiching of the two stories, and redaction of the
summary took place at the same time (this is also Achtemeier's
position: Achtemeier, 1970 pp. 277-8).
/29/ See Achtemeier, 1972.
/30/ Pesch 1 p. 280.
/31/ "The Gospel Miracles", *New Testament Essays* (New York 1965)
p. 228.
/32/ *Ibid*. p. 229.
/33/ Thus Pesch 1 p. 286; and cf. Schweizer, *op. cit*. p. 113.
For the sea miracle Pesch alludes to Jonah (Pesch 1 pp. 270-1),
an allusion important for the narrative model but less so for the
symbolic significance. Pesch 1 pp. 307-11 also stresses the
Elijah/Elisha allusion, and Pesch 1 p. 350 also sees the role of
the eschatological shepherd but omits from his list of O.T. texts
Zech. while correctly stressing a Moses allusion here too. For
the afflicted woman pericope Pesch offers only Lev. 12 and 15;
cf. schema in Pesch 1 p. 279.
/34/ See F. Hahn, *The Worship of the Early Church* (Philadelphia
1976) pp. 50-1.
/35/ This central counterpart story in the second catena shows
signs of conflation of themes from the first catena, e.g. "unclean
spirit" parallel with Gerasene demoniac and gentile setting, woman
as protagonist in both, tassel/scraps parallel, parent appeal for
child with Jairus. The other stories of the second catena (blind,
deaf and dumb) seem to fit a fulfillment of Is. 29.18-19; 35.5-6;
cf. Lk. 7.22.
/36/ Achtemeier, 1972 esp. 209-18.
/37/ Pesch 1 pp. 280-81.
/38/ As liturgical catechesis the closest and proper analogy is
with the later early development in the liturgy of a Johannine
lectionary cycle of the Samaritan woman, the paralytic, the man
born blind (Jn. 4, 5, 9) for use in pre/post-baptismal catechesis
(sse E. Hoskyns, "A Note on the Early Lectionaries", *The Fourth*

Gospel, London 1947, pp. 363-5), and the variant cycle in the
Roman Rite of "Samaritina, Caecus, Lazarus" (Jn. 4, 9, 11) as
pre-baptismal catechesis in connection with the baptismal
scrutinies (see A. Chavasse, "La structure du carême et les
lectures des messes quadragésimales dans la liturgie romaine",
La Maison Dieu 31, 1952, pp. 95-7, 113-14 and cf. p. 76 for
bibliography). As a cycle of lessons for liturgical use the pre-
Marcan miracle catena would no more need an introductory or
concluding summary than does the cycle of lessons read today
either at the Easter Vigil or that read on Good Friday - or the
Johannine lectionary as read today on the 3rd, 4th, and 5th
sundays of Lent in cycle A. The liturgical setting sufficed!
(Note also the co-existence of two similar Johannine cycles, and
tripartite nature of both. According to R. Brown only the
"Samaritina" and the "Caecus" had sacramental significance in
Jn's gospel: "The Johannine Sacrementary", *op. cit.* pp. 106-7.)
/39/ A final point is to justify the presumption followed
throughout that τὸ κράσπεδον means "tassel". It is the technical
term in the LXX for the ritual tassels prescribed by Mocaic Law,
and in the N.T. it has never been questioned that it has any
other meaning than that technical one except in this pericope
and related passages (Mt. 9.20, Lk. 8.44, Mt. 14.36, Mk. 6.56
where the possible Hellenistic Gk. meaning "hem" is suggested as
a possible alternative. Behind the questioning seems to lie the
anxiety to reconcile, assimilate the passages - so that the
"cloak" of Mk. 5.27 will mean basically the same as the other
passages. Certainly Jerome seems to have had no problem. He
translates all the O.T. and N.T. passages with the same word,
fimbria, and employs that same word in only one other passage,
Ps. 43 (44).14 *juxta LXX* where he is translating κροσσωτός, a
rare Gk. word which means only one thing: "tassel".
/40/ A debt of gratitude is owed to Prof. R. Fuller, Virginia
Theological Seminary, for reading both the preliminary and the
finished manuscript, for encouragement and criticism.

Studia Biblica 1978: II, 63-73   63

Legend and Event: The Gerasene Demoniac: An Inquest into History and Liturgical Projection

J. Duncan M. Derrett
Professor of Oriental Laws
University of London

Introduction

     Like the Walking on the Water, the Feeding of the Five Thou-
sand and the Stilling of the Storm (all associated with the Sea of
Galilee), the Gerasene Demoniac and his Swine hover between legend
and fantasy, and the specialists /1/ dismiss the story in so far
as it exceeds, in scope and structure, the healing of the demoniac
in the synagogue at Mk 1:23-26. Here follows a brief attempt to
'peel the onion', i.e. by making a section through the layers of
interpretation adhering to the story, to demonstrate the early
Christian mind at work. The first layer is that of liturgy, Christ
depicted as Saviour, as the Holy Spirit triumphing. The second
layer, moving towards the centre, is the layer of biblical
scholarship: Christ's actions, as would be expected of one
possessed by the Holy Spirit, conform to a scenario which scripture
already contained. Thus the event was in itself a documentation
of the biblical scenario. This is a stage of representation
posterior to informed reminiscence. The third layer is
reminiscence. The story is considered and depicted in a selective
and edifying way, to bring out its significance. There is no
unbiassed, unselective account of anything (contrast the uses,
abuses, and limitations of a photograph). The final, and central,
layer is the event as experienced by the bystanders, intelligible
to them. The inner experience of the man, the core of the story,
can only be conjectured.

I. *The Outside Layer*

     This is a hostile confrontation /2/. Christ is prepared, like
David, to run through a troop /3/. Of the existing vocabulary
many of the key words have military under-senses /4/. The pigs,
implausibly, form up like soldiers, and go to their deaths.

The parallel is the deaths of all Pharaoh's forces (not Pharaoh himself) in the Reed Sea (Exod.14-15). Pharaoh sacrificed to Baal Zephon, and, encouraged by the idol (the last idol of Egypt) attempted to destroy the Israelites. There were tombs there /5/, a cliff, an absence of boats: in fact no way of escape /6/. The guardian angel of the Egyptians was first drowned /7/. At this point all waters were divided /8/. All waters 'are' the Reed Sea at the crisis of redemption, which was also redemption from the idolatry and lasciviousness of Egypt. Had the Egyptians set foot on the opposite shore it too would have been unclean. Moses therefore mediates the passage of the Israelites to purity, a form of baptism. By his great deed God secures that his Name is honoured amongst the heathen.

Note the man's behaviour. It has several senses simultaneously. He cries (though barely conscious of it) for God's mercy /9/. God says, 'Before you call, I answer', which he did most convincingly at the Exodus /10/.

II. *The Second Layer*

We now penetrate below the liturgical (and perhaps lectionary) level, below the level which, according to Mark, should first interest the preacher. The biblical references are rich and numerous, also intriguing. The text used was the unpointed text, ancestor of our Masoretic. But the scholar constantly made use of the LXX and quite possibly alternative Greek versions. Ps. 68:7(6) describes (as it were) Jesus' act: the saved are sent home to their families (one should not be a solitary), while the rest remain in a dry land suitable for tombs and caves. The 'provoking ones' belong in such an ambience. Ps. 107 was a favourite of the early churches since they saw no less than three famous acts of Jesus in it. Did Jesus himself teach that psalm and incorporate it in his 'scenario'? The question remains open. Ps. 107:10-16 belongs to our story. Those that cry out will have their bonds broken (of course our man had the fragments of manacles and leg-irons still on him). The two prophetic passages where swine are spoken of occur at the end of the Song of the Servant: Is. 65:1-7, 66:17-20. These are highly relevant /11/ because the redemption of rebellious and unobservant Jews is mentioned and, simultaneously, the rescue of gentiles. Demons are specially referred to, and worship of demons (amongst which acts we know that seeking for demonic possession was counted). Then comes Zech. 13:2. The names of the unclean spirits and idols will be cut off. But the true scenario for the occasion may be Nahum 1:4,11-15, in which the garbled, ecstatic prophetic pronouncements to two ill-related interlocutors turn out to be highly relevant. Translate as follows:

> 4. He rebukes the sea (cf. Aquila, Symmachus *epitimon*, cf.
> Mk. 4:39) and dries it up, and he makes all the streams
> fail (cf. Ps. 106:9)...
> 11. From thee has come forth a deviser of evil against
> Yahweh, a counsellor of Belial (calculating perversities,
> plotting apostasy).
> 12. Thus said the Lord: 'Even though they are up to strength
> (complete) (cf. Am. 1:6,9) and numerous, they will be cut
> off (razed, or, will disappear), and he has passed across.
> I have afflicted thee, but I shall afflict thee no more.
> (LXX: 'the Lord since he possesses great seas...and thus
> they shall be sent away, and thy sound shall not be heard
> any more'.)
> 13. And now I break his rod from off thee, and I will burst
> thy bonds asunder.'
> 14. And the Lord has given commandment about thee: 'No more
> of thy name shall be sown abroad. From the house of thy
> gods I shall cut off the graven and the molten (image).
> I shall lay thy grave, for thou art nugatory (LXX: they are
> swift)'.
> 15. Behold on the mountains the feet of one who proclaims
> good tidings, who announces peace. Celebrate, O Judah,
> thy festivals, fulfil thy vows, for never again shall
> Belial come into thee, he is completely cut off.

This very difficult passage comes to life when the story of the Swine is told.

The prophetic passages taken together suggest a Jewish mission to the gentiles. The church had a position on whether Jesus conducted such a mission. From the episodes of the Syro-Phoenician woman and the Centurion's Boy /12/ we are entitled to believe that the historical Jesus was prepared to help gentiles either as a matter of charity or if they professed beliefs compatible with Judaism. At that rate a quite different mission could be started in gentile territory, a mission of reclamation in the case of Gadara and Hippos (see below), but at a pace other than that appropriate in Jewish territory. The story insinuates that Jesus could have spread 'peace' in Gadara/Hippos had the public welcomed his initiatives. Here we have a position in answer to the unspoken question, 'Why did not Jesus convert gentiles in Palestine, seeing that gentiles are represented in our churches?'

III. *Reminiscence*

Once a story is told by those who have reasons for telling
it, a certain selection and even exaggeration can be expressed,
in attractive language, so as to make the story meaningful and
edifying. At once numerous themes strike us as belonging to that
layer. In the abyss /13/ the demons are at home, since demons
belong there. The gnawing question, whether Jesus had the right
to cause the loss of so many pigs - a question answered in the
negative by Porphyrius /14/ in the third century - is only a
matter of common sense. Roman law /15/ and Jewish law /16/ are
agreed that Jesus could be liable in damages to the owners,
according to the ideas of the time. A well-known legend of
Pythagoras indicates that a thinker would take care not to let
his religion cost others money /17/. Part of the answer appears
in Ps. 8:7(8). The Son of Man (as the new Adam) has all creatures
subordinated to him /18/, including 'all sheep and "oxen"'. The
word usually translated 'oxen', if read ᵓalpayim instead of
ᵓalaphim /19/ means '2,000'. Thus Jesus was entitled, if he
wished, to exercise sovereign rights over cattle which are *herded*
(as pigs are) to the limit of 2,000.

The conversation between the man and Jesus is all
'reminiscence', i.e. dramatically retold narrative. All of it
must have been plausible and meaningful. The demon speaking
through the man is cunning, vicious, ironical, boastful ('we are
many' is mock-modesty!). He pretends near-equality with Jesus,
in whom he sees the Spirit of God, through whose permission all
demons function during their limited time. Demons do indeed
bargain with their exorcists /20/. The man was an outcast, and
was attempting to stone himself. Demons of death will attempt
to drive a man over a precipice /21/. *Choking* is what one
pretends to do to demons (represented by puppets) when one
attempts to get power over them /22/. Demons choke people. The
pigs, containing the demons, being *choked*, cannot be said to
have been *sacrificed* by Jesus. Strangulating and throat-splitting
are very different in that milieu /23/.

As for the legal problem, there was almost certainly no
treaty between Gadara/Hippos and Galilee, specifically Capernaum,
such as would make a Jew liable for realistic damages for the
destruction of pigs, in a Jewish court, at the suit of a Gadarene/
Hippian /23a/. It was understandable that Jesus should be urged
to leave. God did not intend the gentile followers of Jesus to
be *socially intermixed* with Jews! If the episode could have been

a bridgehead for more of Jesus' activity in the Decapolis
misunderstandings would have ensued on that subject. As it was,
his fame in the Decapolis was useful /24/.

   The man becomes Jesus', and therefore God's, agent. God's
will is fulfilled unpredictably. Our author of the 'reminiscence
level' does understand Jesus' reason for behaving as he did, and
the conversation brings this out. The truth is this, as the tale
projects it (correctly), that the western hypothesis, uttered by
Cicero /25/, that, if one has to debate with oneself the morality
of one's actions, one is presumed to be on the point of illegality
or at any rate immorality, does not operate for Jews. Scrupulous
calculation is proper to their mentality (the parable of the
Unmerciful Servant /26/ shows this very clearly).

   Ps. 8 with its alternative reading *ad hoc* is only a biblical
text to illuminate the story in the hands of a preacher. It has
often been said that Jesus *acquiesced* in the man's request, and
had no responsibility for what transpired; this is wrong. Knowing
the destructive potential of demons (i.e. the semi-controlled
behaviour of possessed persons), he did not *intend* the destruction
of the pigs, which was the unintended result of the man's conduct.
Seen in reminiscence the demons left the man and went into the
pigs. Using the same idiom we must say that Jesus did not intend
the demons to destroy the pigs. The demons' activity was
permitted by God, i.e. it was a phenomenon known to chaos,
imperfectly 'chained' until the 'time'. But at the moment when
it was clear that the pigs might be destroyed Jesus's duty of care
towards the owners and keepers was nullified by two independent
considerations of Jewish law, which law was, *ex hypothesi*, the acme
of righteousness (see below).

IV *The Event*

   Demonic possession is well known /27/. It is a phenomenon
akin to suggestibility under hypnosis. Propensity to possession
is cultural and learnt. It occurs particularly in disadvantaged
persons in stifling, over-rigid societies with little scope for
improvement or recognition of status. It is linked with the
theatre historically /28/, and is a histrionic gift. At the
moment of possession consciousness is by-passed, and great pain
can be tolerated. In general the possessed state correlates with
abnormal energy and power. Rarely possession is spontaneous,
especially with adepts; in such cases it is relatively hard to
terminate, and exorcism is required. More commonly it is self-
induced and therefore 'artificial'. In all cases the subject's

consciousness is present throughout the display, which is a social, not a solitary experience. The subject connives at a pretence, universally accepted, that demons will occupy people, to create illness, or deviance. For several reasons the subjects, while possessed, are violent, obscene, aggressive, and boastful. 'Military' demons, and 'multiple' possession are far from uncommon /29/. Relatives can profit from the subject's possession, but in certain cases the condition of the subject is disabling and also embarrassing /29a/ and possession must be ended by exorcism, otherwise used for healing. *Possessed persons themselves know what will 'de-trigger' them*. This is learnt like the rest of the phenomenon. The exorcist has to discover which demon is at work, and, by reason of having the same demon or a more powerful one (!), expel him, often into an animal or an object /30/. All this is part of a living culture, and is primitive psychiatry.

Pigs in Greece and Rome were favourite sacrificial animals. They, pigs and piglets, were sacrificed to all gods, *excluding Aphrodite* /31/. No Roman tomb was legally protected until a pig had been sacrificed /32/, Pigs and the underworld are closely connected /33/. Our pigs were near a good market, therefore. Pigs are the most human of animals /33a/, often very successfully domesticated. Pigs and piglets were used for *expiation*. The Louvre *crater* depicting the expiation of Orestes is a perfect illustration and Apollonius Rhodius explains the procedure in detail /34/. Circe (there quoted) was after all an expert in pigs. Pigs are used to decoy demons, for demons love pigs /35/. Possessed persons are frequently exorcised by their bargaining with the exorcist for offerings (woman ask for jewellery!). The blood of the victims should be smeared on the subject. If the demon is being expelled into an object this must be brought close, and then cast into a thicket, or river /36/, or burnt. When sacrificing to demons screams and yells are necessary.

We do not know why, but our man was obsessed with death, and impersonated (in the contemporary idiom, was possessed by) the ineluctable Lord of the Dead. His behaviour was a continuous mourning ritual /37/. He was sensible enough not to commit suicide. But he went as near as he could. He represents Death at large amongst men, and Jesus' act is a triumph over death. It is a resurrection-scene. It is a taste of the Passion, and his sympathy with the man is understandable. But in the man's bargaining with Jesus he is enabled to carry out his interest in the pigs: they shall be a substituted sacrifice. He visualises this as his penetration into the pigs, who shall die in his stead. How will he be united with them? Demons are obscene, and so are

the gentiles amongst whom the man lived. Jewish mythology about
gentiles recounted how they loved bestiality /38/. 'Pig' in Greek
and Latin means *pudenda muliebria*. His wish is formulated, at the
level of reminiscence, as a request for bestiality; *in fact* it *may*
have been mere acceptance of an *epipompe* (demon-transfer). Given
permission he attempts to effect this: it is notorious that demons
are sexually active /39/ with creatures of both genders.

Whether he went on all fours to the pigs, or held the piglets
over his head as in the cleansing of Orestes, or both, a few
families of pigs were terrified and went over the cliff. The cliff
is more probably not near Kursi, on the eastern bank (the slope
usually favoured would be in the territory of Hippos), but rather
on the southern bank /40/ within a mile of Tel Qatsir, in the
territory of Gadara. The history of that portion of the Decapolis
/41/ makes it clear that the inhabitants were sensitive about
Judaism (an imperialistic religion in their region /41a/) and about
political freedom from Judaea. The man's possession could
therefore have had several overtones. But he knew that he could be
de-triggered by the 'transfer' of his powerful demon(s) into an
area of death and mourning apart from himself. He sees the pigs in
the water (some of them have died of fright, as pigs will) and he
knows that his demon(s) have left him. He is cured. The exact
number of pigs is neither here nor there.

Jesus' want of care for the pigs is easily explained. (1) All
animals affected by bestiality must be stoned (Lev.20:15-16), and
precipitation is as good as stoning /42/. Pious people would, as a
matter of good order, require the destruction of all animals
reputed to have been affected by attempts at bestiality. (2) All
objects suspected of having figured in idol-worship must be thrown
into the Dead Sea /43/. The Sea of Galilee will do almost as well.
The pigs were destined for sacrifice, and the majority of them for
sacrifice to idols or demons. If any of the actual pigs in the
story were not so destined they were indistinguishably mixed with
those that were. The rule of the majority applies, and all became
prohibited objects /44/. Hence no care could be expended to save
the pigs. Conceivably the disciples could have intervened in time,
or given some warning to the keepers (interested onlookers): we
can see why they did not. Historically, the religious horror of
bestiality and of idolatry are associated /44a/.

Conclusion

Jesus could indeed have gone to the opposite side of the Sea
to rescue this very man. Whether the Storm preceded the episode,

or followed it, is unknown. The evangelist has the Exodus in mind.
But the episode teaches that, so far as demon-possession was
concerned, Jesus was an acknowledged expert, who saw the subjective
condition of *possession* as intrinsically hostile to his mission
wherever it occurred, whether amongst nominally observant Jews or
lapsed Jews (as this one probably was), or gentiles. The mind not
prepared to welcome the Holy Spirit, and to take it as a final and
exclusive guide /45/ is territory into which the ambassadors of
the Kingdom of Heaven must penetrate, land which they must claim
for their Sovereign. We do not know whether Jesus contemplated
the human mind *exempt* from the propensity to be possessed (cf.
Matt.12:45), or indeed whether such a mind exists or will exist.

NOTES

/1/   K. Kertelge, *Die Wunder Jesu im Markusevangelium* (Munich,
1970), pp.102-110; R. Pesch, *Der Besessene von Gerasa* (Stuttgart,
1972); id., *Markusevangelium* I (Freiburg, 1976); D.A. Coch, *Die
Bedeutung der Wundererzählungen für die Christologie des
Markusevangeliums* (Berlin, 1975), esp. pp.78-85.
/2/   J.M. Robinson, *Problems of History...Mark* (London, 1957),
pp.36-7.
/3/   2 Sam.22:30 (not noticed previously).
/4/   ἀποστεύλῃ, ἐπιτρέπειν, ὥρμησεν, even ἀγέλη. λεγιών is
exclusively military. Jewish applied meanings (for the loanword)
are later.
/5/   Exod. 14:11.
/6/   L. Ginzberg, *Legends of the Jews* III (Philadelphia, 1947),
pp.9-31; M.M. Kasher, *Encyclopedia of Biblical Interpretation* VIII
(New York, 1970) pp.128-160; Josephus, *Ant.* iii.320-344; Philo,
Vita Mos. i.167-179; ii.247-257.
/7/   See Kasher, *ubi cit.* The guardian angel was called Mitsraim,
for so the biblical text indicates!
/8/   Ps. 114:3; Is.50:2; 51:10; 63:12; Mekilta, Beš.4:31a;
Mekilta de R.S. 50.
/9/   On κράζειν and κραυγή see lexica and Kittel, *Th.W.N.T.* III
(1938), 899-900. LXX Ps.106 (MT 107): 6,13,19,28.
/10/   Is.65:24. On the relation of this to Exodus see Mekilta *ad.
loc.*; J. Mann, *The Bible as Read and Preached* I (Cincinnati, 1940),
pp.430, 432.
/11/   H. Sahlin, 'Die Perikope vom gerasenischen Besessenen und
der Plan des Markusevangeliums; *Stud. Theol.* xi (1964),pp.159-172.
/12/   Derrett, *Studies in the New Testament* I (Leiden, 1977), pp.
143-169.

/13/   So Luke.   See Greek versions of Exod.15:5; G. Schwarz, *N.T.S.*
xxii (1975/6), pp.214-15.   J. Héring, *Rev. Hist. Phil. Rel.* xlvi
(1966), p.25.   P. Vannutelli, *R.B.* 1925, pp.515, 520.
/14/   Macarius Magnes III.4 (ed. A. von Harnack, *Porphyrius,*
Berlin, 1916, pp.76-8; ed. Blondel, pp.55-57).
/15/   Justinian, *Dig.* 47.2.51 (praecipitata pecora), etc., e.g.
Dig. 9.2.11,5; 19.5.14,3; 9.2.9,3; 9.1.1,7; M. Kaser, *Das römische
Privatrecht*[1] (Munich, 1959), sect. 144, p.519; J.A.C. Thomas,
Textbook of Roman Law (Amsterdam, 1976), pp.363ff.
/16/   Mishnah, B.Q. III.1-7; Maimonides, *Mishneh Torah* XI.IV.vi,
3-9; S. Albeck, 'Torts' in M.Elon, *Principles of Jewish Law*
(Jerusalem, 1975), col. 319.
/17/   Iamblichus (born *c.* A.D. 280), *Vita Pythag.* VIII.36 (ed. A.
Nauck, 1884, p.267).
/18/   So in the Cornfield episode (Derrett, *Studies* I, pp.85-95)
and in the Cleansing of the Temple (Derrett, *Downside Rev.* xcv,
no.319, 1977, pp.79-94).
/19/   By the technique known as ʾal tiqrey: Derrett, *Law in the New
Testament* (London, 1968), pp.180, 224 n.5, 380 n.4; *Studies,* I,
p.92.
/20/   Leiris (cit. inf. n.27), pp.34,60; M. Rodinson, *Magie,
médecine et possession à Gondar* (Paris/The Hague, 1967), p.65.
/21/   Jos., *B.J.* vii.185; Test. XII. Patr., T.Jos. 7:3-4.
/22/   K. Preisendanz, *Papyri Graecae Magicae*[2] (Stuttgart, 1973),
pp.34ff. (Pap.Mag.Par. 2391,II.3,41,44.
/23/   Acts 15:20,29; 21:25; R.A. Rappaport, *Pigs for the Ancestors*
(New Haven and London, 1967), photo 10.
/23a/ H. Bengtson, *Die Staatsverträge des Altertums* II-III (Munich
and Berlin, 1962-9), exemplifies the very varied methods used
between cities (see Nos.558,567,569 as examples).   All such
treaties presupposed a basic Hellenic conception of rightness, not
a scriptural law with supersubstantial overtones.   The Jews could
not collaborate in matters of private law whether as arbitrators,
or as participants in mixed courts, and gentile witnesses, or the
plaintiff's oath, were inadmissible.   Where no treaty exists
reprisals are normal.   It is not impossible that Jesus and his
disciples could have been seized, but their labour and/or their
ransom would hardly compensate for the pigs.
/24/   Mark 7:31.
/25/   Cicero, *de officiis* I.9: aequitas enim lucet ipsa per se,
dubitatio cogitationem significat iniuriae.
/26/   Derrett, *Law,* pp.32ff.
/27/   H.F. Ellenberger, *The Discovery of the Unconscious* (London,
1970), pp.13-15,21; K. Thraede, 'Exorcismus', *R.A.C.* vii (1969),pp.
44-118; R. Kirss and H. Kriss-Heinrich, *Peregrinatio Neohellenika*

(Vienna, 1955), pp.72-3; *Volksglaube im Bereich des Islam* (Wiesbaden, 1960), pp.5-16; J. Beattie and J. Middleton, eds., *Spirit Mediumship and Society in Africa* (London, 1969); M. Leiris, *La Possession et ses aspects théâtraux*...(Paris, 1958). See I. Lewis (infra n.28).

/28/ Leiris is of this view and cites approvingly H. Jeanmaire, 'Le traitement de la mania...', *J. de Psychologie* xlii/1 (1946), pp.64-82; id., *Dionysos, histoire du culte de Bacchus* (Paris, 1951), esp. pp.268-331; A. Metraux, 'La comédie rituelle dans la possession', *Diogène* xi (1955), pp.26-49 (*voudou* in Haïti). A popular and celebrated synthesis is I. Lewis, *Ecstatic Religion* (Harmondsworth, 1975).

/29/ Multiple possession: Leiris, pp.7-8. Military demons: Leiris, pp.21,23,36,47; Rodinson, p.64, M. Griaule, *Le livre de recettes d'un dabtara abyssin* (Paris, 1930), p.130; W. Leslau in *Africa*, 1949, p.205.

/29a/ D.F. Pocock, *Mind, Body and Wealth. A Study of Belief and Practice in an Indian Village* (Oxford, 1973), p.36, shows how persistent possession implies a guilty conscience (in the others) about, e.g. landed property, or unfulfilled vows.

/30/ Thraede, col.52; J.G. Frazer, *Golden Bough. The Scapegoat*[3] pt.IV (London, 1920), pp.31ff,33, 190. Kriss and Kriss-Heinrich, *Volksglaube* (1960), pp.15-16. Prof. J. Middleton (personal communication), reports similarly of the Lugbara of Uganda. Transfer of abnormal physical sensation under hypnosis is notorious. Further: R.A. Ridley, 'Wolf and werewolf in Baltic and Slavic tradition', *J. Indo-European Studies* 4/4 (1976), pp.321-331 (bibliog.).

/31/ G. Wissowa, *Religion and Kultus der Römer*[2] (Munich, 1912), pp.193,194,399 n.2, 411 and n.9, 412 n.1; P. Stengel, *Die griechischen Kultusaltertümer*[3] (Munich, 1920),pp.61,121-2, 124-6; Krause, 'Hostia', P.-W.,*R.-E.* Supp.V (1931), cols. 252-5; Orth, 'Schwein', P.-W., *R.-E.* II A, cols. 811-812, esp. 812,11.21-2; G.E. Mylonas, *Eleusis and the Eleusinian Mysteries* (Princeton, 1961), pp.249f; 1 Macc.1:47; 2 Macc.6:18-21; Frazer, 114-15, 185-6. Cf. Yogesh Atal, 'The cult of the *bheru* in a Mewar village; in L.P. Vidyarthi, ed., *Aspects of Religion in Indian Society* (Meerut, 1961); J. Planalp, *Religious Life and Values in a North Indian Village*, unpublished thesis (Ph.D.), Cornell, 1956 (on practices of *ojhas* [exorcists]).

/32/ Cicero, *de leg.* ii.22,57. F. de Visscher, *Le droit des tombeaux romains* (Milan, 1963), p.144; J.M.C. Toynbee, *Death and Burial in the Roman World* (London, 1971), p.50.

/33/ Rappaport, op.cit. For swine as offering to the dead: M. Andronikos, *Totenkult* (Göttingen, 1968), pp.85-7, 89.

/33a/ Startling information appearing in the *Evening Mail,* Feb.21,

1978 (p.7) (a newspaper that circulates in a wide argricultural
area) confirms persistent remarks on the pig from knowledgeable
persons from ancient times onwards.
/34/   *Argon*. IV.700-718.
/35/   Frazer, op.cit., pp.113,200-1; Celsus, *de medicina* iii.23.
In Bali today the Pig-spirit possesses men!
/36/   All 'scapegoat' information in Frazer; Leiris, op.cit., p.
25; Rodinson, op.cit., pp.65-6.
/37/   R. de Vaux, *Ancient Israel* (London, 1965), p.59; J.B. Segal,
'Popular religion in ancient Israel', *J.Jew.Stud*. 17/1 (1976),
pp.1-22.   See lexica for κόπτω, κόπτομαι, κατακόπτομαι. Also
F.I. Grundt, *Trauergebräuche der Hebräer* (Leipzig, 1868), ch.6,
10; S. Klein, *Tod und Begräbnis in Palästina* (Berlin, 1908), pp.
49-50.   For κραυγή see Rev.21:4; Jer.32:36; 51:49; Esth.4:3;
E. Reiner, *Die rituelle Totenklage der Griechen* (Tubingen, 1938);
M. Alexiou, *The Ritual Lament in Greek Tradition* (Cambridge,
1974).
/38/   Mishnah, A.Z. II.1; Bab. Tal., A.Z. 22b-23a; Jer. Tal.,
Schwab, XI (1889), p.193; Maimonides, op.cit., XIII.II.ii,9.
/39/   On pig as a sexual symbol see T.O. Beidelman, 'Pig...'.
Southwestern J. of Anthropology XX (1964), pp.359,370-1.
Obscenities: Ellenberger, pp.19-21,27-8; O. Böcher, *Dämonenfurcht
und Dämonenabwehr* (Stuttgart, 1970), pp.33-40, 124-30; Kriss and
Kriss-Heinrich, *Pereg. Neohell.* (1975); Leiris, op.cit., pp.41,56,
95.   Of the sexual involvement of demons the best example is the
demon in Tobit. Lewis (op.cit.) predictably refers to incubi and
succubi.
/40/   G. Dalman, *Orts und Wege Jesu* (Darmstadt, 1967), pp.190-3.
/41/   H. Beitenhard, 'Die Dekapolis von Pompeius bis Traian',
Z.D.P.V.lxxix (1963), pp. 24-58.
/41a/ After the plots against the Jews of Caesarea had developed
into a progrom, Jews of Judaea attacked the Greeks of Gadara and
Hippos inflicting losses (Josephus, *B.J.* ii.459); later some of
the latter protected some Jewish inhabitants, when all Greek
cities (except Gerasa) rose against their Jewish residents (ibid.
478) (A.D. 66).
/42/   Luke 4:29; LXX 2 Chr.25:12;   Sus.(LXX),62.
/43/   Deut.13:17-18; Mishnah, A.Z. III.3,9; Ps.106:28; Mishnah,
A.Z. II.3; cf.II.6
/44/   Mishnah, A.Z. V.8-9; III.9.
/44a/ Dr Anthony Phillips draws my attention to his *Ancient
Israel's Criminal Law* (Oxford, 1970), p.121 and E. Neufeld,
Hittite Laws (London, 1951), p.188 (bestiality with a pig, a
sacred animal).
/45/   See Test. XII. Patr., T.Ben. V.2; T.Jos. VII.1; T.Dan.
V.1 (Beliar); T.Naph. VIII.4 (the devil).

The Human Integrity of St John's Jesus

John de Satgé,
Hele Linhay,
Ashburton,
Newton Abbot,
DEVON TQ13 7NW.

Scholars today are far more ready than were their predecessors
to accept an early date for the Fourth Gospel, but far less willing
to take seriously the picture of Jesus which they find there /1/.
Among the factors which contribute to this seeming contradiction
is the widespread view that St John has distorted the humanity
of Jesus in carrying out his purpose in writing: "that you may
believe that Jesus is the Christ, the Son of God, and that
believing you may have life in his name" (Jn 20.31). As Michael
Goulder put it in *The Myth of God Incarnate*, "the full work of
divinizing Jesus falls to John, who has no mere human being but
the Word of God incarnated, striding an inch above the ground" /2/.
The pious intention has been achieved at the intolerable cost of
making Jesus less than human.

I disagree with this judgement. I note that it is not based
on historical or theological arguments, but depends upon assumptions
on what is or is not truly human. In so far as so subjective a
criterion lends itself to scientific control, it comes into the
province of psychology. I do not apologise therefore when I turn
to a psychiatrist for light on St John's Jesus.

* * *

Dr Jack Dominian's book, *Cycles of Affirmation,* is a series of
essays and addresses expounding dynamic psychology. The central
theme is that, to develop properly, each person needs from the
moment of birth the support of at least one other to affirm that
he is fundamentally worthwhile. Time and again Dr Dominian turns
for examples to the Gospel accounts of Jesus and, significantly
for this paper, he uses both the Synoptists and John as if there
were no conflict between their pictures of Jesus.

The scanty records of Jesus' early life are just what dynamic psychology, confronted by the adult man, would have expected. "Christ's identity had a truly human source of influence, that of Mary and Joseph, and a divine one, his Father", writes Dr. Dominian /3/. "Such a complex source of origin might have led to confusion, to what is currently called a crisis of identity." It did not; and the Lucan episode of the boy in the Temple shows why it did not. By the age of 12, Jesus had already reached a stage of self-awareness which enabled him to reconcile the conflicting claims of his earthly and heavenly parentage. The episode marks the transaction known to dynamic psychology as child-parent separation. Seldom can those troubled waters have been so skilfully navigated.

Jesus was therefore able to begin his public life blessed with a clear sense of identity: he "possessed himself" to the full. That self-possession was based on a total confidence in the heavenly Father's affirmation of his worth. It underpins the authority, confidence and insight recorded of his dealings with other people; and its intensity may explain why some things in the record seem alien and even inhuman.

Take for example the ability of St John's Jesus to walk through the crowds and the courts unabashed and unaffected, apparently in control even when he is a condemned prisoner. The key text is the most disconcerting: "Jesus did not trust himself to them, because he knew all men and needed no one to bear witness of man; for he himself knew what was in man" (Jn 2.24-5). Dr Dominian takes that insight to be the quality of empathy, "the capacity to put ourselves into the inner world of another person, recognize their needs, yet remain separate and so available in such a way that their need, their distress or their love does not overwhelm us" /4/. The quality which repels turns out to be the necessary foundation of practical service and love.

Then there are the claims which St John's Jesus makes. "I am the light of the world . . ." When the Pharisees object that he is his own witness, he answers, "Even if I do bear witness to myself, my testimony is true, for I know whence I have come and whither I am going" (Jn 8.12-14). "Who except God", asks Dr Dominian, leaping the theological fence, "can have such self-knowledge at the age of thirty? . . . Such a claim springs either from a paranoid delusion or from a unique and total possession of self . . ."/5/. Divinity, we may say, is expressing itself through a humanity which, far from being damaged, has followed to the full the path of developing personality.

A similar line of though helps to explain the controversy at
the end of chapter 8. "If anyone keeps my word, he will never see
death, claims Jesus. What shocked the Jews was the implied
superiority over Abraham. But Jesus insisted: "Truly...before
Abraham was, I am." "Psychologically", Dr Dominian writes, "this
last sentence is breath-taking" /6/. It expresses "a concept of
continuing and unchangeable identity beyond any circumscribed
human experience and an overwhelming protection against the threat
of death".

Dr Dominian stresses the link which St John always shows bound
such exalted self-possession to an unbroken dependence on the
Father. The Synoptic Gospels record two occasions - in Gethsemane
and on the Cross - when Jesus was assailed by sudden fear and
distress. At both points, the threat of separation from the
Father challenged the Son's confidence in his own identity.
Collapse was averted only when his secure relationship with the
Father overcame the dread of personal disintegration.

St John records no such breakdown, though he shows Jesus
weeping by the grave of Lazarus. He does however imply its
possibility, for without it the prayer would hardly have been made:
"Father, the hour is come: glorify the Son that the Son may glorify
thee" (Jn 17.1). The secure framework of dependence on the Father
shows how it was avoided.

*   *   *

I have introduced the testimony of a psychiatrist for the limited
purpose of questioning the psychological assumption that St John's
Jesus is less than human. I do not suggest that biblical scholars
and theologians should abdicate in favour of psychiatrists: each
to his own trade. But theologians should surely take note when a
psychiatrist applies his insights to the object of their studies,
as Dr Dominian has done, and finds there a human person of
outstanding integrity. There is no psychological need to suppose
that John distorted the picture by divinizing Jesus. There is
nothing against the view that he underlined the divinity which
from the start was there. Thus reassured, theologians may resume
their proper task of interpreting for today St John's message
concerning Jesus the Christ, the Son of God.

NOTES

/1/   John A.T. Robinson, *Redating the New Testament* (SCM 1976),
discusses recent past and present views.
/2/   Ed. John Hick, SCM 1977, p.81.
/3/   Darton, Longman and Todd 1975.
/4/   The comments are on pp.7-8.
/5/   Op. cit., pp.10 and 25.
/6/   Op. cit., pp.8-9.
/7/   Op. cit., p.137.

Matthew and the Divinity of Jesus: Three questions concerning Matthew 1:20-23

Rev. J.C. Fenton,
Christ Church,
Oxford.

The three questions are as follows: (i) Where does the direct speech of the angel end? (ii) Who is referred to as *Emmanuel?* (iii) Why is the text of the Isaiah quotation in Matthew different from LXX? The suggestion will be made that these questions are not independent of each other, but hang together.

(i) *Where does the direct speech of the angel end?*

The usual answer is that the angel stops at the end of verse 21 with the words "for he will save his people from their sins", and that verses 22 and 23 are the evangelist's comment; i.e. it is Matthew who says "All this took place to fulfil what the Lord had spoken." Thus translators who use inverted commas usually close them at the end of verse 21 (RSV, NEB, JB, TEV).

There are two arguments against this punctuation: (a) The way in which Matthew introduces the quotation in verses 22f (τοῦτο δὲ ὅλον γέγονεν ἵνα πληρωθῇ τὸ ῥηθὲν ὑπὸ Κυρίου διὰ τοῦ προφήτου λέγοντος) is very similar to what he has in two other places, namely 21:4f (τοῦτο δὲ γέγονεν ἵνα πληρωθῇ τὸ ῥηθὲν διὰ τοῦ προφήτου λέγοντος) and 26:56 (τοῦτο δὲ ὅλον γέγονεν ἵνα πληρωθῶσιν αἱ γραφαὶ τῶν προφητῶν). In this last passage, the translators usually include the verse as part of the direct speech of Jesus; it is he who says: "But all this has taken place that the scriptures of the prophets might be fulfilled" (RSV; similarly NEB, TEV, but not JB). Matthew's writing has a regularity and consistency about it, so that it is often possible to argue from what he does in one place to what he is likely to have meant in another. It could be, therefore, that we are meant to understand Jesus as saying: "And this has taken place in order that what was spoken by means of the prophet might be fulfilled, saying, Tell the daughter of Zion ..." (21:4f); and the angel as the speaker in 1:22f: "And all this has taken place in order that what was spoken by the Lord by means

of the prophet might be fulfilled, saying, Behold, the virgin
shall conceive...". A modern commentator who takes this view
of the punctuation of Matt. 1:20ff is K. Stendahl, in *Peake's
Commentary on the Bible* (London 1962) p.771; it was certainly
the way that Irenaeus read it *(Against Heresies* III.xxi.4;
IV.xxiii.1). JB acknowledges the consistency of Matthew by
excluding all three passages from direct speech, and making
them all editorial comments.

(b) The other argument against the usual punctuation is that
it creates a problem over the perfect tense (γέγονεν) which is
used in each of the three passages, 1:22; 21:4; 26:56. But
there will be no need to explain γέγονεν as an example of "Perfect
for the aorist", as Blass-Debrunner, *A Greek Grammar of the N.T.*
(Cambridge 1961) sect. 343, or as "Perfect of Allegory" with
C.F.D. Moule, *An Idiom Book of New Testament Greek* (Cambridge
1953) pp.14f; the verb refers to events as they are seen from
the point of view of the speaker (i.e. the angel in the first
passage, the Lord in the other two) who is standing *in medias
res;* the perfect is the appropriate tense.

R.E. Brown rejects the suggestion that the formula-citation
in 1:22f is part of the words of the angel on the ground that
"Nowhere in the Bible does an angel cite Scripture in this
fashion" *(The Birth of the Messiah* [London 1977] p.144 n.31).
Matthew might not have thought it odd; if the devil could quote
scripture maliciously in 4:6, why should not an angel do it
beneficently in 1:22f?

The first question is, Where does the angel stop? and the
suggestion is that he stops in verse 23, either at the word
"Emmanuel", or, so as to include the translation of that word,
at "God with us".

(ii) *Who is referred to as Emmanuel?*

Does the name mean that *God* the Father is *with us,* that is to
say, that he is for us, because of Jesus? Or does it mean that
Jesus is *God,* and he is *with us?* Does it refer to the Father, or
to the Son? The usual answer is that it refers to God the Father,
though the point is not much discussed in the books. Books on
the Christology of the New Testament do not include Matt. 1:23
among the passages in the New Testament where Jesus is referred to
as God. There are the following reasons for taking ὁ θεός in
Matt. 1:23 as a designation of Jesus.

(a) If *God with us* referred to the Father, μετά would have to be understood as "in favour of"; if it referred to the Son, μετά could mean "in the company of". Matthew almost always uses μετά with the genitive in the sense of "in the company of", and seldom in the sense of attitude, i.e. "favour".

(b) Matt. 1:23 is the first Old Testament quotation in the Gospel and it is to be taken with the last words of Jesus in the book, 28:20, as an example of *inclusio:* μεθ' ἡμῶν ὁ θεός / ἐγὼ μεθ' ὑμῶν εἰμι. The ἐγώ at the end of the Gospel matches and explains the ὁ θεός at the beginning. Matthew is saying that Jesus is God.

(c) The presence of Jesus *with* his disciples is a constant theme in Matthew's Gospel, e.g. 10:40; 18:20; 23:8-10; 25:31-46; 28:20. There is no suggestion anywhere that the Father is *with* the disciples; he is *in heaven* (contrast 23:8 with 23:9).

(d) Ignatius is perhaps the earliest surviving writer who has used Matthew, and he refers to Jesus as "our God", ὁ θεὸς ἡμῶν (Eph inscr; 15:3; 18:2; Ro inscr (twice); 3:3; Pol 8:3. For other uses of θεός in reference to Christ in Ignatius, see for example Bauer-Arndt-Gingrich, *Lexicon* (Cambridge 1957) *sub* θεός, 2).

(e) Irenaeus, towards the end of the second century, was certainly taking "Emmanuel" as a way of saying that Jesus is God (e.g. *Against Heresies,*III.xxi.4).

Professor Brown says that "one should not read 'God with us' in a Nicaean sense, as if it were identifying Jesus as God" *(op. cit.* p.150 n.52); but now it begins to look as though one should, and as though Emmanuel refers to him, and not to the Father.

(iii) *Why is the text of the quotation from Isaiah in Matt. 1:23 different from LXX ?*

The only difference is that Matthew has καλέσουσιν where LXX has καλέσεις. Why did Matthew change καλέσεις to καλέσουσιν?

If the speaker is still the angel, then he has already said that Joseph will call the child Jesus and he has explained why: "for he will save his people from their sins" (1:21). The angel now goes on to say that this has happened to fulfil scripture: the virgin will have a son; but there will be more to it than that: the son

whom she will bear will be "God with us", and there will be
people who will call him that. The people who will call him
God will be those who believe that he has saved them "from their
sins". The third person plural (καλέσουσιν) refers back to the
previous last word in the plural, which is "their (sins)",
ἁμαρτιῶν αὐτῶν. Matthew is saying that it is the people whose
sins are forgiven by Jesus who will know that he is God with
them (cf. Brown *op. cit.* p.152).

If this interpretation of Matt. 1:20-23 is on the right
lines: if the passage is a single speech by the angel; if
"Emmanuel" means that Jesus is "God" and "with us"; if "they
shall call" means "his people" shall call him God; then the angel
makes four points, or, as Ignatius might have said, he declares
four mysteries: (a) the conception by the Holy Spirit; (b) the
birth of Jesus; (c) his saving death; and (d) his divinity.
What Ignatius actually said was:

Hidden from the prince of this world were the virginity
of Mary and her child-bearing and likewise also the death
of the Lord - three mysteries to be cried aloud - the
which were wrought in the silence of God... God appeared
in the likeness of man (Ephesians 19; tr. Lightfoot).

Ignatius almost certainly alludes to Matt. 2 in this section of
the letter; is it possible that τρία μυστηρία κραυγῆς refers to
the message of the angel in Matt. 1:20-23, rather as Lipsius
suggested (see Lightfoot, *Apostolic Fathers* [London 1889] Part II
Vol.II p.78)?

The 'Massacre of the Innocents' — Fact or Fiction?

R.T. France
Tyndale House,
36 Selwyn Gardens,
Cambridge, CB3 9BA.

This must be a rather bald summary of an argument which I hope to publish in more detail elsewhere /1/. It concerns the question of the origin of the tradition recorded in Matthew 2:16 that Herod 'killed all the male children in Bethlehem and in all that region who were two years old or under'.

1. A 'Midrashic' Origin?

An earlier tendency to regard this as a typical piece of folk-lore, the murderous jealousy of the threatened ruler and the divinely planned escape of his destined supplanter /2/, is not to be dismissed entirely, but it has rightly been modified by the observation that it is in Judaism that the Gospel of Matthew has its roots, and so it is in Jewish tradition rather than in the wider world of folk-stories that an explanation for the Herod tradition may be sought. In recent years it has become almost obligatory to find this explanation under the heading of 'midrash'.

Without attempting to provide a comprehensive definition of that slippery word /3/, we may agree that Matthew most probably wrote in an environment where scripture was assiduously studied in order to draw out parallels between apparently unconnected passages, and where the stories of great men could thus be elaborated with scriptural motifs which had no historical connection with them. It is therefore often taken for granted that Matthew would freely attach such motifs to the story of Jesus on the basis not of a historical tradition but of this 'midrashic' method, not in order to inform his readers of actual events but to heighten their understanding of the significance of Jesus.

This paper is an attempt to test the plausibility of this general view by exploring the origin of one particular narrative tradition which is widely regarded as a typical midrashic creation.

If the story of the 'Massacre of the Innocents' came into
existence on the basis of scriptural motifs, what were those
motifs, and how did they come to be presented as historical facts.

      One important difference between Matthew's Gospel and midrash
as a literary genre is that the latter is, properly speaking, a
commentary on a given text. The organising principle is the text
itself, onto which other motifs are grafted by way of comment and
expansion. But the Gospel of Matthew has no such basis. There is
no given text, but rather scriptural texts and motifs are brought
in freely as they seem appropriate to illustrate the story. In
other words, the ground-plan of the Gospel is a tradition about
the life and ministry of Jesus (however this may have originated),
not a book or a collection of passages from scripture. When
scriptural texts are introduced, it is because something in the
tradition suggested them as appropriate. If we are, then, to
account plausibly for the Herod tradition as a creation from a
scriptural motif, we must explain why and how that motif found its
way into the tradition in the first place. It may have been
introduced at any stage up to and including the final composition
of the Gospel, but at no point was it a given starting-point, as
it was for the midrashist; there must have been some reason for
its original attachment to the story of Jesus.

2.   *Jeremiah 31:15*

      The most obvious suggestion at first sight is that the story
of Herod's killing arose out of the text which is explicitly cited
as fulfilled in that incident, Jeremiah 31:15 /4/. But on further
consideration this proves unlikely for the following reasons.

      (i) It is generally recognised that the four formula-
quotations of Matthew 2, crucial as they are to its final
structure, are a redactional addition, which can be removed with a
minimal disturbance to the coherence and effectiveness of the
underlying narrative /5/.

      (ii) While two or more narrative sources are generally
discerned behind chapter 2 (at least a 'Magi source' and a travel
narrative involving the flight to Egypt and the return), it has
been strongly argued that these were already combined in a
continuous narrative tradition before they reached Matthew /6/.
If this is so, the story of Herod's coup is an integral feature
of the narrative tradition, providing both the dénouement of the
story of the Magi (which would otherwise end with the unresolved

question of Herod's response to their failure to report back) and the motive and the specific occasion for the escape to Egypt, the subsequent return and the fear of Herod's heir /7/.

(iii) The wording of verse 16 is surprisingly independent of the quotation from Jeremiah 31:15, making no mention of Rachel or Ramah, nor of lamentation or comfort, ignoring the striking οὐκ εἰσίν, using παῖδας rather than the equally suitable τέκνα, and including circumstantial details of time and place which add nothing to the motif of the fulfilment of Jeremiah 31:15 /8/.

(iv) Unless the tradition of the killing of children was already established, there is no reason for Jeremiah 31:15 to come in at all. It is not a messianic passage, and is in itself perhaps the least likely verse in the whole of Jeremiah 31 to catch the attention of a Christian midrashist, with its note of gloom interrupting a chapter of hope /9/. The irrelevant place-name Ramah is an embarrassment rather than an attraction /10/. It is the loss of children which is the only ostensible link with Jesus' childhood, and therefore it could only have been brought into this context on the basis of an already existing tradition of such a loss. The quotation is, then, the *result* of this tradition, not its *source* /11/.

3. *The Moses Traditions*

If Jeremiah 31:15 is eliminated as the scriptural source of the Herod tradition, we are left with the far more plausible suggestion that it derives from a desire to assimilate the story of Jesus' childhood to that of some other great figure of the past /12/.

Thus there are Jewish legends about Nimrod's attempts to kill the infant Abraham, but these are not certainly attested earlier than the medieval *Sefer ha-Yashar*; a still later variant involved Nimrod's slaughter of some 70,000 male children in the attempt /13/. These stories are based on the Moses tradition which we shall consider shortly. They are too late to be relevant to our enquiry.

Much earlier is the statement in the Passover haggadah that Laban attempted to kill Jacob, and thus to destroy the whole nation; but Daube's attempt to trace the Herod tradition to this source depends on the assumption that it envisaged Laban's killing of *children*. This is not obvious: the attempt was

apparently on the adult Jacob, and the intended destruction of
'the whole' (the Hebrew text does not say 'the whole *family*')
seems to be located in the attack on the ancestor of the nation
rather than in a general massacre /14/.

The case for a relevant background in the traditions about
Moses is, however, very strong. According to Exodus, Pharaoh
killed Israelite male children, but Moses escaped. What is
missing from the biblical account as a background to the Herod
incident is the search for a specific potential usurper, and this
is amply supplied by later Jewish traditions that Pharaoh's
massacre was prompted by a prediction (by an astrologer or in a
dream) of the birth of the future liberator of Israel. Such
traditions, witnessed in Josephus and in the Palestinian Targum
/15/, were current by the first century AD. Here then are all the
essential ingredients in the story of Herod, and other echoes of
the Moses traditions in the wording of Matthew 2 /16/ confirm that
here if anywhere is the scriptural background to our story.

4. *The Role of the Mosaic Model in the Development of the
     Tradition*

But to establish a conscious scriptural parallel is not *per
se* to determine the origin of the tradition. We still need to ask
whether the parallel was drawn on the basis of an existing
tradition of Herod's action, or whether the tradition was itself
created on the basis of the scriptural model. Is the Mosaic model
the source of the tradition, or merely a comment on it?

We discounted Jeremiah 31:15 as the source of the tradition
because there seemed to be no reason, without this tradition, for
it to be connected with the story of Jesus. Is there any better
reason for the introduction of the theme of Moses' escape from
Pharaoh? Here the answer is clearly more optimistic. If the
early Christians wished to present Jesus as the new Moses, the
leader of Israel into a new era of spiritual liberation, it would
be natural for them to attribute to him experiences parallel to
those of Moses. Matthew relates the return from Egypt in terms
which explicitly echo Moses' return from exile (2:20, alluding to
Exodus 4:19), and a similar Mosaic typology has been detected
elsewhere in his Gospel /17/. It is therefore argued that the
Herod story is deliberately created to claim for Jesus a divinely-
protected infancy parallel to that of Moses.

But who first coined the story? Not Matthew himself, we may suppose, as he is hardly likely to have both invented the story himself and then paraded it as a factual fulfilment of Jeremiah 31:15. Besides, we have already seen reason to believe that it formed part of a pre-Matthean complex of tradition. For Matthew it was already accepted as factual; its origin must lie further back.

But W.D. Davies' attempt to uncover the New Moses theme in the pre-redactional material of Matthew's Gospel produces surprisingly meagre results /18/. It is in the redactional work of Matthew rather than in his sources that this theme is most clearly present. This suggests that the Mosaic model which is reflected in the wording of Matthew 2 is more likely to be a redactional comment than an integral part of the tradition, still less its source. It is perhaps significant that the most explicit clue to a Mosaic typology in this chapter occurs not in its narrative framework but in the final wording of verse 20. Moreover, the less explicit Mosaic elements in the chapter are found equally in the Herod story and in the narratives of Joseph's dreams, which many scholars regard as originally independent traditions /19/. All of this suggests that the Mosaic typology is not so much a structural element in the narrative framework of Matthew 2 as a redactional gloss on an established narrative tradition, of which the Herod story was already a part.

It should be observed also that the Mosaic typology is not the only christological theme of the chapter /20/. The story of Herod's coup immediately follows the quotation of Hosea 11:1 in verse 15, which presents Jesus not as the new Moses but as the new Israel, and this contrasting typology seems no less fundamental to the chapter. Both in its formal quotations and in its allusive language Matthew 2 is a rich tapestry of scriptural and theological themes, carefully interwoven.

But the warp into which the various threads are woven /21/ is not a meditation on the Exodus story, or any other single typological theme, but rather, as Stendahl has convincingly shown /22/, the sequence of events which led the Messiah from his birth in Bethlehem to his home at Nazareth. The fundamental structure of the chapter is, then, a geographical apologetic, an explanation of Jesus' origins by means of a coherent narrative of his childhood movements. From a literary point of view, therefore, I believe that W.L. Knox judges correctly that 'the fact that the typological correspondence is not more complete suggests that it has been superimposed upon the infancy narrative at a stage in its growth which is not primary' /23/.

Of the two most plausible scriptural origins for the Herod story, then, we have seen that one, Jeremiah 31:15, is almost certainly a redactional comment on an already existing narrative tradition, and that the other, the typological reflection on the story of Moses, is more plausibly accounted for as one of a number of interpretative motifs woven onto the narrative tradition, probably at a relatively late stage in its development, than as itself the origin of that tradition. There is no question of the importance of the Mosaic theme in Matthew 2, but literary considerations do not favour the hypothesis that the narrative arose in the first place from the desire to portray Jesus as the new Moses.

5. *An Apologetic Construction*?

An alternative proposal for the origin of the Herod story has been put forward in some recent studies. Herod's attack foreshadows the ultimate rejection of the Messiah by Israel, for he acts in consultation with the leaders of the people (verse 4), and 'all Jerusalem' shares his fear (verse 3). But the blow falls not on the Messiah, but on Israel herself, represented by the babies of Bethlehem; so Israel's rejection of Jesus will recoil in judgment upon Israel herself /24/.

The supposed parallel is rather forced, in that both Herod and the children of Bethlehem are made to represent the same entity, Israel, so that the punishment for Israel's repudiation of the Messiah, represented in Herod's killing, is visited not on the offender but on his innocent victims. Moreover, Jesus' *escape* from Herod makes a poor symbol for his ultimate suffering, death and vindication.

But if it is hard to detect such an apologetic moral in the story at all, it is still harder to imagine this as its *source*. Would a Christian writer of apologetic fiction willingly choose Herod the Idumaean to represent Israel, or the murder of innocent children to represent Israel's punishment? Given the story, such an interpretation *might* be possible with some surrender of logical precision, but surely no one freely inventing the story could be so embarrassingly clumsy.

It is perhaps salutary to notice that apologetic considerations have also been used to the opposite effect. The story makes Jesus indirectly responsible for the suffering of the Jews of Bethlehem; would a Christian invent an incident so embarrassing for Christian relations with Jews? /25/.

6. *Literary Conclusions*

It is possible, though improbable, that apologetic considerations motivated the inclusion of the Herod tradition in Matthew 2. It is clear that scriptural motifs, particularly from the story of the birth of Moses, have affected its presentation. But in each case it has proved more satisfactory to explain this as the result of reflection on an existing tradition rather than as an indication of the origin of the tradition. Given the tradition, the introduction of the Moses typology and of the quotation from Jeremiah 31:15 are understandable, but the narrative tradition seems in each case necessarily prior, and no adequate starting-point for the tradition has emerged byond the obvious possibility that it derives from an actual event.

It is also significant that the wording of verse 16, terse as it is, contains the surprisingly precise specification of Bethlehem 'and all its district', and of the age of the children as 'from two years old and under', which are not essential to the narrative, and are not suggested by any of the literary models we have been considering. These features are hard to explain on any other grounds than that they record the details of the actual event /26/.

From the literary point of view, then, a historical origin for the tradition seems more probable than an imaginative creation. But is it credible?

7. *Historical Credibility*

A few words must suffice. The number of children involved was probably less than twenty /27/. It was hardly a 'massacre' even by modern standards. By the standards of Herod's reign it was a minor incident. Particularly in the last four years of his reign Herod, by Josephus' account, felt increasingly threatened and took increasingly ruthless measures to eliminate any potential usurper: in these years alone Josephus records three incidents when Herod executed large numbers of actual or suspected conspirators /28/, in addition to the execution of three of his own sons on the same grounds /29/. He was hardly likely to baulk at eliminating a handful of children in order to dispose of a potential threat to his throne /30/. The Bethlehem incident is sometimes regarded as too crude and clumsy for Herod, but there is

plenty of evidence for an increasing irresponsibility, not to say
insanity, in his last years /31/, and other recorded incidents
show a similarly violent and indiscriminate reaction when he was
crossed /32/.

Attempts to find independent accounts of the incident,
particularly in the *Assumption of Moses* /33/ and in Macrobius /34/,
have not been convincing. But how probable is it that such an
event would be independently recorded, when even the crucifixion of
Jesus failed to make any contemporary mark? Certainly if Josephus
had known of it, he would probably have included it gratefully in
his sustained attack on Herod, but it happened, if it happened at
all, nearly a century before the publication of the *Antiquities*;
it would be optimistic to imagine that Josephus had records of
every minor incident in Herod's long reign /35/.

8. *Conclusion*

The Bethlehem incident is no more important to us than it was
to contemporary history. No theological doctrine hangs on it, and
its historicity makes little difference to our historical
understanding of Herod or of Jesus.

Its importance here is rather as a test-case for elucidating
the allegedly 'midrashic' origin of much of the narrative in
Matthew particularly the infancy narratives. It is easy and
attractive to postulate in general terms that Matthew and his
predecessors were not concerned with factual historicity and gave
free rein to their imagination in embellishing the story of Jesus
with suitably edifying tales drawn from scriptural tradition and
folk-lore. But is it plausible? In this one, admittedly trivial,
instance we have found it hard to construct a convincing account
of how this particular story could have emerged from the suggested
scriptural motifs. From a literary point of view it is much
easier to understand it as a reminiscence of an actual event,
written up in the light of relevant scriptural and theological
motifs. And there seems no historical improbability in the event
in itself.

In this case at least, then, it would seem more likely that the
the admitted theological interests of the evangelist and his
predecessors are brought into play not in the creation of
fictional incidents but in the way they report and comment on real
events. The scriptural fulfilment which Matthew claims with such
insistence is not apparently, here at least, in imagination but in

what actually happened. And if in this one instance, so widely
assumed to be legendary, there is reason to find a historical
basis, perhaps we should take more seriously the possibility that
the Matthean infancy narratives as a whole are using actual events
as their starting-point for a theological presentation of Jesus as
the fulfilment of that which was written.

NOTES

/1/   In an article entitled 'Herod and the Children of Bethlehem'
Novum Testamentum 21 (1979) 1-23.
/2/   One of the fullest collections of such stories, drawn from
all parts of Europe and Asia, is G. Binder, *Die Aussetzung des
Königskindes Kyros und Romulus* (Beiträge zur klassischen Philologie
10. Meisenheim am Glan: Anton Hain, 1964). Some of the most
directly relevant are those of Sargon of Akkad (*ANET* 119),
Gilgamesh (Aelian, *De Natura Animalium* XII 21), Romulus and Remus
(Livy I 4), Cyrus (Herodotus I 108-113) and Augustus (Suetonius,
Augustus 94.3).
/3/   See esp. R. Bloch, *DBSup* V (1957) 1263ff; A.G. Wright, *CBQ*
28 (1966) 105-138, 417-457; R. Le Déaut, *Int.* 25 (1971) 259-282.
The debate is usefully summarised by G.M. Soares Prabhu, *The
Formula Quotations in the Infancy Narrative of Matthew* (AnBib 63.
Rome: Biblical Institute Press, 1976) 12 16.
/4/   This is argued by C.T. Davis, *JBL* 90 (1971) 419.
/5/   See G.M. Soares Prabhu, *op.cit.* (note 3) 41 (with detailed
demonstration in his chapters 2 and 4); R.E. Brown, *The Birth of
The Messiah* (London: Geoffrey Chapman, 1977) 100-104. On the
independence of the narrative from the quotations see also E.
Nellessen, *Das Kind und seine Mutter* (SBS 39. Stuttgart: Verlag
Katholisches Bibelwerk, 1969) 48f; A. Vögtle in M. Didier (ed.),
L'Evangile selon Matthieu (BETL 29. Gembloux: Duculot, 1972) 156f.
/6/   See A. Vögtle, *loc. cit.* (note 5) 156-161.
/7/   See G. Strecker, *Der Weg der Gerechtigkeit* (FRLANT 82.
Göttingen: Vandenhoeck und Ruprecht, [3]1971) 51; A. Vögtle, *loc.
cit.* (note 5) 165; M. Hengel & H. Merkel in P. Hoffmann (ed.),
Orientierung an Jesus: für Josef Schmid (Freiburg: Herder, 1973)
140-142.
/8/   See further G.M. Soares Prabhu, *op. cit.* (note 3) 257-261.
/9/   For Christian use of Jeremiah 31 as a whole see C.H. Dodd,
According to the Scriptures (London: Nisbet, 1952) 44-46, 85f;
W.F. Albright & C.S. Mann, *Matthew* (AB. New York: Doubleday, 1971)
LXIII.
/10/   See K. Stendahl in W. Eltester (ed.) *Judentum, Urchristentum,*

Kirche. Festschrift für J. Jeremias (BZNW 26. Berlin: Töpelmann, 1960) 97-100, for the importance of place-names in the overall conception of Matthew 2.
/11/ G.M. Soares Prabhu, *op. cit.* (note 3) 261: 'Here at least, the suggestion that the Infancy Narrative of Mt has been derived from or constructed round the formula quotations must appear absurd'. Cf. E. Nellessen, *op. cit.* (note 5) 46.
/12/ C. Perrot, *RechSR* 55 (1967) 481-504 gives details of several such birth-legends in Jewish tradition. Only those which are possibly relevant to the Matthean story of Herod are mentioned here.
/13/ For the version in *Sefer ha-Yashar* see G. Vermes, *Scripture and Tradition in Judaism* (SPB 4. Leiden: E.J. Brill, 1961) 68-70, 90-95. For the later traditions (*Maᶜaseh Abraham*) see A. Wünsche, *Aus Israels Lehrhallen* (Leipzig, 1907) I 14ff (also I 35ff, 42ff).
/14/ For a translation and discussion of the relevant passage see L. Finkelstein, *HTR* 31 (1938) 291-317. Daube's argument was put forward in his *The New Testament and Rabbinic Judaism* (London: Athlone Press, 1956) 189-192, and in *NTS* 5 (1958/9) 184-186. Cf. M.M. Bourke, *CBQ* 22 (1960) 168-171; C.H. Cave, *NTS* 9 (1962/3) 382-390. For critical comments on Daube's hypothesis see R.H. Gundry, *The Use of the Old Testament in St. Matthew's Gospel* (NovTSup 18. Leiden: E.J. Brill, 1967) 196, n.1; E. Nellessen, *op. cit.* (note 5) 69-72; A. Vögtle, *Messias und Gottessohn* (Düsseldorf: Patmos, 1971) 43ff.
/15/ Josephus, *Ant.* II 205ff (cf. *Ex. Rab.* I 18; *b.Sanh.* 101b); *Tg.Ps.-J*, Ex. 1:15.
/16/ The parallels are set out by R. Bloch in *Moïse, L'Homme de l'Alliance* (= *Cahiers Sioniens* 8 (1954) nos. 2-4. Paris: Desclée, 1955) 164f (and for a full presentation of the rabbinic traditions see *ibid.* 102-118). Cf. P. Winter, *HibJ* 53 (1954/5) 36-42; M.M. Bourke, *CBQ* 22 (1960) 161-166; C. Perrot, *RechSR* 55 (1967) 497-504; E. Nellessen, *op. cit.* (note 5) 64-67.
/17/ For a maximal view of the importance of Mosaic elements in Matthew's portrait of Jesus see H.M. Teeple, *The Mosaic Eschatological Prophet* (JBL Monograph 10. Philadelphia: SBL, 1957) 74ff; F. Hahn, *The Titles of Jesus in Christology* (London: Lutterworth, 1969) 385f; R.H. Gundry, *op. cit.* (note 14) 82f. Other scholars regard this as a much less prominent element in Matthew's christology: see J. Jeremias, *TDNT* IV 870f; W.D. Davies, *The Setting of the Sermon on the Mount* (Cambridge: University Press, 1963) 25-93; J.D. Kingsbury, *Matthew: Structure, Christology, Kingdom* (Philadelphia: Fortress, 1975) 89-92.
/18/ *Op. cit.* (note 17) 25-61.
/19/ G.M. Soares Prabhu, *op. cit.* (note 3) 294ff, designates them 'The Dream Narrative Source' and 'The Herod Source'; cf.

W.L. Knox, *The Sources of the Synoptic Gospels* II (Cambridge: University Press, 1957) 121-123.

/20/ It is, according to W.D. Davies, *op. cit.* (note 17) 92, 'one element in a mosaic of motifs, one strand in a pattern, which equally, if not more, emphasized the Christ as a new creation, the Messianic king, who represents Israel and is Emmanuel'.

/21/ L. Hartman in M. Didier (ed.), *L'Evangile selon Matthieu* (BETL 29. Gembloux: Duculot, 1972) 138f, uses this metaphor: for him the warp (i.e. the primary 'framework') of Matthew 2 is the Mosaic typology; cf. A. Vögtle, *ibid.* 165, 168, who regards it as 'strukturbildend'. On the other hand, W.D. Davies (see note 20) sees it as one strand among others in the final pattern, not as the basic structural principle of the chapter; cf. M. Hengel & H. Merkel, *loc. cit.* (note 7) 161; 'Die Mosehaggada durchzieht das ganze Kapitel 2 wie ein roter Faden'.

/22/ *Loc. cit.* (note 10).

/23/ *Op. cit.* (note 19) 123.

/24/ E. Nellessen, *op. cit.* (note 5) 90; M. Hengel & H. Merkel, *loc. cit.* (note 7) 153, 165; J.D. Kingsbury, *op. cit.* (note 17) 48; G.M. Soares Prabhu, *op. cit.* (note 3) 292f, 300; R.E. Brown, *op. cit.* (note 5) 183. A. Vögtle, *loc. cit.* (note 5) 173f, following W. Rothfuchs, *Die Erfüllungszitate des Matthäus-Evangeliums* (BWANT 88. Stuttgart: Kohlhammer, 1969) 64f, goes further to explain Rachel's weeping as caused by her children's (i.e. Israel's) consequent loss of their status as the people of God.

/25/ P. Nepper-Christensen, *Das Matthäusevangelium: ein judenchristliches Evangelium?* (Acta Theologica Danica 1. Aarhus: Universitetsforlaget, 1958) 153f, following T. Zahn, *Das Evangelium des Matthäus* (Leipzig, 1903) 109f. The incident is represented as used polemically in this way in Acts of Pilate 2:3 (Hennecke, *NT Apocrypha* I 453).

/26/ So G.M. Soares Prabhu, *op. cit.* (note 3) 298 (cf. 259). Cf. also E. Lohmeyer/W. Schmauch, *Das Evangelium des Matthäus* (Meyer Komm. Göttingen: Vandenhoeck und Ruprecht, 1956) 29.

/27/ So P. Bonnard (*Matthieu, ad loc.)* assuming a total population of about 1,000. Albright & Mann, *op. cit.* (note 9) 19, put the total population as low as 300.

/28/ *Ant.* xvi 393-394; xvii 42-44; xvii 167 (cf. *B.J.* i 655).

/29/ Alexander and Aristobulus in 7 BC, *Ant.* xvi 392-394; Antipater in 4 BC, *Ant.* xvii 182-187.

/30/ A. Schalit, *König Herodes: der Mann und sein Werk* (Studia Judaica 4. Berlin: de Gruyter, 1969) 648f n.11, regards the order for the Bethlehem killing, with its political motivation, as entirely in character for Herod's later years. Cf. S. Perowne, *The Life and Times of Herod the Great* (London: Hodder and Stoughton,

1956) 172; M. Hengel & H. Merkel, *loc. cit.* (note 7) 158f.
/31/ See A. Schalit, *op. cit.* (note 30) 648f n.11; E.M.
Smallwood, *The Jews under Roman Rule* (SJLA 20. Leiden: E.J. Brill,
1976) 103f.
/32/ *Ant.* xv 260-266; xv 289f; xvi 379-394.
/33/ E. Stauffer, *Jesus and His Story* (London: SCM Press, 1960)
38f, argues that *Ass. Mos.* 6:4 with its reference to Herod killing
'the old and the young' and executing 'judgments on them as the
Egyptians executed upon them', is a contemporary allusion to the
Bethlehem killing, comparing it with Pharaoh's massacre. But
Herod killed 'the young' on other occasions (esp. the execution
of conspirators πανοικί in 25 BC, Josephus, *Ant.* xv 290), and the
reference to the 'judgments' of the Egyptians is not in fact
directly related to killing.
/34/ The setting provided by Macrobius (*Saturnalia* II 4.11) for
Augustus' *bon mot* that it would be better to be Herod's pig than
his son is clearly a garbled reference to this incident. But even
if Macrobius was not himself a Christian (he makes no reference
to Christianity in his writings, though this would not be
unparalleled for a Christian writer on non-theological subjects in
this period: see W.H. Stahl, *Macrobius: Commentary on the Dream of
Scipio* [New York: Columbia University Press, 1952] 6-9), as an
educated man, perhaps in government service, about AD 400 he was
inevitably in close contact with Christianity. His knowledge of
the incident need not, therefore, be regarded as independent
evidence, but is more probably derived from Christian tradition.
/35/ Josephus' main source for the period, Nicolaus of Damascus,
was Herod's friend and close associate, and so was not likely to
record minor incidents which were discreditable to him.

Studia Biblica 1978: II, 95-109

Jesus and Sectarian Judaism

Jack Freeborn,
7 Pinfold Road,
Worsley, Manchester, M28 5DZ.
England.

It seems to me that in Matt. 5:17-20 Jesus was taking the Torah very seriously; he was warning his followers that they should achieve a higher degree of practical observance of the Torah than that which was currently being achieved by the Pharisees and scribes. I am aware that some experts take a different view of this passage. Some claim that it was wholly or partly fabricated many years later by a legalistic wing of Jewish Christianity /1/; by analysing the context and form in the Matthaean and Lucan versions some scholars contrive to maintain that the passage does not mean what it appears to mean. I do not propose to examine all these arguments closely. It is rather that I find I can go about my daily business of study and faith with this working assumption, namely that Jesus did in fact recommend adherence to the Torah, indeed that he did so with an urgency which was unusual in his time, and, furthermore, that this intensification of Torah-obedience is the key to any understanding we may have of his whole vocation.

My contentions run parallel to the work of Heinrich Graetz. He was a German Jew who failed to find a German publisher for his work on Jesus: *Sinai and Golgotha* /2/. It therefore had to be translated into French and was published in 1867. For Graetz, Jesus was an Essene-type Jew for whom renunciation of life was a dominant theme. An aversion to marriage, total disavowal of oaths, esteem for self-inflicted poverty, scorn for worldly riches and a special expertise in casting out demons - all are characteristics of the Essene sect, known to scholars long before the Dead Sea Scrolls were discovered. Add to this, as Graetz did, concern for outcasts, emphasis on the more fundamental precepts of Torah, ardour in calling Jews to turn to God in filial love and the freedom of a Pharisaic style of interpreting scripture

- and here I believe we are at the best starting-point for an
historical appreciation of Jesus. It is significant that
Heinrich Graetz was a Jew. He stands near the beginning of a
long and honourable succession of Jewish scholars who have
found themselves so much at home in the Synoptic Gospels that
they have been convinced of their basic authenticity. It is
unlikely that Graetz was innocent of biblical criticism. He
knew that Strauss rejected all miraculous and mythological
elements in the New Testament /3/; the anti-semitic Bruno Bauer
had even claimed that the Gospel-writers invented Jesus altogether
/4/. Not so the Jewish Graetz. While remaining strongly antagon-
istic to Christianity, he felt that the Synoptic picture of Jesus
was too convincing, too unmistakably Palestinian, to have been
fabricated by the early church.

     I cannot myself rival the impartiality of a learned Jew. I
persuade myself that I have no axe to grind. At least I have
tried to avoid the luxury of discarding those parts of the
Synoptic Gospels which do not fit in with my picture of Jesus.
It is certainly no part of my faith that the whole Bible must be
literally true because it is inspired by God. It would be
nearer the mark to say that I find the opposite view even more
incredible, namely that many parts of the Synoptic Gospels
originated in the minds of Christians long after the time of
Jesus. In this instance I just wonder what sort of person
Matthew was, what sort of church would have welcomed his version
of Christ's message. Some say he was a tax-collector before his
conversion. I would not have thought that such an occupation
would have predisposed him to turn the liberal, outcast-loving
Jesus into a legalistic fanatic.

     Let us look at the example of marriage. After the discussion
on divorce Matthew is supposed to have inserted a "hard saying"
which suggests that some people may feel it right to renounce
marriage altogether for the sake of the kingdom of Heaven,
Matt.19:12. Not a very popular text for sermons, roughly on a
par with the more easily mocked : "Better be married than burn
with vain desire", 1 Cor.7:9. Of which, more later. Meanwhile
let us return to Matt.19. Still struggling to be open-minded,
the student is told that Matthew has inserted the words "other
than unchastity", Matt.19:9, in order to soften Christ's ruling
on divorce; the same can be said of Matt.5:32, whereas no such
ground for divorce is permitted in the Marcan and Lucan parallels.
What has happened? Have there been two Matthaean redactors, one
liberal and one legalistic? I may be a teacher of gymnastics but

I do not care for the theological gymnastics required of a New
Testament student. They strike me as both inelegant and
dangerous. I certainly cannot explain all the motives which
produced our four Gospels; I recognise that each has its own
character, reflecting perhaps idiosyncrasies of the author or
the *Sitz im Leben*. But to turn a liberal into a legalist - or
vice versa - is a different matter. Can we not assume for the
time being that Jesus did recommend renunciation of marriage - for
those who can accept it (Matt.19:11)? Can we not assume that
Jesus took a strong line on divorce - with the shocking suggestion
that the all-powerful male should have no more right than the
submissive female had of divorcing a marriage partner - which, of
course, was no right at all? Does the so-called "adultery clause"
make Jesus a liberal? Not necessarily. Jesus may well have
included the phrase on some occasion when a firm stand was needed
on adultery. I do not know when Matthew wrote all this down - or
when the tradition reached a fixed form, oral or written. I do
know that Paul wrote to the Corinthians about 55 A.D., i.e. less
than 30 years after the crucifixion. Some Christians at Corinth
were convinced that they should renounce marriage; they
certainly took this line on account of their faith in Christ,
perhaps especially in view of the coming end of the world (1 Cor.
7:26). Did Paul reject this attitude as contrary to the freedom
of the Gospel? Not at all. He agreed with it repeatedly throughout this chapter (1 Cor.7). If anything, he qualified the position
along the same lines as Matt.19:12, i.e. renunciation of marriage
is only for those who can accept it. Curiously, Paul made his
one clear quotation from the words of Jesus in this very context -
not about celibacy, but about divorce, which, of course, he was
against, 1 Cor.7:10. It is obvious from the chapter that Paul
himself wanted to discourage over-enthusiastic asceticism, but he
could not deny what must have been a firm tradition in the Corin-
thian church, namely that "celibacy is a good thing". And this,
I repeat, within 30 years of the time when Jesus spoke. Do we not
remember the views of a parent or teacher quite clearly after
30 years, perhaps word for word at crucial moments but certainly
in their general trend?

So, back to my working assumption: Jesus did recommend
renunciation of marriage and he did say most of what the Synoptic
Gospels suppose him to have said. Questions of consistency may
arise, but even these should be seen in their right perspective.
After all, which public speakers give the same emphasis in their
every utterance throughout their careers? Personally, I find the

picture of Jesus which emerges from this assumption to be more
credible than if we pretend that his words were invented by various
rival groups within the church many years later.

The case of teaching on marriage is worth taking further.
What about the context in contemporary Judaism? Rabbinic
literature suggests that celibacy was unusual. Ben Azzai,
disciple of Akiba, had to excuse himself for being unmarried /5/;
when he claimed that he was too busy with the Torah, R. Elazar ben
Azariah retorted that he had diminished the divine image by not
marrying. On the other hand, periods of sexual abstinence were
observed: for instance, Noah and his sons were supposed to have
kept apart from their wives while they were in the ark /6/. There
was also a tradition of sexual abstinence required of a warrior.
It seems that sexual abstinence became normal and life-long at
Qumran when the sectaries felt they were in a continual state of
Holy War. Josephus regarded Essene celibacy as life-long although
there was also a married order /7/. Broadly speaking, life-long
celibacy was an Essene characteristic, not a rabbinic one. Where
can we place Jesus? Some members of the Jesus-movement gave up
their wives as well as their property, Luke 18:29; some, it seems,
did not. The kind of celibacy Jesus recommended, i.e. life-long
celibacy, was Essene rather than rabbinic. The kind of celibacy
which some early Christians practised was obviously life-long,
like the 144,000 men who had not defiled themselves with women,
Rev.14:4. The reason for the celibacy, i.e. the imminence of God's
kingdom, also reminds us of the Hasidaean warrior and it was this
Hasidaean puritanism which appeared later in the Essene community
/8/.

Here I have a problem of terminology. I wish to draw
comparisons on a broad canvas between three groups: first, Jesus
in the Synoptic Gospels, second rabbinic literature probably
representing Pharisaic teaching, third, the sectarian puritanism
to be found in the Dead Sea Scrolls, the Damascus Document and
in the Essene community as described by Josephus, Pliny, Philo and
Nippolytus. Some scholars make a sharp distinction between
Essenes and the sectaries of Qumran and Damascus. I am sure there
are important differences but I am inclined to agree with Dupont-
Sommer that the similarities are greater /9/. I will differentiate
whenever possible. I hope I will be forgiven if in describing
a tendency as Essene I have in mind features which the Essenes
shared with the other forms of sectarian puritanism. This applies
to the next example, that of scriptural interpretation. The way
Jesus used scripture can be compared with the methods of the other

two groups. "Male and female created he them" (Gen.1:27) is
quoted by Jesus to emphasise the indissolubility of marriage.
The very same words are used in the Damascus Document /10/ to
make a different point, namely that polygamy is wrong. It was
an Essene style to re-interpret scripture in order to harden
the rule /11/. The style of Jesus is comparable; in this
instance he sets Genesis over against Moses in order to prohibit
divorce. In contrast to this, the rabbis used Gen.1:27 much as
we would, i.e. to establish the male/female character of the first
human being /12/. Jesus was like the Essenes and he was not like
them. His extremism seems to be paralleled in sectarian
puritanism - perhaps we might say only in that part of Judaism - but
Jesus was not an Essene. Both points are important if we are to
understand him correctly.

A final point on the question of marriage. The sectaries at
Damascus were very concerned about 'kindred and affinity' -
which relations one is not allowed to marry. Ask Jesus a
question about marrying one's dead brother's wife (Mark 12:18-26)
and the answer is clear: he is just not interested! There is no
such thing as marriage in heaven, he says. Now turn to John the
Baptist. He was rather too interested. He accused Herod of
marrying his brother's wife (Mark 6:17). In actual fact Herod had
married his niece but someone got it wrong! My point is that
Mark was very concerned to tell us about John the Baptist but
neither he nor the other evangelists seemed to understand the
Baptist's position on 'kindred and affinity'. From this I infer
that not only the Jesus movement but also Jesus himself was not
interested in the more ritual aspects of marriage law. I am also
convinced that Jesus gave a special status to women in his
movement, a status already implied in his prohibition/of divorce.
It was not normal in rabbinic circles to consort publicly with
women, some of them of dubious reputation, as Jesus did. It was
utterly unthinkable in the Essene sects.

I believe this picture - I dare not call it a pattern - can
be repeated in areas other than marriage. Exceptionally high
standard of behaviour and dedication to God, sometimes to the
point of total reununciation of life, to this end a high-handed
use of scripture. Combine this with freedom of choice: every
individual is left in his own relationship with God, not in the
security of a disciplined organisation. Always remember the
urgency of the present crisis. Add to this a disregard of
convention, sometimes explicit repudiation but sometimes
unconscious neglect. The parallels with rabbinic literature must

be a constant warning to us not to make premature judgements.
But I am equally sure that we shall not understand Jesus unless
we compare him seriously with sectarian Judaism.

What is sectarian Judaism? The Essenes, indeed, along with
the sects at Qumran and Damascus. But there is more to it than
that. It would have been better to say the various groups,
parties, tendencies within contemporary Judaism. Josephus names
four groups: Pharisees, Sadducees, Essenes and a fourth group
whom we might call freedom-fighters though they are sometimes
known as Zealots /13/. For the benefit of his Hellenistic
readers Josephus called these groups philosophies. Whatever else,
they were not co-operating denominations within a World Council
of Judaism. In effect, each claimed that they alone were right.
In addition, there were more groups and more distinctions. About
5% of Jews seem to have been Pharisees. Sadducees and Essenes
together made up 2% /14/. The freedom-fighters were more of a
tendency than a continuing group. Who were the others? There
were the scribes, more a profession than a party, but playing an
important role in the community. Amongst the schools were the
liberal Hillel from Babylon and the conservative Shammai from
Galilee. Their disciples were so much at odds with each other that
they would not worship together. And there were the Samaritans
who had their own place of worship but in other respects remained
close to a Sadducean type of conservatism. The Samaritans were
like the sectaries of Qumran and Damascus in that they set up their
own priesthood to rival Jerusalem, but unlike these sectaries in
their involvement with commerce and their repudiation of apocalyptic.
Were the Samaritans within Judaism or were they a separate religion?
Surely they were within it /15/. So were the Therapeutae, rather
similar to the Essenes but living in Egypt. Nor should we forget
John the Baptist who had a movement of his own; nor the
Hellenistic Jews such as Philo and the authors of the Sibylline
Oracles. My question is: how far did one have to go to be
repudiated by Judaism as a whole? Surely there was no recognised
limit. Where did Jesus stand in this scheme of things? I feel
I must say immediately that Jesus stood clearly inside Judaism.
I do not say inside mainstream Judaism because I am not sure that
such a concept is appropriate. It was more a matter of different
movements or trends, varying in influence and numerical strength,
with a silent majority carried along by one current or another.
I cannot take seriously any suggestion that there was an unholy
alliance of all the Jewish parties against Jesus. In fact, I
suspect that Pilate heard about the miracle-worker who was being
hailed as a king. Romans seem to have been particularly

susceptible to sensational miracles, far more so than the shrewd
rabbis /16/. I am sure Pilate would have been jealous of
Christ's obvious popularity. That is why Jesus tried to keep his
Messiahship secret. It is possible that Pilate had received
garbled reports of Christ's apocalyptic language and jumped to
the conclusion that people took it literally, i.e. as a political
claim. All that Pilate had then to do was to instruct the
quisling Sadducees to identify this dangerous rebel, have him
arrested secretly and rush through the trial and crucifixion
before the Passover crowd realised what was happening. Such is
the behaviour we would expect from the devious, underhand bully
whom Josephus describes on other occasions /17/.

If the evangelists draw a different picture of Pilate - a
confused, vacillating seeker after justice - it would be easy to
say that they were not present at the trial and were merely trying
to commend Christianity to the Romans many years later /18/. I
do not know where the evangelists obtained their information but
I wonder whether there is another explanation. Once he came face
to face with his Messianic rival, Pilate had second thoughts about
the apocalyptic language. Could Jesus really be king of another
world, a spiritual one? R.T. Herford, specialist on the Pharisees,
thought at first that apocalyptic literature was entirely for
Zealots. After further years of study he came to the conclusion
that it was more widely valued /19/. In fact some of it was
written by peace-loving Pharisees. It seems perfectly reasonable
to me that the Sadducees, who started the operation as Pilate's
stooges, then became actively prosecuting counsel. The Sadducees
would have argued: 'Of course these apocalyptic visions of a
transcendent kingdom are political and dangerous; Jesus must be
crucified!' So, as the evangelists put it, Pilate gave way. It
would have been more accurate to say that he reverted to his original
policy of ruthless extermination. Philo's description of Pilate
seems to support this image of a callous bully who could sometimes
be frightened into changing his mind /20/. Pilate's thinking went
like this: 'Wait a moment. If this Jesus were really a Pharisee
with a new, subtle kind of teaching and massive popular following,
his martyrdom might do more harm than good!' But Pilate could not
be bothered to pursue the matter.

Of course, the sentence was grossly unfair. Jesus was not a
political leader, though with the amount of apocalyptic language
he used it is hardly surprising that some of his followers had
Zealot sympathies. I believe this situation made life difficult
for the Jesus movement. Josephus has described how badly Pharisaic

moderates were treated by fanatical nationalists /21/. For
three years during the Jewish war of 66 to 70 A.D. the Romans left
the Jewish groups in Jerusalem to fight it out among themselves.
At one stage the moderates, who wanted peaceful co-existence with
the Romans, had to contend with two other groups, themselves also
opposed to each other. One of the latter was a priestly group who
occupied the inner temple, murdered the high-priest and established
their own truly Zadokite priesthood. Another seems to have been a
nationalist group from rural parts of Israel. At any rate Jesus
had very good grounds for weeping over Jerusalem. The sectaries
of Qumran and Damascus would surely have supported the priestly
Zealots. Jesus also wanted reform of temple worship but he would
surely have been counted amongst the moderates for he and his
followers had not broken away from temple worship (Acts 2:46) - at
least prior to Stephen's death. If Northern Ireland and indeed
modern Palestine are anything to go by, 40 years may not bring much
change in the relationship between contending parties. I guess
that the Jesus movement did suffer in Christ's own time at the
hands of political agitators of various kinds. Repeated
references in the Gospels to persecution are not therefore
fabrications by a later church. Furthermore, the danger from
Romans and Herodians was a real one (Matt.10:17,etc.).

    So this is how things stood at the time of the trial. Pilate
was terrified by the Triumphal Entry into Jerusalem. The
Sadducees were embarrassed to the point of exasperation by the
Cleansing of the Temple. What about the Pharisees and scribes? No
doubt, some individuals were offended by the devastating criticism
which Jesus directed at the Pharisees. After all, Jesus was not
good at tactful diplomacy. I cannot believe that the Pharisees and
scribes turned against Jesus as organised groups. Jesus obviously
visited the home of Pharisees. Some Pharisees gave Jesus a kindly
and well-founded warning about the danger of the Triumphal Entry
(Luke 19:39). Perhaps Joseph of Arimathea was of similar
inclination, for not all members of the Sanhedrin were Sadducees.
Is it not one of the tragedies of history that the Gospels give an
overwhelming impression of a head-on collision between Jesus and
the Pharisees? As the rabbinic parallels indicate, much of Christ'
teaching would have been warmly welcomed by Pharisees: they too
advocated humility, kindness, gentleness, forgiveness, doing God's
will thoroughly, justice for the needy, do-as-you-would-be-done-by.
The Pharisees also discouraged revenge, any expression of anger,
insincere or ostentatious worship /22/. Yes, give way to those
who disagree with you, avoid lustful thoughts as much as adultery
/23/, - this is what the Pharisees taught also.

But after all that, Jesus was not a Pharisee. Can we attempt
to define the Jesus movement in relation to the other forms of
contemporary Judaism? I have deliberately called it a movement
because it was not a sect. By no means all the people whom Jesus
influenced were expected to renounce their old life to follow him.
There was apparently no ceremony of initiation. That came later.
It was certainly a campaign to prepare the whole of Judaism for
the coming crisis; it was a reform movement but rather loosely
organised. This looseness derives from the fact that each
individual was to be guided by God in his decisions about
marriage, family relationships, property, etc. The rich young
ruler was left to decide whether to give away his possessions; as
the AV puts it: "If thou wouldst be perfect" (Matt.19:17). Notice
also that he was to give to the poor, not, as with the Essenes, to
the leaders of the movement. On occasions, however, instructions
were precise and exacting. On their preaching mission the
disciples were to heal the sick and tell people about God's
kingdom; they were to take no food nor money nor bag for
belongings; they were to go barefoot with no spare coat and they
were to be unarmed (Luke 9:3;10:3-4 par.). The Essenes were also
required to travel light, in old clothes but with weapons in case
of brigands/24/. The comparison is illuminating. Like the
Essenes, but not like the Essenes.

Each movement - or break-away group when we may call it
that - claimed to go further in the direction of radical obedience
to God. It started with the 'pious ones', the *chasidim,* the
remnant in Maccabean times who resisted attempts to water down
the Jewish faith under Hellenistic pressure. Out of this
movement emerged the Pharisaic party as a distinct group with
recognised standards of Law-observance. But the Pharisees were
prepared to compromise; they tolerated a priesthood contaminated
by foreign influence and themselves conducted business with
Gentiles. Both Essenes and Zealots were not so tolerant. The
Zealots were resolved to remove the contamination by force. The
Essenes escaped from the contamination and established their own
higher standards of Torah-observance; this included renunciation
of property and marriage and strict discipline imposed by their
overseers. I believe it is in this context that we must take
seriously Christ's instruction that his followers should achieve
a higher standard of Torah-observance than that achieved by
scribes and Pharisees (Matt.5:20). As with the Qumran sect it
was the urgency of the crisis which required such drastic action;
unlike them, however, Jesus did not conceive of the coming
salvation in purely political terms. Yet the yearning for fuller

obedience, even for deeper intimacy with God, is analogous to
the Essene demand for increased purity.

At this point we must return to the question of consistency.
Can a man contradict himself without losing his integrity? Do
the contradictions appear sharper to us than they did at the
time? I suppose the matter would have been simpler if Jesus had
been like John the Baptist. John, too, did not belong to the
Qumran sect, but at least he was consistently ascetical. His
baptism was different; it was a public, once-only ceremony,
whereas the Essene lustrations were secret and repeated. Above
all, it was a baptism of repentance for all sorts and conditions
of men, who then returned to their daily lives. Whereas the
Essenes turned their back on the wicked world, it seems that
baptised tax-collectors were to be honest tax-collectors and
baptised soldiers were to be gentle soldiers, even content with
their wages (Luke 3:14)! Prostitutes were also baptised
(Matt.21:32) and presumably improved their lives appropriately.
Meanwhile, back in the wilderness, John maintained his life of
prayer and purity. In passing we note that the Jesus movement,
though loosely organised, was in some respects stricter than
John's; some at least of Christ's followers had to leave their
fishing nets - and their families - to follow him. But the
point I want to make is that the baptist movement already
contains a certain inconsistency. Can one maintain one's new,
higher standard while continuing to be fully involved in the
world - or is it necessary to withdraw into the wilderness? We
know that Jesus chose the former way, the way of involvement, despite
the ridicule it brought. How could a drunkard and friend of
tax-collectors be Messiah (Luke 7:34)? In fact, the principle of
withdrawal is there. Jesus not only kept the prayer times
required by the Torah; he also added longer periods of prayer or
fasting as occasion required /25/.

Besides marriage, divorce, family ties and property, there
are other areas in which it can be shown that Jesus expected more
than the Pharisees demanded. Take swearing. In an age of
superstitition one can well imagine how oaths could be misused.
A poor man might feel compelled to make an oath which bound him
to an unfair contract. Pharisees advised caution in the matter /26/
Essenes were against oaths but members were required to make one at
the time of admission /27/; the Damascus Document allowed swearing
before judges or at their decree /28/. The position of Jesus is
more radical. He banned swearing altogether.

Take love of neighbour. The Qumran sectaries were to love other members but hate outsiders /29/. Followers of Jesus were to love all men, including non-Jews, members of despised trades, even enemies. It seems that some Pharisees had begun to widen the circle of those who deserved to be loved, as the rabbinic parallels suggest /30/; Jesus went further. Incidentally, no holy scripture said, "Love your neighbour, hate your enemy" (Matt.5:43). It was the Qumran sectaries who said that and we need this background if we are to understand the Sermon on the Mount.

There I could conveniently leave the question of love for enemies. As in the case of sabbath-observance, Jesus quotes the narrow view of Qumran in order to reject it. The relationship between Jesus and the Essenes would be one of total opposition. If we want a parallel we would have to look amongst the more broad-minded Pharisees. But a further look at the documents makes one wonder. In the Dead Sea Scrolls we read: "I will repay no man with evil's due; with good will I pursue a man" /31/. Hardly a parallel, one might say, but it could be the seed of a new concept: respond to evil with love. Josephus in his account of the Essenes is straightforward: they were told to "hate the wicked always" /32/. But why does Hippolytus follow Josephus almost word for word up to this point, where we read that the Essenes were to "hate no man, neither the unjust nor the enemy, but to pray for them" /33/? Hippolytus was a learned, argumentative rigorist of the third century. I can think of no reason why he should have "christianised" the Essenes in a work devoted to refuting heresies /34/. Once again I have the temerity to trust the early Christian copyists until they have been proved wrong. Just suppose that some Essenes, unknown to Josephus, did pray for their enemies. For myself, this would not detract from the challenging originality of Christ's command: "love your enemies". What it would do is to put this new commandment in its proper setting, i.e. sectarian puritanism. Loving one's enemies was just one more example of "going the extra mile", of observing the Torah more fully than other Jews did.

My speculation could be extended by reference to the *Testament of the XII Patriarchs*; this work is quoted repeatedly in the Damascus Document and a couple of times in the Dead Sea Scrolls /35/. Scholars are not sure whether the work as we now have it contains Christian interpolations. In it we read: "if a man wishes to harm you, do good to him and pray for him" /36/; "the good man can conquer evil by doing good... He loves the unjust as himself" /37/. Some experts believe the book was written by Essenes /38/.

This heightening of the Torah's demands can be seen also
in the way Jesus treats the concept of reward. Pharisees stressed
the reward, usually in heaven, to be given to the pious /39/.
Jesus also spoke much about heavenly reward but with the
significant addition that even this reward cannot be claimed by
the law-keeper as of right. "We are servants and deserve no credit,
we have only done our duty", Luke 17:10. For both the Essenes and
the Pharisees special virtue was attached to those who did more
than their duty /40/; such goodness atoned for the faults of
others. In contrast, the followers of Jesus were to renounce any
such claim; those who work longer hours in the vineyard achieve
no special status in God's eyes, Matt.21:14. Greatly daring, I
suggest that in the parable of the prodigal son the elder son's
mistake may not be exactly that of a legalist. As part-owner of
the farm, I suppose, he did have a right to be consulted before
the fatted calf was killed. His real mistake was the disrespect he
showed to his father. He broke the far greater law of the Ten
Commandments. We know in any case that Jesus accused the
Pharisees of evading the rule: "Honour your father and your
mother", Mark 7:10. I could also suggest that the parable of the
unjust steward is an attack on the Pharisaic practice of usury;
the rogue put charity before customary business rules (Luke 16:1-14
/41/! But again I over-state my case. My plea is that we try out
the hypothesis that Jesus was a law-keeping extremist. Much that
he said and did can then be seen in a new light.

But what about the occasions when Jesus openly violated the
Torah? Did he really make all meats clean, Mark 7:19? I admit
that this is only Mark's comment, but he surely had grounds for
making it. Why did Jesus allow himself to be defiled by contact
with Gentiles, Samaritans, prostitutes and others with whom a
Pharisee would refuse to associate? Why did Jesus break the
Sabbath? With our Pauline spectacles we may not have asked these
questions as persistently as we should. On the Sabbath question I
would say that Jesus did observe it in the sense of worshipping
in the synagogue and resting from his weekday journeys. He did
not wish to destroy the Sabbath rule but to set alongside it the
pre-eminent commandment of love, to save life and care for the
needy. It may even be that Jesus had a background of exceptionally
strict sabbatarianism. When Jesus referred to the absurdity of
not drawing an animal out of a well on the Sabbath, Luke 14:5 =
Matt.12:11, he was virtually quoting, albeit with disapproval, the
extraordinarily strict rule of the Damascus Document: "If the anima
fall into a pit it may not be drawn out on the Sabbath" /42/. At
one point Jesus was a thorough-going sabbatarian: he hoped that his

followers would not have to flee from their homes on a Sabbath,
Matt.24:20; for most Jewish nationalists permission to fight on
a Sabbath had been granted since Maccabean times.

However, it does seem that Jesus ignored the ritualistic
aspects of the Torah, as in the case of marriage law. Perhaps
Jesus felt that rules about defilement from sinners were of no
importance compared with the infinity of God's love and the
urgency of the crisis. How unusual was this in the Judaism of
his time? Very unusual but perhaps not unique. R. Johanan ben
Zakkai remarked confidentially to his students: "it is not the
corpse that pollutes" /43/. Dr Vermes has compared Jesus with
another near-contemporary, R. Ḥaninah ben Dosa /44/. I do not
agree with all that Dr Vermes says. For instance, he claims that
Jesus was not an expert in Jewish law. Personally I believe that
Jesus was exceptionally knowledgeable on the Hebrew scriptures.
Sometimes Jesus took it for granted that a questioner knew his
Bible; the rich young ruler, for instance, got his answers right
although he was no scribe. The really strange thing is that, unlike
the Pharisees and Essenes, Jesus did not demand regular Bible
study. But the comparison with Ḥaninah ben Dosa is interesting.
Although not specially learned, his prayers for healing were more
often answered than those of more renowned scholars; this was
thought to be due to his outstanding honesty and his intimate
relationship with God. Haninah began his Sabbath observance
earlier than the Torah required, but what is specially remarkable
is his attitude to defilement. He seems to have ignored it.
After killing a serpent (he had a special line in killing serpents)
he took it to the local school, saying: "My sons, it is not the
serpent that kills, but sins kill" /45/. A dead serpent would
surely have been a defiling object, to be disposed of as skilfully
as possible. My point is that a Jew could be noted for his
specially strict observance of the Torah and yet he might, perhaps
unconsciously, neglect the rules on defilement. Like Jesus,
Ḥaninah was a Galilean. Dr Vermes thinks that the Pharisees
exercised less influence in Galilee than in Judaea. If so, that
might explain why ritual matters, some of which even worried John
the Baptist, did not concern Jesus. It could also possibly
explain why Jesus seems not to recognise the amount of common
ground he shared with Pharisees.

Was Jesus always consistent? Perhaps not. Single-minded
fanatics have a total dedication which commands our admiration.
Other, richer characters are less consistent or at least they
appear so to lesser minds; this may be due to their greater

sensitivity towards various points of view or to the needs of
different situations; it may be due to a greater profundity of
thought, for truth is not always neat. I believe that Jesus was
a rich, many-sided personality of the latter kind.

NOTES

/1/   G. Barth in G. Bornkamm, G. Barth, H.J. Held, *Tradition and
Interpretation in Matthew*, 1963, pp. 129ff. Variations on the same
theme in G. Strecker, *Der Weg der Gerechtigkeit*, FRLANT 82 (1962),
pp. 143-7; W. Trilling, *Das wahre Israel*, 1964, pp. 167-186.
/2/   A summary can be found in his *History of the Jews*, 1891,
vol. II, pp. 149-157.
/3/   D.F. Strauss, *Leben Jesu*, 1835-6.
/4/   *Kritik der evangelischen Geschichte der Synoptiker*, 1841-2.
/5/   Yebamoth 63b.
/6/   Gen. R. xxxv.1
/7/   Jos. B.J. II. 120.
/8/   M. Black, Hasidaean-Essene Asceticism, *Aspects du Judéo-
Christianisme*, 1965, pp. 19-32.
/9/   G. Vermes, *The Dead Sea Scrolls*, 1977, pp. 125-330 ("the
Essene theory is relatively the soundest").
/10/ CD iv.21.
/11/ H. Braun, *Spätjüdisch-häretischer and frühchristlicher
Radikalismus*, 1957, vol.II, pp.3-6; 111 note 2.
/12/ Strack-Billerbeck, *Kommentar zum NT aus Talmud und Midrasch*,
1924/61, I, p.801f.
/13/ Jos. Ant. XVIII.i.1-6; B.J. II.viii.2.
/14/ T.W. Manson, *The Servant-Messiah*, 1956, p.11.
/15/ R.J. Coggins, *Samaritans and Jews*, 1975, p.163.
/16/ I. Abrahams, *Studies in Pharisaism and the Gospels*, First
Series, 1917, p.111.
/17/ B.J. II. 172-179.
/18/ P. Winter, *On The Trial of Jesus*, 1961, p.61.
/19/ *The Pharisees*, 1924, p.188; *Talmud and Apocrypha*, 1933, p.193.
/20/ *Legatio ad Caium*, 299.
/21/ B.J. IV. 196ff., et al. A. Finkel in *The Pharisees and the
Teacher of Nazareth*, 1964, p. 143, suggests that the Zacharias
mentioned in Matt. 23:35 was a pacifist Pharisee who negotiated
with the Romans and was illegally murdered by Zealots after a
Jewish court had failed to convict him.
/22/ Yoma 72b, for example.

/23/ Lev.R. Ahare Mot xxiii.12.
/24/ Jos. B.J. II. 124-6.
/25/ J. Jeremias, *The Prayers of Jesus,* 1967, p.75.
/26/ Tanchuma B.I. Mattoth 19a.
/27/ CD xix.1.
/28/ CD ix.9.
/29/ 1 QS i.10.
/30/ Pesikta R 195a-b.
/31/ 1 QS x.18.
/32/ B.J. II.139.
/33/ *Refutatio,* ix.23.
/34/ M. Black, The account of the Essenes in Hippolytus and Josephus, in *The Background of the NT and its Eschatology,* Studies in honour of C.H. Dodd, 1956, p. 175.
/35/ A. Dupont-Sommer, *The Essene Writings from Qumran,* 1961, p. 301.
/36/ *Test. Joseph,* XVIII.2.
/37/ *Test. Benjamin,* IV.4.
/38/ See D.S. Russell, *The Method and Message of Jewish Apocalyptic,* 1964, pp.56-7.
/39/ R. Aboth ii.1.
/40/ 1 QS v.6.
/41/ J.D.M. Derrett, *Law in the NT,* 1970, pp.48-77.
/42/ CD xiii.23.
/43/ Pesikta de R. Kahana 40b.
/44/ *Jesus the Jew,* 1973, p.27.
/45/ A. Büchler, *Types of Jewish-Palestinian Piety,* 1922, p.89.

Jesus and the Exilic Soteriology

Paul Garnet
Department of Theology,
Concordia University,
Montreal,
Quebec, H4B 1R6, Canada.

By the term "exilic soteriology" I mean salvation ideas, during the period of the Second Temple, which were based on the conviction that Israel was still in Exile as far as the accomplishment of God's purposes for a national restoration was concerned. A restoration would depend upon the fulfilment of Lev. 26:39-42 (a perfect doxology of judgement, accepting God's exilic punishment as righteous), of Ezek 20:33-40 (a separating of the submissive from the rebellious in Israel) or of Dan. 9:24 (the passage of a predetermined period of time). I have shown elsewhere /1/ that this concern dominated the soteriology of Qumran, but there are signs of it in most strands of second-temple Judaism /2/.

An important link between Jesus and the type of Judaism exemplified at Qumran is the teaching of John the Baptist and in what follows I shall attempt to show:

1.   that the exilic theme was an important element
      in John's ministry,
2.   how it was elaborated by John,
3.   how Jesus understood John's ministry in terms
      of the Exilic Soteriology.

The Baptist led the people to expect the promised restoration of Israel through his programme. According to Q he used the image of gathering to describe the saving work of the Coming One whom he proclaimed (Mt. 3:12, par. Lk. 3:17). Matthew summarizes his message in the same terms as that of Jesus: "Repent, for the Kingdom of Heaven is at hand" (Mt. 3:2), whilst Luke calls his message "good news" (Lk. 3:18). The Benedictus, which probably reflects the understanding of the significance of John's ministry among his own disciples as well as early Christians, speaks of his work as the first step towards the redemption of Israel and

deliverance from her enemies. Restoration passages such as Isa. 9
and 40 are clearly alluded to (Lk. 1:68, 74, 76, 79). Even
Josephus, who regularly down-played the eschatological expectations
of Judaism /3/, uses language which betrays the Baptist's underlying
restorational emphasis, for he refers to the people "coming
together" for baptism and to John's concern that this baptism might
be "acceptable" to God. Also such an emphasis would explain why
Antipas felt threatened by his movement /4/.

        John's programme for Israel's restoration seems to have owed
something to Ezek. 20:33-44 where it is stated that God would bring
Israel again into a wilderness experience after her exile among the
nations and there purge out the rebels from her midst. Thus not
all who left the land of exile would actually return to the land
of Israel. The Baptist expected the separation of the wheat from
the chaff before the gathering of the former. Everything
unfruitful would simply be destroyed (Mt. 3:10, 12[Q], par. Lk.
3:9, 17). Qumran reproduced the prophesied separating process in
their community and even referred to their geographical location
in the desert by Ezekiel's term, "the wilderness of the peoples"
(1QM 1:3). The Baptist did not attempt such separating himself,
but ascribed it to the Coming One. He seemed to identify this
final winnowing stage of the exile with the Woes which were to come
upon Israel in the last days just preceding her restoration /5/.

        In chapter 36 Ezekiel elaborates upon God's acceptance of
Israel after the restoration: God would sprinkle clean water upon
her (vss. 25, 29), give her a new heart, put his own spirit within
her and cause her to obey his Law (vss. 26f.). The Baptist's
teaching retains the elements of restoration, water, spirit and
obedience, but he has them in a different order: water, obedience
("fruits worthy of repentance"), spirit and restoration. Because
Ezekiel wished to emphasise the grace of God, he put repentance
after salvation. John's concern was to obtain a commitment to
righteousness from the people before it was too late, so he put the
water rite first.

        John's baptism was a sign of repentance. This is clear not
only from the Markan material (Mk. 1:4; Mt. 3:11), but also from
the Lukan infancy tradition (Lk. 1:16f) and Josephus /6/. This
repentance may or may not have been genuine (Mt. 3:7f[Q], par.; Lk.
3:7f.). "Fruits worthy of repentance" would show if it was.
Luke's special material gives us a glimpse of what such fruits
might be: sharing with the needy and refusing to take unfair
advantage of a position of power (Lk. 3:11-14). John's
condemnation of Antipas is further evidence for his emphasis on

practical righteousness (Mk. 6:17; Lk. 3:19).

Mark calls John's baptism a baptism of repentance for the
forgiveness of sins (εἰς ἄφεσιν ἁμαρτιῶν Mk. 1:4). How is this
forgiveness to be understood? Is it a national or an individual
forgiveness? In the light of the restorational emphasis we have
already noticed it probably means a national forgiveness. In
Luke's birth narrative, John is to prepare "a people ready for the
Lord" (1:17) and in the Benedictus he is "to give a knowledge of
salvation to His people in the forgiveness of their sins" (Lk. 1:
1:77), emphasising the corporate aspect. In the LXX the term
ἄφεσις is used for the jubilee general amnesty (Lev. 25:10ff.) and
the phrase εἰς ἄφεσιν for the scapegoat rite (Lev. 16:26). In
Qumran's thinking the day of atonement and the year of jubilee were
linked with the idea of restoration /7/.

When we come to the teaching of Jesus about John, we find a
stress on the exilic soteriology. When the Baptist asked whether
Jesus was the Coming One of whom he had preached, Jesus was
satisfied to answer by referring to his own ministry in terms drawn
from the restoration prophecies of Isaiah /8/. The testimony
attributed to Jesus in Lk. 7:27 (Q) imports into the prophecy of
Mal. 3:1 the language of Exod. 23:20 which referred to an angel to
lead Israel into the promised land. Mt. 21:31 refers to the tax
collectors and the harlots *entering* the Kingdom as they responded
to John's ministry. This is territorial imagery.

Jesus taught that the very act of submitting to John's baptism
was itself an implicit doxology of judgement: justifying God in his
counsel and wisdom (Lk. 7:29f., 35[Q]). This is also what the
sayings reported in Matthew are probably referring to when they
speak of fulfilling all righteousness (Mt. 3:11) or of accepting
the way of righteousness brought by John (Mt. 21:32). Jesus spoke
of John's baptism as being from heaven (Mk. 11:30), that sphere
where God is obeyed perfectly. It is likely, therefore, that the
baptismal confession took the form of a doxology of judgement.

Some other conclusions we have reached also agree with the
witness of Jesus concerning John. The Baptist marked the beginning
of the new conquest of Canaan as violent men seized the Kingdom
(Mt. 11:12[Q]). His work, as well as that of Jesus, separates two
groups: the Pharisees who rejected God's will and the tax
collectors who justified God (Lk. 7:29f.; Mt. 11:35; 21:28-32). The
The parable of the two sons refers implicitly to John's emphasis on
repentance (Mt. 21:30:32) and explicitly to his emphasis on
righteousness (Mt. 21:30, 32).

A major question which interested Jesus's contemporaries was
"How and when will God restore Israel in fulfilment of his
promises?" The exilic motif involved here was not a major concern
for the early church, which would be unlikely to insert material
relating to this into the tradition. I have used throughout this
essay the criterion of multiple attestation, but I believe this
material also satisfies the dissimilarity criterion along the lines
of reasoning I have just given.

NOTES

/1/   *Salvation and Atonement in the Qumran Scrolls, W.U.N.T.*,
Series 2, No. 3, Mohr, Tübingen, 1977.
/2/   E.g. the exilic doxologies of judgement in the Prayer of
Azariah (Gk. Dan. 3:26-45), the Prayer of Esther (Addns. to Esth.
14:6ff) and the Prayer of Baruch (Baruch 1:15-3:8). Tobit 14:5-7
states that the restoration under Zerubbabel was not the
restoration promised through the prophets. As for the
preconditions, Tobit 13:5 states that on the very day Israel truly
repents she will be gathered from dispersion, Jub. 23:17-21 demands
that a whole generation study the Law perfectly, Text. Jud. 23
declares that the captivity will end when Israel repents with a
perfect heart and walks in God's commandments, whilst Test. Naph.
8 ascribes the restoration to the activity of God himself through
priestly and kingly messianic figures. Even Philo has allusions to
the exilic soteriology (Praem. Poen. xiv 79ff., xvi 95, xix 186f.,
xxviii).
/3/   See e.g. C. Scobie, *John the Baptist,* S.C.M. Press, London,
1964, p. 111.
/4/   Ant. XVIII, 116-118.
/5/   1QM 1 envisages first a return of the Sons of Light from the
"wilderness of the peoples", then a war described in terms of the
eschatological Woes. Following this there would be eternal peace
and joy for the Sons of Light. Clearly the last item alone
constitutes the promised restoration. John's equivalent is the
final gathering into the garner.
/6/   Loc. cit. Josephus states that John demanded practical
righteousness as a prerequisite, not just as a sequel to baptism.
This statement though probably motivated by opposition to
Christian baptism (Scobie, loc. cit.), is nevertheless evidence
for the Baptist's emphasis on repentance for candidates.
/7/   1Q DM 3:6f.; 11Q Melch.
/8/   Lk. 7:19-22(Q). Cf. Isa. 35:5, 1O; 61:1.

Studia Biblica 1978: II, 115-127

St. Mark's Attitude to the Relationship between History and the Gospel

M. E. Glasswell,
Department of Religion,
University of Nigeria,
Nsukka,
Nigeria.

Ever since Wrede asserted in 1901 /1/ that St. Mark's Gospel did not make sense as history there has been an ever-increasing momentum to explain the construction of that Gospel theologically, sometimes as if it had little or no connection with history at all. More recently, the Finnish scholar Räisänen has asserted, in a very instructive survey of the discussion of the messianic secret in Mark since Wrede and a very careful redactional analysis of the text of Mark /2/, that Mark does not make sense as theology either. For Räisänen there is no single key to Mark's theology and the work is a collection of assorted traditions under no single consistent viewpoint /3/. Where Mark does introduce something himself, such as the command to silence after Peter's confession /4/, there is no obvious relation to other parallel redactional elements in the Gospel, such as the commands to the demons to be silent /5/, nor is the significance of these elements explained /6/. They are to be distinguished from the commands to silence after the miracles which are regarded by Räisänen as being from the tradition. For Räisänen, any attempted explanation of the theme of secrecy as a whole runs up against problems and contradictions which demand as much reading between the lines for their resolution as the historical reconstructions of the liberals queried by Wrede. Mark is therefore for Räisänen a collector of often contradictory traditions rather than a theologian. But for what end?

This is a question, unanswered by Räisänen, which we must ask if we grant that Mark's Gospel is neither straight history nor a sophisticated theological construction. We must ask what Mark thought he was doing in writing as he did and what he expected his readers to conclude from reading what he wrote.

Presuming that Räisänen's analysis of tradition and redaction
in Mark is correct and presuming that Mark's readers were
equally aware of what Mark simply took over and what he added
or subtracted, some significance should be apparent. Of course,
it is highly probable that the whole work as it stands was
something new, apart from the originally isolated traditions
or traditional units which it contains. But, if so, we must
presume that this combination was intended to make sense as a
whole and to be seen to do so. If this was not intended to be
purely historical or purely theological, then what was it intended
to say? Why indeed was the particular form of quasi-historical
narrative chosen? Räisänen's conclusion is unsatisfactory even
if the alternative explanations Räisänen discusses are inadequate
answers to these questions (which Räisänen himself does not
discuss and seems to rule out as unnecessary). Lack of an
adequate explanation does not mean there is none, even if we grant
that Mark does not spell it out.

I take it for granted that the form of St. Mark's Gospel
presumes an attitude to history on the part of the evangelist,
even if the content is not straightforward history. But I also
presume that the connections between the traditions which are
incorporated have a theological basis, in a broad sense. This
theological basis I also presume discloses the attitude to history
of the evangelist, i.e. to the particular history referred to.

Since Wrede the theological explanations of St. Mark's Gospel
have in fact been largely concerned with Mark's attitude to
history. Of course this has often meant that various schools of
thought have thereby displayed *their own* attitude to history, as
is the case with the existentialists and the proponents of the
so-called new quest of the historical Jesus. Too much has
undoubtedly been read into Mark, as Räisänen rightly protests.

Much of the attitude to history which has been adduced for
Mark has in fact been negative, reflecting what Wrede thought was
the evidence of the pre-Marcan tradition concerning Jesus'
messiahship, whereas Wrede's original idea of Mark's purpose was
positive, viz. to present a messianic life despite an unmessianic
tradition. The false idea that Wrede's explanation of the secret
in Mark was apologetic has already been corrected, though it
persists /7/. Conzelmann rightly reversed Wrede's order by
showing that Mark was reducing messianic tradition, not filling
out unmessianic tradition /8/. This had a positive theological
purpose. Other approaches such as those of J.M. Robinson /9/

and T.A. Burkill /10/ have discerned a definite view of history, or a philosophy of history, in Mark, which for Robinson reinforced the new quest but which Burkill saw as a theological construction.

I will assert in this paper that Mark's attitude to history is not a simple one, i.e. to history as such, but one which sees it in its relation to the gospel proclaimed by the Church and that Mark's concern is not so much with history at all as with the person of Jesus (i.e. Christology) as the one who provides the proper link between history and the gospel. Thus I will wish to show that Mark's account is indeed neither pure history nor pure theology but a conscious combination of the two without identifying them.

It is perhaps the greatest merit of the recent book by H.C. Kee /11/ to recognise that the right word for the *genre* to which Mark's Gospel belongs, or the nearest we can get to it, is apocalyptic. This provides the requisite background in Mark's own day for the understanding of Mark's work I wish to present, though this is in other respects not the same as Kee's and independent of his. In my contribution to *New Testament Christianity for Africa and the World* /12/ I discussed Mark's first verse as being significant for his whole Gospel in terms of seeing it as presenting the relationship between the Church's gospel in Mark's own day and its historical beginning in Jesus' life right up to the crucifixion and empty tomb. I asserted that history (or the historical Jesus) and the gospel are seen as being related to each other, yet that after the resurrection the gospel was seen as taking over from him whilst proclaiming *him* rather than his own original message of the kingdom of God; or, in other words, that his own original message was understood now in terms of his person. He is also seen as fulfilling his own message at the end. Thus Christology is seen as being the key to both history and eschatology. This is largely achieved through use of the Son of man title for Jesus' continuous role. Kee has provided a valuable background in apocalyptic thought for this use of the concepts of ἀρχή and τέλος and for the relationship set up between them /13/ - though I must admit that I had been previously led to mistrust apocalyptic through that current prejudice noted by Kee /14/. If the term can be applied to the mainly christological interest I see in Mark all well and good, but I still do not see Mark's interest as being mainly eschatological, as in Marxsen's view /15/, for the reasons I gave in that article. Mark does distinguish between Jesus' preaching of the nearness of the kingdom and the gospel of Jesus' identity as the Son of man and

Son of God, even though he sees that preaching as being fulfilled
in that later gospel. Mark sees the significance of the past
history of Jesus' life and ministry in terms of the Church's
gospel in his own day. Central to that gospel is the person of
Jesus who relates the beginning to the end, irrespective of when
that will be. This viewpoint needs now to be more fully explained.

But first I wish to take issue with the views of J.M. Robinson
and T.A. Burkill to which I have already referred, views which see
Mark as having a particular attitude to history as such. This will
help to show the reasons for my own view.

J.M. Robinson sought to avoid "the dissolution of the Marcan
history of Jesus into Mark's religious experience" or "the
petrification of the Marcan *kerygma* into objective historiography"
/16/ (i.e. either pure theology or pure history). He substitutes for
these a theological, or, rather, an eschatological view of history.
I have already, in my article referred to above /17/, disputed
Robinson's understanding of the relation between Mk.1:15, Jesus'
preaching of the kingdom of God, and Mk.1:1, the beginning of the
gospel, insofar as the interest of Mark in Jesus' proclamation lies
not so much in the historical fact of the proclamation itself as in
its relation to the gospel about Jesus Christ in Mark's day.   The
gospel about Jesus Christ is seen as arising out of and depending
upon the preaching of Jesus but the relation between them is "not
temporal but christological". Mark is not concerned so much with
the historical context of Jesus' preaching as with the context of
the gospel about Jesus Christ in which Mark wrote, and with the past
history, including Jesus' preaching, as the ἀρχή of that gospel.

Since I see Mark's concern as being christological, rather
than historical (or eschatological), I take issue with Robinson's
statement that "in the Marcan presentation they /i.e. the exorcism-
narratives/ depict a cosmic struggle in history to inaugurate the
eschatological reign of God" /18/, so that Mark wrote "cosmic
history". The secrecy-theme in the exorcisms, as Mark explains
it in 1:34 (cf. 3:12), shows that his interest in these stories is
primarily christological rather than in "an affirmation of the
presence of eschatology in history", as part of an "affirmation of
the truth of history" /19/. Mark's intentions were not to reaffirm
history but to affirm what the gospel says about Jesus with
reference to history, recognising at the same time the limitations
of history.

Robinson's concern with the "new quest of the historical Jesus"
seems to be behind his preference in exegesis for seeing Mark's role

as "historiciser" of the oral tradition and as such dependent on
a real history at the centre of Christian theology and at the
heart of the kerygma. But the alternatives are not simply either
to seek a "haven of refuge for contemplating eternal truths" or
to recognise a "cosmic struggle taking place in history", since
the basis of the gospel is neither. The basis as well as the
content of the gospel is found in Jesus Christ, who is himself
the link between history and eschatology /20/. I believe it is
the function of the Son of man sayings of Mk.2:10, 28 in the
debates to proclaim this fact. Yet Mark does not thereby present
Jesus "as the one who acts truly in history" in order to set "the
record straight" /21/. Rather, for Mark, the gospel proclaims in
the present the significance of the historical Jesus for the
future salvation to be brought by the Son of man, and he explains
how this depends on the passion, death and resurrection of Jesus
by which alone it is possible to call him Messiah and identify him
as Son of man. Fuchs' interpretation of Jesus the Christ as the
end of history and of its successive continuity as standing within
it /22/ is nearer the truth because it is Christology which answers
for Mark the questions connected with both history and eschatology
and brings them together. The context of the gospel, between the
beginning, in Jesus' life in history, and the end, prevents Mark,
however, from identifying history and eschatology in the way
Robinson suggests /23/. Mark brings history and the gospel into a
dialectical relationship by associating Jesus' action in history
with the authority of the Son of man. This is not to historicise
the kerygmatic tradition but to show its relationship to the
historical Jesus, using, admittedly, the language of apocalyptic.

Despite Räisänen's earlier study /24/, which I reviewed in the
Journal of Theological Studies /25/, I believe that in the present
combination of passages in Mk. 4 we get the message of Mark,
whatever the process of accretion, and that the sayings material
added to the parables make them in some way programmatic for the
relation between history and the gospel in Mark's own day (see
Mk. 4:11, 12, 21-25). By this means the life and ministry of
Jesus are seen as standing in a similar relationship to the
preaching of the gospel as they stood in relation to the coming of
the kingdom of God in Jesus' original parables of contrast /26/.
For Mark, however, the mystery of the kingdom of God is not
eschatology present in history (which would contradict what I
believe to be the original point of the parables) but the secret
of Jesus' identity and of his relationship to the kingdom (which is
in keeping with the original point of the parables) which the
gospel discloses to those within. The point is then christological.

Thus I wish to assert that in Mark there is no simple
concern with history as such but with history in its relation
to the gospel /27/. The secrecy-theme as a whole, whatever its
varied origin in its different aspects, witnesses to the fact that
history alone will not suffice and cannot be appealed to on its
own, even in terms of a hidden meaning. Mark is certainly aware
of a difference of time between Jesus and the gospel of the
Church, and sees them as being separated and related to each other
by the cross and resurrection (see Mk.2:19, 20). Continuity is
found in the person of Jesus himself.

In Burkill, instead of an historical understanding of Mark's
Gospel we have an attempt to give the Marcan understanding of
history. Burkill admits that Mark's Gospel is not biography and
that Mark was conscious that Jesus was not adequately recognised
during his earthly life but asserts that despite this Mark wished,
by using the doctrine of the secret, to affirm that Jesus really
was the Messiah, although Jesus' lifetime was a period of
concealment followed by one of open proclamation by the Church /28/.
For Burkill inconsistencies in the narrative reflect Mark's concern
to present the real truth behind the historical appearance. The
resulting contradictions arise from the difficulties Mark made for
himself by asserting Jesus' actual messiahship in history over
against awkward facts which he does not suppress /29/.

Burkill makes valid criticisms of historical explanations of
the secret such as that of Vincent Taylor but by transferring the
difficulties in a historical explanation to Mark's account he does
not adequately explain the theme of secrecy. He simply makes Mark
appear to write something inconsistent. But why should Mark try
to prove the gospel from history or assert that Jesus *was* the
Messiah when he was aware of contradictions? Rather Mark
acknowledges an apparent inconsistency between history and the
gospel with his doctrine of the secret, which is not explained
because it simply testifies to this absolute distinction between
history and gospel whilst still making it possible to affirm the
truth of the gospel about Jesus Christ in relation to and over
against history as a whole. Proof from history is however
forbidden, despite traditions of miracles and of the historical
confession of Jesus as Messiah and the false accusation that he
was a messianic pretender. This implies an ambivalent attitude to
Jesus within history, however, rather than to history as such and
supports the view that Mark's main concern is christological rather
than historical, even in his recognition of a distinction of
periods between Jesus' lifetime and that of the Church. The latter

point is itself connected with the apparent inconsistency between
history and the gospel, which Mark acknowledges, even, or
precisely, in relation to messianic tradition, by his doctrine
of the secret. Thus the secret cannot be meant to open the way
for a messianic life of Jesus (despite Wrede and Burkill), but
to affirm the truth of the Church's later gospel. It is not a historical theory but a hermeneutical device /30/. The point may well
be that miracles, messianic confession, and even messianic claim
cannot and could not make Jesus the Messiah, but only God, by way
of the cross and the empty tomb. Only then can those who were with
Jesus know and proclaim the truth which God alone, as in the
heavenly voice, rightly reveals to them about Jesus. Only then
does the story which can now be told make sense. The absoluteness
of the secret, expressed in blindness of foes and disciples, as
well as in explicit commands to silence, has this significance,
and is therefore given no historical explanation. It is presented
as an aspect of the history itself.

Thus Mark maintains a distinction between history and the
gospel in his narrative, only relating them to each other in the
person of Jesus. The gospel lies between the ἀρχή of Jesus'
earthly life and his return in glory at the end, and explains the
relationship between them in christological terms. Here we have a
total view of history seen in terms of the Church's gospel of Jesus
Christ. It is a view which is eschatological in its scope, with
Christology as its basis. Apocalyptic may be the right word for
this approach though it does not fully explain it.

The contradictions in Mark's account should be seen as
resulting partly from a combination of previously existing
traditions but they are maintained precisely because the work is
neither pure history nor pure theology but an attempt to relate
history and the gospel to one another whilst distinguishing
between them. The secret has its role in all this, as I have
explained, in relation to Christology, as we see from its
redactional introduction after Peter's confession and the cries
of the demons (cf. Räisänen's analysis) /31/, but is itself
unexplained. It is Matthew and Luke who attempt to historicise
the theme.

The fact that, in Mark, the secret, though absolute, is not
capable of being kept hidden in a historical sense shows that it
is not a historical concept with a historical function, but rather
that it stands over against history as such. Thus a command to
silence is disobeyed without the full truth of the gospel being

disclosed because the theme of lack of understanding maintains the
secret despite any disclosure. The motif of revelation despite
concealment is not therefore meant to assert the full truth of the
gospel in history - which would be another form of the apologetic
explanation of the secret rightly rejected by Wrede, but a claim
that the gospel is true despite the history and that it can be seen
to be true in relation to history if viewed from the right
perspective. This means that history cannot be substituted for
the gospel and that the person of Jesus, present in history, is
only properly proclaimed by that gospel. It is in these terms that
Mark's Gospel can be said to fit with the "new quest of the
historical Jesus". The Son of man sayings provide the required
continuity, which is christological and not "heilsgeschichtlich".
Mk.8:38 in its Marcan context makes the point that the crucified
Jesus, whose identity is historically concealed, must be confessed
before the end when the Son of man comes in glory because that Son
of man has already suffered, died and been raised in the person
of Jesus of Nazareth.

Mark is thus drawing attention in his work to Jesus *from
within history,* as being still the context of the Church's own
preaching, rather than to history itself. He also acknowledges
that within that history as a whole there is *still* a secret with
regard to Jesus' identity, even when the gospel is proclaimed.
This is one reason why the distinction of periods, though playing
some role, is not the real point of the secrecy-theme in Mark /32/.
The real distinction of times in Mk.8:38 is between history as a
whole, where the crucified Christ must be confessed, and the end.
Mark is therefore not directing our attention in his Gospel to
Jesus' lifetime over against the time of the gospel. It is for
this reason, I suggest, that he does not draw attention to any
such transition at the end of his Gospel, but rather points from
the empty tomb to the future parousia as the time of full and
final revelation, even if it is not necessarily near.

The relation between history and gospel which Mark is concerned
with is not then simply one between past and present, but has its
context in his own day, in the preaching of the gospel itself. The
whole account which he describes as the ἀρχή of the gospel belongs
then in the context of the Church's preaching, just as it is
derived from that preaching. It is then neither pure history nor
pure theology but an account of the relation between history and
gospel *in that preaching.* It looks back to Jesus' lifetime to
establish the nature of that relationship, and is therefore a
presentation of that preaching in historical form without

identifying the gospel with that history as such. If it were
doing that the first verse could have read - The Gospel of Jesus
Christ /35/.

Probably Kee is right that the word apocalyptic is the
correct description for a writing which refers to a figure in the
past and contains historical narrative but the context of which is
the time of writing and which looks to a future consummation.
Chapter 13 represents the time of writing, with its reference to the
preaching of the gospel (verse 10). The main message is not
however the nearness of the end but the identification of Jesus
with the Son of man who guarantees the fulfilment of his message
in Mk.9:1.

Thus I see the significance of the theme of secrecy in Mark's
Gospel as a whole as a device which discloses Mark's attitude to
the relation between history and the gospel. The subject-matter
of his own Gospel is the basis (or beginning) of the gospel,
which was preached by the Church at the time of writing, over
against the end, but not so much in order to draw attention to
the distinction of times between Jesus' lifetime and his own day
but to show how that gospel can and should proclaim Jesus who
relates the beginning to the end. Mark recognises in his account
the historical difficulties of proclaiming Jesus by incorporating
into his narrative the theme of secrecy. Since these historical
difficulties concern not only the historical tradition about Jesus
but also the continuing historical context of that proclamation
itself, the secrecy is not simply concerned with a distinction of
periods between then and now but remains a constant factor. The
gospel and history remain in constant tension, and this explains
the inconsistencies or contradictions in the narrative with regard
to concealment and revelation. Mk.4:11, 12 in their present
context reflect this relationship between concealment and
revelation and are explicable on the basis of the observation that
Mark's Gospel should not be viewed on one plane as either pure
history or pure theology. The words do not belong for Mark simply
in the context of Jesus' lifetime but relate that to the time of
writing as the true context of the proclamation of the gospel
itself. The whole historical tradition of Jesus' eschatological
preaching, casting out devils, miracles and even messiahship is
set in relation to the gospel which depends on Jesus' death and
resurrection and points to his return as Son of man in glory.
That expectation is Mark's main concern as the proper outcome of
what preceded and made it possible. What preceded is therefore
presented as a veiled witness which must not detract from the

necessary progress of the history itself through death and
resurrection. There were sufficient elements of secrecy in the
tradition already for Mark to highlight them in a christological
direction and use them to block out aspects of the historical
tradition which might contradict a true understanding of Jesus'
destiny, or emphasise the historical background itself to the
detriment of the later gospel. It is the complementary theme of
the disciples' lack of understanding in the context of Jesus'
lifetime which emphasises the potential wrongness of what is
concealed but nonetheless known in the historical tradition. The
fact that Jesus did work miracles and was regarded as the Messiah
was not and is not a *historical* secret, but neither is it the
content of the gospel. This is, I believe what Mark is saying.

     Thus Mark is not trying to prove anything about the history
he describes, indeed quite the reverse. He is trying to say
something about the gospel to which the history he records
pointed and to which it led. But he does not thereby identify
his account of the history with that gospel. He shows how Jesus
fits in, in terms both of history and gospel, as the one to whom
the gospel witnesses within history and to whom it points at the
end. There is then an ambivalent attitude to history with
regard to the person of Jesus which, I believe, Burkill has
wrongly interpreted. Mark's attitude to history cannot be of
the gnostic kind, however, because of the emphasis on the cross
as a necessary precondition for the gospel. Prior to the end to
which we are pointed forward, there is still a concealment, except
for those with eyes to see and ears to hear, of which Jesus'
preaching of the kingdom of God in parables is symbolic. God's
purpose in all this is expressed in Mk.4:21-25.

     Whether my explanation of the secret is right or wrong will
depend on how well it does explain all aspects of Mark's book
as a whole, but I believe that some total explanation of Mark's
understanding of what he is writing is necessary and must involve
an explanation of the relation between the gospel and the
historical tradition as part of Mark's conscious purpose. His
motivation is less easy to discover, but I believe that the
circumstances referred to in Mk.13 must have led him to reaffirm
the truth of the gospel over against historical events, if not
history as a whole, with reference back to Jesus, as well as
forward to his return. His message is that the Church must in
the meantime remain faithful to Jesus on the way of the cross,
whenever the end will come. The guarantee of the fulfilment of
Jesus' message lies, according to Mark, in Jesus' person, not in

signs and wonders, which should not be relied on now by an
emphasis on them then. The call now as then is to follow him
so that the beginning will be confirmed by the end when the one
who was crucified is manifested in glory for those who remain
his disciples.

NOTES

/1/   *Das Messiasgeheimnis in den Evangelien* (Göttingen 1901, 1913,
1963), trans. J.C.G. Greig, *The Messianic Secret* (Cambridge and
London, 1971).
/2/   *Das "Messiasgeheimnis" im Markusevangelium. Ein redaktions-
kritischer Versuch* (Schriften der Finnischen Exegetischen
Gesellschaft 28, Helsinki 1976).
/3/   Cf. Räisänen's conclusion (*ibid.*, p.168): "So wird man es
sich gefallen lassen müssen, im ältesten Evangelisten mehr
einen Tradenten und weniger einen Theologen bzw. Hermeneuten zu
sehen, als die neuere Forschung im allgemeinen vorausgesetzt hat".
/4/   *Ibid.*, pp.103f.
/5/   Räisänen notes only a parallel pattern in that a command to
silence always follows a confessional formula, *ibid.*, p.118.
/6/   E.g. *ibid.*, p.118: "Leider sagt Markus nicht *warum*" (his
italics), and p.162.
/7/   See e.g. Räisänen, *ibid.*, p.35, n. 2. Cf. Wrede, *op.cit.*,
p.224. Wrede rejected the apologetic explanation because it
should not have been necessary if it was an established fact that
Jesus became Messiah only at the resurrection. If there was a
wish to assert Jesus' foreknowledge, direct statement of this
would be all that was required. However, Bousset came to hold
this view, *Kyrios Christos* (Göttingen 1913, 1921, 1926*, 1965*),
p.66, trans. J.E. Steely, (1970), pp. 107f. But Bultmann
rightly pointed out ("Die Frage nach dem messianischen Bewusstsein
Jesu und das Petrus-Bekenntnis", *Zeitschrift für die
neutestamentliche Wissenschaft* 19 [1919-20], p.167; *Exegetica*
[Tübingen 1967], p.2) that an apologetic purpose in the secrecy-
theme in Mark does not fit the juxtaposition of concealment and
revelation in the Gospel which Wrede had pointed out, nor explain
either the disobedience of the commands to be silent or the
disciples' lack of understanding.
/8/   "Gegenwart und Zukunft in der synoptischen Tradition",
Zeitschrift für Theologie und Kirche 54 (1957), p.294.
/9/   *The Problem of History in Mark* (London 1957).
/10/ *Mysterious Revelation. An Examination of the Philosophy of
St. Mark's Gospel* (New York 1963).

/11/ *Community of the New Age* (London 1977).
/12/ Ed. M.E. Glasswell and E.W. Fashole-Luke (London 1974): "The Beginning of the Gospel. A Study of St. Mark's Gospel with regard to its First Verse" (pp.36-43).
/13/ *Op.cit.*, pp.66ff.
/14/ E.g. pp.106f, 145f.
/15/ *Der Evangelist Markus* (Göttingen 1959), trans. *Mark the Evangelist* (New York 1969).
/16/ *Op.cit.*, p.45.
/17/ "The Beginning of the Gospel", pp.38f.
/18/ *Op.cit.*, pp.39ff.
/19/ *Op.cit.*, p.46.
/20/ This is why Mark could make Jesus affirm his messiahship at his trial and follow this immediately with a reference to the future Son of man in glory (Mk.14:62). After all Mark did not deny history but wished to set it in relation to the Church's gospel and future hope. Jesus' messiahship is here both affirmed and qualified (cf. J.R. Donahue, *Are you the Christ*, [SBL Dissertation Series 10, 1973], p.180) or rather transcended with reference to the Son of man.
/21/ Robinson, *op.cit.*, p.47 where he speaks also of "the reality of the *eschaton* within history".
/22/ *Zur Frage nach dem historischen Jesus* (Tübingen 1960) pp.219ff. He speaks on p.236 (trans. *Studies of the historical Jesus*, p.46) of a relation ('beieinander') between history and kerygma as against a mere succession ('nacheinander'). This is what, I think, we have in Mark's Gospel.
/23/ The parables of contrast - which are not to be called 'parables of growth' - in Mark 4 show this. For Mark, the relation between the kingdom of God and Jesus' original preaching of it is as enigmatic as that between Jesus and the gospel which later proclaims him. Yet it is there for those with eyes to see.
/24/ *Die Parabeltheorie im Markusevangelium* (Schriften der Finnischen Exegetischen Gesellschaft 26, Helsinki 1973).
/25/ N.S. XXVI (1975), pp.455-457.
/26/ The summaries at the end of chapter 4 of Mark's Gospel (vv.33f.) serve the usual generalising function of summaries in Mark and give the historical point of reference, but they do not contradict vv.11f since those verses relate the historical point of reference to the ultimate result or goal of Jesus' preaching in the effects of the gospel and function therefore on a different plane. This is why they are different from other references to parables in Mark. They concern the parables as part of the ἀρχή of the gospel.

/27/ Cf. the same point with regard to the miracles in my essay,
"The Use of Miracles in the Markan Gospel", *Miracles. Cambridge
Studies in their Philosophy and History*, ed. C.F.D. Moule (London
1965). See K. Kertelge's agreement with this approach in
Die Wunder Jesu im Markusevangelium (SANT 23, Munich 1970), pp.202f.
/28/ *Op.cit.*, pp.2, 69, 158ff, 175ff, 319ff.
/29/ *Ibid*, pp.177ff, 209, 321ff.
/30/ Cf. Conzelmann, *op.cit.*, p.295: *"Die Geheimnistheorie ist
die hermeneutische Voraussetzung der Gattung 'Evangelium'"* (his
italics)
/31/ *Das "Messiasgeheimnis" im Markusevangelium*, pp.105, 159.
For Räisänen, the commands to silence must come in for Mark over
against any statement of Jesus' identity, statements which Mark
accepts as correct.
/32/ Cf. Räisänen, *ibid.*, pp.165f, where he says that the
salvation-history explanation of the secret in Mark is the least
beset with difficulties, yet not a satisfactory explanation of all
aspects of the secrecy-theme.

Studia Biblica 1978: II, 129-149

Meditations in Matthew

Rev. Dr. J. Marsh
Rannerdale Close,
Buttermere,
Cockermouth,
Cumbria, CA13 9UY

On these four mornings of Congress I propose to offer an
exposition of parts of Matthew's gospel. I hope that the four
passages we review will enable me to present to you, and to gain
your sympathy for, an understanding of Matthew that indicates his
relevance both to his own day and to our own.

This morning I want to expound chapter 3. With this chapter
Matthew takes up the story of Jesus as told by Mark. He has
prefaced this with some important interpretative material. Using
interesting historiographical devices he has made his readers aware
that in the person of Jesus God will be creating in human history a
new and final people of God. He has done this in part by his
genealogy, tracing Jesus' descent from Abraham (the father of all
Israel) through David (whose ideal kingdom will be renewed at the
divinely appointed end) and in part by showing how the pattern of
Israel's destiny has been revealingly repeated in the story of
Jesus. For, like Israel of old, he has descended into Egypt, and
been delivered from it, crossing the Jordan and entering the
(geographical) land of promise.

Against that background Matthew tells his story of John the
Baptist. John was evidently a figure indispensable to the gospel
story, for each of the four evangelists writes of him, and it is
therefore important not to miss any clues they give of his
significance, so as to see his advent and mission against the
politico-religious situation of his time.

Matthew states that John 'appeared as a preacher in the Judean
wilderness'. His message was 'Repent; for the kingdom of Heaven is
upon you!' (I confess my gratification that the NEB prefers 'upon
you' to 'near' or 'at hand' as a translation of ἤγγικεν to describe
the relationship of the kingdom of Heaven to men). Matthew sees
John's appearance as the entry point into human history of the

actuality of life in the final and perfected people of God, or, in other words, of the kingdom of Heaven.

John appeared in the Judean wilderness wearing 'a garment of camel's hair,, and a leather girdle around his waist', thereby indicating to his Jewish contemporaries that he was cast in the role of Elijah, the anticipated herald of Messiah; for it was this selfsame description of Elijah that had enabled king Ahaziah to identify the man who had prophesied his imminent death (2 Kings 1.5-8).

Two small items of information provided by Luke help an assessment of John's public appearance and message. First, in 1.80 Luke records that 'as the child grew up he became strong in spirit; he lived in the wilds until the day when he appeared publicly before Israel'. Dr. Caird has speculated whether John's sojourn in the desert brought him into contact with one or other of the ascetic communities whose life and thought the Dead Sea Scrolls have so illuminated for us. Much earlier Dr Plummer denied such contact: 'He preached the kingdom of God; they preached isolation... They abandoned society; he strove to reform it'. But perhaps Dr. Plummer has formulated his antitheses inaccurately, for the difference between John and the sects was not that he believed in the kingdom and they did not, but that they had quite divergent views as to how the kingdom would come into history.

At the time there were in circulation three views from which John's own position can be distinguished. The Pharisees and Sadducees held that the kingdom would come in the future, and that as its essential precondition Israel would have to observe all the requirements of God revealed in the Mosaic law. Hence their stress on observing the law, so that Israel might come to enjoy the blessings of the kingdom. The Zealots likewise believed that the kingdom was a future reality, but held that its arrival would be achieved by a successful campaign for Jewish independence. The sectaries held that however much the public manifestation of the kingdom was a future reality only after tribulations and wars, it was nevertheless an experience open in the present, provided that the indispensable disciplines of the community life were zealously observed. In clearly conscious distinction from these three positions, John proclaimed that the kingdom was a present reality, and had in fact 'come upon' Israel. But entry did not depend upon the practice of an ascetic communal but isolated life, but upon Israel's radical repentance for her long failure to be

a true people of God in the world. The failure had been
evidenced in two ways: first, by not fulfilling the mission to the
Gentiles so often laid upon them by the great prophets ('Don't
presume to say to yourselves, "We have Abraham to our father'");
and second, by the failure to achieve or maintain a society where
all injustice and unrighteousnesses were abhorred and abolished
('Prove your repentance by the fruit it bears').

John's call for repentance was thus much more than for
individual moral renewal; it was a summons to disown all the
rebelliousness of the past, and to seek once more a true worship
of God, not only in the Temple, but in the ordering of justice in
public as well as in private life.

The second piece of Lukan information is in 3.15: 'The
people were on the tiptoe of expectation, all wondering about
John, whether perhaps he was the Messiah'. So even though John
by his very dress proclaimed himself an Elijah figure, the message
he brought and the impact he made produced a strong suspicion in
the public mind that he was in fact himself Messiah.

Two conclusions may thus be stated about John the Baptizer:
first, his message to Israel as a nation as to the present reality
of life in the kingdom of God through repentance and forgiveness
was good news to the inhabitants of an occupied territory, and in
clear contrast to other views current at the time. Second, that
in so speaking about the kingdom, he was understandably and
inevitably reckoned himself to be Messiah. But if that has to be
said of John the Baptizer, must it not equally be said about
Jesus?

That John's ministry was to his people as a nation rather
than as an agglomeration of individuals is indicated in the way
that Matthew records the response he evoked: 'They flocked to him
from Jerusalem, from all Judea and the whole Jordan valley'. When
they responded they were baptized in the Jordan, confessing their
sins. Baptism was a rite that John adapted from the sects. But
in Qumran it was a repeatable ritual of purification, while for
John it was a once-for-all reality. This probably means that just
as Israel's forefathers had long ago crossed the geographical
Jordan to enter the geographical Land of Promise, so now, in
ritual symbolism present Israel was to cross the non-geographical
Jordan and enter the non-geographical kingdom of God. Such entry,
like that of their forefathers, was meant to be once-for-all; and
as they were now to be admitted on repentance by divine forgivness,
so for the future they would be kept in the kingdom by repentance

and forgiveness.

Matthew tells that 'Jesus arrived at the Jordan from Galilee,
and came to John to be baptized by him. John tried to dissuade
him. "Do you come to me?" he said. "I need rather to be
baptized by you". Jesus replied, "Let it be so for the present;
we do well to conform in this way with all that God requires [AV:
to fulfil all righteousness]". John then allowed him to come.'

Jesus' response to John is not easy to translate, though
English scholars are remarkably unanimous about what it means.
Yet I confess a dissatisfaction, ultimately theological and
resting on how the word 'righteousness' is to be understood. It
could be here, as often, and as most translators have supposed,
something that God requires of men: but it could be, as it often
is in Second Isaiah, something that God does for men. God
proclaims through Isaiah "My righteousness is near" and means
thereby that his deliverance of Israel has actually begun (cf.
Isa. 46.13; 51.5,6,8; 56.1 etc). This would make Jesus' response
to John read, 'Let your objections lie just now; our present duty
is to bring to fulfilment all the promised deliverance of God'.
In view of Matthew's report that John's message was that the
kingdom of God had 'come upon' Israel, this is a quite natural
sequence of ideas, indicating that at Jesus' baptism the great and
final deliverance of God began to be realized in the actualities
of human history. This is supported by Matthew's account of the
baptism of Jesus.

The two significant points of Matthew's story of the baptism
are that Jesus saw the Spirit of God descending like a dove to
alight on him, and that a divine voice proclaimed, 'This is my Son,
my beloved, on whom my favour rests'. The symbolism of a dove is
uncertain. Rabbinic tradition compared Israel to a dove, and in
the Talmud the brooding of the spirit in Gen. 1 is compared to the
brooding of a dove. In the Babylonian Talmud the 'Bath Qol' or
voice from heaven, is heard 'mourning like a dove'. The symbolism
may suggest that Jesus will work in the spirit of gentleness
finally to inaugurate God's new creation. But it may be that the
clue is really to be found in the Hebrew word for dove, 'Jonah',
so that in this vision Jesus saw himself filled with the spirit of
Jonah, to carry the good news of repentance and forgiveness to
Gentiles as well as Jews. That would not be an alien idea in a
gospel that records how Gentiles were the first to worship Jesus,
and ends with a charge to the eleven to 'make disciples of all
nations'. So far the story of the baptism has affirmed either the
inauguration in human history of God's new and final creation, or

the completion of the neglected task of taking the good news about
God to the Gentiles. In either case the baptism is clearly
invested with strong eschatological significance.

The voice which declared, 'This is my Son, my Beloved, on
whom my favour rests', is also concerned with historical
fulfilment. What is meant by 'Son'? It is all too easy for
modern Christians to read into the word a good deal of what was
seen to be implied by it at the Councils of Nicea and Chalcedon.
But they were much later. Jesus, who heard these words, and
Matthew who recorded them, knew nothing of the Great Councils.
They would have understood 'Son' in Old Testament terms, where
'Son of God' means the whole people of God. Indeed Matthew has
already provided such a clue, when he saw the life pattern of the
old Israel being fulfilled in the life pattern of Jesus as he was
taken into Egypt. 'Out of Egypt have I called my Son' he quotes
in appropriate illumination from Hosea 11.1, where it is plain
that the prophet is speaking of Israel as a whole corporate
entity. Similarly when Solomon is called a Son of God (2 Samuel
7.14) it is because he will establish the kingdom of David and
build a temple for God. So it is interesting to recall that the
inscription on Jesus' cross stating the grounds of his
condemnation read, 'This is Jesus the king of the Jews' (27.47),
and that it was at his crucifixion that the temple curtain was
torn apart, for a new temple was being erected through the cross
in the person of Jesus Christ. In both these senses 'Son' is
used corporately, not referring to Jesus as an individual, but as
the embodiment for the time being in one person only, of the whole
corporate society of the people of God. So Matthew indicates once
more that the baptism of Jesus is a means of his identifying
himself with the disobedient people of God: he repents with them
and for them of their sinful failure to be a true people of God,
and receives signal recognition that in him the new life of the
final people of God in history has at last begun. The kingdom
of heaven has been inaugurated. The time of the end has come.
Eschatology is realized. The kingdom of God has indeed 'come
upon' men.

2

Today I shall consider three separate passages though I
believe they contribute to the development of one common theme.

What can an ordinary reader make of the Sermon on the Mount?
It appears to be a series of impossibly idealistic demands on
human nature that make murder and adultery almost unavoidable

crimes, interspersed with some outdated regulations for life in
occupied Palestine of the first century. Is it then a series of
impossible imperatives held up as an ideal, or a picture of life
in a heavenly kingdom that has not yet really arrived, or is it
an 'Interimsethik', regulations for the relatively short interval
between the present age and the actual arrival of the kingdom of
Heaven? Each of these suggestions has some validity, and each
can be given due weight if the so-called Sermon be regarded as
descriptive of the sort of existence that belongs to the citizen
of the heavenly kingdom as he now lives in some kingdom of this
world of which he is also a citizen. It would indeed have been
strange that Jesus, who followed John in announcing the the
kingdom of Heaven had 'come upon' Israel, and that Israel could
enter it forthwith, upon true repentance and by God's forgiveness,
had himself never described what life in the kingdom was like, or
that, having done so, his description had been neither recorded
nor preserved.

I propose then to look at some of the Beatitudes and some of
the expositions of the Law; but to that I propose to add a
consideration fo some verses from chapter 23. For it seems that
just as the Beatitudes are congratulatory descriptions of the kind
of existence involved in becoming and being a citizen of the
kingdom of Heaven, so the 'Woes' on the scribes and Pharisees in
chapter 23 are condolatory descriptions of the kind of existence
involved in declining the invitation to God's people to repent
and believe the good news of God's forgiveness and the open
entry into the kingdom of Heaven.

What is a Beatitude, what is a 'Woe'? A Beatitude, I suggest,
is a congratulatory description of an enviably propitious
condition or situation in which some persons or class of persons
are to be found; while conversely, a 'Woe' is a condolatory
description of an unenviably ominous condition or situation in
which some person or persons are to be found. Let us review some
of the quite astounding assertions Jesus made.

To be congratulated, Jesus said in a statement clearly
factual and descriptive, 'are the πτωχοὶ τῷ πνεύματι, for theirs
is the kingdom of Heaven'. Who are these fortunate people already
living in the heavenly kingdom? The NEB at first named them as
'Those who know they are poor', but in a second edition changed
this to 'those who know their need of God'. The change is less
drastic than it sounds, for the man or society that is poor in
spirit is precisely one that knows man's need of and ultimate
dependence upon God; while the rich in spirit are those men or

societies who do not know man's need of or dependence upon God,
but suppose that men can supply all their needs from their own
resources. So the really fortunate men or societies, whatever
temporary fluctuations of fortune may otherwise suggest, are those
that live in trust and dependence upon God, knowing that he is
all-sovereign. The unfortunate society or man tries to be self-
sufficient, an attitude sooner or later doomed to destruction. So
to be in this sense 'poor in spirit', to know one's need of God,
is to be fortunate indeed.

The fourth Beatitude speaks of the fortunate hungry: 'How
blest are those who hunger and thirst to see right prevail; they
shall be satisfied', the NEB helpfully translates; for to hunger
and thirst after righteousness is far more than to want to be a
'better person'; it is rather to want right to be vindicated
everywhere. Yet righteousness, individual or social, cannot be
attained by men on their own, or even known in their unaided
wisdom. Higher standards of righteousness cannot be attained
without divine aid. God's grace is available to individuals, so
he can be trusted to forgive and renew the penitent man, and also
to vindicate justice in a society that practises injustice. So
the heavenly citizen, being, like all his fellow men, an imperfect
man in an imperfect society, does not yield to cynicism or
despair, because he trusts God for his own personal salvation and
justification, and also for the public vindication of justice in
his earthly society. Evil powers, he knows, are not sovereign in
this world, for God comes even now to men and nations in voices
and movements that vindicate justice and righteousness. The
kingdom of Heaven is not just a chronological successor to the
kingdoms of the world, but within those kingdoms justifies and
vindicates its life to its own citizens. So in all types of
earthly society the citizen of the kingdom is fundamentally a
happy and fortunate man.

The eighth Beatitude closes the series with an affirmation
about the fortunate persecuted. Of them as of the poor in spirit
it is said that the kingdom of Heaven is theirs, which may
indicate another general classification of heavenly citizenship.
It is certainly clear by now that the citizen of the kingdom must
be ready to suffer for his good fortune. Such suffering is to be
seen as inevitable, and a cause for rejoicing. It was the
uncomfortable destiny of Jesus himself (Luke 12.50), and the
disciple cannot expect to have it otherwise (John 15.20). Yet
Jesus' destined path was not wholly dark (John 13.13; Heb. 12.2),
and the Christian can likewise properly derive joy from his own
suffering (1 Pet. 4.13). The heavenly citizen knows that he can

(and must!) 'in everything give thanks' (1 Thess. 5.16). How
fortunate such a person is.

To round off the Beatitudes Matthew describes the real
situation and good fortune of the heavenly citizen as he lives in
a world that so readily menaces and maltreats him. But whenever
he is falsely charged with wrongdoing as a disciple, he will have
at that very time, not at some unspecified future date, a truly
beatitudinous good fortune. For he will know that he lives not
only in a world where men can make him suffer, but also in a
world where any such suffering is, in God's grace and providence,
undergirded and transformed into joy. This is not an assurance
of post-mortem bliss, but of a joy given in God's presence with
those who suffer and are persecuted for the sake of the gospel.
They become heirs to the suffering joy and the joyous suffering of
the Old Testament prophets. So does God deal with those who enter
the kingdom, and he does it even while they live in the present
unredeemed world. The kingdom of Heaven has indeed 'come upon
them'.

I now turn to the next section of the Sermon, where Jesus
says what links the old order and the new. a necessary link, since
the new order of the kingdom has come while the old order
continues. Some consequent ambiguities are here resolved.
Heavenly citizens, though members of the new order, are not by
that fact exempted from the requirements of the old law, which
has not been abolished but shown to be in need of fulfilment.
Contemporary Judaism knew very well the inadequacy of the old law,
and by the tradition of the scribes and Pharisees tried to keep
it 'up to date'. But no extension of legal requirements can cover
the innumerably variant situations in which men find themselves.
So statutes do not and can not give a full indication of God's
will for men, though they do offer a reliable guide to its
general direction. So Christians are required to have a
righteousness greater than that of the scribes and Pharisees,
discerning for what purpose God gave his laws, and allowing that
purpose always to govern their actions. Commandment obedience,
or, to use Luther's phrase, 'legal righteousness', is not a
piecemeal observance of an ever-expanding and unattainable legal
code. For example, consider the probhibition of murder.

'You have learned that our forefathers were told, "Do not
commit murder'", said Jesus, using a theological passive to
indicate the divine origin of the law. The parallel to that comes
in Jesus' 'But what I tell you is this:...' - and no claim to

divine authority could be clearer than that! The God who give the
old law through Moses is not giving heavenly citizens a new law,
but a new way of receiving and understanding the old law, not
only through but in the person of Jesus. So neither the old law
or the new is meant to be an impersonal and arbitrary imperative
given to unconsenting individuals or communities, but rather to
express a relationship which a loving creator offers to his
creatures so that they may find and enjoy the fellowship with
their creator for which they were made.

     So the heavenly citizen is brought to a new attitude to
goodness and the law. A commandment is no longer linked to just
one human action, but is a point of reference to a whole range
of moral situations. Confronted with the sixth commandment he
will not plead guilty only when he has murdered another human
being; rather will be acknowledge guilt whenever he nurses anger
(a murderous emotion) against his brother man, when he abuses his
brother man ('raca' in this instance is an obscure term, and
involves regarding another person as less than human, as a 'thing')
and again whenever he 'sneers at' his brother man, for that too is
to deny him truly human status, and so to 'kill' him. To this
more-than-legal insight into the sixth commandment is joined a
positive duty of reconciliation. Heavenly citizens will not go
through life without having personal relationships sometimes
going awry, perhaps even by their own fault. But in any such
deterioration of relationships the heavenly citizen will work for
reconciliation, else he will be unable with integrity to worship
God the reconciler. For Jesus it was clear that no man can
rightly offer a gift to God while being unreconciled to a brother
man.

     Sometimes distorted relationships will lead to the search for
remedy by civil law. Even then, on the very way to court,
reconciliation must have absolute priority; for once a legal
process starts it must grind its way to its legal non-merciful end
end, with the disputants 'dead' to each other, as unreconciled as
ever - or worse, as v.26 states so forcibly. Law and grace,
revenge and forgiveness, are opposites, and the heavenly citizen is
is one who, by divine grace and the reconciling power it bestows,
even in the present age abandons revenge and the law, seeking to
live with other men as God has shown in Christ that he lives with
all men, in forgiveness and reconciliation. So once more it is
clear that even in the present age the kingdom of Heaven 'comes
upon' men.

     The Beatitudes began the first book of teaching in Matthew;

the seven 'Woes' of chapter 23 are near the beginning of the fifth
and final book of teaching. They sound strange to ears that have
heard the Beatitudes, but they turn out to be an understandable
contrast to them, giving a description of the unfortunate and
unenviable state of those who continued to be religious Jews
without becoming citizens of the heavenly kingdom. They are not
curses uttered by a maledictory Jesus on those who rejected him,
but objective assessments of the true unbeatitudinous
circumstances in which those who rejected Jesus had perforce to
live their lives.

Each 'Woe' has an introductory 'Alas for you', which means
'How unfortunate you are', just as each beatitude began with 'How
blest are they', i.e. 'how fortunate they are'. The first three
Woes concern the teaching of those unfortunate persons, and the
latter four their excessive legalism.

23.13, 14: Lawyers and Pharisees 'shut the door of the king
kingdom of Heaven in men's faces' and fail to enter themselves.
They focussed attention on outward conformity with the law, as if
that, and not undisturbed community and communion with God in
his kingdom, were the true end of the law. They kept men from
entering the realm where God dwells with men, and failed to
respond to God's invitation themselves. An unfortunate position
to be in indeed!

23. 15: Unfortunate indeed to have great evangelical zeal
(as Hillel had urged) and then, when a convert was made, to make
him a narrow-minded fanatic insisting on every Pharisaic
peculiarity in what was, by divine intent, meant to be a universal
religion. An unfortunate situation indeed!

23.25,26: How unfortunate to be 'fussy' about eating and
drinking from vessels not ceremonially cleansed or properly
washed, and not realize that if what was put into even a clean
vessel were obtained by unfair means, it mattered little that
the agent had all his crockery properly washed. An unfortunate
state to be in indeed!

23.29-36: Finally, among the Woes, how unfortunate to be
among those who care about the tombs of prophets and national
heroes, boasting that if one had lived in earlier days, one would
not have persecuted those whose graves one now honoured, and yet
to be falling a victim to the easy self-deception that they could
avoid the errors of the past: for when the prophets are sent to
the present generation, it will kill the prophets as did the

fathers of old. Indeed, Jesus asserted, the present generation
would become the focus-point and the great finale of all the
killings of innocent men, from Abel to Zechariah (i.e. throughout
all the Old Testament period).

So it is clear that Jesus is contrasting two orders, each of
them available and open to men in the present. The kingdom of
Heaven is not something yet to come; it can be entered, or turned
away from, now.

3

On the first two mornings of this all too brief look at
Matthew's gospel, we have been concerned with what Matthew
reports as the central theme of the message of Jesus - that the
kingdom of Heaven has 'come upon' Israel. Those who repent and
by the gracious forgiveness of God are admitted to the Kingdom
become its earthly citizens; but they will not on that account be
exempted form the 'slings and arrows of outrageous fortune' that
afflict humanity at large; on the contrary, they will have
special misfortunes of their own, in suffering for the sake of
the kingdom. Yet whatever they may suffer in the world, their
lot can still, in the great assertions of the Beatitudes, be
truly called 'blessed'. They will also know more than other men
what God asks of them, since the teaching of Jesus enabled them
to use the law already received through Moses in such a way that
its original purpose would be fulfilled in the community of the
heavenly citizens, the new Israel or people of God, which Jesus
was calling into existence by his words and works.

This morning I want to look at another statement about Jesus'
mission, given in a summary characteristic of the synoptic
gospels, in Matthew 9.35-38. It reads: 'So Jesus went round all
the towns and villages teaching in their synagogues, announcing
the good news of the kingdom, and curing every kind of ailment
and disease. The sight of the people moved him to pity; they
were like sheep without a shepherd, harassed and helpless; and
he said to his disciples, "The crop is heavy, but labourers are
scarce; you must therefore beg the owner to send labourers to
harvest his crop"!

The summary is quite compact, and fairly comprehensive.
Jesus is depicted as teaching in the synagogues, announcing the
'good news of the kingdom' pitying the people in their
shepherdlessness, seeing a plentiful harvest alongside a scarcity
of harvest labour, and calling for prayer that labour may yet be

found. For all the indubitably apparent diversity, I believe
there is a profundity here to be discovered.

If Jesus 'went round all the towns and villages' of Galilee
it is clear that a considerable time was spent in what might be
termed an 'evangelistic tour' of the province; and that fact, with
the added information that Jesus taught, announced the kingdom and
healed every kind of disease, makes it certain that by this time
he was already an outstanding person.

It is perhaps not an unfair assumption that his teaching in
the synagogues would comprise the sort of teaching that Matthew
has already summarized in the Sermon on the Mount. It is equally
not an unfair assumption that his announcement of the good news
(or 'gospel') of the kingdom was not different in essentials from
the description of it given in a previous summary (4.17), 'Repent;
for the kingdom of Heaven is upon you'. Jesus was saying, what
John the Baptist had said before him, that Israel must repent of
her failure to be a true people of God in the world, both in her
failure to fulfil her mission to the Gentiles (the claim to have
Abraham as father no longer could be advanced as entitlement to
be the true people of God) and in her failure to establish a just
and moral society (repentance must be demonstrated by the fruit
it would bear). But where God found repentant people, there he
was, in and through the mission of Jesus, re-establishing finally
and for all time, the true people of God, the very kingdom of
Heaven on earth.

One thing that Jesus observed for himself on his tour of
Galilee was the state of God's Israel as it then existed in its
unrepentant state. He was moved to pity by what he saw, which
Matthew described as the people being like sheep without a
shepherd. This was a pastoral imagery easily comprehended by the
rural population of Galilee, but understood theologically also by
the Jews, who would hear in the metaphor echoes of, say, Ezekiel's
condemnation of the national leaders of his day, who, though
exalted to be the shepherds or leaders of God's flock, were sadly
deficient in the execution of their duties, neither feeding God's
flock with the proper food of his word, nor securing a proper
defence against their enemies. Jesus evidently viewed his
contemporaries as in similar plight, being neither fed with their
proper food, nor given a rightful protection against their enemies.
Religiously and politically they were being misled. This national
condition could equally be described as God's people being
prevented from living as citizens of the kingdom of Heaven,
because in their earthly existence they were not being offered the

privileges and opportunities that God had provided for them.

And yet, at the same time, and as a result of the same tour, Jesus said to his disciples, 'The crop is heavy, but labourers are scarce; you must therefore beg the owner to send labourers to harvest his crop'. So, paradoxically enough, at the very time when Israel's 'shepherds' were depriving God's flock of their proper food and security, the true situation was one which could only be described in a change of metaphor as a 'harvest'. The metaphor of sheep and shepherd had exposed the falsity of those who were privileged to be leaders of God's flock; the new metaphor expressed Jesus' conviction that, looked at as a field in which God had sown his seed, the true people of God was now ripe for harvesting. And the yield would be more than abundant. One thing only was lacking - labourers to work in the harvest field.

Seed sown annually in the field produces an annual crisis of its fulfilment at the time of harvest. Crisis is the right word, for as Jesus and the Galilean peasants knew full well, and as modern farmers equally recognize, gathering the best harvest means deciding to reap at precisely the right moment. But God's seed is not concerned with an annual agricultural crisis of that sort; so what are the implications of Jesus' using such a metaphor to elucidate a crisis so uniquely final as that of God's purpose in the world?

The dominant answer to that question within the Christian tradition has been substantially the same as that advanced by Jewish prophecy and apocalyptic. It is that the ultimate reckoning of God with his world would and could only come at the end of the whole process. Indeed it may well be asked, Could any other view be seriously taken? For there could not be two 'ultimates', one of history and time, and another of God in his dealings with men in time. So the dominant theme has remained: The harvest, the ultimate reckoning, cannot take place before the end of time; all historical occasions can be no more than penultimate occasions, however filled they may be with God's dealing with men in history, and all historical occasions are penultimate to the great ultimate occasion when time ceases and eternity supervenes.

But however unavoidable that view seemed, and seems, it appears not to have been the view of Jesus as depicted in this Matthean summary. The crop is heavy: the harvest is ripe now. The fulfilment of God's purpose and his judgement on human

history is being enacted now. The ultimate is here and all other
historical occasions are penultimate to this ultimate reality that
has appeared in the mission and life of Jesus of Nazareth.

So God's harvest is ready for reaping. But labour is scarce;
it is then surely of considerable significance that Matthew
follows this summary with the statement that Jesus 'called his
twelve disciples to him and gave them authority to cast out
unclean spirits and to cure every kind of ailment and disease; and
of no less significance that he sent them out on a mission with
the injunction 'as you go proclaim the message, "The kingdom of
Heaven is upon you"'. The disciples are to be labourers in the
harvest.

But is a disciple's work really of that kind? Does he really
act as a harvester in God's field, in announcing the arrival of
the kingdom of Heaven? The parable of the wheat and the tares
(13.24-30) tells of a farmer sowing his field with good seed, but
while everyone was asleep his enemy came and sowed darnel among
the wheat. When the weedy growth was noticed the farm hands asked
if they should forthwith pull out the darnel and so free the crop
from the alien growth. But the owner said 'No', and let the two
grow together until the harvest, when both could be pulled up and
a final separation made. It is not surprising that this parable
has been interpreted in accordance with the dominant eschatology
of Christian interpretation, and the reference has been taken to
be to the last great judgement on the last day, when angels would
separate the weeds from the wheat, i.e. those who belong to the
kingdom of Heaven from those that do not. But if we take what I
believe was Jesus' own understanding of the harvest of God's
field, then the work that the disciples have to do is precisely
by their preaching and compassionate action to separate out those
who respond in penitence and hope and enter the kingdom of Heaven
from those who do not. And surely this is a true description of
the commissioned disciple of Jesus. The same considerations can
be given to the parable of the drag net (13.47-50) from whose
catch the good fish are taken and the bad thrown away.

The eschatological openness of each present moment finds
fuller expression in the later chapters of Matthew. The 'trusty
servant' of 24.45 is not one who thinks that the master will come
only at the end of time, and that therefore his coming need not
be reckoned with until the moment is near; nor would he be one,
we may suppose, who spends his time on the watch tower looking
for distant signs of the approach of his master's entourage. He
would quite fail, in Matthew's phrase, to 'manage his master's

household staff and issue rations at the proper time'.

It seems to me that the basic difficulty that modern man, and the modern Christian, have in adopting this 'realized eschatology' of Jesus is the understandable but nevertheless erroneous conviction that the kingdom of Heaven cannot have come since there is so much evil still in the world. But such a conviction would certainly not have counted with Jesus, as even a cursory reading of the Beatitudes will show. The heavenly citizen is not preserved from the troubles that afflict mankind in general; but in the world where troubles come, he also lives in another world, or to put it differently, in the same world with a new knowledge about it, that in it and over it, God still reigns, and that he can make even the wrath of man to turn to his praise. That trust gives the heavenly citizen a sense of values utterly different from his secular contemporaries.

I am also inclined to think that the same basic difficulty has made many a translator of the New Testament fight shy of translating ἤγγικεν in any sort of context by any word that indicates actual arrival rather than 'drawing near'. One notable exception is the NEB, but Dr Dodd had a good deal to do with that particular version! To take one example from Matthew: in 26.45, 46, RSV renders 'the hour is at hand', and 'my betrayer is at hand'; NEB improves on this with 'The hour has come' and 'the traitor is upon us', though that is a clumsy phrase for the occasion, but at least avoids the fault I regret. Good News Bible improves even more with 'The hour has come' and 'Here is the man who is betraying me'. I cite another instance from Luke and his story of the Easter walk to Emmaus. In v.15 RSV translates 'Jesus himself drew near and went with them', while NEB much more happily renders 'Jesus came up and walked along with them'; GNB not quite so happily as before says 'Jesus himself drew near and walked along with them'. And in the later stage of that walk, in v.28 Luke, according to RSV, wrote, 'They drew near to the village to which they were going. He appeared to be going further; NEB has 'They had reached the village, and he made as if to continue his journey'; while GNB states, 'As they came near the village to which they were going, Jesus acted as if he were going further'.

I leave you to ponder how far the reluctance to translate ἤγγικεν by any term of arrival has manifestly affected the translation of passages where the notion of arrival is by far the most defensible meaning to adopt. Since that is so, it is surely worth trying to see what sort of difference the meaning of

'arrival' would make to what Jesus had to say about the kingdom of
Heaven. It would, in my view, and in holding it I cannot do other
than acknowledge a great debt to C.H. Dodd, at least bring us to
think about the kingdom in the same way that Jesus himself thought
of it in his own lifetime, and even, as we shall see to-morrow, in
the shadow of his imminent death upon the cross.

                                   4

     In today's concluding glance at Matthew's gospel I shall
consider not so much a passage as a personage of the gospel, the
person of the Son of Man. Not that I can exhaustively examine the
material, but that I might set it in a not too implausible
perspective.

     I begin with three assumptions: First, that Matthew, and Jesus
about whom he wrote, knew full well the use of the term Son of Man
as the means by which God addressed his prophet Ezekiel. Second,
that Matthew, and Jesus about whom he wrote, were familiar with the
figure of the Son of Man (and of other figures and features) in
contemporary Jewish apocalyptic. And third, that if Jesus made any
use of the idea of the Son of Man from any source, he would have
stamped upon it his own highly creative and original meaning. To
these three suppositions I would add what I take to be a fact, that
Jesus regarded himself, and spoke of himself, as the Son of Man (16
14ff; 17.9,22; 20.18). What then can be learnt from Matthew about
Jesus as he is identified, and self-identified, as the Son of Man?

     There is no literary indication that Jesus used the phrase in
terms of its use in Ezekiel. Yet for the Christian it is at least
interesting that, like Ezekiel, Jesus knew himself to be
commissioned to speak divine if uncomfortable words to a wayward
people and their false shepherds. Like Ezekiel, he suffers
misunderstanding, misrepresentation and rejection, though, like
Ezekiel, his mission was essentially to bring new life to a people
that had become no better than a skeleton carcase.

     Matthew has two sayings about the Son of Man peculiar to his
gospel. The first is in the explanation of the parable of the
wheat and the tares: 'The sower of the good seed is the Son of Man.
The field is the world; the good seed stands for the children of
the kingdom, the darnel for the children of the evil one. The
enemy who sowed the darnel is the devil. The harvest is the end of
time [or, in my preference, the consummation or fulfilment of the
age]. The reapers are angels [or, in less celestial terms,

messengers]. As the darnel, then, is gathered up and burnt, so at
the end of time [or, fulfilment or consummation of the age] the
Son of Man will send out his angels [or, messengers] who will
gather out of his kingdom everything that causes offence, and all
whose deeds are evil.... Then the righteous will shine as
brightly as the sun in the kingdom of their Father." That
explanation is generally taken to be more the product of Matthew's
pen than of Jesus' speech. It certainly creates difficulties, and
one has been made unavoidable by the NEB renderings, 'The harvest
is the end of time' and 'At the end of time the Son of Man will
send out his angels [or, messengers]'. These two phrases firmly
fix the parable to the chronological end of the history of the
world. But in the light of Jesus' word about the harvest in 9.37f,
a very different possibility emerges. If the harvest is the
'fulfilment' of the age, it is the point at which it is possible
to pass from this present age into the new age, the one that is
to come; and that is precisely what is possible to those who have
heard and responded to the teaching of Jesus. The kingdom of
Heaven has 'come upon' them. They have repented and believed the
good news. This was the theme of Jesus' own preaching; it was
also that of his messengers, who were thus already sorting out the
righteous from the unrighteous, or, to pass from the agricultural
figure of 9.37f to the piscatorial one of 13.47f, they are, as
fishers of men, already sorting out the good fish from the bad,
the children of the kingdom from the children of the evil one.

The 'last judgement' is also the theme of the other saying
about the Son of Man peculiar to Matthew. It occurs in 25.31:
When [or, perhaps better, 'whenever'] the Son of Man comes in his
glory and all the angels with him, he will sit in state on his
throne, with all the nations gathered before him. He will
separate men into two groups.' Then follows the remarkable
narrative in which neither those who serve nor those who neglect
the Son of Man have been an any way aware of his presence among
them, yet are judged on how they treated him in his successful
incognito as a human being in need. It is legitimate, as Jeremias
has shown, to assume that v.31 is closely related to 16.27: 'The
Son of Man is to come in the glory of his Father with his angels,
and then he will give each man the due reward for what he has done.
I tell you this: there are some standing here who will not taste
death before they have seen the Son of Man coming in his kingdom.'
Can this saying also be related to the understanding of
eschatology disclosed in 9.37 by the saying about the harvest?

There seem to be two chief difficulties: first, the
chronological difficulty of thinking of the 'end' of a temporal

series as coming during its course. Yet Paul and John should
enable this to be accepted as an authentic New Testament mode of
thought. To Jesus' assurance to Martha that her brother would rise
again, she responded, 'I know that he will rise again at the
resurrection on the last day'. Jesus met that with the momentous
words, 'I am the resurrection and I am life. If a man has faith in
me, even though he die, he shall come to life; and no one who is
alive and has faith shall ever die.' The transition from this age
to the next will not be made on some unspecified date in a
chronological future, but is made whenever a man comes to believe
in Jesus Christ. The border of the eternal runs alongside every
chronological moment. Paul wrote that 'upon us [Christians] the
fulfilment [lit. the ends] of the ages has come'. Christian life
is always lived where the boundaries of the temporal and eternal
meet. The 'final' things are always taking place.

     The second obstacle is the absence of glory and majesty that
is thought to be an inevitable accompaniment of a final divine
judgement. But again, if the testimony of John be heeded, it is
clear that the expectation of 'glory' and 'majesty' undergoes
radical change for Christians. John portrays the death of Jesus
not as an inglorious defeat on Good Friday transcended by a
glorious victory on Easter Day, but rather sees the cross itself
as the place where true divine glory is manifested. So the glory
of the last judgement need not be manifested in pageantry and
impressive ceremonial, but rather in the seriousness and finality
of the Father's words and acts. So the Christian has little excuse
for a reluctance to banish from his imaginative structures the
glorious paraphernalia usually associated with the judicial
activities of the Son of Man. Admittedly Jewish apocalyptic came
to see him in that role as a heavenly and glorious figure; but
Jesus, himself a Jew, believed that the humiliation of the Son of
Man was the true manifestation of his glory.

     But it is time to return to the theme and ask what place the
idea of the Son of Man played in the life and ministry of Jesus.
Matthew gives more copious evidence than the other evangelists,
but neither from him nor from any other source is there sufficient
data clearly to indicate a development in Jesus' use of the term,
though differences in its use there certainly are.

     The first use of the term is in the word spoken to the
prospective disciple, a doctor of the law, who offered to follow
Jesus wherever he went (8.19). 'Foxes have their holes', Jesus
replied, 'the birds their roosts; but the Son of Man has nowhere
to lay his head.' If this be an Ezekiel-like comment on the

discomforts of a prophet it is not startlingly new; but if already
Jesus is linking suffering and victory together in the destiny of
the Son of Man, his distinctive insights may already be finding
expression. The same applies to the saying that 'The Son of Man
came eating and drinking and they say "Look at him! a glutton and
a drinker, a friend of tax-gatherers and sinners"' (11.19). Other
such sayings, varying in intensity from reference to the Son of
Man being spoken against (12.32) to a foreshadowing of betrayal
and death (17.22 etc.) are sufficient indication of the significant
variation of the use of the term in Matthew.

Another series of sayings reflects the divine status and
authority of the Son of Man that is present in the ministry of
Jesus. The Son of Man is to appear at the end of the age (its
fulfilment or consummation) and send out his messengers to do the
work of harvest, separating the children of the kingdom from the
children of the evil one. The Son of Man is also one who comes,
not to be served, but to serve, and in the execution of his mission
brings men to a 'last judgement' of God upon men and nations, a
function to be performed within the lifetime of some of Jesus'
contemporaries (16.28).

But it is in sayings that indicate the destiny of the Son of
Man that Jesus' most radical contribution is to be discerned.
The Son of Man is seen as one who by his own suffering and death
will finally achieve the 'inauguration' or 'arrival' of the kingdom
of his Father. It is in this area more than anywhere else that a
development in the thought of Jesus seems possible to trace,
however inexactly.

Matthew's first summary of Jesus' teaching was that Israel
should repent, for the kingdom of Heaven had 'come upon' them
(4.17). The next summary stated that he went round all the towns
and villages...announcing the good news of the kingdom' (9.35).
It seems that at this period of the ministry the arrival of the
kingdom was unadulterated good news. Yet before the second summary
Matthew has made it clear that Jesus knew that the citizens of the
kingdom of heaven would suffer for their citizenship (5.11f) and
immediately after the second summary Matthew tells how Jesus sent
out the twelve on an 'evangelistic campaign' with clear foreboding
that their path would not be smooth (10.16-39). With the
introduction of the figure of the Son of Man Matthew prepares the
way for understanding what Jesus meant in 16.27 and 25.31. The
Son of Man is less fortunate than the foxes of the countryside,
though he has the divine prerogative to forgive sins on earth
(9.6). He sows God's good seed in the Father's field, but an enemy

sows darnel there too (13.24-30). His mission will be neither
immediately successful nor unopposed.

It would be culpable obtuseness to deny that there is a real
element of 'vaticinium ex eventu' in the predictions of the
passion that Matthew records (16.21; 17.22f; 20.18f; 26.2), as in
other such sayings (e.g. 12.40). But it is impossible to deny
that there was a time when it became quite apparent to Jesus
himself that the destiny of the Son of Man (himself) was to be a
tragic one. This is certainly so, in Matthew's picture of Jesus
in Gethsemane, where he says to his disciples at the approach of
Judas, 'The Son of Man is betrayed to sinful men'. But the most
illuminating comment of the Son of Man was made in the course of
Jesus' trial before the Sanhedrin. The Jewish authorities had
already decided, says Matthew, that Jesus must be arrested and
executed (26.3ff). Arrested duly he was, and put on trial for
his life. He proved an awkward prisoner, saying nothing to the
charges made against him. At last the High Priest said to him,
'By the living God I charge you to tell us: Are you the Messiah,
the Son of God?' Jesus replied 'The words are yours. But I tell
you this: from now on, you will see the Son of Man seated at the
right hand of God and coming on the clouds of heaven.' This was,
reports Matthew, denounced as blasphemy, and Jesus judged guilty
of death. At that moment Jesus and the High Priest knew that what
lay ahead for Jesus was death. But while the High Priest naturally
believed that death would be the end of Jesus and his messianic
claims and community, Jesus himself saw a future for himself beyond
death, one in which, in the words of Daniel Jesus himself quoted,
'one like a [son of] man "came" with the clouds of heaven; he
approached the Ancient in Years and was presented to him.
Sovereignty and glory and kingly power were given to him, so that
all people and nations of every language should serve him; his
sovereignty was to be an everlasting sovereignty, and his kingly
power such as should never be impaired.' The Son of Man might
be put to death; but that would prove only to be the path to his
true glory. Per crucem ad coronam could hardly be more clearly
stated.

It is tempting, and not unilluminating, to ask what all this
means for understanding the figure of the Son of Man in Matthew's
gospel. I cannot resist the speculation that, although chapter 28
contains no explicit reference to the Son of Man, verses 16-20
were nevertheless intended by Matthew to provide the climax to the
story of the Son of Man in his gospel. If it be so read, much
light is cast upon it, and upon previous sayings, some of them
otherwise enigmatic in the extreme. For here Jesus, as the Son of

Man, comes with his messengers, after he has received full
authority in heaven and on earth, and sends his messengers out on
their universal mission which will in fact separate the children
of the kingdom from the children of the evil one; and that 'final'
coming and the mission to gather in the children to the kingdom of
their Father has taken place within the life-time of those who
were contemporary with Jesus in the days of his flesh. And he,
the Son of Man, will be with his own community until the end of
the age, always available to those who live where Paul said
Christians do live, at the point where this age and the one to come
overlap in the person of Jesus, incarnate, risen glorified, and
come at and for the end.

I do not suppose that this will be a popular view; perhaps my
best course is to leave it with you for consideration and prayer.
Dominus vobiscum, which after Christ's last words in Matthew 28.20
is not a prayer, but a proclamation! *Laus Deo.* Amen.

*As on a previous occasion, I was invited to give a number of Bible
readings to the Congress, though on this occasion, instead of
speaking to a small group, it was arranged that I should address
any members of Congress who wished to listen. In preparing them
I was therefore not attempting to make a learned contribution to
the scholarly discussions of the Congress, but rather to suggest
by some sort of example how one student of the New Testament
had found his study contributing to his religious understanding
both of the biblical text and of the person with whose life and
work the text is concerned. I can only hope that even the scholars
may find some value in this somewhat different approach.

New Quest — Dead End? So What about the Historical Jesus?

James I.H. McDonald
23 Ravelston House Road,
Edinburgh, EH4 3LP,
Scotland.

When one considers the range of approaches to the life of Jesus - over the years from Strauss to Bornkamm and from A. Schweitzer to E. Schweizer, or even today from Stauffer to Vermes /1/ - the question is raised (quite seriously) whether all are participating in the same game or whether we should frankly recognise that several different sports are involved. Yet, despite the enormous variety of approaches encompassed by the term *Leben-Jesu-Forschung,* there is - rather like Hinduism from the Upanishads onwards - an overarching unity, a unity that comprehends rich diversity. Thus, the most recent new quest is not to be taken in isolation from what has gone before - nor does it claim otherwise, for its starting point is the *kerygma* and the negative stance which Bultmann and his co-kerygmatists have taken in relation to the quest of the historical Jesus. The 'No Entry' sign which Bultmann erected at the approaches to *Leben-Jesu-Strasse* was itself a response to the historical quest of a century or more which had preceded Bultmann's work. The study of the historical Jesus, indeed, is characterised by new quests and dead ends. It resembles a gigantic maze in which there is broad agreement about the starting point, even if it is variously described (e.g., the four gospels, Christian tradition, the *kerygma,* christology); and hopeful questers have often journeyed along the same or parallel paths for part of the way, eventually diverging in their search for the final goal. In their much travelling 'in the realms of gold', if they have 'many goodly states and kingdoms seen' and circumnavigated 'many western islands' (a rare one, like R. Otto, also including a few eastern ones in his itinerary), yet their reward has been false dawns and chimeras, even if sometimes they were deluded into thinking they were breathing the 'pure serene' of Nazareth, c.29 A.D. Nevertheless, until the combined weight of Barth and Bultmann blocked the entrance gate, most scholars seemed

convinced of the worthwhileness of the pursuit. Even if one might
not arrive, it was preferable to travel rather than remain immobile.
Bultmann was the stay-at-home. Purchasing his work permit from
Kähler, he believed that one should live and labour in the *kerygma*,
through which one was addressed by Jesus as Lord and brought to
the decision of faith. Anything else comes of evil! The quest-maze
is one in which one may lose oneself and one's faith. It represents
an illegitimate and futile attempt to buttress faith in the *kerygma*
by appeal to historical facts, for kerygmatic foundations cannot rest
on the shifting sand of historical research. The significance of
the new quest is that it accepts Bultmann's premises but disagrees
with his conclusions. It is possible, indeed necessary, to be
concerned with the historical Jesus, for the *kerygma* itself, by
the nature of its message, propels us in that direction.

There are, to be sure, a number of issues which we must
discuss in due course: not least, whether the procedures of the
new quest represent a genuine historical quest or whether they are
a cunning piece of apologetics. We must also enquire whether they
are logically successful. Meanwhile, there is more to say about
the dialectic of new quest - dead end.

When one is caught in the maze and finds to one's chagrin that
the path so hopefully pursued has led to a dead end, there is a
temptation, if not to give up in disgust, at least to cancel out
one's entire experience of that course and start *de novo*. Others
making parallel attempts reach the same conclusion. Something has
been learned - but that 'something' is a negative result. In the
history of the quest, it has frequently been the case that the
route declared to be a dead end becomes totally despised. Yet
this is hard to understand, except in terms of the psychology of
the scholars. A charge of liberal Protestantism brought against
Bultmann is like the proverbial red rag to a bull. Yet Bultmann
began his scholarly career under the tuition of W. Herrmann, J.
Weiss and E. Troeltsch, and drank deep of the Marburg Neo-Kantianism
of H. Cohen /2/. Before coming under the influence of Heidegger,
he was sympathetic enough to the *Leben-Jesu-Forschung* to write his
own book on Jesus /3/, in which a certain affinity with Harnack is
discernible in the way he structures the material; and his
purposive view of history - his 'dialogue with history' - is
certainly not without significance for the historiographical
problems raised by the quest. If Bultmann saw the 19th century
quest as a dead end, one must ask in all seriousness - how dead is
'dead'? Doubtless, some aspects of it are moribund, although we
must examine them carefully for signs of life and insist on a

certificate specifying the precise cause of death before burying
them once and for all. Again, to return to our famous maze: it
is not true to say that all results are negative. The *voyageurs*
have discovered certain important signs - directional or procedural
indicators which effectively delimit the range of options open to
us. The 19th century quest conceived, if not Lachmann, then
certainly Weisse and Holtzmann, so that source criticism became a
major guide through the maze. No less, it spanned J. Weiss and
A. Schweitzer with their rediscovery of eschatology (a sign which -
remembering Reimarus - had been around for a long time but had not
been treated with sufficient seriousness). And M. Kähler himself
is of this ilk. Rightly he tells us that we live and move and have
our being within a kerygmatic ambience. To be sure, his attitude
to the 19th century quest is negative. He will have no truck with
the historical relativism which presumed to rediscover the historical
Jesus and present him as an object of faith. He attacks the 'papal
pretensions' of wolfish dogmaticians in historians' clothing. Yet
all this can be construed, at least in part, as a plea for right
historical method. However much he attacked them in practice, he
did not break off diplomatic relations with the historical
questers. With his sharp distinction between *Historie* and *Geschichte*
(for which it is sometimes hard to forgive him), he might occasionally have been guilty of obscurantism, never of scepticism.
Indeed, he takes the gospels to supply 'the irresistible impression
of the completest reality'. It is the total work *(Werk)* or
achievement of Jesus that is *geschichtlich*, and that is precisely
what is expressed in the Easter faith and the New Testament as a
whole /4/.

It might not be unfair to say that the 19th century quest is
a dead end in relation to its intentions but not in relation to its
achievements. Out of it has come a whole series of indicators,
some of which might suggest the total abandonment of the original
intention and a reappraisal of priorities, while others are
consistent with the continuation of the quest in modified form
and with more sophisticated aids to navigation. The first set of
indicators was elaborated in three distinct phases: (i) source
criticism, which eventually reached its crowning glory in the
massive work of B.H. Streeter /5/; yet what appeared to be a gift
to the historian - the 'Q' sayings and the Markan outline - turned
out, in the light of further criticism, to be something of a Trojan
horse, fashioned by the evangelists and theologians of the early
Church, to the ruin of much painstaking work by T.W. Manson and
C.H. Dodd, as well as a host of lesser mortals; (ii) form criticism,
which pointed to the necessity to identify the *Sitz im Leben* of the
material - to be found, in an indefinite number of cases, in the

early congregations but, in an indefinite number of others, in
the ministry of Jesus; and (iii) redaction criticism, fostered by
Wrede /6/ and compatible with source and form criticism (not to
speak of kerygmatic theology), but maturing late as a determining
factor in gospel criticism. Of these, form criticism is pivotal,
but none of the three is disposable. Here then are guides (albeit
not for the faint-hearted), to help us penetrate more effectively
into the maze, although we do not yet by any means see with
assurance the road through to a historical objective.

However, there are other indicators which have been taken to
be of no less importance. Chief among these is eschatology, to
which there may be said to be four broad responses. (i) Consistent
eschatology (also known as thorough-going or futuristic eschatology)
the tradition of Weiss and Schweitzer, variously developed by
later scholars, including Bultmann. (ii) Realised eschatology,
of which the protagonist was C.H. Dodd: 'The eschaton has moved
from the future to the present, from the sphere of expectation
into that of realised experience' /7/. (iii) Proleptic eschatology;
as R.H. Fuller put it, what Dodd called realised eschatology is
better described as 'proleptic instalments of the final blessings
of the End' /8/; J. Jeremias called it *eine sich realisierende
Eschatologie*; J.A.T. Robinson, like E. Haenchen, spoke 'not of a
realized, but of an inaugurated eschatology' /9/. (iv)
De-eschatologizing: the arch-exponent of this procedure is
E. Stauffer, who strips away eschatology with the rest of the
superimposed lumber of secondary interpretation, Jewish and
Christian, in his positivistic quest for Jesus 'as he really was'
/10/.

That the responses to the single factor of eschatology should
virtually career across the whole spectrum of possibility suggests
the operation of other powerful presuppositions. Among these,
philosophical presuppositions rank high. Is the critic to adopt
as his own standpoint, for example, the idealism of Hegel, coupled
perhaps with some form of Neo-Kantianism, as befits an upholder of
ethical monotheism? If so there are two main possibilities.
Either one de-eschatologizes the kingdom of God in the teaching
and ministry of Jesus, so that it becomes realised as a this-worldly
monistic and ethical reality - perhaps sociologically conceived as
in Ritschl, or individualistically as in Herrmann; or one takes
eschatology consistently through the life of Jesus but interprets
his death as, in effect, the de-eschatologizing agent, so that one
is free - as in the case of Weiss - to arrogate to oneself a
Ritschlian position (or whatever), or - as in Schweitzer's case -

to remove eschatology from further theological concern by a kind
of semi-Hegelian *tour de force* /11/. Of these two options, the
second has at least the advantage of distinguishing between the
presumed standpoint of Jesus (i.e., determined by eschatology)
and the standpoint of the scholar, thus establishing the
possibility of a criterion of differentiation. Consequently,
there is less chance of the scholar creating Jesus in his own
image - the recurrent reproach of the 19th century quest.
Bultmann's position, on the other hand, gives rise to disquiet,
not simply because he wants to close the door on the Jesus quest
but because, when he allows it to open to admit a chink of light
what we find is not Jesus but 'Jesus and the Word', summoning us
to decision in much the same way as the *kerygma* itself, except that
in the latter the proclaimer has become the proclaimed. It is as
if the historical Jesus were not so much the presupposition of the
kerygma, rather its echo. It may be fair, despite appearance to
the contrary, to see Bultmann's interpretative procedure as
effectively de-eschatologizing both Jesus and the *kerygma*, for
they do not so much proclaim the future kingdom as call men to
the decision of faith and obedience to the Word. As it has been
put tersely:

> 'Eschatology becomes nothing more nor less than disguised
> ethic, and the whole interpretation of Jesus becomes
> ethicised throughout. The views of Bultmann the dialectician
> and existential philosopher are not so fundamentally different
> from those of Bultmann the pupil of Herrmann in 1917' /12/.

Of course, there are other ways of playing the game. If one
has had a respectable Oxbridge upbringing and has drunk deep of
the Platonic springs, purified perhaps by an infusion of English
incarnational theology, then the kingdom of God is essentially a
timeless reality, the Eternal paradoxically manifesting itself in
history. Such was the way of C.H. Dodd; and unless it is
seriously held that Jesus was a Platonist, it will be necessary -
if Dodd's general picture of Jesus is viable at all - at least to
de-philosophize his interpretation /13/. This was partly
accomplished by proleptic eschatology and its variants; but here
the danger is rather one of theologizing Jesus' standpoint, so
that it becomes a facet of biblical theology or 'bible realism'
(a tendentious title if ever there was one) - Jesus' own position
being confused once more with Christian attempts to make sense of
it. Or finally, one can say, in effect, with Stauffer: a plague
on all your houses! We must strip away every kind of overlay,
including that of Jewish eschatology and apocalypticism, and lay

bare what actually happened: *wie es eigentlich gewesen ist*.
Unfortunately, in doing so one reads into the material a whole
new set of assumptions and dreams of the uninterpreted 'facts' of
the historical positivists, along with von Ranke, Niebuhr and Lord
Acton, if not with Auguste Comte.

All this is just a trifle discouraging. It looks like the
proverbial 'fly in a flybottle' or 'Catch-22' situation. When we
are trying to penetrate the maze, we succeed only in going round
in circles, no matter which way we turn. Should we, after all,
retire with Bultmann behind the entrenchments of the *kerygma* and
rule out of order any suggestion of a foray in the direction of
the historical Jesus on the grounds that, at best, it must fail
in any particular not already given in the *kerygma* and that, at
worst, it can seriously weaken the kerygmatic defences? The
post-Bultmannians, kerygmatists to a man, have said 'No!'. The
new quest they launched is unique in that it starts out from the
givenness of Bultmann's negative and attempts to overcome it.
Its beginning is thus characterised by the motif 'Dead End - New
Quest', rather than the reverse; and as such it deserves a hearing.

E. Käsemann led the first sortie - tempering his natural
verve, as a good commander should, by a sober assessment of the
strategic situation /14/. The *Historie-Geschichte* puzzle is
foremost in his mind. *Historie* has about it an element of
petrification. To put it baldly, if we were to ask, 'Lord, can
these bones live?', we should receive the answer, 'Not if you
simply enumerate them and hand down a statistical record to your
successors!'. Passing on the *bruta facta,* Käsemann says, may
very well obstruct a proper understanding of history. Here we
pause. There may be profound truth in his observation, and
Käsemann has many wise things to say about the problem of the
historical element in the gospels. But it would be easy to parody
the above statement. It reminds one of the business man who is
alleged to have said, 'I have made up my mind. Don't confuse me
with the facts'. *Bruta facta* may be a positivistic shibboleth,
but you cannot have historical significance in detachment from
historical *data*. In short, the German linguistic puzzle may not
be the most helpful means of handling the historical problem of
Jesus and the gospels. It might have been more profitable (at
least to the non-Germanic mind) to demonstrate the inappropriateness
of historical positivism for the renewed quest and the advantages of
employing the procedures of existentialist historiography. For
that, as I understand it, is what Käsemann proposes.

Like a commander in the field again, Käsemann finds himself
lamenting the dilemma in which technological warfare has placed him.
The form-critical kit, which is regulation issue to all combatants
these days, fails to provide any kind of formal criterion by which
to identify authentic Jesus material. In particular, the criterion
of dissimilarity, with which he believes he can partially operate,
is largely disarmed because an essential element is missing, *viz.*,
'a conspectus of the very earliest stage of primitive Christian
history'. No wonder Käsemann speaks of the embarrassment of
critical research! Here is, potentially, the ultimate weapon, and
it fails because no one has been able to design a suitable fuse!
And he has no illusions about where this leaves him. On the basis
of form criticism, he says, the task is 'to investigate and make
credible not the possible unauthenticity of the individual unit of
material but, on the contrary, its genuineness' /15/. If these are
the terms on which the battle against scepticism must be fought,
then there is more than a question mark against the adequacy of
weapons.

What can be done, of course, is to delimit the scope of the
conflict. Don't expect me, Käsemann says in effect, to 'reconstruct
something like a life of Jesus', even 'with the utmost caution and
reserve'. We know nothing about the 'interior development' of
Jesus' life, and next to nothing about his 'exterior development'.

> 'Only an uncontrolled imagination could have the self-
> confidence to weave out of these pitiful threads the
> fabric of a history in which cause and effect could be
> determined in detail /16/'.

Yet Käsemann cannot yield to scepticism, for he believes he would
then be untrue to the *kerygma,* which identifies the exalted and
the humiliated Lord, and he would be defenceless against docetism.
He finds 'certain characteristic traits in his [sc. Jesus']
preaching' which cohere with the *kerygma*, and from these he develops
a surprisingly powerful picture of the 'one who transcends all
categories', whose 'But *I* say to you ...' goes far beyond rabbi
or prophet or mere integration with Jewish piety, who overrides
'with an unparalleled and sovereign freedom, the words of the
Torah and the authority of Moses', who consorts with sinners and
thus breaks down the distinction between sacred and secular, who
puts the demons to flight as he ministers to man, and whose
reverberating 'Amen' 'signifies an extreme and immediate certainty,
such as is conveyed by inspiration'. All this and inaugurated

eschatology too! So impressive is Käsemann's overrunning of the
commanding heights of scepticism that one wonders if somewhere
he has employed a secret weapon - so unlikely is it that he could
conjure up so full a picture out of the minimal resources he has
described to us. It would appear that the many other criteria
that Käsemann says we have have at least supplemented the
criterion of differentiation in important ways. All such criteria,
however, require close scrutiny.

One last point: the concept of Jesus as one who fits no
formula has its dangers - not least because it is so acceptable to
Christian ears.

> 'He cannot be classified according to the categories
> either of psychology or of the comparative study of
> religion or, finally, of general history. If he can
> be placed at all, it must be in terms of historical
> particularity /17/'.

Fair enough - the scholar must accept Jesus as he finds him or
discovers him to be. He must not force him into a Procrustean
bed fashioned by the presuppositions of his discipline. However,
since the *data* for a psychological classification are not
available, the reference to psychology is somewhat gratuitous -
probably a defence against charges of reviving the 19th century
quest. Comparative religion is an altogether different
proposition. It is its business to take account of Jesus!
As already indicated, it must not do so by forcing him into an
alien mould; it must treat its *data* with integrity. But there is
no way by which a theologically based hermeneutic can deny to
comparative religion and phenomenology the right of handling Jesus
material in ways appropriate to these disciplines. If the
contribution of such disciplines were taken seriously by
theologians, it might well be that their total understanding of
Jesus would be enhanced thereby. Nor can one claim to be concerned
with 'the historical Jesus' without engaging with 'general history'
and its methods.

Käsemann's essay, the first significant contribution to the
new quest, was the early crop in an abundant harvest in which the
prize exhibits are probably the work of G. Bornkamm, E. Fuchs and
G. Ebeling - with H. Braun something of an autumn variety. But
our task here is not to review the already well publicised
features of the new quest, but rather to make a critical appraisal
of some of its crucial, operational assumptions.

For the proposed sortie from the entrenchments of the *kerygma*, the tactical criteria mean the difference between success and failure. Yet the criteria on which the new quest appears to depend are gravely defective. There is, it is generally felt, a sense in which the criterion of dissimilarity (N. Perrin's phrase /18/) can and should operate: e.g., to bring out what is distinctive in the ministry of Jesus as compared with ancient Judaism or the early Church, and thus to afford a critically assured minimum of authentic material - even if a substantial element of common ground might be presumed to exist between Jesus and the Church that called him Lord. Yet, apart from a few limited areas (e.g., parables), the confident application of this basic criterion would appear to be ruled out by the fact that our knowledge, if not of first century Judaism, then of the early Church, falls far short of the required level. In that case, it is rather like building a bridge to nowhere! Again, even if it were workable, it would produce a caricature of Jesus, for the wholly unique would be wholly incomprehensible. Jesus' identification with the broad tradition of Judaism is almost as important historically as his break with it and is an indispensable element in any account of his ministry. It would therefore be more true to say that if any material in the gospel tradition could not be related to a Palestinian ethos (assuming that we could make an adequate identification of the latter), its authenticity would be suspect. On this basis, a whole range of possibilities, to which a carefully stated criterion of differentiation is relevant, opens out before us. In a given case, Jesus might have quoted or rein-forced some aspect of Judaism (or is it more probable that this material comes from the Palestinian Christian Church - whatever that was?); he might have applied Jewish teaching in a distinctive way (or is it more probable that we have here an echo of the hermeneutical debate between Christians and various groups of Jews?); or he might have wholly denounced some particular tendency in Judaism (or do we have here a reflection of later first century confrontations between Jews and Christians?). Notice, however, how much we need to know - on the one hand about the Palestinian situation and the religion of the Jews, and on the other, about how Jesus related to this ethos and in what roles or capacities he related to it - *before* we can apply the criterion of differentiation. We need a general backcloth against which to set individual utterances. We cannot consider them in isolation or piecemeal. In short, this criterion may well be a useful secondary tool but, generally speaking, it is not capable of primary application.

Yet we might be excused for thinking that the new quest looks to this criterion precisely for this primary function. It is the

criterion for which Käsemann is searching, although he admits to
finding it elusive. It is the criterion which N. Perrin takes as
basic; but if the hull is as defective as we have found it, the
ship cannot take on board additional cargo like the criteria of
coherence, multiple attestation and others besides, unless one
entertains the unlikely hope that such cargo will add to buoyancy.

To return to our original question: is the new quest a dead
end? In some ways, perhaps it is. Apart from the fact that it is
methodologically unsatisfactory, it is not, in the strict sense of
the term, a dialogue with history at all. It is essentially a
dialogue with the *kerygma*. To be sure, it finds, in the content of
the *kerygma,* the ineradicable tones of Jesus of Nazareth, summoning
men to faith and obedience. It is concerned to delineate more
sharply the *given* historical elements in the *kerygma* (i.e., in the
gospels), and to present the picture of 'this real Jesus' (Käsemann
term) compounded of his words and sometimes also his conduct
(cf. Fuchs). Indeed, for the later Käsemann at least, the earthly
Jesus rises up through the *kerygma* to become its spearhead, the
eternal liberating liberal (Harnack, art tha sleepin' there below?)
To be frank, one finds oneself stimulated by Käsemann's enthusiasm
and sincerity, and rejoicing that the *kerygma* has regained the
human face it should never have lost. And one listens no less
intently when Bornkamm talks of the essential mystery of Jesus in
terms of his making present the reality of God, an event which
'signifies the end of the world in which it takes place'. But
Bornkamm's book might more aptly have been entitled, 'A Christian
View of Jesus of Nazareth', and Käsemann's essay 'The Problem of
the *Kerygma*'. In short, the post-Bultmannian quest is incorrigibly
theological. It takes place within a specifically Christian frame
of discourse, and it employs historiography as the tool of faith-
hermeneutics. As such, it has doubtless made, and will continue
to make,a timely and major contribution to New Testament
interpretation. But, in their determination to avoid any
contaminating truck with the old 19th century quest, and in
serving so loyally under the colours of the *kerygma* (with such
inhibitions as that entails), the post-Bultmannians have in fact
side-stepped the essential problem of the historicity of Jesus of
Nazareth. They found him entombed in the *kerygma,* and they sought
to roll away the stone so that his full humanity should be given
back to the Church's life and proclamation. R. Barbour writes
thus of Käsemann's procedure:

'"Factors of faith" and "factors of history" are here
indissoluble, and it can be argued that the historical

realism of this approach is due to theological or
psychological factors rather than to any careful
consideration of the difficulties involved in the
philosophies of many of his fellow-scholars' /19/.

Be that as it may, if the post-Bultmannians rest content with this
kind of historification of the *kerygma*, they may well be accused -
with some justification - of 'wearing the blinkers of their trade'.
There is an important sense in which Jesus cannot be handed over
completely to the *kerygma* or the Church's memory, for he belongs
to the broad secularity of history. In relation to *this* Jesus,
historiography must not merely subserve faith-hermeneutics but must
be given its head, so that it can show us (not indeed 'Jesus as
he was' but) Jesus as we can encounter him in history. A byproduct,
if not an essential part, of this approach will be dialogue with
Christian interpretation or hermeneutics on the one hand, and
non-Christian historiography on the other. In relation to the
historical quest, however, the so-called new quest is, if not a
dead end, then tangential. Its future contribution probably lies
in the realm of christology and the relation of the humanity of
Jesus to such questions as the nature of God, salvation and
discipleship. In this realm, its importance is hard to over-
estimate.

But if the new quest is unable to cope with the historical
problem of Jesus as we have identified it, the range of alternative
options open for us to pursue is not extensive. On the conservative
side, which often excels in exegesis, the capacity to grapple with
fundamental problems of historicity is neutralised by the determined
attempt simply to historify what might be called, at best, an
enlightened biblicism. On the biblical-theological front, the
weighty scholarship of, for example, J. Jeremias and O. Cullmann,
while achieving notable results in some areas of historical
research, finally evaporates in the theological stratosphere of
Heilsgeschichte. We may look to W. Pannenberg for his theology of
history, and rub our eyes as we discern Hegel *redivivus* /20/.
Scandinavian scholarship has underlined and illuminated the
operation of tradition, especially in a Jewish setting, and in so
doing has prodded and found reaction in some tender spots of the
formgeschichtlich constitution; but the value of this research for
historical purposes has been diminished by the range of unsubstan-
tiated, dogmatic assumptions which are made in the by-going /21/.
The liberal approach, which always had a genuine concern for
historicity (however poorly it may have expressed it in
practice) and whose obsequies have often been indelicately

celebrated by a variety of theological schools, is nevertheless
alive and as well as can be expected - a circumstance that is in
itself remarkable in view of the fact that the liberal quest has
included in its itinerary more dead ends than it is normally
possible to visit in one life-time without expiring prematurely
through sheer exhaustion. While liberals in Europe have had to
throw in their lot with a wider post-liberal coalition in order
to survive the cold prevailing winds of dogmatism and docetism
(thus partly succumbing to them), the American climate has been
kinder to their *genus,* even if the soil of Rauschenbusch was
hospitable to its ranker growth habits. In fact, the biological
weakness of the liberal organism has been its proneness to .
ideological infestation, as can be seen in the social-historicism
of S.J. Case and even some of his distinguished successors in the
Chicago school - a movement which badly needed the correctives
given to it be scholars like F.C. Grant and A.N. Wilder. Yet,
despite its imbalances, this liberalism was concerned with the
method of historical research - Case expounded his own criterion of
differentiation as early as 1927 - as well as with the empirical
goal of the quest. As H. Anderson has put it,

> 'In the socio-historical approach among American Biblical
> researchers, we see what is, I think, a valid protest
> against the abstraction of the kerygma from the historical
> context in which the believer and interpreter are situated'
> /22/.

If we find in such liberalism less than the complete answer, we do
not on the other hand encounter it as a dead end - rather, as a
pointer to the direction of travel, even if our course must be set
in still closer relation to the signals we receive from all kinds
of *data* - social, economic, political and religious. New Testament
scholarship is littered with the shipwrecks of mariners less fully
informed about the waters in which their passage lay.

     The procedure which we tentatively advance here in the
briefest of sketches may be described as phenomenological or
structural, operating in accordance with the well established
principles of *epoché, Einfühlung* and eidetic vision /23/. The
cumulative evidence of our sources suggests that Jesus was a
religious figure, a *homo religiosus* in the broadest sense, who
lived in Palestine at a particular time which our sources indicate
fairly precisely. One can give an account of the combined social,
religious, political and economic forces which formed the
particular ethos in which his life and work lay; and in that
setting one can distinguish the roles and procedures which

characterised his ministry, examine how he related to the
commanding heights of the socio-religious landscape that formed
his world, and deduce something of the purpose underlying his work.
It is also important to account for his death in terms of forces
immanent in his ministry and the responses it evoked; and to
understand the faith-response of his disciples to him and the
faith they subsequently had in his ultimate triumph, i.e., the
resurrection faith.

All this, I should have thought, is fairly unexceptionable;
but, to avoid misunderstanding, it may be well to spell out what is
and what is not implied in this minimal sketch. To take the
negative first. It is *not* a resumption of the old liberal quest.
No use is made of the Markan framework as a biographical outline;
no attempt is made to give a psychological or developmental
interpretation of Jesus' self-consciousness; and, true to the
principle of *epoché*, no extraneous philosophical or theological
assumptions are read into his ministry or made the interpretative
basis of his life and teaching. In this latter respect, therefore,
our proposals differ from the new quest also; for, despite its use
of the criterion of differentiation and its much vaunted disavowal
of all attempts to penetrate the self-consciousness of Jesus, it
has made Jesus into the prototype of the Christian theologian.
Bornkamms procedures, it has been hinted, lead to a Christian
Kalimah: 'There is no god but God, and Jesus is his first
theologian' /24/. Reflect also, if you will, on the 20th century
philosophizing and theologizing of eschatology - producing various
concoctions that, one can safely say, never were on sea or land!
Again, our suggested procedures represent neither a simple
continuation of the social-historicism of Chicago, although they
relate well enough, I think, to its later, more highly developed
forms, nor a simple reversion to the *Religionsgeschichte* of
Bousset or Otto, whose work was in any case conditioned by
philosophy. Yet one cannot help reflecting that if the encounters
of Otto and Bultmann at Marburg had taken the form of genuine
dialogue rather than confrontation, the parameters of the new
quest today might have been drawn very differently, and the
problem of the historical Jesus might not have been as intractable
as it has proved.

On the positive side, we propose to employ in full the
resources of the traditio-historical criticism of the gospels and
the historical investigation of the relevant Palestinian milieu.
We propose also to use as catalyst a phenomenological method of
organising the *data* (cf. the principle of 'eidetic vision'), so as

to produce a meaningful framework within which to view the
significance of Jesus. In relation to such a framework, the
criterion of dissimilarity might at last become fully operational
for individual *logia* and *pericopae*.

A few examples must suffice.

We can plot the *religious movements* with which our sources
are concerned. Apart from Jesus' own movement, the most
significant – amid the growing sectarianism of first century
Judaism – was that of John the Baptist. We can examine the
characteristics of such movements and their hinterland. To do so,
we may have to de-theologize our evidence, if the movement has
subsequently become the object of Christian theological
interpretation, as John did. We can examine the relationship
between movements (e.g., those of John and Jesus). Even the
Christian theologizing (i.e., what the Christians made of John)
is a religious phenomenon and can be charted.

We can plot the *religious roles* involved – with the focus
upon Jesus himself. Remembering that the wholly unique would be
wholly incomprehensible, we ask what role or roles the first
century Palestinian observer could properly have attributed to
Jesus. The most obvious candidate is the prophetic role. The
propriety of this attribution can be defended not only directly
from our sources (to which the criterion of unintentional reference,
among others, may also be usefully applied) but also on a formal
analysis of some of Jesus' utterances. It is to be noted that
the question here is not whether our sources regard 'prophet' as
an adequate description of Jesus (for in this respect they may
well reflect Christian interpretation), nor whether Jesus himself
regarded the attribution as appropriate (for that we shall never
know with certainty). What is much more to the point is the
structure of prophetic mission, including Jesus' 'Amen' to God's
approach, the sense of being commissioned by God, of being
entrusted with the divine message, and the urgency to deliver it.
Also relevant are prophetic actions, and the total involvement of
the prophet in his mission. Above all, his mission and message are
eschatological: their central point of reference is that which is
complete, *teleios*. In the light of this analysis of the prophetic
role, the whole gospel tradition about Jesus must be re-examined.
But other possible roles have also to be investigated. Was he a
charismatic? Does he relate to a Galilean charismatic movement?
There is a hint of this (no more) in the gospels, and some external
evidence of charismatics in Galilee – all of which has been ably

exploited by G. Vermes /25/. While the whole matter is worthy of
careful investigation, we might briefly comment here that this
appears to be at most a subsidiary motif in Jesus' ministry and
one which can be subsumed under the prophetic. Again, did Jesus
fulfil the role of a rabbi? Not that there is any suggestion that
he was a trained rabbi in the sense that Saul of Tarsus was; but
what were the rabbinic standards in the Galilean synagogues, to
which Jesus seems at one point in his life to have had free access
as teacher and expositor? Was he recognised for a time locally as
a rabbi because of a certain interpretative flair, the flashing
insight of prophetic involvement? At any rate, it is possible to
relate a remarkable proportion of Jesus' exegesis and paraenesis,
including some of the parables, to just such a *Sitz im Leben*. All
of this raises another issue of importance: what was Jesus' relation
to tradition, especially scriptural tradition? What kind of
hermeneutic did he employ? If, as we are told, it was not 'as
the scribes', then of what kind was it? How do we map this
exousia, by which he was distinguished?

We can plot Jesus' *use of major religious symbols*. In a
Palestinian milieu, no religious figure could avoid encountering
them. In Judaism, they may be taken to include Law, Temple, King
and Land (whatever else). Jesus' attitude might be expected to
exhibit a certain polarity in relation to them, in the sense that
he scrutinised them radically in the context of the *eschaton*, that
which is complete, and consequently affirmed their deepest purpose
or function while attacking all temporizing accommodations of
them. Thus, in relation to the first of these, Jesus' attitude is:
God's Law (Torah) is perfect (complete), hence one is not to
detract from it by circumventing its deepest purpose and intent
but to respond to it as a child of God. God's Temple is a house
of prayer for all the nations; it is not to be made a robbers'
den. As a child of the Father, one observes its true function in
his service. God is King of Israel. The basic concept of Israel
is that of a theonomy, and consequently the *eschaton* is also
theonomous. Jesus therefore rejects the basis of the claim of
the rulers of this world if they do not submit to God as King
(although as a temporal subject one still has to reckon with
Caesar). On the other hand, the mission of the eschatological
prophet is to give expression to this theonomy in the midst of a
world which does not recognise God's kingship: to express completion
in the midst of the yet incomplete, and thus bring it near to
others and make it possible for them, here and now, to engage
with it (enter into it). The total transformation, however, is
yet to come: those who 'enter in' are taught to pray, 'Thy Kingdom

come ...'. What of the Land, defiled as it was by the oppressor?
Jesus certainly came to terms with the question of how one should
react to the occupying power - he was not a mere dreamer,
possessed of transcendental irresponsibility. But he does not
appear simply to have endorsed the Zealot goal of a land cleansed
of the oppressor, still less the Zealot methods of achieving it /26/
His vision or goal was the Land reformed as part of a total cosmic
transformation, so that it is the meek who inherit the earth.

        Even if we confine ourselves to a consideration of the above
symbols, Jesus' radicalism triggers off such explosive potential
that there was hardly an element in the establishment to which he
did not pose a threat. Here was no crazy charismatic. Here was
one who relentlessly exposed the pretences of men, who stripped
them of their defences and saw into their innermost being. As
secular totalitarian states today cannot abide the critical
individualism of the intelligentsia or *literati,* so the religio-
political totalitarianism of Judaea could not indefinitely
withstand the prophetic radicalism of Jesus. His involvement in
religio-political issues was so complete that, when the Jewish
authorities were finally persuaded to move against him and haul
him before their hastily summoned kangaroo court, they could
'throw the book' at him and make the most unlikely charges stick -
at least as far as a none too scrupulous Roman governor was
concerned.

        As an extension of the above, we can plot in particular
Jesus' use of symbols for God. One of them - King - we have
already discussed. Closely associated with it is the symbol of
Judge. Jesus makes use of the prophetic forms of judgement,
usually governed by the condition of repentance. One of the most
important symbols is Father, *Abba.* A crucial text here is the
'Q' saying (Matt. 11:25ff.) which, however, it is necessary to
de-christologize, for as it stands in the tradition it can hardly
be other than a Christian version. Perhaps our phenomenological
method enables us to apply the criterion of differentiation in a
new way, so that we can focus on the Father-son or child
relationship as a basic symbol of Jesus' discourse. All who
respond to God - all who say 'Amen' to his approach - enter into
this relationship as his sons or children and say 'Our Father ...'.
Again, God alone is *agathos* and *teleios,* calling men to
corresponding goals and aiding them in their quest. It is also
possible to explore the negative correlatives of such symbols:
Satan, Beelzebub, Mammon ...

Finally, we can survey the *faith dimension* which our
material presupposes. From Jesus' use of religious symbols one
can deduce something of the faith by which he lived. Even more
accessible, perhaps, is the disciples' faith, which (stumbling
as it was) is to be found in their response to Jesus throughout
his ministry - a response which discerned in his life, work and,
eventually, in his death, something of the numinous and the
theonomous. In essential continuity with this response is the
resurrection faith, the mainspring of which might well be charted
in terms of a prophetic-like perception of the crucified Christ
as the Son who has learned obedience through his suffering and,
now *teleios* in every sense, is the source of eternal salvation
to all who obey him (to follow out the Hebrews model in this
instance: cf. Heb. 5:8f.). Here is the Christ of faith who
underlies all Christian *kerygmata*.

Our final comment is therefore appropriately given to the
'Jesus of history'- 'Christ of faith' problem. As each evangelist
makes clear in his own way, it is essential to hold the two
together. Mark's way is particularly relevant. For him, the
life and death of Jesus - everything prior to his exaltation -
form 'the beginning of the gospel' (along with God's saving work
in Israel, and the ministry of John the Baptist). Thus,
theologically speaking, God's saving work is accomplished in
history. The correlative is that Jesus' life, ministry and death
are part and parcel of this worldly historicity. As such, they
are open - completely open - to historical research. What then
of the problem that has troubled generations of biblical critics?
Is the believer totally at the mercy of the historical critic?
I think not. We must distinguish two kinds of procedures. The
decision the believer makes when he freely confesses Jesus Christ
as Lord is, in fact, complex in nature. An important strand within
it, so to speak, is the judgement that Jesus was a real historical
figure who lived a particular kind of life and died a particular
kind of death in Palestine about two thousand years ago. Thus,
an integral part of the faith system of the modern Christian is
the affirmation of the essential historicity of the gospels'
witness to Jesus - an affirmation which includes Kähler's
'irresistible impression of the completest reality' as well as
Macquarrie's 'minimal core of factuality' /27/. Paul wrote that
if Christ is not raised, then Christian faith is in vain (cf. 1
Cor.15:14). It could equally be said that if Jesus did not live -
and live a Christ-like life at that - then Christian faith is in
vain. Other possibilities would remain - some kind of Christian
ideology, perhaps, or a gnostic version of Christianity; but not

the Christian faith that 'the Word became flesh and dwelt among
us ...' (John 1:14). That certainty comes through Christian
proclamation and hermeneutics - 'rightly dividing the word of
truth' (2 Tim. 2:15). The secure Christian, accepting that we
know what matters about Jesus, can suspend judgement on innumerable
historical problems (e.g., was Jesus born in Bethlehem or
Nazareth? Was he actually tempted forty days in the wilderness?
Did he perform all the miracles with which he is credited? Was
the last supper a Passover meal or some other kind? Is the story
of the empty tomb historical or legendary?). The Christian's
faith - to speak generally - is not dependent upon a 'successful'
resolution of such problems, but upon responding to the figure who
addresses him through the gospels. The other side of the coin,
however, is that Jesus as a historical figure is properly the
object of historical investigation. No inhibition can be placed
on such historiography (provided that proper historical method,
which takes account of the nature of the sources, is always followed). While to some Christians such technical research is of
little relevance, to others it may have more than parenthetical -
though perhaps not critical - significance. They may recognise that
an element of risk necessarily attaches to a historical faith, just
as an element of relativity necessarily attaches to historical
judgements. Perhaps the model we are looking for is that of a
dialogue between historiography and faith-hermeneutics, in which
each performs its appointed task in its proper context and thus
obviates the confusion which arises when one seeks to dominate or
despise the other. However this may be, New Testament scholarship
cannot escape the problem of the historical Jesus simply by
shouting *'kerygma'*. If Christ did not live, he did not rise to
glory! The quest of the historical Jesus is an inescapable part
of the responsibility of the New Testament scholar. It is high
time that it was resumed wholeheartedly.

NOTES

/1/   The works cited here simply exemplify the diversity of the
'quest'. They are: D.F. Strauss, *The Life of Jesus Critically
Examined*, Eng. tr. (1846, 1892) London, 1973; G. Bornkamm, *Jesus
of Nazareth*, Eng. tr., London, 1960; A. Schweitzer, *The Quest of
the Historical Jesus*, Eng. tr. London, 1910, 2nd ed., 1922; E.
Schweizer, *Jesus*, Eng. tr., London, 1971; E. Stauffer, *Jesus and
His Story*, Eng. tr., London, 1960; G. Vermes, *Jesus the Jew*, London,
1973.

/2/   Cf. the essay 'Autographical Reflections' in S.M. Ogden (ed.), *Existence and Faith*, London, 1961, pp. 283-8.

/3/   *Jesus and the Word*, Eng. tr., New York 1934, London 1958.

/4/   *Der sogenannte historische Jesus und der geschichtlich, biblische Christus*, Leipzig, 1892 (new ed., München, 1956); Eng. tr., *The so-called Historical Jesus and the historic Biblical Christ*, Philadelphia, 1964.

/5/   *The Four Gospels*, London, 1924; (5th imp.) 1936.

/6/   Cf. *Das Messiasgeheimnis in der Evangelien*, Göttingen, 1901; *The Messianic Secret*, Eng. tr., London, 1971.

/7/   *Parables of the Kingdom*, London, 1935 (3rd ed. 1936), p. 50.

/8/   *The Mission and Achievement of Jesus*, London, 1954, p. 48.

/9/   *Jesus and his Coming*, London, 1957, p. 81.

/10/   Op. cit.

/11/   Cf. G. Lundström, *The Kingdom of God in the Teaching of Jesus*, Eng. tr., Edinburgh & London, 1963, p. 76.

/12/   G. Lundström, op. cit., p. 154.

/13/   For Dodd's Platonism, cf. R.H. Fuller, op. cit., p. 33; M. Burrows, "Thy Kingdom Come", J.B.L. 74, 1955, pp. 1-8; E. Jüngel, *Paulus und Jesus*, Tübingen, 1962, pp. 107-120.

/14/   "Das Problem des historischen Jesus", Z.T.K. 51, 1954, pp. 125-53; Eng. tr., "The Problem of the Historical Jesus", *Essays on New Testament Themes*, London, 1964, pp. 15-47 (from which the following quotations are taken).

/15/   Op. cit., p. 34.

/16/   Op. cit., p. 45.

/17/   Op. cit., p. 46.

/18/   *Rediscovering the Teaching of Jesus*, London, 1967, pp. 39-45.

/19/   *Traditio-Historical Criticism of the Gospels*, London, 1972, p. 47.

/20/   "If Bultmann's intellectual ancestor was Soren Kierkegaard, Pannenberg's was Hegel": H. Zahrnt, *The Question of God*, Eng. tr., London, 1969, p. 285.

/21/   Esp. H. Riesenfeld and B. Gerhardsson. For criticism of underlying assumption, cf. W.D. Davies, *The Setting of the Sermon on the Mount*, Cambridge, 1964, pp. 464-80; A.J.B. Higgins, *The Tradition about Jesus*, Edinburgh, 1969, pp. 7-14.

/22/   *Jesus and Christian Origins*, New York, 1964, p. 75.

/23/   *Epoché* means "holding back" - i.e., suspending or bracketing our own value judgements in order to understand and treat with integrity the positions which others hold and which may be foreign to us. *Einfühlung* is broadly "empathy" and involves an imaginative effort to "get inside" another world-view. *Eidetic vision* (cf. Gk. εἶδος , form, shape) denotes the attempt to see a given phenomenon as a whole, to detect the coherence of the parts in the totality, or (as some would put it) to grasp the essentials

or essence of a situation. The phenomenological method goes
back to E. Husserl. Modern exponents of it include G. van der
Leeuw (cf. his *Religion in Essence and Manifestation,* London,
1948), M. Eliade (cf. *Patterns in Comparative Religion,* London,
1958), and W.B. Kristensen (cf. *The Meaning of Religion:
Lectures in the Phenomenology of Religion.* The Hague, 1960).
For a brief introduction to the phenomenological method, cf.
E.J. Sharpe's discussion of modern approaches to the study of
religion in the Open University course book *Seekers and Scholars,*
1977, Unit 2, Part II, esp. pp. 78-82.
/24/   Cf. O. Piper's review of Bornkamm's *Jesus of Nazareth:*
"A Unitary God with Jesus as His First Theologian", *Interpretation*
XV, 1961, pp. 473ff.
/25/   Op. cit., pp. 58-82.
/26/   Cf. S.G.F. Brandon, *The Fall of Jerusalem and the Christian
Church,* London, 1951; *Jesus and the Zealots,* Manchester, 1967;
The Trial of Jesus of Nazareth, London, 1968.
/27/   J. Macquarrie, *The Scope of Demythologizing,* London, 1960,
p. 97.

Mark 9:33-50. Catechetics in Mark's Gospel

James I.H. McDonald,
23 Ravelston House Road,
EDINBURGH, EH4 3LP.

As a glance at the commentaries will show, it is widely
accepted that Mark 9:33-50, the most obscure part of Mark
(according to J. Weiss), includes material 'compiled under a
catechetical impulse' /1/. The criteria that prompt this
conclusion are, in the main, purely formal: for example,
recurring catchwords like 'in (my) name', 'cause to stumble',
'little', 'it is good for...', 'fire' and 'salt', which combine
to produce an impression of artificiality when viewed in terms
of narrative quality, but are congruent with the mnemonic and
didactic devices of the catechists. The unity that comprehends
this remarkable diversity is illustrated by the linkage between
the disciples' contentiousness at the beginning (9:33f.) and the
final exhortation to 'be at peace with one another' (9:50).
But, even in those who put forward this catechetical hypothesis
with some confidence, there is to be detected more than a hint
of exegetical hesitancy or uncertainty; and it is rarely the
case that such a hypothesis, advanced on formal grounds, is
tested against material criteria. In this brief paper, an
attempt is made to do precisely that. Let us assume for the
moment that both Mark and his source were concerned to use this
material primarily for the *catechesis* of the church. Their
intention (or Mark's intention, at least) was to press home the
notion of placing aside worldly goals and taking up one's cross
as a disciple of Christ (cf. 8:34ff.). Can such a hypothesis
be sustained throughout the passage? Does it illumine its
admitted obscurity? And does the experience we gain by testing
this hypothesis lead us to understand more clearly the
possibilities and limitations of the methods of form and
redaction criticism?

In the first group of verses (9:33-37), we are concerned
with the *leading dominical symbol* of the catechism. It is
fourfold: (i) Jesus questions the disciples: "What were you
arguing about on the way?" (v.33f.); (ii) 'the first shall be
last of all and servant of all' (v.35); here, the abrupt manner

in which this saying is introduced probably indicates a separate
source /2/; (iii) the *paidon* symbol (v.36); whatever the earlier
history of this material, here it marks 'a new stage, possibly
a new beginning', as V. Taylor observes, following Holtzmann
and Schmidt /3/; (iv) the third saying - 'whoever receives one
of such *paidia* in my name receives me, and whoever receives me,
receives... him who sent me' (v.37) - is unexpected in this
context, and exegetes have questioned whether it truly belongs
here. Would not 10:15 (receiving the kingdom as a child) be
more appropriate to the narrative, as C.H. Turner argued /4/?
We must stress again that the pre-history of this tradition is
not our primary concern here, although it is both complex and
fascinating. What we note is the remarkable synthesis which the
catechist has effected. He has brought together four disparate
traditions to form his basic dominical symbol. In this way, the
question Jesus puts to his disciples is effectively addressed
to the church - tacitly rebuking its false values, its power
structures ('it shall not be so among you') and all that the
late Ian Henderson called 'ecclesiastical thuggery'. Jesus
then firmly sets before the church the transvaluation of all
worldly values, so that the first becomes last and service
(*diakonia*) becomes preeminent. The *paidon* symbol is brought in
to exemplify this revolution. Finally, the church learns to
show acceptance to 'such children' (children generally?
children of widows? or the weak and dependent?) and to understand
Christ's identification with them. Indeed, the church will
receive Christ - nay, God - into its very being as it receives
them (9:37).

Here one pauses only to underline that, while exegesis is
strained to breaking-point when it attempts to treat 9:33-37 as
straightforward narrative, a thoroughgoing catechetical
hypothesis not only highlights the synthetic unity of these
verses but also releases their dynamic and challenge. And we
seem to be learning quite a lot about the operation of form and
redaction criticism in an ecclesiastical *Sitz im Leben*.

The next unit (9:38f.) represents the first practical
outworking of this dominical teaching. It is concerned with
ecumenical relations! A tradition about John in the form of
an apophthegm or pronouncement story is the vehicle used to
raise the question of the independent operator, the born
separatist, the determined free-churchman, who does not hesitate
to claim to work in Jesus' name though he rejects formal
apostolic authority (9:38). Needless to say, apostolic
authority is all set to prohibit him! One thinks at once of

Paul's contention with the apostles of Jerusalem, although there
is no suggestion here that his case is directly in view. The
dominical word prohibits the prohibitors and is in line with the
strain of ecclesiastical openness that recurs in the gospels.
'Other sheep I have, who are not of this fold...' The
additional saying of 9:40 - 'For he who is not against us is
with us' - is a gnomic utterance which the catechist no doubt
felt was as appropriate as it was memorable /5/. A further
saying (9:41) underlines how dependent the Christian missionary
is on the sympathiser who is prepared to perform the simplest
of acts to help him on his way. Truly the blessing of God
rests on all who show such goodwill, however obscure they are
/6/.

    In 9:42, the catechist takes up a series of solemn warnings
about courses of conduct which, if left unchecked and
uncorrected, would destroy the nature of the church as Christ's
people and totally neutralise its mission. The first concerns
offences against 'one of these little ones who believe...'.
The dominical symbol about the acceptance of *paidia* is relevant
here /7/ but the catechist's (and Mark's) concern in this
context is not so much for children as such as for those well
disposed to Christ and his followers who nevertheless need
support, guidance and encouragement in the faith, like the new
member wrenched from his pagan background or perhaps even the
rival exorcist who is cited here as a weaker brother to whom
one should show goodwill. The values of the church are
expressed in *its nurture, its care of the weak and dependent* -
those who need to be fed with milk, since they are not yet able
for a heavier diet (cf. Heb. 5:12). They have priority in the
church's *diakonia,* in accordance once again with the leading
symbol. If instead of nurture the church gives offence (causes
to stumble), then the judgment of God is pronounced in vivid
metaphor against whoever is responsible - a form carried over
from prophecy to *catechesis.*

    A noticeable feature of this passage is the alternation of
the singular and the plural. As we have already noted, reference
is made at the beginning and the end to the community of
disciples or believers. Singular references, when introduced,
are indefinite or general: for example 'if anyone (τις) wishes
to be first...' (v.35), or 'whosoever..." (ὃς ἂν) in vv.37,41,
42. Clearly such references are intended primarily to guide
individuals within the community, and as such they have a
natural place in church catechetics. The same is true of vv.
43-48, in which the second personal singular pronoun is used

consistently. Therefore, after the stern warning in v.42, the
catechist applies traditional sayings of Jesus (concerned with
removing obstacles to "entering into life" or "entering the
kingdom of God") to *the question of the discipline* - indeed,
the *self-discipline* - required of the individual member of the
community who would be a disciple of Christ /9/. To respond to
the major symbol set before the church at the beginning of the
passage, the individual, like the disciples, must be prepared
to sacrifice unproductive or counter-productive areas of his
life.

Thus, throughout the passage, the catechist is concerned
both with the believing community as such and with the
responsibility of the individual member to it. Can it be that,
even when the instruction is formally couched in the singular,
the reference is also corporate? For example, might not vv.43-
48 evoke the familiar figure of the church as body and suggest
that amputation of limbs is sometimes necessary for the well-
being of the whole organism? In that case, the reference might
be to the necessary but distasteful process of *purging the roll*.
The major difficulty in this view arises from the use of the
second person singular. In the case of the 'body' metaphor,
the plural is strictly required: ὑμεῖς δέ ἐστε σῶμα Χριστοῦ
(1 Cor. 12:27), even if the individual is a limb or member. No
one, however, is suggesting that the σε or σου of 9:43ff. refers
grammatically to the church; that is clearly impossible. On
the other hand, one must make allowance for the fact that, if
we are dealing here with church catechetics, then what we have
is in telescoped and minimal form. While the *Stichwörter*
survive the redaction, the exegesis which the catechist himself
supplies (so important in a teaching situation) has been lost.
It is therefore by no means impossible that the catechist
applied these *logia* not only to the self-discipline of the
individual but to ecclesiastical discipline (cf. 1 Cor. 5:5,13).
In terms of early Christian exegesis, that would be an easy
step for him to effect!

Whether this suggestion is valid or not, the catechist is
alarmed at the possibility of the total corruption of the
members and thus of the community; for wholly corrupted members
are fit for nothing but to be thrown out and consumed like so
much offal in the valley of Gehenna. Such a dreadful fate,
however, does not apply to the faithful church, as the catechist
now mames clear, even if he requires an extraordinarily mixed
metaphor in order to do so! Instead of being ravaged with
unquenchable fire, every member will be 'salted with fire'

(v.49): a phrase which has given the textual scholars and the commentators acute difficulty. Once more, the thoroughgoing catechetical hypothesis makes more sense than most. The catechist, having the church in mind throughout, recoils from the horrific prospect of judgment falling upon a wholly corrupted church and underlines the fact that his concern - and that of Christ - is for a purified, mature church, a well-seasoned community ('have salt in yourselves', v.50). The fire which affects every member of such a community is not that of judgment but that which tests his mettle, which purifies him of imperfections and which makes his spirit stronger, more mature - like the fire of persecution, or personal trial, or suffering. But the standard figure which expresses this concept in the tradition is that of salt; hence the mixed metaphor and the extolling of salt in v.50. At this point, however, the catechist's mind has moved one further stage, to pick up yet another originally independent saying brought into the catechism by word association /10/. Salt stands for a quality of the true church. The seasoned church is a fine thing; a church that has lost its seasoning is useless. Incidentally, this concept explains the curious language of 'salt that has lost its seasoning'. As V. Taylor observes, salt cannot really become saltless (ἄναλος) /11/. Apply the church metaphor and the difficulty is resolved: if the church has lost its seasoning, with what will it season the world? Have such seasoning in yourselves, the catechist urges. The next imperative, which refers back to the original dominical symbol, probably stands in conditional parataxis to the first: 'then you will be at peace among yourselves'.

The catechetical hypothesis stands up well to the test of consistency and to the criterion of dissimilarity which we have tacitly applied throughout. It also makes better sense of this passage than the more common historicising efforts. Two observations may be made briefly in conclusion.

(i) Our study suggests that one model of Christian catechetics found its centre in a major dominical symbol or symbols. It may be useful to contrast this with another catechetical model, in which the focal point of reference came from scripture, a Christian hermeneutic being applied to it. For example, in 1 Cor. 9:3-12, the focus is put upon the citation of the Law of Moses: 'You shall not muzzle the ox that treadeth out the grain'. Is this really about oxen? asks Paul - and, following a not unusual exegetical procedure, he relates the text to the maintenance of the ministry! In Mark 9:33-50,

the scriptural focus is replaced, as we have seen, by a
suggestive grouping of traditions relating to Jesus - traditions
which tend to have a more direct meaning than the scriptural
allusiveness of 1 Cor. 9:3-12 but which also give a lead to the
interpretation of no less allusive sayings which the catechist
attaches to them. By opening up the latent meaning of such
symbols for the catechumen in the church, the catechist is
instrumental in effecting a disclosure situation in which the
pupils do not simply learn doctrine but are placed under the
judgment of the word of Christ. Here indeed is 'the nurture
and admonition of the Lord'. The whole church - not merely the
catechumen - is simultaneously placed in the same position; and
the instruction is geared not only to spiritual enlightenment
but to mission.

    (ii) Our study indicates that form criticism, working as
it tends to do with an ecclesiastical *Sitz im Leben*, illumines
the tradition at a comparatively late stage in its development.
It is not a difficult matter to deduce earlier applications of
some of the material - like the 'salt' symbol, for instance.
Perhaps the time has come to make a new effort to trace the
history of the gospel tradition, in which the main concern is
not simply to classify or categorise its forms but to elucidate
the fluidity of living traditions, to show the focal points
round which they tend to cluster and to indicate the
transformations that occur in an expository and didactic
tradition in which the processes of transmission and exegesis
are closely linked.

NOTES

/1/   V. Taylor, *The Gospel According to St. Mark*, London, 1952,
p.408. For an outline of the features of early Christian
catechesis, cf. J.I.H. McDonald, *Kerygma and Didache*, Cambridge,
1979, chapter 3.
/2/   'Abrupt', because Jesus is already talking with the
disciples; a new source has therefore been suspected: cf. K.L.
Schmidt, *Der Rahmen der Geschichte Jesu*, Berlin, 1919, p.230;
H. Anderson, *The Gospel of Mark*, London, 1976, pp.233f.
/3/   Op. cit., p.405. Cf. T.F. Glasson, *Expository Times* 59,
1947-48, p.166. The comments on the passage by C.G. Montefiore,
The Synoptic Gospels I, London, 1909, are still worth reading.
/4/   C.H. Turner, *The Gospel according to St. Mark*, London,
1928, p.48.
/5/   '...he doesn't belong to our group' - probably he was a

charismatic: cf. E. Schweizer, *The Good News According to Mark*,
Eng. tr., London, 1971, pp.194f.
/6/   Cf. R. Bultmann, *History of the Synoptic Tradition*, Eng.
tr., London, 1968, pp.24f.
/7/   Mark's propensity for adding verses (no doubt reflecting
a general tendency in the tradition to acquire appendages) is
admitted even by cautious scholars like V. Taylor (op. cit.,
p.408); other examples cited include 2:21f., 27f., 3:27ff.;
4:21-5; 7:14-23; 10:10ff.
/8/   In fact, Matthew 18:5f. combines Mark 9:37a with 9:42.
/9/   Cf. S.E. Johnson, *A Commentary on the Gospel According to
St Mark*, London, 1960, p.166; E. Schweizer, op. cit., pp.198f.
/10/   Cf. H. Anderson, op. cit., p.239; E. Schweizer, op. cit.,
pp.199f.
/11/   Cf. V. Taylor, op. cit.; p.414.

'Paradisial' Elements in the Teaching of Jesus

David L. Mealand,
Department of New Testament,
University of Edinburgh.

In this paper I wish to consider some possible Paradisial motifs in the Gospels, especially in the poetic denunciation of cares in Luke 12:22-32 par.

In Isa. 11:6-9 we find a vision of the future in which the lion is to become vegetarian and eat straw like an ox, and in which hurting and destroying is to cease in all God's holy mountain. The author expects the future to mirror the tranquillity of Eden, and believes that the harmony of Paradise will be regained. Even when stripped of pseudo-historicity, the myth of a lost era of innocence and bliss continues to haunt the imagination. It serves as a foil to the present era of mortality and guilt. The expectation of a future return to the conditions of Paradise has been the stock in trade of Utopian movements down the ages, and of 'Millenarian' movements across the globe /1/. It plays on a basic human dissatisfaction with the present and a desire for something closer to the dream of perfection. It is perhaps no accident that Isa: 51.3 and Ezek. 36:35 speak of Zion's post-exilic wilderness becoming like the garden of Eden.

In the New Testament the term Paradise is used to refer to a region of the celestial geography to which the repentant thief is to depart (Luke 23:43) /2/ or to which an ecstatic might be snatched up /3/. But we also find the motif of a future return to Paradisial conditions in Jewish and Christian texts /4/. The Qumran sectarians spoke of a return to the glory of Adam /5/, and Jeremias detects Paradisialism in several passages in the Gospels. These include Mark 10:2-12, which I grant, and Mark 1:13; 7:37, and Matt. 11:5 par., in all of which the connection is less obvious /6/. It is, however, not unreasonable to see a connection between the expectation of the Reign of God and that of a return to the conditions of Paradise. It is with this in mind that I wish to look briefly at the Mission Charge, and in more detail at the

Denunciation of Cares.

It is widely though not universally agreed that the Mission
Charge appeared both in Mark 6 and also in Q (cf. Luke 10:1-16
par.). Common elements include the rule that disciples are to
travel without money and without a bag or wallet (which would be
used for carrying food, or as a begging bag). Q probably forbade
staff and sandals. Mark prohibited taking of food or additional
clothing. Luke 10:4 forbids greetings on the journey. Is it
possible to find a consistent rationale for these injunctions?
Many of the forbidden items were standard equipment for travellers
in the period in question /7/. Their omission would have seemed
very striking to the people of the time. Presumably the absence
of a staff indicated defencelessness and peacefulness of purpose
/8/. The absence of a bag and of money marked out the envoy as in
a state of helpless dependence even for his next meal. Taking no
food and no additional clothing would also have signalled
dependence on the customary hospitality of the ancient Near East.
Walking barefoot might indicate either fasting or poverty /9/.
Though the early Christians did suffer poverty there are
difficulties about both of these explanations. Commentators have
often noted a further factor which may be important. This is that
Rabbinic rules about the Temple Mount forbade the wearing of
sandals, the carrying of a staff, and the carrying of money in
cloth or bag or moneybelt /10/. All of these things were
inappropriate on the holy mountain. Perhaps the similarity of
these rules to those of the Mission Charge is no accident, and may
offer a further clue to their significance.

The prohibition of greetings on journeys is also striking.
It might simply signify haste (as in 2 Kings 4:29), or else that
the peace-greeting had special significance (Luke 10:5-6) and was
not to be uttered idly to all who passed by on the road. But
Rabbinic rules may again provide a clue. These debate the
circumstances in which one might interrupt prayer in order to
greet someone passing by /11/. If the Christian mission was seen
as a holy task of considerable urgency, then one can understand
that idle interruption should be discouraged.

In their present form these rules reflect the practice of
early Christian mission, but behind that we might be able to
detect an earlier concern with the proclamation of the Reign of
God during the ministry of Jesus. Hahn judiciously noted that the
insistence on the absence of equipment is in tune with the
attitude of Jesus /12/. Taken together the injunctions
distinguish the envoys from ordinary travellers and from beggars.

The disciples were sent out to announce the Kingdom, and their
very appearance was a prophetic parable. They travelled in haste
and without resources. They had to display trust and to be
dependent on the hospitality of others for their needs. The
similarity between these wandering messengers and Temple pilgrims
would suggest that the approach of the Kingdom made the time a
holy season, and the whole land a holy place. Such a time would
be a time for total trust and total dependence on God /13/.

So far anything approaching a Paradisial feature has only
emerged rather tentatively. That element emerges more strongly
when we consider the denunciation of cares (Luke 12:22-32 par.)
which is, in fact, often associated with the Mission Charge by
commentators. There are variant versions in Thomas (log. 36) and
in Pap. Oxy. 4.655, but these add little. It is probably Luke
rather than Matthew who retains the position of the passage in Q,
but both canonical versions need to be studies in order to
reconstruct the basic unit. In fact scholars as different as
T.W. Manson and E. Fuchs reach surprisingly similar conclusions
in identifying the core of the passage as the following:

I   Consider the ravens,
        That they neither sow nor reap,
        They have no barn or storehouse;
        And God feeds them;
        How much better are you than the birds!

II   Consider the lilies,
        How they neither toil nor spin,
        Yet I tell you that Solomon in all his glory was not
            arrayed like one of these.
        But if God so clothe the grass
        Which today is in the field
        And tomorrow is cast into the oven;
        How much more you, O ye of little faith?   /14/

Some think that the passage reflects the hardships of early
Christians facing either persecution or the general difficulties of
the early years of the Church. But others, probably correctly,
see a more specific reference to the insecurity of Apostles and
wandering prophets. These had to abandon ordinary means of
support, and depend on converts or on well-wishers for food and
other necessities /15/. The original poem might be thought to
envisage a more radical dependence on nature, but it is probably
correct to see a connection with the life-style of wandering
charismatics. It is less likely to be a homily telling Galilean
farmers not to worry so much about their crops. Nor is it simply

a piece of popular piety inculcating trust in providence /16/.
Käsemann comments that 'the Jewish belief in Providence is
modified in a very odd fashion' /17/. Indeed it is.

Miraculous feeding by God appears in the story of Elijah and
the ravens in 1 Kings 17, and in the Manna tradition of Exodus 16.
But in Jewish tradition the latter was also linked with the
abundant provision of food for Adam in the garden of Eden.
According to the myth in Genesis the need to worry about clothing,
and the need to work for food came after the Fall. This point is
put vigorously in a Rabbinic debate in the Mishnah where R. Simeon
b. Eleazar is reported as saying:

> 'Hast thou ever seen a wild animal or a bird practising a
> craft? - yet they have their sustenance without care and
> were they not created for naught else but to serve me? But
> I was created to serve my Maker. How much more then ought
> not I to have my sustenance without care? But I have wrought
> evil, and forfeited my sustenance' (i.e. forfeited my right
> to sustenance without care) (Kid. 4.14, tr. Danby).

This Rabbinic passage reaches the opposite conclusion from the
saying of Jesus. The Mishnah follows Gen, 3:17-19 and argues that
because humanity has sinned it has been condemned to earn bread
with toil and sweat. The saying of Jesus seems to disregard the
emphasis on the fall. Jesus calls for faith (Luke 12:28 par.)
/18/ and urges a simple dependence on God characteristic of
Paradisial conditions. But how is this radical demand for trust
and freedom from care to be construed?

In early Christian teaching cares are spoken of as care for
things of the world, or as cares of this aeon (1 Cor. 7:32-3; Mark
4:19). This suggests that to live without such cares is to live
in the new age. The Reign of God was seen as a time for total
trust and total dependence on God. It is not surprising that such
thoughts provoked disorders, and the Epistles to the Thessalonians
may well reflect the havoc which such apocalyptic enthusiasm
aroused (cf. 1 Thess. 4:11; 2 Thess. 3:10-12) /19/.

In the saying about the ravens and the lilies we find an
appeal to nature. But that appeal conflicts with the conventional
wisdom of a text like Prov. 6:6 with its hard-headed observations
about the diligence of the ant. The gospel passage declares that
anxious striving for food and clothing is no longer appropriate.
We cannot, of course, be sure that such an atttitude must be
attributed to Jesus rather than to early Christian enthusiasm.
But we can compare it with the boldness of the act of plucking ears

of corn on the sabbath (Mark 2:23-28) and the appeal behind Moses
to 'the beginning' in the saying about marriage in Mark 10:5-9.

The Reign of God was seen as bringing healing and
forgiveness, and an end to Satan's rule. It is described as a
feast, and compared to priceless treasure. It is a time for
simple trust, defencelessness and dependence; a time which
recaptures the fabled bliss of the beginning of things. Though
the Reign of God is not simply seen as a return to the beginning,
it may well be that there are Paradisial elements in the teaching
about the Reign of God. We might go on from this tentative
conclusion to argue that these elements invite comparison with
other Utopian and apocalyptic movements /20/, but that is another
story.

NOTES

/1/ The term 'Millenarian' is here used not in the strict sense
familiar to theologians, but in the wider sense employed by
sociologists and Mediaeval historians; hence the inverted commas.
/2/   Cf. Jub. 4.23; T.Abr.20; Aboth 5.20.
/3/   2 Cor. 12:2-4; cf. Hag. 14b-15b.
/4/   1 Enoch 24.4-25.7; Apoc. Mos. 13.4; T.L. 18.10-11; T.D. 5.12;
4 Ezra 8.52; Rev. 2.7; Papias acc. Irenaeus *Haer*. 5.33. 3-4; cf.
J. Jeremias in *T.D.N.T.* 5.765-773.
/5/   1QS 4.23; Z.D. 3.20; 1 QHod. 17.15; cf. 2 Bar. 73.6-7.
/6/   Jeremias, *T.D.N.T.*, 5.772.
/7/   Jeb. 16.7; B.B. 133b; cf. Epictetus 3.22.10.
/8/   R. Pesch, *Das Markusevangelium* I (Freiburg: Herder, 1976)
328.
/9/   Cf. Ta⁀an 13a; Sabb. 152a.
/10/ Ber.9.5; b Ber. 62b; T.Ber. 7.19 (17); j Ber. 9.8; cf.
P. Hoffmann, *Studien zur Theologie der Logienquelle* (N.T.Abh. 8)
(Münster: Aschendorff, ²1972) 322-3.
/11/ Ber. 5.1; also j Ber. 5.9a.24; Ber. 14a, 32b; cf. Ber. 2.1.
/12/ F. Hahn, *Mission in the New Testament* (London: S.C.M., 1965)
46.
/13/ Pesch, *Markus*, 328; Hoffman, *Logienquelle*, 327.
/14/ T.W. Manson, *The Sayings of Jesus* (London: S.C.M., 1950)
112; cf. E. Fuchs, *Studies of the Historical Jesus* (London: S.C.M.,
1964) 106.
/15/ H.J. Degenhardt, *Lukas Evangelist der Armen* (Stuttgart: Kath.
Bibelwerk, 1965) 81-85; G. Theissen, *Soziologie der Jesusbewegung*
(Munich: Kaiser, 1977) 19.
/16/ R. Bultmann, *The History of the Synoptic Tradition* (Oxford:

Blackwell, 1963) 104.
/17/ E. Käsemann, *Essays on New Testament Themes* (London: S.C.M.,
1964) 41.
/18/ Fuchs, *Studies,* 108, 158-166.
/19/ E. Best, *The First and Second Epistles to the Thessalonians*
(London: Black, 1972) 175-8, 337-341; also see Augustine *Retr.* 21
(P.L. 32. 638-9).
/20/ See J.G. Gager, *Kingdom and Community* (Englewood Cliffs:
Prentice-Hall, 1975).

From Cana to Cana (John 2:1-4:54) and the Fourth Evangelist's Concept of Correct (and Incorrect) Faith

Francis J. Moloney S.D.B.,
Salesian Theological College,
Oakleigh,
Victoria 3166, Australia.

It has been said before that the opening chapters of the Fourth Gospel follow a careful logic /1/. What that logic is, however, has by no means been decided. The paper that follows is an attempt to trace the mind and the hand of the Evangelist, as he assembled his material according to certain literary conventions, so that he might convey his particular theological point of view.

I

Whatever one makes of the pre-history of the Prologue (1:1-18), it belongs to the Gospel as we have it now. As R.H. Lightfoot has insisted, it is "designed to enable *the reader* to understand the doctrines of the book" /2/. I would take this further, and suggest that John opens his Gospel with a page which tells *his readers* the full facts about the origin and role of Jesus, so that throughout all the dramatic encounters which will take place between Jesus and his various interlocutors in the Gospel "story", the reader will be called to make his own decision in the light of what he has read in the Prologue. He can no longer be indifferent. That the book was written to call *the readers* to a growth in true faith is expressly stated in 20:31: "These things are written that *you* may go on believing" /3/.

The second section of the book runs from 1:19-51. This section must be understood as one of promise and expectation. The promise of Jesus opens with the Baptist's pointing away from himself towards Jesus, to whom he gives witness, fulfilling what was said of his role in 1:7,15 /4/. Jesus is indicated as "the Lamb of God" (v.29) and "the Son of God" (v.34). It is important to notice that this witness is given in the face of a series of

queries concerning his status.   "Who are you?", ask "the Jews" from
Jerusalem (v.19).   They then go on to suggest that he may be one
of their expected eschatological or messianic figures.   At first
they suggest two precursors to the Messiah: the returning Elijah,
promised in Mal. 4:6, or "the Prophet" promised in Deut. 18:18
(v.21).   As the Baptist refuses to accept this identification,
they assume that he is not "the Christ" (v.25).   This atmosphere
of Jewish "guessing" about the person of John the Baptist, within
the horizons of Jewish messianic speculation, is important, as
exactly the same process takes place when the scene shifts, and
some disciples of the Baptist "follow" Jesus (vv. 35-51).   Again
we find a series of guesses - this time about who Jesus might be:
Rabbi (v.38), Messiah and Christ (v.41), "him of whom Moses in
the law and also the prophets wrote" (v.45), Rabbi, Son of God,
King of Israel (v.49) /5/.   It is most important to notice that
Jesus neither accepts nor refuses these titles.   His answer to
their guessing takes the form of a promise of "greater things"
which they "will see" (v.50): the revelation of the heavenly in
the person of the Son of Man (v.51) /6/.

     Thus, it appears to me, John brings Jesus on to the stage of
history by placing him firmly within the context of current Jewish
speculations about the Messiah.   These speculations, however, are
transcended by the witness of John who points to Jesus as the Lamb
of God who takes away the sin of the world and as the Son of God
(1:29,34), and then by the direct promise of the Son of Man (1:51)
/7/.   Jesus appears as someone who will reveal "greater things" to
those who see with the eyes of faith (v.50) /8/.   This "seeing" is
very important in the Fourth Gospel, as Jesus reveals his Father
through his ἔργα, his obedient presence among men, and especially
through the ἔργον of the Cross.   There is another "sight",
however, which sometimes leads people astray /9/, and it is
mentioned for the first time in 2:23-24:

     "Now when he was in Jerusalem at the Passover feast, many
     believed in his name *when they saw the signs* (τὰ σημεῖα)
     which he did; but Jesus did not trust himself to them".

It appears that the "sight" of Jesus and the things which he did
would not necessarily lead to true faith.   There must be some
further criterion for correct faith which goes beyond the "seeing"
of the "signs" of Jesus /10/.

     Taking my lead from 2:23-25, a piece of Johannine redactional
commentary which comes as a most important signpost in the section

of the Gospel which runs from Cana to Cana (2:1-4:54), I believe
that the whole section, the Johannine version of the beginning of
Jesus' public ministry, sets out to establish an all-important
criterion for correct faith: a radical openness to the "word" of
Jesus. While there will always be a *visible* aspect to the
revelation of God in Jesus, there is also the danger that one
might settle for the materiality of the "sign". A careful study
of 2:1-4:54 shows that John has assembled his material with great
skill to present, through a series of examples, his own point of
view about the nature of correct faith. I hope to show that he
uses the criterion of a radical openness to the "word" of Jesus
to judge whether his examples come to a stage of disbelief, partial
belief, or full belief in the saving revelation which Jesus has
come to bring. It must be stressed, at this stage, that I am by
no means exhausting the message of Jn. 2:1-4:54 in this analysis.
The Fourth Gospel can be compared to a symphony where a bar or
two can drop a hint of a theme which will later dominate a whole
movement. There are many Johannine themes mentioned for the first
time in the Cana to Cana section which I will not even consider.
I am attempting to draw out the structure used by the Evangelist
to present his major theme: faith in the word of Jesus /11/.

II

Is this section, from Cana to Cana, a literary unit? The
major problem for the defence of the unity of 2:1-4:54 is the
theme of "days" which seems to run from 1:19-28 (see v.29: "The
next day") through to 2:1: "On the third day there was a marriage
at Cana in Galilee". Older commentators (e.g. J.H. Bernard and
M.-E. Boismard) argue that the frequent mentioning of "days" in
chapters 1 and 2 shows that the Evangelist wished to use a week of
seven days to open Jesus' public ministry /12/. This device makes
Jesus' appearance a "new creation", just as the first creation
in Gen. 1:1-2:3 took place within the framework of seven days.
R.E. Brown sees this as a "possible interpretation", but still
divides the Gospel with Cana to Cana as a literary unit /13/.
Brown, who sees the first Cana miracle as both completing the
sequence of ch. 1 and opening that of ch. 2, expresses concern
lest we read into the Gospel "something that was never even thought
of by the evangelist or by the redactor" /14/.

The theory has been taken up from another point of view in the
period since the appearance of Brown's commentary by A.M. Serra,
J. Potin and B. Olsson /15/. These scholars do not work on a neat

scheme of a week which is not found in the text (e.g., the Cana
miracle is said to take place on the third day, not the seventh!),
nor do they link it with the concept of a "new creation" which
is Pauline (see 2 Cor. 5:17; Gal. 6:15; Col. 1:15-20), rather
than Johannine. These scholars have traced a series of traditions
in Targumic and Rabbinic literature in which the encounter with
God at Sinai takes place only after a week's preparation. The
theophany begins on the seventh day (Potin /16/), and the high
point of God's revelation at Sinai, the actual giving of the
Torah, takes place "on the third day" of the theophany (Serra /17/).
A particularly important aspect of this theory is its contribution
to a further development of John's argument that the revelation of
Jesus goes over and beyond the Torah and the cult of Judaism, an
argument already initiated by the expectations and promises of
1:19-51. The high point of God's revelation to Israel, carefully
prepared for, as the nation waited seven days at the foot of
Mt Sinai, then given "on the third day" of the theophany, is
used as background for the first revelation of the δόξα of Jesus
(see 2:11). All through 1:19-51 there has been an attempt on the
part of others ("the Jews" and the future disciples) to explain
both John the Baptist and Jesus in terms of Jewish messianic hopes.
At the end of it all they are told that they will see greater things
(v.50). The sight of those things is a revelation, as the Torah
was a revelation, but the δόξα is no longer found in the Torah,
but in the miraculous activity of Jesus. As John has told us in
the Prologue: "The law was given through Moses, the gift of the
truth came through Jesus Christ" /18/.

      While this theory shows a close link between 1:19-51 and 2:1-11,
the Cana miracle must remain as an integral part of 2:1-4:54. The
themes just mentioned certainly continue into 2:1-11, but there is
something quite different happening in 2:1-11. Jesus is now
actively involved in his task of revealer. While 1:19-51 promises
that this will happen, 2:1-11 is the first of a series of episodes
where it in fact happens. In 1:31 John the Baptist indicated that
his activity was that Jesus "might be revealed (ἵνα φανερωθῇ) to
Israel". In 2:11 we are told that Jesus "manifested (ἐφανέρωσεν)
his glory". In 1:49-50 Jesus remarks on the poor nature of
Nathanael's (and the other disciples' - see the change from singular
to plural in v.51) faith. In 2:11 we are told "and his disciples
believed in him". There is an obvious qualitative leap from what
was hoped for and promised in 1:19-51 to what in fact happens in
2:1-11.

      Similar difficulties arise from 4:46-54. We have already seen,
from a cursory glance at 1:19-51, that this Gospel seems to present

Jesus as the substitution of the "old gift" which was given
through Moses (see 1:17). If this is the major theme of 2:1-4:54
also, then how does the story of the gentile official's act of
faith fit in? This question has led several scholars (e.g. C.H.
Dodd, E.C. Hoskyns and especially A. Feuillet) to argue that
4:46-54 is a sort of parable about the giving of life and the
power of the word which serves as a preface for the discourse in
5:19-47 /19/. These scholars see the theme of Jesus' surpassing
all Jewish expectations as the central theme of the passage we
are considering, but I hope to show that it is concerned with the
matter of correct and incorrect faith. Within this vision of
things, the two Cana miracles will play a vital role as a "frame"
around the whole series of episodes /20/.

                                   III

     Introducing his study of 2:1-4:54, S.A. Panimolle argues
that 2:1-12 and 2:13-22 must be understood as "signs", the former
of the glory of Jesus and the latter of the resurrection. These
two signs are then followed by a triptych of faith in chs. 3-4:

     1.   Nicodemus, a figure representing orthodox Judaism, can
          only accept Jesus within his own categories, as a miracle
          worker and a teacher from God. This is not enough.

     2.   The heretical and schismatic Samaritans, even though
          they have seen no "sign", come to understand Jesus as
          the saviour of the world.

     3.   The pagan official believes immediately in Jesus' word
          and is thus a model of perfect faith /21/.

There is a lot in this theological presentation of the question
of correct faith, but it appears that there may be more to it than
the two signs followed by three examples of faith. What are we
to make of the reactions of John the Baptist in 3:22-31 and the
Samaritan woman in 4:1-26?

     Recalling what we said earlier about the incomplete nature of
this study, we must open our survey of the structure of 2:1-4:54
by looking at the two passages which John sets as a "frame" around
his various other pieces of narrative material: 2:1-11 and 4:46-54.
This parallel is not always recognised, but a careful analysis
shows a number of very interesting correspondences.

2:1:   "On the third day there   4:43,46: "After two days he
       was a marriage at Cana   departed to Galilee... So
       in Galilee".   he came again to Cana in
                                             Galilee".

By referring to "two days" in the introductory v.43, John may want
the reader to see that Jesus comes again to Cana "on the third
day" /22/. However, even if the chronological references are
not as close as I am suggesting, the indication of the place as
Cana in Galilee, and the use of the word πάλιν /23/ are clear
indications that the author may be rounding off an inclusion /24/.
A look at the two miracle stories will show that the link between
the two scenes runs even deeper than an identity of place, and
perhaps of chronology.

    Breaking the form-critical rules for miracle stories /25/,
John constructs *both* stories in a most interesting, parallel
fashion:

            2:1-11   *4:46-54*

1. *Problem:* "The wine failed"   *Problem:* "An official whose son
    (v.3).   was ill" (v.46).

2. *Request:* "The Mother of   *Request:* "He went and begged him
    Jesus said to him, 'They   to come down and heal his son"
    have no wine'" (v.3).   (v.47).

3. *Sharp rebuke:* "O woman,   *Sharp rebuke:* "Unless you see
    what have you to do with   signs and wonders you will not
    me?" (v.4).   believe" (v.48).

4. *Reaction:* "His Mother said   *Reaction:* "'Go, your son will
    to the servants, 'Do   live'. The man believed *the
    whatever he *tells* you'   word* that Jesus spoke to him
    (ὅ τι ἂν λέγῃ ὑμῖν   (ἐπίστευσεν ὁ ἄνθρωπος τῷ λόγῳ
    ποιήσατε)" (v.5).   ὃν εἶπεν αὐτῷ ὁ Ἰησοῦς)" (v.50)

5. *Consequence:* A miracle   *Consequence:* A miracle which
    which leads to the faith of   leads to the faith of others
    others (disciples) (vv.   (the household) (vv.51-53).
    6-11).

Both scenes are rounded off with a redactional comment which again
shows that John is attempting to draw his readers' attention to
his deliberate inclusion:

2:11: "This, the first of his   4:54:   "This was now the second
    signs, Jesus did at Cana   sign that Jesus did when he
    in Galilee".   had come from Judea to
                                          Galilee".

    The two passages have been constructed with great care, to form
an obvious inclusion. What must also be seen, however, is that
Jesus' interlocutors in each case (his Mother and the official)
commit themselves to his word. In both cases we have the
background of the word λόγος: "Do whatever he *tells* you" in 2:5,
where the verb λέγειν is used, and "He believed *the word*" in 4:50,
where the noun λόγος is used. There can be little doubt that in
the midst of the multitude of theological innuendos that scholars
find in these passages (particularly in the first Cana miracle /27/),
a most important point is that the Mother of Jesus and the official
are used as examples of correct Johannine faith. They do not need
"signs" to come to faith; they commit themselves to *the word* of
Jesus /28/. That this is important for a correct understanding of
the two clearly parallel passages is indicated by the sharp
rebuke directed at the official: "Unless you see signs and wonders
you will not believe" (4:48). The fact of the matter is that
neither the Mother of Jesus nor the official "see" signs and
wonders, yet they believe.

    The various scenes which fill Jn.2:12-4:45 must be considered
from the point of view of the people who are involved in them, in
some sort of personal encounter with the person of Jesus. This
means that we have to consider "the Jews" (2:13-22), Nicodemus
(3:1-21), John the Baptist (3:25-36), the Samaritan woman
(4:7-15,16-26) and the Samaritan villagers (4:27-30, 39-42). Also
in the section there are various transitional passages which
arrange the time and the place of each event, and give John a
chance to add his own comments (2:12; 3:22-24; 4:1-6; 4:43-45).
These passages are very important, as the Evangelist uses them
to shift people from place to place, situating his scenes according
to his overall plan, and also to add his own running commentary as
he assembles his material. However, we will not consider them in
this particular study /29/. There are two other pieces of
material which I have not yet listed: 2:23-25 and 4:31-38 /30/.
These two passages are used by John in a manner similar to the role
of the chorus in a Greek tragedy. He punctuates his narrative of
dramatic encounters between Jesus and various interlocutors with
these two reflections, in an attempt to indicate to the reader
exactly what he is trying to do through his series of dramatic
encounters.

Jn. 2:23-25 is universally recognised as a Johannine comment
about correct and incorrect faith: "Many believed (ἐπίστευσαν) in
his name when they saw the signs which he did; but Jesus did not
trust (ἐπίστευεν) himself to them". This is clearly a criticism
of a faith based purely on the σημεῖα /31/. The function of
4:31-38 is more complex and it is impossible to go into great
detail here. The passage obviously reflects the missionary
situation of the Johannine Church /32/, but it must also have a
sense in its present context. It is most important to catch the
full implications of vv.31-34, as here the reason why Jesus can
present himself as the unique revealer is explained: he is one
with the will of the Father, and this will eventually lead him to
bring his task (τὸ ἔργον) to its perfection (τελειώσω). This is
an unmistakable reference to the hour of the Cross and resurrection
(see 2:4,18-22), often described in the Fourth Gospel in terms of
"the perfection" (τέλος and related words. See 5:36; 13:1; 17:4;
19:28,30) and Jesus' "work" or "task" (τὸ ἔργον. See especially
5:36 and 17:4 where the two terms are closely united) /33/. The
point of this second redactional addition is to call attention to
the Cross. In a passage (2:1-4:54) which will insist heavily on a
radical openness to the word of Jesus as a criterion of true faith,
John speaks to his own community at the end of the first century,
already involved in a missionary activity, as is clear from the
placing of this discussion with his disciples in a period when the
Samaritan villagers are "coming to him" (v.30), and his command to
"look up" (v.35) to see the harvest ready for reaping. By adding
this discussion with the disciples, John reminds his Church that
there is one visible "work" which stands behind all missionary
activity and success (see especially vv.37-38), the Cross and the
resurrection. The best explanation of this passage is found later
in the Gospel: "And I, when I am lifted up, will draw all men to
myself" (12:32) /34/.

These two comments play a most important role in 2:1-4:54. In
2:23-25 the theme of the whole section is stated in negative terms,
as John criticises an incomplete faith, based purely on the
externalities of the "signs". Yet in 4:31-38 another chord is
sounded. This "faith in the word" must be balanced by a
presentation of the sign that is beyond all signs, the "hour" of
the death and resurrection of Jesus (see also 2:4,18-22, which
makes the same point). One need not look too far to find a
motivation for this second Johannine comment if (as I believe is
the case) one of the more serious problems that the Johannine
community had to face after being expelled from its Jewish roots
was a nascent docetic Gnosticism /35/.

It remains now to survey the passages 2:13-22; 3:1-21; 3:25-36; 4:7-15; 4:16-26 and 4:27-30,39-42. As I mentioned above, we will be concerned with the personalities involved in each of these scenes, and how they react to the word of Jesus. Thus, we are interested in "the Jews", Nicodemus, John the Baptist, the Samaritan woman and the Samaritan villagers.

a. *"The Jews" (2:13-22)*

Again we find ourselves faced with a passage fraught with all sorts of difficulties. What is its relation to the Synoptic Gospels' use of the same scene? When did it take place in the life of Jesus? What is the relationship between vv.18-20, clearly a prophecy about the resurrection of Jesus, and the events of vv.13-16? These questions, and many others, are of great importance for a complete understanding of the passage, but we must look to the encounter between "the Jews" and Jesus and its outcome. We will leave aside all other considerations.

Jesus here encounters "the Jews" for the first time /36/. After their request for a σημεῖον to give authority to what he has just done (v.18), Jesus answers, "Destroy this temple, *and in three days I will raise it up"* (v.19). The reaction of "the Jews" is a complete refusal to accept the revelation which has been communicated to them through the actual "words" of Jesus (direct speech is used). They throw the words of Jesus back at him, refusing to take the leap outside their own categories of "sticks and stones" which Jesus demands of them: "It has taken forty-six years to build this temple, *and will you raise it up in three days*?" (v.20). It is vitally important to notice that it is the actual *words* of Jesus that are taken up and thrown back at him in a mocking question:

Jesus	*Jews*
καὶ ἐν τρισὶν ἡμέραις	καὶ σὺ ἐν τρισὶν ἡμέραις
ἐγερῶ αὐτόν.	ἐγειρεῖς αὐτόν;

The redactional explanation which follows makes it clear that John is concerned here with a question of faith. Later, after the resurrection, the disciples "believed (ἐπίστευσαν) the scriptures and the word (τῷ λόγῳ) which Jesus had spoken" (v.22). This is precisely what "the Jews" refused to do. The verdict on the first example of faith between the frame of the two Cana miracles is that there is *no faith*.

b. *Nicodemus (3:1-21)* /38/

There is a clear progression and change of attitude in our next example: Nicodemus. He seeks out Jesus in the midst of darkness - "This man came to Jesus by night" - and he is prepared to make a limited confession of faith, calling Jesus a Rabbi, a teacher come from God, one who works signs; and he believes that God is with him, precisely because he has done wonderful miracles (3:2). Nicodemus, within the limitations of his Judaism (see v.1: "a man of the Pharisees", "a ruler of the Jews"), is prepared to accept Jesus, as long as Jesus fits into his categories. However, he cannot or will not understand the message of rebirth from above in the spirit. This is not the end for Nicodemus (see 7:50-52; 19:38-42), but John clearly uses him here as an example of a man with an incomplete faith. He can only accept Jesus within his own categories, just as he could only accept the notion of rebirth within his own categories. Again it is important to notice how the words of Jesus are taken up by Nicodemus. This time, however, they are not thrown back at Jesus, but they are misunderstood:

Jesus speaks to Nicodemus saying: "Unless one is born *anew* (ἄνωθεν), he cannot see the kingdom of heaven" (v.3).

Nicodemus answers: "How can a man be born when he is old? Can he enter *a second time* (δεύτερον) into his mother's womb and be born?" (v.4).

Jesus speaks of one's being born "again/from above" (ἄνωθεν), but Nicodemus, unable to go outside the categories which he himself can measure, can only reply in chronological terms of "a second time" (δεύτερον) /39/. Nicodemus, our second example of faith, must be judged as having *partial faith* /40/.

c. *John the Baptist (3:25-36)*

The third personality, John the Baptist, brings back the discussions of 1:19-34 concerning the identity of the Messiah. Whatever may have been the original tradition which stands behind vv.25-30, the Evangelist uses it to show the relationship between the Baptist and Jesus. It has often been pointed out that there was a problem with a Baptist-sect in the Johannine Church /41/. While there may be an element of truth in this theory, it is an exaggeration to claim that this Gospel is anti-Baptist. If we are correct in seeing the Cana to Cana section of the Gospel as a series of examples, leading the reader to a full appreciation

of correct faith, then the figure of the Baptist is used here in
a very positive sense. He declares that he is not the Messiah,
but the one sent before that figure (v.28). He then goes on to
describe his relationship with the Christ. Recalling our
criterion of true faith, given to us from the examples of the
Mother of Jesus and the pagan official, then the Baptist's point
of comparison takes on an important light within the context of
the Cana to Cana section of the Gospel. The Baptist describes
himself as:

> "The friend of the bridegroom who stands and
> *hears him* (ἀκούων αὐτοῦ)",

and as one who,

> "Rejoices greatly at the bridegroom's voice
> (τὴν φωνήν)" (v.29).

It is because of this that the Baptist is full of joy, and ready
to decrease as Jesus appears upon the scene (vv.29-30). The
Baptist is presented as a figure who sees his relationship to
Jesus as a listener, as one who hears Jesus' voice, and accepts
the consequences: "He must increase, but I must decrease" (v.30).

It seems strange that there is no use of λόγος or any related
words. If I am correct in my suggestion that the criterion being
used in openness to "the word", then why did John use φωνή and not
λόγος or ῥῆμα in v.29? We can never be certain of just why an
author chooses certain words, but there is a great deal of evidence
which indicates that John is here using material which came to him
from very old John the Baptist traditions. The Evangelist has
retouched it here and there, but on the whole, "it is highly
probable that we are here in touch with pre-canonical tradition"
/42/. I would suggest that the tradition already said what the
Evangelist had in mind. As such, he left the traditional words
as he found them. John the Baptist displays a radical openness
to the word of Jesus and, as such, this third example shows us
the Baptist's *complete faith* /43/.

In the examples which we have seen so far, we have found a
complete cycle of possible reactions to Jesus: no faith ("the
Jews"), partial faith (Nicodemus) and complete faith (John the
Baptist). It has now become clear that there is another element
which should be noticed. All of these examples of faith come from
Judaism, and this has been made clear by the Evangelist in every

case. "The Jews" (2:20), Nicodemus, a man of the Pharisees and
a leader of the Jews (3:1) and John the Baptist, called Rabbi
(3:26) and involved in a discussion over the Jewish Messiah
(3:28), are the three figures involved in the drama so far.
This section has been highlighted by a redactional note in 2:23-25,
criticising certain Jews who are in Jerusalem for the Passover.
The link with Judaism here is as strong as it could possibly be,
and our first series of examples shows a movement from no faith
to complete faith within Judaism. The frame which opened the
whole Cana to Cana section of the Gospel (2:1-11) was also
closely linked with Judaism. It told of the faith of a Jewish
woman at a Jewish feast in a Jewish region. It must be stressed
at this stage that the whole "progression" from one state to
another is not a condemnation or canonization of any group or
person. The examples are used as a model of various types of
faith, *all of which* could be the experience of the reader.
John's point is that a full movement, from no faith to complete
faith, is possible within Judaism. He asks his readers from a
Jewish background: "Where do you stand?"

In an introductory passage, rather clumsily joining 4:1-3
with 4-6, and clearly showing the work of an editor, John places
Jesus outside Judaism. He is now geographically in a non-Jewish
world. The Samaritan woman is then introduced /44/. We are now
in the land of the heterogeneous and heterodox Samaritans, and
Jesus is carrying on a dialogue with a woman of that race. While
2:1-3:36 took place in a Jewish context, 4:1-42 is entirely
concerned with Samaritans. The Johannine addition in 4:31-38 in
a missionary context is determined by this, just as 2:23-25 was
directed at certain Jews in Jerusalem. The second part of the
Cana to Cana "frame", closing the whole section (4:46-54), must
also be seen as the reaction to Jesus of someone outside Judaism.
There a non-Jew comes to full faith in Jesus /45/.

a[1] *The Samaritan Woman (4:7-15)*

There appear to be two different moments in Jesus' encounter
with the Samaritan woman. In a first moment Jesus offers the
woman "living water" (vv.7-15), and in the second the woman comes
to suspect that Jesus might be the Messiah, as he has told her the
secrets of her private life (vv.16-26) /46/. We will study these
passages separately, as it appears to me that they offer a
progression of faith similar to the movement from "the Jews" to
Nicodemus in our first trio of examples.

The point of the first discussion is Jesus' offering the woman "living water". Jesus reveals himself as one who can dispense eternal life, and he explains this in terms of water:

> "Whoever drinks *of the water that I shall give him will never thirst;* the water that I shall give him will become in him a spring of water welling up to eternal life" (4:14).

The reaction of the woman is a *complete* misunderstanding of what has been said to her. Notice again that this revelation has come through the actual "words" of Jesus (direct speech is used). She now throws these words back to Jesus, refusing to take any leap which will lead her outside her own categories. In v.14 Jesus spoke of "living water" and a spring of water "welling up to eternal life". The woman then replies, using Jesus' own words, but unable to go beyond ordinary water and ordinary springs:

> "Sir, *give me this water that I may not thirst,*nor come here to draw" (v.15).

As in the case of "the Jews" in 2:13-22 /47/, it is important to see how the very *words* of Jesus are used in the woman's reply:

Jesus	The Woman
ἐκ τοῦ ὕδατος οὗ ἐγὼ δώσω αὐτῷ οὐ μὴ διψήσει	δός μοι τὸ ὕδωρ ἵνα μὴ διψῶ

The woman, in this first instance, fails to grasp the opportunity which Jesus presents. She is no way open to his words, merely repeating them back to him in a completely mistaken sense. Therefore, like "the Jews" in the parallel passage from the Jewish triptych, she must be judged as having *no faith* /48/.

b[1] *The Samaritan Woman (4:16-26)*

Unlike "the Jews", the Samaritan woman is given a further chance /49/. There are two very important points being made in this section: the revelation of Jesus (vv.16-19,25-26) and the reference to true cult (vv.20-24). We are concerned here with Jesus' revelation of himself, and the woman's reaction to this revelation.

As the woman has not been able to go beyond material water and geographically situated springs, Jesus now questions her on

something well within her own experience - her marital situation.
This is something which she can understand, and her reaction to
Jesus' telling her about her private life leads her to confess
that Jesus is "a prophet" (v.19). After the section on true cult
the woman comes back to the fact that he has shown her wonderful
things (v.25), and so she hesitatingly suggests that he may be
the Messiah (v.25) /50/. Again it is important to notice the
parallel between this second example of faith and the corresponding
scene in the first triptych - Nicodemus (3:1-21). In that passage
Nicodemus was prepared to accept Jesus according to the
categories which his Jewish hopes would allow, and he sought him
out because he did signs (3:2). Exactly the same thing is
happening here. The Samaritan woman sees that he is able to do
wonderful things, and is prepared to accept him as "a prophet"
(v.19) and perhaps as "the Messiah" (v.25) because he was able
to tell her about her private life.

The parallel runs deeper. The incomplete faith of Nicodemus
was corrected by a discourse from Jesus, the Son of Man and the
Son of God, the unique saving revelation of God (3:11-21). In
the case of the Samaritan woman there is no discourse, but Jesus'
first use of his most important Christological title: ἐγώ εἰμι.
Unfortunately, many commentators and translators make this final
statement from Jesus into an acceptance of the woman's suggestion
that he might be the Messiah: "I who speak to you am he" (v.26 RSV)
This is not the case. Over against the woman's suggestions that he
may fulfill *her* expectations of prophet and messiah, Jesus reveals
himself as someone who exceeds such hopes in his reply: ἐγώ εἰμι ὁ
λαλῶν σοι: "I am (is) the one speaking to you" /51/. It is
important to notice the woman's part in the following scene with
the villagers. She is not convinced by Jesus' self-revelation.
In v.29 she wonders with the villagers, "Can this be the Christ?".
She remains within her partial categories. In perfect parallel
with the Nicodemus scene, this "second chance" given to the Samaritan woman provides the Evangelist with a model of *partial faith*.

c[1] *The Samaritan Villagers (4:27-30,39-42)*

The example here, running parallel to the example of complete
faith given by John the Baptist (3:25-36), is very clear, obvious
at a first reading. The woman goes back to her village and
communicates her partial faith in v.29: "Can this be the Christ?".
This leads the villagers to go out towards Jesus (v.30). Many
Samaritans, in a first moment, share the woman's partial faith.

They believed because of the woman's telling them (διὰ τόν λόγον τῆς γυναικός) of his miraculous reading of her private life (v.39). However, after staying with them for two days, "many more believed because of his word" (ἐπίστευσαν διὰ τόν λόγον αὐτοῦ) (v.41) /52/. Just in case the reader has missed the point, John has the villagers themselves announce their new-found faith: "It is no longer because of your words that we believe, for we have heard (ἀκηκόαμεν) for ourselves, and we know that this is indeed the saviour of the world" (v.42).

Even though the language of the John the Baptist section was conditioned by the tradition which John received, while the Samaritan section is more "Johannine", there is a correspondence between the two parallels in the use of the verb ἀκούειν in 3:29 and 4:42. Like John the Baptist in 3,25;36, the Samaritan villagers show a radical openness to the word of Jesus, and as such are an example of *complete faith*.

                                    IV

Various conclusions could be drawn from this analysis /53/. I merely wish to outline the two that are most immediate: the literary structure of Jn.2:1-4:54 and the Johannine concept of correct (and incorrect) faith, as it is presented through this passage.

1. *The literary structure of Jn.2:1-4:54.*

It appears that we have uncovered a most interesting Johannine teaching technique. After his encounter with Jewish expectations and a promise indicating what true believers would "see" in him (1:19-51), the Evangelist then proceeds, by means of the Cana to Cana passage, to indicate to his readers what is meant by true faith. He does this through a series of dramatic episodes in which various people react to the word of Jesus in various ways. On two occasions he pauses along these dramatic encounters to comment, and to direct the reader's attention to the point which he is trying to make. On one occasion (2:23-25) he is critical of those who believe in Jesus merely because of his "signs", while on another occasion (4:31-38) he reminds his readers that there is one "sign" which goes beyond all "signs" and which will always remain the object and source of faith: the τελείωσις of the ἔργον of the Cross and resurrection of Jesus.

The whole section can be seen in the following structure /54/:

FROM CANA TO CANA (Jn. 2:1-4:54)

2:1-11: The marriage feast at Cana. The example of the Mother of Jesus. *Complete faith* in a Jewish context.

    a. 2:12-22: The expulsion of the vendors from the temple.
The example of "the Jews":
No faith.

2:23-25: John comments, criticising a faith based on signs

    b. 3:1-21: The encounter with one of the Pharisees, a ruler of the Jews.
The example of Nicodemus:
Partial faith.

    c. 3:22-36: The discussion with John the Baptist.
The example of the Baptist:
Complete faith.

a^1 4:1-15: The first discussion with the Samaritan woman who refuses "living water".
The example of the Samaritan woman:
No faith.

b^2 4:16-26: The second discussion with the Samaritan woman who is now prepared to accept Jesus as a prophet and possibly as the Messiah.
The example of the Samaritan woman:
Partial faith.

4:31-38: John comments, through Jesus, recalling the essential "work"

c^1 4:27-30,99-42: The advent of the Samaritan villagers who eventually believe because of the word of Jesus.
The example of the Samaritan villagers:
Complete faith.

4:43-54: The official at Cana. The example of the Official. *Complete faith* in a non-Jewish context.

Left-margin labels:
INCLUSION: Complete faith in a Jewish and in a non-Jewish context.
The movement to faith in a Jewish context.
The movement to faith in a non-Jewish context.

In this remarkably simple structure we have a frame of two examples of complete faith: the Mother of Jesus in a Jewish context, and the official in a non-Jewish context. Set within that frame we have a two-fold repetition of a series of examples which move from no faith ("the Jews" and the Samaritan woman) to partial faith (Nicodemus and the Samaritan woman) to complete faith (John the Baptist and the Samaritan villagers), and this movement takes place first in an entirely Jewish world, linked with the first example in the "frame", the Mother of Jesus, and secondly in a heterodox (missionary?) world, linked with the official in the second part of the "frame" around the whole series of episodes. John's own comments are also symmetrically inserted: 2:23-25 comes *after* the first example of faith ("the Jews") while 4:31-38 comes *before* the last example ("the Samaritans").

Much more could, and should, be said at this point. It strikes me that this is a superb example of teaching technique, drawing the reader through a series of events which move dynamically from one situation of faith to another, continually asking him where he stands. The sharp division between the Jewish world and the Samaritans also needs further investigation. It is equally important to notice that there is a movement to faith within Judaism; thus "the Jews" are not a figure of Judaism as such. Any further investigation of these suggestions would take us well beyond the scope of this paper. As such I merely indicate them as fields for possible further investigation.

2.   *The Johannine concept of correct (and incorrect) faith.*

There is little need for me to spell this out at length. What I have uncovered through this investigation does not bring anything startlingly new into current discussions of the Johannine concept of faith. R.E. Brown (among others /55/) has pointed out that there are "types" of faith in the Fourth Gospel /56/. He sees four types of faith, adding one which I have not considered here: those who see the signs and come to understand their full significance. He quotes the disciples' faith in 2:11 as an example of this type of faith /57/. I would understand 2:11 as a consequence of the "faith in the word" of the Mother of Jesus, leading to the faith of others, just as the faith of the official led to the faith of his household (4:53). As Brown himself points out, these same disciples still have a long way to go before they arrive at complete faith /58/.

For John, true faith means a radical openness to the word of Jesus, i.e. to all that he has come to reveal. Anyone who will not accept this revelation (e.g. "the Jews" or the Samaritan woman) has no faith. The signs must not be understood within the categories which men, history and culture can determine (neither Jewish: Nicodemus, nor non-Jewish: the Samaritan woman). Ultimately, it is taking the risk of accepting this revelation without condition (John the Baptist and the Samaritan villagers) which produces true faith. John himself explains that the high point of this revelation which must be accepted is not found in the externality of the "signs" (2:23-25), but in the event of the Cross, where Jesus will bring to perfection the revealing task which the Father had given him (4:31-38. See also 5:36; 13:1; 17:4; 19:28-30).

If I am correct in seeing the Cana to Cana section of the Fourth Gospel as a carefully structured passage, leading the reader through a series of examples of faith, then we must agree with David Deeks whose study of the structure of the Fourth Gospel led him to conclude that: "The Fourth Evangelist was not only a brilliant theologian; he was also a master of a very specialised literary technique" /59/. I am not convinced by Deeks' own structure, however, as it is indeed "very specialised". I hope I have shown that the highlight of the Cana to Cana passage is not the Evangelist's use of *complicated* literary techniques, but his careful blending of traditional material with his own contributions to lead us, the readers, through a *simple* reflection on the nature of true faith, that we might understand Jesus' summary statement at the end of his public appearance:

> "If anyone hears my words and does not keep them, I do not judge him; for I did not come to judge the world. He who rejects me and does not receive my words has a judge; the word that I have spoken will be his judge on the last day" (12:47-48).

NOTES

/1/   See, for example, I. de la Potterie, "Structura primae partis Evangelii Johannis (capita III et IV)", *Verbum Domini* 47 (1969), 130-131. A similar position to that of de la Potterie is found in a most recent study of Jn.1-4, S.A. Panimolle, *Lettura Pastorale del Vangelo di Giovanni*, Lettura pastorale della bibbia (Bologna, Dehoniane, 1978), Vol. I. See also R. Schnackenburg, *Das Johannesevangelium*, I. Teil, HTKNT IV,1 (Freiburg, Herder, 1965),

pp. 270-272; H. van den Bussche, "La Structure de Jean 1-12", in
L'Evangile de Jean, Recherches Bibliques 3 (Bruges, Desclée de
Brouwer, 1958), pp. 76-88. K. Hanhart, "The Structure of John I
35 - IV 54", in *Studies in John*. *Presented to Professor Dr. J.N.*
Sevenster on the Occasion of His Seventieth Birthday, SNT 24
(Leiden, Brill, 1970), pp. 21-46, argues that Jn. 1:35-4:54 is a
deliberate use of Matthew, Mark, and especially Luke. Although he
makes some very interesting suggestions, I do not find his
argument convincing. He claims that the finished Synoptic Gospels
were used by John's community and that John's use of them was
determined by a liturgical interest. One moves from one unprovable
(improbable) hypothesis to another.
/2/   R.H. Lightfoot, *St. John's Gospel* (Oxford, University Press,
1956), p. 11. Stress mine. See also his further insistence on
p.78: "These verses give the key to the understanding of this
Gospel, and make clear how the evangelist wishes his readers to
approach his presentation of the Lord's work and Person".
/3/   There is a well known textual difficulty associated with
the verb πιστεύειν in 20:31. Both the present subjunctive,
indicating that the readers already believe and that the book is
written that they may continue in that belief, and the aorist
subjunctive, indicating that the book is written to bring them
to faith, are well attested. Our interpretation (and our
understanding of Cana to Cana) accepts the use of the present
subjunctive, which appears to be the better reading. See R.E.
Brown, *The Gospel according to John XIII-XXI*, The Anchor Bible
29a (New York, Doubleday, 1970), p. 1056; R. Schnackenburg,
Das Johannesevangelium, III. Teil, HTKNT IV,3 (Freiburg, Herder,
1975), pp. 403-404.
/4/   See I. de la Potterie, "Giovanni Battista e Gesù testimoni
della verità", in *Gesù Verità* (Torino, Marietti, 1973), pp.167-178;
M.D. Hooker, "John the Baptist and the Johannine Prologue", *NTS*
16 (1969-70), pp.354-358; C.K. Barrett, *New Testament Essays*
(London, SPCK, 1972), pp.27-48.
/5/   See R. Schnackenburg, *Johannesevangelium* I, pp.321-328.
/6/   This movement towards Jesus' self-revelation is often missed.
See, for example, D. Deeks, "The Structure of the Fourth Gospel",
NTS 15 (1968-69), p.112 note 4, where the author argues that v.49
"grounds Jesus' status in his eternal relation to the Father".
V.51 is not discussed. See F.J. Moloney, *The Johannine Son of Man*,
Biblioteca di Scienze Religiose 14 (Rome, LAS, 1976), pp.23-41, for
a full discussion of this question. I believe that the encounter
between the expectations of Judaism and the Johannine presentation
of Jesus as someone who surpasses these expectations reflects the
situation of the Johannine Church. See F.J. Moloney, "The Fourth

Gospel's Presentation of Jesus as 'the Christ' and J.**A**.T. Robinson's
'Redating'", *The Downside Review* 95 (1977), pp.239-253. Too often
the "corrective" nature of 1:50-51 is overlooked, and 1:35-51 is
seen as the disciples' discovery of the Messiah in a wholly
positive sense. See, for example, S. Sabugal, *CHRISTOS*.
Investigación exegética sobre la cristologia joannea (Barcelona,
Herder, 1972), pp.194-206; S.A. Panimolle, *Lettura Pastorale*,
pp.184-185.

/7/   One must be careful in understanding the term "the Son of
God" in the Fourth Gospel. In general, it is the title *par
excellence* for Jesus, as we find it used by the Baptist in 1:34.
However, it is also used as an incomplete confession of faith,
when it is clearly conditioned by Jewish messianic ideas of "a son
of God". This is the sense in which it is found in 1:49. See on
this, F.J. Moloney, "The Johannine Son of God", *Salesianum* 38 (1976)
pp.71-86, esp. 79-80.

/8/   On the connection between "seeing" and "believing" in the
Fourth Gospel, see F. Hahn, "Sehen und Glauben im Johannesevangelium"
in H. Baltensweiler and Bo Reicke (eds.), *Neues Testament und
Geschichte. Historisches Geschehen und Deutung im Neuen Testament:
Oscar Cullmann zum 70. Geburtstag* (Tübingen, Mohr, 1972), pp.125-141;
C. Traets, *Voir Jésus et le Père en Lui selon L'Evangile de Saint
Jean*, Analecta Gregoriana 159 (Rome, Gregorian University Press,
1967). On 1:51 see pp.125-128.

/9/   See especially F. Hahn, "Sehen und Glauben...", pp.126-36.

/10/ Here we are touching on the difference, in the Fourth Gospel,
between the ἔργα of Jesus and the σημεῖα. We cannot enter into
the details of this discussion here. See, for a good summary and
further bibliography, R.E. Brown, *John*, pp.525-532 and R.
Schnackenburg, *Johannesevangelium* I, pp.347-356, and especially
pp.347-350, where the distinction between the two is clearly
indicated. Briefly, the "signs", although showing the active
presence of God in the deeds of Jesus, can be understood in a
material fashion, and this is criticised by John (see 2:23-25).
The "works" of Jesus are ultimately associated with the whole
reason for his being sent by the Father, fulfilled in the "work" of
his death. On the relationship between the ἔργα and the ἔργον see
F.-M. Braun, "La Réduction du Pluriel au Singulier dans l'Evangile
et la Première Lettre de Jean", *NTS* 24 (1977-78), pp.40-67 (45-47).
See also the important works of W. Thüsing, *Die Erhöhung und
Verherrlichung Jesu im Johannesevangelium*, Neutestamentliche
Abhandlungen 21,1 (Münster, Aschendorff, 1970²), pp.58-63;
W. Nicol, *The Sēmeia in the Fourth Gospel* SNT 27 (Leiden, Brill,
1972), pp.113-124; S. Hofbeck, *Semeion. Der Begriff des "Zeichens"
im Johannesevangelium unter Berücksichtigung seiner Vorgeschichte*

(Münsterscharzach, Vier-Türme-Verlag, 1966), pp.67-72; 147-155; 178-185.

/11/ Other scholars have pointed out that the theme which follows is "true faith". See, for example, S.A. Panimolle, *Lettura Pastorale*, p.201; I. de la Potterie, "Structura...", pp.139-140; H. van den Bussche, "La Structure...", pp.83-88; R.E. Brown, *John*, pp.cxliii-cxliv. In what follows I will refer indiscriminately to "the Evangelist" and "John" without any intention of identifying the author(s).

/12/ J.H. Bernard, *A Critical and Exegetical Commentary on the Gospel According to St. John*, ICC (Edinburgh, T. & T. Clark, 1928), pp.33-34; M.-E. Boismard, *Du Baptême à Cana (Jean 1,19-2,11)*, Lectio Divina 18 (Paris, Editions du Cerf, 1956), pp.14-15.

/13/ R.E. Brown, *John*, pp.105-106.

/14/ *Ibid.*, p.106.

/15/ J. Potin, *La fête juive de la Pentecôte*, Lectio Divina 65 (Paris, Editions du Cerf, 1971), Vol. 1, pp.314-317; A.M. Serra, "Le tradizioni della teofania Sinaitica nel Targum dello Pseudo-Jonathan Es. 19,24 e Giov. 1,19-2,12", *Marianum* 33 (1971) 1-39. Although critical of some of Serra's theological conclusions, B. Olsson has largely followed these scholars in his *Structure and Meaning in the Fourth Gospel. A Text-Linguistic Analysis of John 2:1-11 and 4:1-42*, Coniectanea Biblica, New Testament Series 6 (Lund, Gleerup, 1974), pp.102-109. See the serious criticism of these attempts to find an Old Testament "grid" for the New Testament in B. Lindars - P. Borgen, "The Place of the Old Testament in the Formation of New Testament Theology. Prolegomena and Response", *NTS* 23 (1976-77) 59-75 (64-65).

/16/ J. Potin, *La fête juive*, pp.314-316. See also B. Olsson, *Structure and Meaning*, pp.103-104. Olsson, in fact, argues for a six day period.

/17/ A.M. Serra, "Le tradizioni...", pp.8-22; 36;39. See also, B. Olsson, *Structure and Meaning*, pp.102-103.

/18/ For this interpretation of 1:17, see S.A. Panimolle, *Il dono della legge e la grazia della verità (Gv 1,17)* (Roma, AVE, 1973); F.J. Moloney, "The Fulness of a Gift which is Truth (Jn. 1,14.16-17)", *Catholic Theological Review* 1 (1978), pp.30-33; *id.*, *The Word became Flesh*, Theology Today 14 (Cork/Dublin, Mercier, 1979), pp. 50-53.

/19/ C.H. Dodd, *The Interpretation of the Fourth Gospel* (Cambridge, University Press, 1953), pp.318-319; E.C. Hoskyns - F.N. Davey (ed.), *The Fourth Gospel* (London, Faber & Faber, 1961), p.249; A. Feuillet, "La signification théologique du second miracle de Cana (Jn IV, 46-54)", in *Etudes Johanniques* (Bruges, Desclée de Brouwer, 1962), pp.34-46. This article from Feuillet is an excellent summary of

the whole question. The criterion of the surpassing gift of
Jesus is also used for 1:19-4:54 by D. Deeks, "The Structure...",
pp.111-113. He suggests a heading for the section: "Witness to
Christ; Christ supersedes all earlier expectation" (p.111).
Feuillet (art. cit., pp.37-38) finds it difficult to accept the
theme of "faith" as a determining principle for the division of
the material as "il n'y a pas progression d'un cas à l'autre". It
is precisely a "progression" which convinced me that 2:1-4:54 was a
unit, and that the question of faith is the major issue.
/20/ Some recent scholarship still sees 2:1-12 as belonging to
the opening stage of the Gospel. See, for example, B. Lindars,
The Gospel of John, New Century Bible (London, Oliphants, 1972),
pp.76-133, where he studies 1:1-2:12 under the heading: "The
manifestation of the divine glory in Jesus". See also R.H. Lightfoot
St. John, pp.90-105.
/21/ S.A. Panimolle, Lettura Pastorale, p.201. He is following
the suggestion of I. de la Potterie, "Structura...", pp.137-140.
/22/ While scholars sometimes see a connection between "the third
day" of 2:1 and the resurrection, very few pay any attention to
the "after two days...Jesus came again" in 4:43,46. C.H. Dodd,
Interpretation, p.320 and R. Schnackenburg, Johannesevangelium I,
p.331 are among the few who see a possible contact with the resurrection stories. M.-E. Boismard, Du Baptême à Cana, p.107, makes the
link via the "after two days" of Hosea 6:2. This seems somewhat
unlikely. I would like to take this discussion further, insisting
that both references to "days" (2:1; 4:43) connect the Cana
miracles with the resurrection. Recently, B. Lindars, "Two
Parables in John", NTS 16 (1969-70), pp.318-324, argued that there
are traces of a parable of Jesus in Jn.2:10 which was originally
quite independent of the miracle story. The "story" part of the
Cana episode had its origins in a story about Jesus similar to
much folk-lore which concerns itself with the childhood of a great
man. There is, of course, abundant evidence of this sort of
material in the apocryphal gospels (see, for example, the Infancy
Gospel of Thomas). Lindars points to Lk.2:41-51 as evidence for
this sort of material within the canonical Gospels. Most recently,
R.E. Brown, The Birth of the Messiah. A commentary on the infancy
narratives in Matthew and Luke (London, Geoffrey Chapman, 1977),
pp.487-488, has picked up Lindars' point, adding a further most
interesting suggestion. The reference to "on the third day" in
Jn.2:1 was added by the Evangelist as a guide to the reader that
he must understand the passage in the light of the resurrection,
just as the Lucan example of the same sort of material (Lk.2:41-51)
has "after three days" in 2:46 for the same reason. Turning now
to the second Cana miracle, we find a very close parallel
reference to "two days" in Jn.11:6. There Jesus delays his going

to Bethany "for two days", thus arriving on the third day. This
is clearly a link with the resurrection, and I would suggest that
the act of faith in 4:46-54 is also presented under a hint of
resurrection. Of course, the link between resurrection and faith
is made explicit for this section in 2:22.

/23/ The word is very popular with the Fourth Evangelist. He
uses it more often than any other Evangelist, and it is most frequently found in very Johannine transitional scenes. It is
repeated at the end of the second Cana miracle. On this second
πάλιν see K. Hanhart, "The Structure of John I 35 - IV 54", p.29:
"The curious word order πάλιν δεύτερον implies that this second
sign is a reiteration of the first sign or forms its logical
complement". See a similar use in 4:3; 6:15; 8:12; 10:7; 19:40.

/24/ This inclusion has often been noticed. See, for example,
B.F. Westcott, *The Gospel According to St. John* (London, John
Murray, 1908), p.79; A. Schlatter, *Der Evangelist Johannes. Wie
er spricht, denkt und glaubt* (Stuttgart, Calwer, 1948), p.139;
R.H. Lightfoot, *St. John*, p.128.

/25/ See, for an excellent summary of these "rules" and the
various history of religions parallels which have helped the form
critics to establish them, W. Barclay, *The Gospels and Acts*
(London, SCM Press, 1976) Vol. I, pp.33-41. All the necessary
references to Bultmann and Dibelius can be found in Barclay.

/26/ This parallelism was noticed, in passing, by W. Bauer,
Das Johannesevangelium erklärt, HZNT 6 (Tübingen, J.C.B. Mohr,
1933), p.78.

/27/ See the commentaries, and also E. Malatesta, *St. John's
Gospel 1920-1965. A Cumulative Bibliography of Books and
Periodical Literature on the Fourth Gospel*, Analecta Biblica 32
(Rome, Biblical Institute Press, 1967), Nos. 1321-1428. I stress
again that I exclude none of these possibilities. I am trying to
indicate what I believe is the major theme through the whole
section, but not the only theme.

/28/ It is important to notice that everything happens because of
the Mother of Jesus. The use of the same terms ("Mother of Jesus",
"woman"), the link with "the hour" and her association with the
Beloved Disciple in 19:25-27 lead me to see the Mother of Jesus as
a model of faith for this Evangelist. See especially M.-E. Boismard,
Du Baptême à Cana, pp.154-159. He writes, "Marie ne met pas en doute
la puissance de Jésus-Messie, et la preuve en est qu'elle commande
aussitôt aux serviteurs: 'Faites tout ce qu'il vous dira.' *Avant*
qu'aucun miracle ait été accompli par Jesus, Marie croit parfaite-
ment en sa mission, et sur sa seule parole elle croit qu'il a la,
pouvoir de remédier au manque de vin. Par là,
elle mérite mieux qu'aucun autre cet éloge: 'Heureux ceux qui
croient sans avoir vu" (Jo., 20,29)" (p.159). See also K. Hanhart,
"The Structure...", pp.39-42. Hanhart compares Jn.2:5 with Mary's

"fiat" in Lk.1:35. In the second Cana miracle, the official is
strangely said to "believe" as a result of the sign in v.53. Here
we may have remnants of the older story. I would insist that
the *Johannine* point of view is expressed in v.50: Jesus speaks
and issues a command. The official, without any comment, believes
in the word and does exactly as he is told. This is correct
faith, in no way dependent upon the sign which follows.
/29/ It should be noted that one of the many features of
R.E. Brown's commentary is the care he gives to these transitional
passages. It would need a further study concentrating exclusively
on these passages to prove my case. I believe that the transitional
passages add considerable weight to the case which I am arguing
through my study of the persons involved.
/30/ It is clear from a superficial reading that 2:23-25 is
redactional. The author draws back from the action and makes a
comment. Although it is not as clear, the same thing is happening
in 4:31-38. Here John uses the questions of the disciples over
"food" as his prop for Jesus' reply concerning the whole reasons
for his presence among them. On the redactional nature of this
passage, see U.C. von Wahlde, "A Redactional Technique in the Fourth
Gospel", *CBQ* 38 (1976), pp.520-533, esp. 530-532. See also
B. Lindars, *John,* pp.192-193. Too often the word "redactional" is
taken to mean that the passage is of little importance. In fact,
the opposite is the case. It is precisely in the redactional
passages where the author shows his hand and reveals his overall
plan.
/31/ See F.J. Moloney, *Son of Man,* pp.46-47.
/32/ See R. Schnackenburg, *Johannesevangelium* I, pp.482-488;
B. Lindars, *John*, pp.192-193.
/33/ See E.C. Hoskyns, *Fourth Gospel,* pp.246-247. Hoskyns'
treatment of the whole passage is most helpful. See also, in a
similar vein, I. de la Potterie, "Gesù e i Samaritani", in *Gesù
Verità,* pp.39-53, esp. pp.47-52. I mentioned above (note 10) that
this section of the Gospel points up the difference between the
σημεῖα and the ἔργα of Jesus. Faith based on the σημεῖα was
criticised in the first redactional comment (2:23-25), while the
ἔργον was described as the purpose of Jesus' presence in the
second reflection (4:34).
/34/ A glance at the commentaries will show that vv.37-38 are
somewhat a "crux". I have merely touched on what appears to me as
its solution. Jesus is the one who sows (v.37). The reaping is
done by "others", down to the time of the Johannine Church, which
also "enters into their labor" (v.38).
/35/ See, for this position, and a comprehensive study of the
question, R. Schnackenburg, *Johannesevangelium* I, pp.101-153.

Notice the link between "words" and "works" in 14:10. This link
is never made with the "signs". See R.E. Brown, *John*, p.527;
W. Nicol, *The Semeia in the Fourth Gospel*, pp.116-117.
/36/ This is another serious problem. Who are "the Jews" in
the Fourth Gospel? They must not be identified with a nation,
but within a group (certainly belonging to Judaism of the 1st
century) who refused to accept the revelation of Jesus. John's
use of the term must also be understood in the light of the
Johannine Church's relationship to the Synagogue at the end of
the century. For a useful summary of this discussion, see R.
Leistner, *Antijudaismus im Johannesevangelium, Darstellung des
Problems in der neueren Auslegungsgeschichte und Untersuchung der
Leidensgeschichte*, Theologie und Wirklichkeit 3 (Bern, Herbert
Lang, 1974), pp.17-67. Unfortunately, Leistner concentrates
almost exclusively on the German discussion. See further R.E.
Brown, *John*, lxx-lxxiii; F. Festorazzi, "I Giudei e il Quarto
Evangelo", in *San Giovanni. Atti della XVII Settimana Biblica*
(Brescia, Paideia, 1964), pp.225-260. Festorazzi links the
question with the situation in the Johannine Church very well.
/37/ R.E. Brown, *John*, pp.127 and 530-531, has recognised
various levels of faith in the Fourth Gospel. He would call this
example "hostile blindness". In the light of Jesus' first
attempt to reveal himself to the Samaritan woman (see below), I
would maintain that it is only "the Jews" who are presented as
"hostile", as this was the situation in the Johannine Church.
However, even without any hostility, there can still be blindness,
and thus no faith. On Johannine "faith" see also the excellent
syntheses of J. Painter, *John: Witness and Theologian* (London,
SPCK, 1975), pp.71-85, and R. Schnackenburg, *Johannesevangelium* I,
pp. 508-524.
/38/ For a detailed study of the structure and meaning of Jn.3,
see F.J. Moloney, *Son of Man*, pp.42-51.
/39/ R. Bultmann, *Das Evangelium des Johannes*, Meyer Kommentar
(Göttingen, Vandenhoeck und Ruprecht, 1968[10]), p.95 note 2,
explains this well: "Die Zweideutigkeit johanneischer Begriffe und
Aussagen, die zu Missverständnis führen, liegt nicht darin, dass
eine Vokabel zwei Wortbedeutung hat, sodass dass Missverständnis
eine falsche Bedeutung ergriffe; sondern darin, dass es Begriffe
und Aussagen gibt, die in einem vorläufigen Sinne auf irdische
Sachverhalte, in ihrem eigentlichen Sinne aber auf göttliche
Sachverhalte gehen. Das Missverständnis erkennt die Bedeutung
der Wörter richtig, wähnt aber, dass sie sich in der Bezeichnung
irdischer Sachverhalte erschöpfe".
/40/ R.E. Brown, *John*, p.127, would call this reaction
"intermediary". See also pp.530-531. See J. Painter, *John*, pp.81-83.

/41/ See especially, R. Bultmann, "Die religionsgeschichtliche
Hintergrund des Prologs zum Johannes-Evangelium", in *EUCHARISTĒRION*.
*Studien zur Religion und Literatur des Alten und Neuen Testaments
Herman Gunkel zum 60. Geburtstag dargebracht von seinen Schülern
und Freunden,* FRLANT 19 (Göttingen, Vandehoeck und Ruprecht,
1923) Vol. II, pp.3-26. As is well known, Bultmann argues that
the Johannine discourses (and especially the Prologue) come from
proto-Mandean sources which honoured the Baptist. When John
"christianised" this source, the figure of the Baptist had to be
played down. I do not accept this direct influence of proto-Mandean
hymns, but there is evidence within the New Testament itself of a
Baptist group (see Acts 19:1-7).
/42/ C.H. Dodd, *Historical Tradition in the Fourth Gospel*
(Cambridge, University Press, 1963), p.287. See his discussion of
3:22-30 on pp.279-287. See also M. Black, *An Aramaic Approach to
the Gospels and Acts* (Oxford,Clarendon Press, 1967[3]), pp.146-149.
Black suggests that the whole passage may be "a Greek sayings-group,
translated from Aramaic sayings of the Baptist", and used by John
(p.149).
/43/ R.E. Brown, *John*, p.531 would describe this as "the reaction
of those who believe in Jesus, even without seeing the signs".
See J. Painter, *John*, pp.83-85.
/44/ See R.E. Brown, *John*, pp.164-169; 175-176. Brown claims that
"the *mise en scene* is one of the most detailed in John".
/45/ It is not clear from the term used ($\beta\alpha\sigma\iota\lambda\iota\kappa\acute{o}\varsigma$) whether the man
was an official in Herod's army, as is the centurion ($\acute{\epsilon}\kappa\alpha\tau\acute{o}\nu\tau\alpha\rho\chi o\varsigma$)
in Matt. 8:5-13; Lk.7:1-10, or someone attached to the royal family.
In the latter case he would most likely be a Jew, but in the former
he could be either a Jew or a gentile, as mercenaries were commonly
used. Some scholars point out the difficulty, but do not see it as
significant. See, for example, R. Schnackenburg, *Johannesevangelium*
I, pp.497-498; B. Lindars, *John*, p.202. If I am to pursue my
argument, his being a non-Jew would have been of great importance
for the Evangelist. For this interpretation see J.H. Bernard,
St. John, p.166; E.C. Hoskyns, *Fourth Gospel*, pp.259-261. C.K.
Barrett, *The Gospel according to St. John* (London, SPCK, 1954),
p.206. These scholars come to this position by linking the
Johannine story with the Synoptic "centurion" account, as also
does K. Hanhart. "The Structure...", p.30, who argues that John
is using the Synoptics to compose chs. 1-4. Josephus uses the word
(in the plural) to refer to special forces in Herod's army in
Jewish Antiquities X,123; XV,289; XVII,266.270. 281 etc. Even
here,however, it is not explicitly stated that they were
mercenaries, although the hostile contexts indicate that they may
well have been. A. Schalit, *König Herodes. Der Mann und sein
Werk,* Studia Judaica IV (Berlin, Walter de Gruyter, 1969), pp.167-183,

describes the structure and composition of Herod's army. On
pp.173-183 Schalit shows how the non-Jew Herod, because of his
suspicious nature, gathered non-Jewish elements around himself
for protection, and how he even "planted" ex-soldiers who were
non-Jews in his cities (e.g. Sabaste). Is the βασιλικός one of the
gentile officials in one of Herod's χώρα βασιλική? See, on this,
ibid., pp.702-703. In this light, Ant. XVIII,281 certainly looks
as if it refers to foreign mercenaries, where the βασιλικοί are
mercilessly killed by the strong man Athronges and his four
brothers, along with the Roman soldiers. See further, A. Schalit,
op. cit., pp.181-182 and note 122; p.212, note 250. The least
one can conclude is that there is every possibility that the
βασιλικός was a non-Jew. This movement from a Jewish to a
non-Jewish world was noticed by A. Guilding, The Fourth Gospel and
Jewish Worship. A Study of the Relation of St. John's Gospel to
the Ancient Jewish Lectionary System (Oxford, University Press,
1960), p.50. See also K. Hanhart, "The Structure...", p.29.
However, both Guilding and Hanhart see this section of the Gospel
as a Johannine use of the theology of Acts 1:8, which I regard
as improbable.
/46/ See R.E. Brown, John, pp.166-181; B. Lindars, John, pp.
177-191; C.H. Dodd, Interpretation, pp.311-315. The treatment by
E.C. Hoskyns, Fourth Gospel, pp.233-248, is again very satisfactory.
/47/ R. Schnackenburg, Johannesevangelium I, pp.462-467, continually draws parallels with the Nicodemus passage. This is
certainly the case with 4:16-26, but in vv.7 15, even though one
cannot speak of "hostility" from the woman, "the Jews" of 2:13-22
are paralleled. As I mentioned above (note 37), even though one
cannot speak of "hostility", the woman shows neither readiness nor
capacity to accept "the words" of Jesus. I would again suggest
that the hostility of "the Jews" comes from the actual situation
of the Johannine Church. This was not the case with a missionary
audience, even where there was no faith (see below, note 49).
/48/ J. Marsh, Saint John, Pelican New Testament Commentaries
(Harmondsworth, Penguin Books, 1968), pp.213-214, misses this
point completely, as he breaks the first encounter with the woman
at v.14, and opens the second with v.15.
/49/ If my understanding of this section of the Gospel is correct,
then Jesus' perseverance with the Samaritan woman may also reflect
a missionary situation, in which perseverance was necessary. The
case with "the Jews" was different. If we understand "the Jews"
as "the Synagogue across the street", as Krister Stendhal has
graphically described the situation at the end of the first century
(K. Stendhal The School of St. Matthew [Philadelphia, Fortress
Press, 1968[2]] p.xi), then John writes of a group of people who have

already closed their doors to Jesus (and his missionaries) as a
consequence of the *birkat ha-minim*. See, on this, J.L. Martyn,
History and Theology in the Fourth Gospel (New York, Harper and
Row, 1968). Also important, alongside these historical questions,
is John's technique, well described by R. Schnackenburg,
Johannesevangelium I, p.436: "Dem Evangelisten geht es nicht um
eine pädagogisch-seelsorgerische Einwirkung Jesu auf die Frau,
sondern um die stufenweise Selbstoffenbarung Jesu".
/50/ It is often suggested that the Samaritan idea of the
Messiah or the Ta'eb is reflected here. He was expected to be
(among other things) a prophetic revealer. This appears to be
based on Deut.18:18, and is reflected in the 3-4th century
Samaritan document Memar Markah IV:12. See R. Schnackenburg,
Johannesevangelium I, pp.475-476 and R.E. Brown, *John*, pp.170-173,
for more detail and further bibliography.
/51/ Some scholars see this, but still suggest that the passage
is the proclamation of Jesus as the Messiah. See, for example,
S.A. Panimolle, *Lettura Pastorale*, pp.394-398, and J.H. Bernard,
St. John, p.151: the phrase "if not an assertion of the Speaker's
Divinity, is at any rate an assertion of his Messiahship". This
is only true if we see John's idea of Messiahship as something
which transcends all other expectations - Jewish or Samaritan.
See, on this, F.J. Moloney, "The Fourth Gospel's Presentation...",
pp.245-253, esp. pp.247-248.
/52/ I suggested above (note 22) that the reference to "two days"
in conjunction with v.46 may refer to the "third day" resurrection
motif. There may also be a further hint of perseverance in a
missionary situation.
/53/ One that immediately comes to mind is the argument against
any sort of rearrangement theory.
/54/ Although in my analysis I have only examined the episodes,
and the people involved in them, in the structure I will also
include the various transitional passages. I believe that they
also indicate the same theme, but that case will have to be argued
elsewhere.
/55/ See, for example, O. Cullmann, "Εἶδεν καὶ ἐπίστευσεν. La
vie de Jésus, objet de la 'vue' et de la 'foi' d'après le quatrième
évangile", in *Aux Sources de la Tradition Chrétienne, Mélanges
Goguel* (Neuchâtel, Delachaux & Niestlé, 1950), pp.52-61;
W. Grundmann, "Verständnis und Begegnung des Glaubens im Johannes-
Evangelium", *Kerygma und Dogma* 6 (1960), pp.131-154.
/56/ R.E. Brown, *John*, pp.530-531.
/57/ Brown cites 6:69; 9:38 and 11:40 as examples of this arrival
at true faith through signs. I think that a case could be made
against this suggestion. 6:69 must be understood in the light of

6:68; 9:38 is not really the reaction to a miracle, but to Jesus himself, presented as the revealer in vv.35 and 37 (see F.J. Moloney, *The Son of Man*, pp.154-159), while 11:40 places the act of faith *before* the seeing of the glory.

/58/ R.E. Brown, *John*, p.531.

/59/ D. Deeks, "The Structure of the Fourth Gospel", p.126.

Studia Biblica 1978: II, 215-218

The Beloved Disciple Again

M.B. Moreton,
The Rectory,
Middleton Cheney,
Banbury, Oxon, England.

References in the Fourth Gospel to the 'beloved disciple' or to the 'other disciple' form a complex question, and I do not propose to make an overall review of the problem. But two particular instances have forced themselves upon my attention: the first of these references, in the story of the Last Supper, in 13:18-30, and the last of them in the proto-Gospel, in the story of the running to the tomb, in 20:2-10.

* * *

First, the running to the tomb. This passage in John has obvious affinities with the dubious and now mostly-unread verse in Luke, 24:12: *But Peter rose and ran to the tomb; stooping and looking in, he saw the linen cloths by themselves; and he went home, wondering at that had happened.*

Canon John Drury, in a recent review in the *Journal of Theological Studies* /1/, rightly warns against any assumption that Luke and John rely on common sources, rather than allowing for the possibility that one knew the other. For my immediate purpose here, I do not think that the form of the relationship is critical. Indeed, 'one knowing the other' might even sharpen my point. Yet, given any faith in the reality of 'oral tradition', I think it more reasonable to suppose that an evangelist knew some branch of a pluriform oral tradition than to suppose that he was dependent on a particular crystallization of that tradition in the more restricted circulation of another written Gospel, and himself introduced considerable changes in order to make the tradition suit his own purposes. My knowledge of specialized New Testament studies is, I admit, nearly all at second-hand, but I do not cease to be astonished at how reluctant the critics of the old solutions to the synoptic problem seem to be to abandon the basis of documentary hypotheses. But to return to this particular instance, my *feeling* is that Luke (or deutero-Luke) and John are

here separately dependent on earlier tradition, rather than that
either John knew a version of Luke with this doubtful verse in it,
or that he knew the verse before it was interpolated, or that
either Luke or the interpolator knew John.

Of the 'other disciple' in this running to the tomb, John says
that he προεδραμεν... και παρακυψας... βλεπει... τα οθονια, and
then, of them both, απηλθον προς αυτους. Luke says of Peter that
he εδραμεν και παρακυψας βλεπει τα οθονια... και απηλθεν προς
εαυτον. The verbal coincidences are considerable; but the
important point is that Luke's single disciple, Peter, is
identified by these coincidences not with John's Peter, but with
ὁ ἀλλος μαθητης.

The conclusion seems inescapable, that ὁ ἀλλος μαθητης was
Peter's *alter ego*. Perhaps this originated in a simple duplication,
just as in Matthew one blind man and one angel turned into two of
each. The converse process, two disciples being merged into one as
the tale was retold hardly seems likely; especially if the
distinctive characters of the two disciples had already been worked
out.

What then, we must ask, is the purpose of John's version? I
suggest that it is not a glorification of this 'other disciple'.
His 'seeing and believing' is not set in any necessary contrast to
Peter's failure to believe; rather, it is but a natural and minor
development of the 'seeing' and 'wondering' that we find in Luke's
version; and it may have been so developed even before the duplication
of the disciples. As the tale stands, both in itself and in
context, this 'belief' can be of no final nature: as such it would
be contradicted immediately by 'As yet they did not know the
scripture', and it would also make the remainder of the proto-
Gospel (i.e. the story of Thomas) redundant. The story has not
acquired a polished finish; it has been developed, perhaps over-
developed, in an *ad hoc* manner, and its joints are showing.

                            *   *   *

The story of the identification of the betrayer at the Last
Supper lacks conviction in any of the Gospels, but in none of them
is this more marked than in John. Why did the disciples fail to
take the hint from the giving of the morsel? And more to our
immediate point, why didn't Peter ask his question directly?

The introduction here of 'another disciple', εἱς ἐκ των
μαθητων, is achieved in a rather back-handed fashion. There is no

straight-forward ὁ μαθητης ἀγαπητος. And that ὃν ἠγαπα ὁ 'Ιησους
is put in almost as an afterthought, a development of the tale
rather than something basic to it.

Bultmann's exegesis /2/ of this whole passage (which I take
to include 13:18f, *He who ate my bread* has lifted his heel
against me', as well as the undoubtedly fresh start with ταυτα
ειπων in 13:21) leaves our two questions unanswered. That the
disciples persistently misunderstood Jesus's words is no
sufficient explanation of this particular instance in vv. 26-30.
And even if, with Bultmann, we take out vv.28f ('Now no-one...
knew why [Jesus] said this. Some thought that... [he] was
telling [Judas], "Buy what we need for the feast"') as 'one of the
evangelist's characteristic comments', this still leaves an
original contradiction between question, answer, and understanding,
that is wholly incredible.

I suggest that it may be possible to argue that John has
conflated two separate stories, one concerning the question, and
anther giving a quite different account, in which there was no
prophecy of betrayal, let alone any questioning as to the identity
of the betrayer. Instead, Jesus' foreknowledge was shown only in
the private word of command to Judas, accompanied by the giving of
the morsel. If this is so, then the real difficulty in the
passage is seen to lie in John's own development in v.26a, Jesus'
answer: 'It is he to whom I shall give this morsel...'.

This analysis disposes of only one of our problems; but it
serves to emphasize the independence of the second, that of
Peter's indirectness.

The verses which speak of the 'other disciple', vv.23-25, may
be seen as a parallel to Mark 14:19, *They* began to say to him...
"Is it I?"'. This is a question whose answer seems to develop
with the telling, so that John's v.26a is best seen as a parallel
development to Matthew's "You have said so", but one that has lost
all its ambiguity.

A comparison of vv.23-25 with the synoptic accounts suggests
that in the earliest tradition there was a direct question. So
what then has happened here? As in our first instance, no real
emphasis falls on this beloved disciple. Here, Peter is Naaman,
the other is merely Gehazi, the go-between. His function in the
story is surely nothing other than to introduce a certain
distance, a reverential separation, either between the prince of
the apostles and his Lord, or between an earthly and traitorous

Peter and the heavenly Master.

* * *

Thus these two passages do have something in common. We have
found sufficient reason to think that the beloved disciple may be
an insertion in both of them, following an expansion of the earlier
forms of the tales. This reinforces the common observation that,
except in 19:26f, the beloved disciple and Peter go hand in hand.
The exception is, of course, a problem - but even that passage is
not wholly beyond explanation by some association with Peter. In
the Gospels he frequently appears as a representative of the Church,
a role often said to be played by the beloved disciple in the
Fourth Gospel, and nowhere more strikingly than in this exceptional
passage, 19:26f.

I submit, therefore, that the figure of the beloved disciple
in the Fourth Gospel is basically a device, intended to correct a
growing reverence for Peter; just as in Matthew the statements
exalting Peter are usually accompanied by others showing his
weakness and failure. And yet it is tempting to go beyond the
evidence in asking to whom 21:24 refers, 'This is the disciple who
is bearing witness...': for the Fourth Gospel is the most Peter-
centred of them all.

NOTES

/1/   *JTS* XXVIII.2, October 1977, p.551.
/2/   *The Gospel of John*, Oxford 1971, pp.479-86.

Studia Biblica 1978: II, 219-226

The Cross and the Revelation of Jesus as
ἐγώ εἰμι in the Fourth Gospel (John 8.28)

Rev. J.E. Morgan-Wynne
Regent's Park College
Oxford.

I

If, as I believe, the lifting up of the Son of Man in Jn.
8.28 refers primarily to Jesus' death, then this verse contains a
problem which most commentaries and monographs seem to ignore, or
at best lightly touch and pass on.

First, then, let me seek to substantiate the view that the
lifting up of Jn. 8.28 refers to the death of Jesus /1/:

(a)   Jesus says, "When you lift up the Son of Man...". Elsewhere
in John ὑφοῦν is used in the passive voice; only here is the
active voice used. It is natural to take this in the sense "When
you bring about the crucifixion of the Son of Man..."; that is,
the reference is to Jesus' death in the first place /2/.

(b)   If we look back to the first occurrence of ὑφοῦν in John at
3.14, we find that the reference to the Son of Man's being lifted
up is in the first place to the cross - only so can the analogy to
the lifting up of the serpent on the pole by Moses make sense /3/.

(c)   If we look forward to the final occurrence of the verb at
12.32-33, we find that the evangelist adds a comment to the
assertion, "If I be lifted up from the earth, I will draw all men
to myself". His comment runs "Now he said this in order to
signify *by what manner of death* (ποίῳ θανάτῳ) *he should die*".
Here, then, on the threshold of the passion, the evangelist in
unambiguous fashion has sought to focus his readers' attention on
the death, on the cross of Jesus /4/.

This does not, of course, preclude a double-entendre - namely
that, paradoxically, the death is the means of his exaltation, his
lifting up in a metaphorical sense /5/. What it does mean is that
we ought not to glide off the cross into talking about the

resurrection and exaltation when ὑψοῦν occurs in the fourth gospel, as is often the case /6/.

In the light of this brief survey of the evidence we may maintain that the primary reference of 8.28 is to the cross.

II

Secondly, we turn to examine ἐγώ εἰμι. R. Bultmann argued that this should be expanded with "the Son of Man" /7/. His arguments were:
(i)   ἐγω cannot be subject and predicate.
(ii)   Why would the Jews ask, "Who are you?", since ἐγώ εἰμι would be gross blasphemy on its own.

E.N. Freed maintained that 8.28 was parallel to 4.25f where by Jesus' own admission he is the Christ (to which 9.35-37 is a variant form).

R. Schnackenburg attempted to counter this as follows: /8/
(i)   The ἐγώ εἰμι of 8.28 connects up with that of 8.24.
(ii)   Jesus never says directly, "I am the Son of Man", in Jn. (perhaps John held firmly to the knowledge that Jesus had only spoken of the Son of Man in the third person).
(iii) The Son of Man is linked to a definite complex of ideas, especially that of exaltation and glorification, and will be introduced here ad vocem ὑψοῦν.

The link with 8.24 seems to me to be decisive /9/. Bultmann's second point seems a strange piece of "historicising". The question, "Who are you?", is a means whereby the evangelist can build up to the important statement of 8.28. Freed's reference to 4.25f and 9.35-37 is interesting but not necessarily decisive - the evangelist was not bound to follow one particular build-up and he must be allowed a freedom to modify and develop as he saw fit.

Accordingly, we assume that ἐγώ εἰμι should be taken absolutely and that it recalls the formula of Yahweh's self revelation, Yahweh's autokerygma, in Second Isaiah /10/. The phrase ἐγώ εἰμι embodies the claim that Jesus is in some way the manifestation of God and that he has the right to use the divine self-revelatory formula /12/.

III

If these two positions are correct, then our problem is this:
how in John's thought is the *cross* the revelation of Jesus as the
divine presence? How can the main clause, "You will know that
ἐγώ εἰμι" be derived from "When you lift up the Son of Man"? How
does the death of Jesus reveal the truth of his claim to be the
manifestation of God? F.J. Moloney wrote, "For the fourth gospel,
the death was a proof that Jesus as 'I am'" /13/ - but why? /14/.

Before we try to elucidate this question, let us note that
the remainder of 8.28 plus v.29 asserts the unity of the Father
and Jesus. Jesus' teaching is not done on his own authority but
reproduces what the Father has taught him. "He who sent me is
with me: He has not left me alone, because I always do what is
pleasing to him". Jesus' union with the Father is grounded in
his obedience to the Father. He always does what pleases his
Sender (cf. 4.34 etc. and 8.16 where Jesus asserts that his
judgment is true because μόνος οὐκ εἰμι, ἀλλ' ἐγώ καὶ ὁ πέμψας με,
i.e. there is a continual union between himself and God).

The cross, then, will not reveal something new but will
further reveal what has been true of the ministry as a whole /15/
- that Jesus is ἐγώ εἰμι and that his union with the Father,
grounded in God's will and Jesus' obedience, entitles Jesus to
make this claim.

IV

I now want to bring 16.31-32 into the discussion to elucidate
the problem which lies behing 8.28 /16/.

16.31-32 follows a kind of confession of faith by the
disciples: "We believe that you have come forth from God". Jesus
replies, "Do you now believe? Look, the hour is coming and has
come when each of you will be scattered to his own home and you
will leave me alone."

The evangelist seems to emphasise this aloneness of Jesus at
the cross, and indeed he builds up to this by showing what we may
call a "sifting process" through which the inadequacy of human
faith before the cross becomes manifest.

(i) 2.23-25. Many in Jerusalem believed because of his signs
but there was something unsatisfactory in a faith based on signs
alone (cf. 4.48), so Jesus did not entrust himself to them.

(ii)   6.60 ff. Many leave off following him after the Bread of
Life Discourse.
(iii) 8.31 ff. Jews who had believed on Jesus turn against him,
make many sharp accusations against him in the dialogue and wish
in the end to stone him to death.
(iv)   12.36b ff. We have the depressing summary of the results of
Jesus' ministry by the evangelist, backed up by the two Isaianic
quotations (53.1 and 6.9ff) and followed by the comment that,
though many of the ruling classes believed, they did not openly
confess Jesus as the messiah for fear of excommunication from the
synagogue.
(v)   13.1 ff. Jesus is pictured as concentrating on his own, but
soon one of these goes out to betray him (13.30), another's denial
of him is predicted (13.38), and now, at 16.32, it is said that
the rest will abandon him and will leave Jesus on his own to face
death /17/.

        Jesus is, then, humanly speaking, on his own /18/. As he
faces the cross, he is left on his own. 16.32b corrects this
stark picture: "Yet [adversative καί] I am not alone, *because the
Father is with me*". The same phrase μετ'ἐμοῦ ἐστιν is used here
as in 8.29 /19/. At the cross the union of Jesus and the Father
is more evident than ever in John's view /20/. The desertion of
the disciples only serves to off-set with sharper relief the union
between Jesus and the Father, a union based on the will of the
Father and Jesus' obedience /21/.

        For the fourth evangelist the cross is clearly willed by God:
   (i)   the hour texts (2.4; 7.30; 8.20; 12.23, 27; 13.1; 17.1)
point to this.
   (ii)   δεῖ of 3.14 grounds the cross similarly in the divine will.
   (iii) According to 10.17f the power to lay down his life, and to
take it again, is a command which Jesus has received from his
Father (cf.14.30-31).
   (iv)   At the arrest Jesus speaks of the cup which the Father has
given him to drink.
   (v)   The OT quotations in the passion story, while probably
belonging to a pre-Johannine account, are taken over by John and
point to God's will (13.18; 19.24,28, 36-7).

        Jesus now goes to that cross in obedience to the Father. It
will be recalled that he put aside the momentary desire to escape
the hour (12.27) and that he rose from supper to depart and
encounter the prince of this world so that the world might know
that he loved the Father and that he continually did what the
Father commanded (14.31).

As in his earthly ministry he only said and did what the
Father gave him to say and do, *so in his death he does what is
willed by the Father and so shows his oneness with the Father.*
Because of the failure of "his own", Jesus' oneness with the
Father comes across with tremendous emphasis in 16.32. Precisely
because of this oneness between Jesus and the Father, the claim
ἐγώ εἰμι is justified. The cross reveals the validity of the
claim. The cross is the proof that Jesus is ἐγώ εἰμι.

16.32 provides the clue by which we may understand the two
halves of 8.28.

V

Finally, I wish to make two brief points.

(i) Of whom is John thinking when he wrote "you will know..."?
I do not think that this presents too great a difficulty. What
is asserted is that true knowledge, and we may legitimately add
true faith, comes after the cross. There is fairly clear
evidence that some of John's church had belonged to the synagogue
/22/. For John, then, the cross had proved the means of revealing
the true nature of Jesus to at least some Jews /23/.

(ii) Why does the evangelist stress Jesus' being left on his own
at 16.32, when he goes on to record the presence of the Beloved
Disciple at the foot of the cross? The issue of the Beloved
Disciple is, of course, a thorny one in Johannine research. I can
only baldly state here that I think that (a) John is asserting
that all the disciples left Jesus and he interprets this
christologically in 16.32; (b) in the scene at the foot of the
cross he is speaking a message to his church which concerns the
significance for the church of the Beloved Disciple who had
truly seen (spiritually) the significance of the cross as the
saving event for mankind and had borne his witness to it (cf.19.
34b-35). In addition he thereby also secured the continuity
between the disciples of the ministry and the church of the post-
Easter era.

NOTES

/1/ B. Lindars, The Gospel of John (N.C.B.), London, 1972, p.
157: "To 'lift up'... becomes almost a technical term for
crucifixion, while retaining the notion of exaltation". F.J.
Moloney, The Johannine Son of Man, Rome, 1976, p.62: "It is clear

that this moment [i.e. of the cross] is uppermost in John's mind
when he uses ὑψωθῆναι". W. Thüsing, Die Erhöhung and
Verherrlichung Jesu im Johannesevangelium (N.A. 21), Münster,
1970[2], p.12, goes so far as to say, "The only content of the
Johannine ὑψωθῆναι which can be ascertained with certainty is,
therefore, the crucifixion of Jesus".

/2/   Among commentators who accept a reference to the cross
(wholly or in part) at 8.28 are Lagrange (239), Strathmann (148),
Hoskyns-Davey (337), Bultmann (350), Barrett (284), Wikenhauser
(173), Lightfoot (191), Marsh (359), Schnackenburg (II. 396),
Brown (i. 351), Lindars (322), Fenton (100), Sanders-Mastin (225);
cf. too Moloney, op. cit., pp.136, 139; J.T. Forestell, The Word
of the Cross (A.B. 57), Rome, 1974, p.64.

/3/   Among commentators who accept a reference to the cross
(wholly or in part) at 3.14f. are Schlatter (95-96), Lagrange (81),
Hoskyns-Davey (217), Bultmann (152[4]), Barrett (178), Brown (I.
145-6), Lindars (157), Sanders-Mastin (128); cf. Moloney, op. cit.,
pp.62, 135 (he argues against any inclusion of the idea of the
ascension); Forestell, op. cit., p.62; T. Müller, Das
Heilsgeschehen im Johannesevangelium, Zurich, 1961, p.61.

/4/   Among scholars who accept a reference to the cross (wholly
or in part) at 12.32 are Schlatter (272), Lagrange (335), Hoskyns-
Davey (426), Bultmann (ET 432), Barrett (355-6), Brown (I. 468),
Lindars (434), Sanders-Mastin (297); Moloney (62, 182-4),
Forestell (63).

/5/   See the quotation from Lindars in note 1 and compare R.
Schnackenburg I. 396 (ET) where he says that "Jn sees the cross
itself as 'exaltation'... For Jn the Pauline 'scandal of the
cross' is not overcome only by the subsequent resurrection but by
the majesty and saving power of the cross itself... Though the
'exaltation' also means the crucifixion, the crucifixion itself,
in the Johannine perspective, is already so rich in theological
meaning that it at once implies the 'glorification'". Lagrange
(81) wrote "La croix était déjà pour Jésus une exaltation".
Brown, who believes that the return to the Father includes
crucifixion-resurrection and ascension, nonetheless says (I. 145):
"The phrase 'to be lifted up' refers to Jesus' death on the
cross". Alan Richardson (73) is also worth quoting: "The
exaltation of Christ is his crucifixion; the cross is the throne
of the King of Israel. The expression 'lifting up' ('exaltation')
becomes in the fourth gospel a technical expression for the
crucifixion".

/6/   E.g. Schlatter (211), Wikenhauser (174), Fenton (100),
Richardson (119), Forestell (64, 197).

/7/   Das Evangelium des Johannes, Göttingen, 1941, p.248(5),
265 (4,7) (ET Oxford, 1971, 327(5), 348(6), 349(3). He had been

anticipated by J.H. Bernard (I.C.C.), Edinburgh, 1928, II. 303.
He has been followed by Widenhauser (173), Lindars (322), and E.N.
Freed, The Son of Man in the Fourth Gospel, J.B.L. 86 (1967), pp.
405-6. Lindars writes: "The Passion will confirm what Jesus has
already said about his identity... It will not only be apparent
that Jesus is the Son of Man (Bernard), or rather the Agent of
Salvation in its fullest sense, as indicated when the phrase was
used in verse 24". (Cf too, The Son of Man in the Johannine
Christology, Christ and Spirit in the N.T., ed. B. Lindars and
S.S. Smalley, Cambridge, 1973, p.53).

/8/   II, p.256.

/9/   So also Moloney, op. cit., p.138: "To make 'the Son of Man'
the predicate of v.28a would cause the loss of the obviously
intended repetition".

/10/ See H. Zimmermann, Das absolute ἐγώ εἰμι als
neutestamentliche Offenbarungsformel, B.Z. 4 (1960), pp.54-69,
266-76; R.E. Brown I, Appendix IV; J.T. Forestell, op. cit., p.47;
"The context of the absolute ἐγώ εἰμι in Jn. 8.28 and 13.19 is
exactly similar to the usage in Dt-Is... [It] identifies Jesus in
his person as the revelation of Yahweh to men". Cf. too S.S.
Smalley, The Johannine Son of Man Sayings, N.T.S. 15 (1968-69), p.
295.

/12/ C.H. Dodd, Interpretation of the Fourth Gospel, Cambridge
1953, p.248: "The solemn affirmation ἐγω εἰμι, here as elsewhere,
is an echo of the ἐγώ εἰμι, אני הוא, but which in the Second
Isaiah Jehovah declares himself as the Self Existent, and is to be
taken as declaring that in Christ the Self-Existent is fully
revealed". Cf. also p.377.

/13/ Op. cit., p.137.

/14/ Müller, op. cit., pp. 34f wrote: "The basis for knowing
certainly lies in Jesus' death... The reason why Jesus' death
means the decisive hour for such knowledge will in truth not be
said here."

/15/ Cf. B. Lindars, op. cit., p.322: "The Passion will confirm
what Jesus has already said about his identity... The Passion will
thus reveal the true relationship between Jesus and God"; but he
does not elucidate the point. Sanders-Mastin, op. cit., pp.225f
comment: "The death of Jesus will demonstrate that his present
actions and words are not the expression of his own self-will but
of his submission to the will of God (cf. 5.19; 6.38; 7.16)".

/16/ B. Lindars, op. cit., p.322 is the only commentator known to
me to have noticed the link with 16.32 (though the Nestle text has
a marginal reference to 16.32 at 8.29, while the B.F.B.S.[2] has in
the margin of 16.32 a reference to 8.29 but not vice versa!):
"The fact that Jesus is not alone even in the darkness of the
cross will be emphasised in 16.32". Lagrange (433) on 16.32

merely noted a link with 8.29.

/17/ G.B. Caird, The Will of God. II In the Fourth Gospel, E.T.
LXXII (1960-61), p. 116, has written: "...we find a large group of
initial believers, which gradually melts away and finally
disappears, leaving Jesus alone... The manifestations of God in
the life and ministry of Jesus *have not produced a saving faith
even in his most intimate friends*" (italics mine).

    Writers have often represented the history of salvation
diagrammatically like two triangles, one on top of the other,
beginning with Israel at Sinai and narrowing down to the meeting
of the two points, representing Jesus on his own at the cross,
and then widening out into the church, the new Israel. This is
very like John's picture of Jesus on his own (16.32).

/18/ There is surely a link between this emphasis and the grain
of wheat picture at 12.24, where the grain remains on its own
(μόνος) unless it falls into the earth and dies, and then it bears
much fruit.

/19/ B. Lindars, op. cit., p.514: "The vocabulary (i.e. of 16.32)
has a close parallel in 8.29".

/20/ Thus we believe that R.E. Brown's comment, (I, p.146), "The
justice of Jesus' claim to the divine name 'I AM' ... was scarcely
evident at the crucifixion" (made by Brown to support his claim
that the crucifixion does not exhaust the concept of being lifted
up), proves invalid. The death of Jesus did prove the correctness
of the use of 'I AM" - proved it, that is, to the eye of faith.

/21/ Cf. Sanders-Mastin, op. cit., pp.225-6, comment that Jesus'
death is the supreme example of his obedience to the Father.

/22/ Cf. J.L. Martyn, History and Theology in the Fourth Gospel,
New York-Evanston, 1968.

/23/ Cf. Hoskyns-Davey, p.337: "The thought here is of those Jews
who were converted to... the church"; Barrett (284); Fenton (100);
Marsh (360); Moloney, op. cit., p.137: "If they [the Jews] wish to
be saved from their sins, they can still find that salvation in
the cross of Christ whom they themselves have crucified".

Studia Biblica 1978: II, 227-241

Limits to the Understanding of John in Christian Theology

Joseph Stephen O'Leary,
5 rue des Irlandais,
Paris 5e,
France.

I propose to study the use made of St. John's Gospel in the
De Trinitate of St. Hilary of Poitiers as a minor contribution
towards an understanding of the history of Christian thought. The
value of the exercise will lie in the remarks of a methodological
and speculative kind which it occasions and I shall have to deal
gingerly with the exegetical alternatives whose baffling
multiplicity, in the case of the Johannine text, can make
such general reflections seem a premature venture. There are
three reasons why I may presume to do this with some confidence:
(i) Many of the exegetical difficulties may be seen as due to an
error of method, in that adequate attention is not first given to
the literary integrity of the text as we have it. How many
ingenious theories of dislocation have been thought necessary to
explain the obscurities of John 10, for example, yet when a literary
analysis reveals the rigour and clarity of its composition it is
found that the text itself explains these obscurities far better
than any such hypothesis. (ii) If literary sensitivity can thus
supply a control for the speculation of exegetes, perhaps a further
similar one may be found in the recognition of the contemplative
rhythm and purpose of the Gospel. C.K. Barrett has observed
that Johannine thought does not move in straight lines and it is
to be regretted that many exegetes continue to behave nonetheless
as if it must be made to do so. I trust it will be possible to
indicate in this paper a coherence in Johannine thought every bit
as satisfying, seen in the light of its contemplative intention, as
the coherence of discursive logic. (iii) Even if the models
proposed in this paper should turn out to be slightly caricatural
representations of the thought of John or Hilary, this would not
undermine their necessity and validity. If the task of grasping
Christian tradition as a history of *thought* is ever to be
accomplished, and if theology is even to assume its own history in

the way that the philosophical tradition has done in Hegel and
Heidegger, then one must cut the Gordian knots of exegesis and
resist the terrorism of scrupulous erudition which would reduce
the history of Christian thought to a collection of atomised and
uninterpreted facts. Armed with the best hypotheses one can find,
tested again and again against the facts as historical research
reveals them, one must proceed to a critical and theological
interrogation of history under pain of being crushed by it. And
that unpleasant fate can take one of two forms: one can be crushed
by history into an unthinking conservatism, where past words
usurp the place of present realities, or one can succumb to
historical relativism, in which history becomes a nightmare of
uncertainty from which it is impossible to awake. If faith is to
build on history and at the same time not to be its slave it must
have the courage to interpret it - hence the need of models and
hypotheses which are bound to be simplifications. Of course one
can ignore history altogether - a dash of Scripture and a dash of
'experience' goes a long way - and I do not intend to argue here,
what I feel strongly to be the case, that this is a form of
theological suicide and that 'only through tradition, tradition is
conquered'.

        One of the problems of Christian thought is the unsolved
riddle of its origins. For one seeks in vain amid the misty
philosophy of German theologians or the elusive personalism of
French ones for an adequate account of what is meant by Revelation.
The account of the matter given in Scripture itself and repeated
by Church authorities is deserving of a closer phenomenological
study than it has yet received, but cannot be expected to
provide the resolution of our perplexity. The absolute distinction
we tend to make between Scripture considered as Revelation and
everything else as mere commentary operates in practice, in any
case, as a source of mystification in theology, causing us to
under-estimate the value and originality of every creative moment
in the history of Christian thought and to forget that religious
insight is a perennial source of new and important visions of
truth, whether they pass as Revelation or not. When subsequent
tradition is seen as developing under the sign of some kind of
original sin - the Hellenisation of dogma or the rise of 'early
Catholicism' - in exile from the lost paradise of Scriptural
Revelation, it is clear that the attempt to understand history has
been deflected in a mythic sense by the influence of a theological
a priori. I shall thus put the whole question of Revelation in
brackets and consider the dialogue between John and Hilary as one
between two religious thinkers in the same tradition, which is

also ours, and I shall also decline to consider the status of
the Nicene dogma presiding over Hilary's work. Insofar as this
paper touches on the truth of Hilary's thought it will be in a
merely phenomenological sense, the somewhat schematic character
of his vision of Christ being contrasted with the fullness and
immediacy of John's, and the question 'by what authority?' will
be eschewed, though it is in the end probably the fundamental
question for a history of Christian thought.

The central idea of Hilary's work is the eternal generation
of the Son, implying a unity of nature between Father and Son and
expounded in opposition to the Sabellian misinterpretation of this
unity and the Arian denial of it. Hilary's processes of
composition reveal his literary apprenticeship as exegete of
St. Matthew, for most of the work consists of commentary on
scriptural passages, particularly from the Fourth Gospel. Hilary
finds a lucid correspondence between the biblical text and his
dogmatic convictions so that his reading of John is one which
almost determines in advance what the evangelist has to say. It
is the mark of our inability to espouse the elusive horizon of
Johannine vision that the same can be said of all other theological
readings of John, from Origen to Bultmann. But side by side with
his dogmatic clarities Hilary develops a rhetoric of nescience and
silence, an apophatic current which is to be seen, no doubt, as an
attempt to recapture the sense of mystery which his reading of the
scriptural text has lost. Now in John there is no need of such
apophatic developments. The mystery is in the words of Jesus, not
behind them in the depths of divine infinity; it is revealed not
hidden. John 1:18a - 'no one has ever seen God' - casts no
aspersions on the revelatory adequacy of the words of Jesus and
does not suggest that they need to be supplemented by a 'negative
theology' which would bring to awareness the distance between
speech about God and the reality of God. Rather are they a
guarantee of the unsurpassable plenitude of the knowledge of God
conveyed by the Word Incarnate. It is in Him - not behind or
beyond Him - that the unseen God is 'made known' (1:18b). 'He who
has seen me has seen the Father' (14:9). The apophatic streak
indicates the bad conscience of dogmatic theology which has lost
the contemplative integrity of biblical language. In Aquinas and
Augustine this negative moment is thought out in a dialectical
unity with the positive exposition of doctrine, whereas in Hilary
such lucidity has not yet been attained and the evocations of the
'infinity of faith' (DT I 12), which alone can embrace the hidden
depths of God through its generous acceptance of the mighty
paradoxes of Revelation, come as a recurrent afterthought rather

230 Studia Biblica 1978: II

than as an intrinsic element of the doctrinal argument. The
dissociation which one can detect in germ here comes to fruition
in decadent theology where a mute nescience becomes the preserve
of mystics while dogmatics, having run through all its possibilities
of conceptual play, soon discovers it has lost the art of thinking
about God. Already in Hilary's stress on the unity of nature
between Father and Son we feel we are at a tangent to the religious
meaning of John's text and in his sense of mystery we feel that a
compensatory reflex is at work.

I think that one can also detect the beginnings of another
dissociation, a split between subjective (fides qua) and objective
(fides quae) in that the content of faith tends to present itself
as an objective bloc over against the subjective apprehension of
the believer. This can be seen in Hilary's so objective summary
of John 1:1-14, which also shows that the subjective-objective
split is connected with the Latin language. Latin relative to
Hebrew or Greek is an exophrastic rather than endophrastic
language, i.e. it presents the speaker with prefabricated formulae
in which anything he wants to say has already been almost said for
him, whereas an endophrastic tongue provides plastic roots which
the speaker shapes creatively as he forms sentences. Listen now
to the Johannine prologue as the Latin language synthesises it into
a set of formulae:

Proficit mens ultra naturalis sensus intelligentiam et plus
de Deo quam opinabatur edocetur. Creatorem enim suum Deum
ex Deo discit. Verbum Deum et apud Deum in principio esse
intelligit.. Venientem quoque in sua a suis non receptum,
recipientes autem sub fidei suae merito in Dei filios
profecisse cognoscit, non ex complexu carnis neque ex
conceptu sanguinis neque ex corporum voluptate, sed ex
Deo natos. Deinde Verbum carnem factum et habitasse in
nobis et gloriam conspectam eius, quae tanquam unigeniti a
Patre sit perfecta cum gratia et veritate (DT I 10).

Note first of all how the weight of John's diction, the grandest in
the biblical repertory, is lost in this transcription. The solemn
emphasis that falls on the words *doxa, charis* and *aletheia* is
trivialised by the lightness of 'et gloriam conspectam eius' and
'perfecta cum gratia et veritate'. And the great paradox of John
1:14 is quite taken for granted in the summarising accusative
'deinde Verbum carnem factum'. Next consider how the contemplative
rhythm and perspective of, for example, 1:1-2 are obliterated when
these verses are taken as conveying doctrinal information. John

began his Gospel in a Jewish key with three contemplative moments causing us to dwell successively on the creative divine Word in its primordiality (memories of Genesis 1:1), in its intimate connection with God and in its own divine status. 1:2 marks a pause as if to keep us from passing too quickly over these difficult and near inconceivable themes for contemplation. The language is hymnic and mythic and no doubt John is well aware that what he presents for contemplation is something that can never be clearly grasped; it is much less accessible than 'incarnate' utterances like 'I am the way' or 'I am the bread of life'. Yet it is necessary to hold this moment of contemplation in order to register the import of the climax at 1:14. We are not being supplied with information but we are being initiated into a contemplative exercise whose movement should bring us to a renewed vision of Jesus of Nazareth. Perhaps the paradoxical identity stated in 1:14 - 'the Word became flesh' - all the more paradoxical in that the word 'became' has been used as the mark of the creaturely realm up to this point in contrast to the 'was' which indicates the Logos in his primordial being, perhaps this astonishing intuition should be regarded as abolishing the perspectives that led up to it rather than as adding a new fact to those already established. Parallels to such a procedure could be sought in 14:6, 'I am the way', which both completes and bewilderingly alters the meaning of the more dualistic representations of 14:1-5, or in 10:30, 'I and the Father are one', a similar startling emergence of identity where the parabolic language of 10:1-18 had worked with a more naive model of the relation of Father and Son. For John each new recognition of what God is like seems to knock from under our feet the ladder that helped us attain it. Some such theory - I put this forward only *gymnastikos* - may yield the key to the coherence and effectiveness of Johannine discourse.

But to return to Hilary's reading of 1:1-14, a third criticism that may be made of it is that the objectifying overview that allows Hilary to summarise with such elegant wordplay as in 'venientem quoque in sua a suis non receptum', which quite mistakes the function of Johannine repetition as if it were a mere turn of style, and that allows him to make the whole content of the prologue the object of such verbs as 'discit', 'cognoscit', 'intelligit', that this 'bird's eye view' of the economy of salvation afforded by a dogmatic stance puts the believer outside the events he accepts, so that instead of accepting the invitation to join the 'we' which is the subject of the prologue's vision - derived perhaps from a communal hymn - Hilary reads it as a message in the third person and then, only subsequently, subjectively

appropriates it in the first person singular. Scripture is as
a musical score that is lit up from within only in performance,
i.e. in the liturgy. Here is another possible clue to the
purpose and nature of the Johannine text - read it in the third
person singular rather than in the first person plural and you
put yourself outside the circle into which it invites you.

It may be objected that this objectification is only Hilary's
way of representing the first impression of a reader who is a
stranger to the text. It is true that the next paragraph (DT I 11)
gives a more participative reading of the text, in which Hilary
insists on the salvific import of each of its affirmations, in a
series of dogmatic notes. The heresies he wards off here are seen
as excluded by the wording of the text - this almost Rabbinic idea
of the all-sufficiency of the Bible, seen as magically pre-containing
the answers to future theological problems, is still a source of
mystification in theology. The first three heresies have to do
with the status of the Son who is neither (i) a second god nor (ii)
a lesser being of a different nature nor (iii) coming after the
Father. Two other heresies concern the reality of the Incarnation
which is (i) an Incarnation of the Word and of none other and (ii)
in our flesh, so that he is 'in suis perfectus et verus in nostris'.
Thus is secured the hinge on which our salvation turns. This
correlation of dogma and salvation certainly offers Hilary a way of
interiorising the Johannine text and of reproducing in his own
language its message: 'divini sacramenti doctrinam mens laeta
suscipit, in Deum proficiens per carnem et in novam nativitatem per
fidem vocata', but one suspects that this dogmatic mediation tends
to transfer the focus of hope from the loving action of God to the
security of fixed metaphysical schemata. When these become the
primary object of faith, or are undialectically equiparated with
the primary object of faith, the Johannine severity towards the
unbelief of the Jews becomes hard to understand and the Johannine
meaning of faith becomes opaque. The leap of faith is interpreted
in too narrowly dogmatic terms in such accounts as the following:
'ratio communium opinionum consilii coelestis incapax hoc solum
putet in natura rerum esse, quod aut intra se intelligit aut
praestare possit ex sese' (DT I 12), and the rationalism here
attacked is but the mirror-image of the intellectualist model of
faith opposed to it. The clash of dogma and rationalism is a
stylisation of the clash of faith and unfaith. St. John could
serve as a guide back to the basic issue. Hilary's second
paraphrase of the prologue also seems to introduce a subtle
division between the eternal Word in his intra-trinitarian history
and the Jesus who acts on the stage of our history, the supreme

dissociation of classical theology, both orthodox and heretical, and one which the discretion of the mythic backdrop in the Johannine prologue does not occasion. This duality in the Christ may be seen as a vanishing one in the movement of Johannine contemplation, which once again may guide us to an integral perspective. If careful limits are set to the work of imagination and to the invalid speculative use of such words as 'eternity', 'omniscience' and 'divine substance', whose meaning may not be regarded as transparent, then the validity of the dogmatic gesture of Nicea can be safeguarded without forcing us to a dualistic view of Christ.

In II 13 Hilary again introduces St. John as a fisherman miraculously gifted with supernatural insight and pretends to be trying to catch him out in some mistake as he scrutinises the text of 1:1-14, only to be astonished every time by the sagacity of the fisherman's replies. Some of these difficulties concern the same points of doctrine as in I 10ff and verify once again that the plenitude of Scripture suffices to show the emptiness of all heresies. Others are a more tortured aporetic, which it would be both difficult and futile to analyse, and which shows how a certain ruminative playing with the text, carried to extreme lengths later by Augustine, is often a substitute for a clear grasp of its drift. It is clear too that it is often as a result of such a hermeneutic impasse that the Fathers lean so heavily on dogma as an aid to interpretation. The strained rhetoric of the 'Fisherman' theme, taken over from the very apophatic sermons of Eusebius of Emesa, is also relatory of the dissociative elements in Hilary's attitude to Revelation which we have noticed. Hilary's system has a grandeur and coherence of its own, the full appreciation of which must be reserved for another occasion. But the bias of its dialogue with the Johannine text indicates clearly what are the subtle displacements which tend ultimately, in lesser minds, to put Christian language out of joint with respect to its primary sources and with respect to the Mystery of which it intends to speak.

Time presses, so I move directly to DT VII where Hilary comes to the heart of his argument - 'septimus hic...liber... ad perfectae fidei sacramentum intelligendum aut primus aut maximus' (VII 1) - and also undertakes his most sustained commentary on Johannine texts. At VII 9 he promises to show that the Son is God, arguing from his name, his nativity, his nature, his power and his own claims for himself. In 9-12 he is busy showing that the name 'deus' given to the Son in John 1:14 and 20:28 is to be

taken at its face value. In 13-14 he moves to the argument from
nativity, concluding: 'Tenet itaque nativitas eam ex qua substitit
naturam et filius Dei non aliud quam quod Deus est subsistit'. Then
he invokes John 5:18, 'He called God his Father making himself
equal to God'. This proves first of all the true nativity of the
Son: 'Anne naturalis nativitas non est ubi per nomen patris
proprii naturae aequalitas demonstratur?', and from thence is
deduced the perfect equality of nature. Suspicions of circularity
in the argumentation are somewhat allayed when one recalls the
exhaustive demonstration of the true nativity of the Son given
in the preceding Book. In any case Hilary drops his plan of five
arguments for the Son's divinity in VII 16 for he realises that
this argument from nativity includes all the others. Thus in the
exegesis of John 5:19-23 which follows he is not bound to the form
of argument from nativity to divinity and equality of nature.
Instead he takes a global view of the passage as an exposition
of 'omne sacramentum fidei nostrae' (VII 17) and reads it as a
piece of Trinitarian catechesis. Jesus confirms his true sonship
when he says 'The Son can do nothing of himself except what he sees
the Father doing' and indicates his divine nature when he adds
'Whatever the Father does the Son does likewise'. Hilary expresses
an interesting view of the consciousness of Jesus in this context:
'Per virtutis ac naturae in se paternae conscientiam...', 'tantum
sibi ad faciendum praesumeret quantum in conscientia sua esset
inseparabilem a se Dei Patris ... posse naturam' (VII 17). Hilary's
high metaphysical reading of the text thus colours his picture of
Jesus's own mind in a distorting way. A scrupulous exclusion of
such metaphysical horizions is necessary to capture the movement of
Johannine contemplation here. The deeds of Jesus are captured
here in the perspective of his loving relation with the Father, a
relation presented in the language of parable, for 5:19-20a like
10:1-5 can be read as mere homely parable with no explicit
theological content - though John does not confine our reading to
this level. The authority of Jesus is seen as founded on his
filial obedience. Hilary sees rather his divine nature as founded
on his eternal sonship. Such is the inflational effect of dogmatic
presuppositions on the text of Scripture.

        Jesus' awareness of his eschatological role: 'and greater
works than these will he show him', sc. the works of raising
the dead and of judging, is subsumed by Hilary under his awareness
of his divine status. Where John slowly and meditatively expounds
a series of identities - (i) the identity between Jesus's work of
healing and the loving creative action of God, 5:17, (ii) between
the authority of his deeds and his filial submission, 5:19-20a,

(iii) between his eschatological deeds - death, resurrection, judgement - and the work already begun in the healing of the paralytic, so that these too are to be seen in the filial perspective, 5:20b, (iv) between the lifegiving activity of Father and Son, 5:21, (v) between the judgement of Jesus and the eschatological judgement of God, the identity in this case being so absolute that it can be shockingly said that the Father 'judges no one but has given all judgement to the son', a statement that leads to confusion and to accusations of inconsistency against John when taken as conveying information rather than expressing contemplative insight, 5:22-23 - this series of mighty paradoxes is reduced to monochrome metaphysics in Hilary's reading. By referring everything to its transcendental background he obscures the picture of God breaking into history through the activity of Jesus, a picture which in John implies no preceding or superintending picture of God's action above or beyond history, for that is another of the distinctions that tend to vanish in the non-duality of Johannine contemplation. The one creative-historical action of God is identical with the action of Jesus and this identity becomes manifest above all in the eschatological dimensions of Jesus's action. Alas that dogmatic theologians, even in these post-scholastic times, regard the perspectives of Scripture, in their lack of clear explicitation of the transcendental background of the merely 'economic' relations they display, as inferior to the grander and deeper view of a completed dogmatic system. What is needed is a clearer understanding of how much revelation is bound to history and to the human modalities which convey it. To recapture the truth undoubtedly contained in such dogmatic constructs as Hilary's account of the eternal sonship, we must think it out from its historical roots, controlling its development and purifying it of hermeneutic simplifications and distortions until its validity can be established in a modified form as an aspect of the presence of Christ, a horizon opened up, but only perhaps as the elusive 'ultimate' implication, by his appearance in history. In the meantime the concept of eternal generation must not be allowed to keep us from grasping the revelation of Jesus's sonship *in the flesh*. Our pre-understanding of Father and Son should not impede the ever-new discovery of who the Father is across and in the earthly career of the Son.

Moving on now to DT VII 22, and leaving much that should be thought out more thoroughly behind us, we come to Hilary's treatment of the verse that is the locus classicus for all the limits to the understanding of John in Christian theology and in exegesis, John 10:30, 'I and the Father are one'. Loisy exemplifies

them to perfection when in the second edition of his commentary
he suggests that the verse has no relation to its context and was
interpolated to annoy the Jews by its Sabellian overtones. This
shows that read impatiently, at the wrong pace, the Fourth Gospel
can become as meaningless and as aesthetically displeasing as a
slow movement of some sublime quartet would be if played at
breakneck speed. Let us attempt to view John 10:30 instead as a
peak of paradoxical insight prepared by all that has gone before,
from 10:1ff. True, this point is not reached by the consecutive
logic of our habitual objectifying discourse, for the rhythm that
would set up would keep us from pausing over each statement as a
single intuition to be appropriated and entered into in a meditative
way. We may none the less reconstruct the ladder of insights that
prepares for this climax. The first explanation of the parable of
10:1-5 dwells on the theme 'I am the door' (7-10), the second, with
a fine twist of perspective that serves to confuse a too simple
logic in favour of a deeper spiritual insight, begins with the
statement 'I am the good shepherd', i.e. the one who lays down his
life for the sheep. This is developed in vss.14-15 where between
the two clauses of 10:11 are now chiastically inserted the words
'and I know mine and mine know me, as the Father knows me and I
know the Father'. Here then Jesus' relationship to his sheep is
grasped in a richer perspective as one of mutual intimacy and is
then founded on his relationship with his Father. In 10:17 this
involvement of the two relationships is presented in descending
rather than ascending order: 'For this reason the Father loves me,
that I lay down my life ....', so that the divine initiative which
is the ultimate perspective on all that we have heard so far now
comes clearly to the fore. In this perspective Jesus can now
present the full dimensions of his own action as empowered by this
divine initiative: 'I lay down my life, that I may take it up again.
No one takes it from me, but I lay it down of myself. I have
authority to lay it down and I have authority to take it up again.
This command (one might read 'mandate') I have received from my
Father.' Here already is clearly implied a profound unity of
action between Jesus and the Father.

In 10:22ff Jesus replies to the question 'Are you the Messiah?',
first straightforwardly, 'I have told you so already but you do not
believe' (i.e. it is your unbelief that makes matters obscure to
you and makes it necessary to keep asking that question), adding
that his works witness to him, and then he points to the Messianic
function he fulfils for those who believe in him: 'You do not
believe because you are not of my sheep. My sheep hear my voice and
I know them and they follow me, and I give them eternal life that

they may not perish for ever, and no one will snatch them from my
hand' (10:26-28). Here the shepherd parable provides the terms
for a statement of Messianic authority and the eschatological
nature of the life Jesus gives is for the first time clearly
stated. In the following verses Jesus founds this claim, once
again, in his relationship to the Father: 'My Father who gave
them to me is greater than all and no one can snatch them from
the hand of the Father. I and the Father are one' (10:29-30).
What does this add to the previous glimpses of the Father-Son
relationship? 10:29 presents a closer identity between Father and
Son in their care for the sheep than we have yet seen and it also
tightens the bond of the sheep to the Father, in a wake of 10:28
which had similarly stressed the inviolability of their relation
to the Son. The strength and unity of the saving action of God
through Jesus emerges here with maximum force. But John will not
leave us with simplifying notions of this unity, aware as he is
that even this language remains parabolic. 10:30 asks us to raise
our eyes yet higher and to see a unity between Father and Son that
is more profound than their unity in a saving action (or even than
their mutual love as glimpsed in 10:15). Yet this unity is still
not a consubstantiality within the divine nature, as the classical
reading would have it. It is a unity to be discerned in
contemplating the human figure of Jesus in his historical presence
and, more importantly, in his post-Paschal presence to the faithful
(for the contemplative anamnesis of John sublates the past of the
Jesus of history into the present of his Risen Life - thus,
incidentally, solving the problem of the 'positivity' of Jesus
and freeing faith from bondage to a 'historical Jesus' who would
be doomed to ever-greater obsolescence with the passing of the
centuries ...; but in what form was John aware of such problems?
cf. 2 Cor.5:16). Jesus is one with God in an absolute sense. Nicea
is here in germ, but also a greater truth than that of Nicea, a more
concrete and central vision of the status of Jesus.

Hilary catches well the tone of this discourse: 'Consciae
potestatis haec vox est, imperturbatae virtutis libertatem per id
quod nemo oves de manu sua abripiat confiteri' (VII 22), but he
begins from a dogmatic viewpoint which sabotages the contemplative
progress of the discourse by making all of Jesus' claims seem quite
obvious. There is the same stylisation of Jesus' consciousness -
'unigenitus ... Deus naturae in se suae conscius' - which bypasses
the incarnational perspective of the discourse, a discourse which
even at its theological highpoints tells us less what God is in
himself than what God is in himself for us. John 1:18 is sufficient
assurance that there is no vision of God not ineluctably filtered

through the incarnate presence of the Lord and that to 'go behind
the scenes' is to reach only the abstractions our own mind may
forge; nor does any church dogma entitle us to do so. 'Quomodo
quod non rapitur de manu Filii non rapitur de manu Patris?', asks
Hilary, and tells us that 10:30 is the logical answer, and that
because Father and Son are one their hand is one. True, the
text of 10:28-30 bears this logical interpretation, but it is
misguided. John does not intend a logical riddle in speaking
first of Jesus' hand and then of 'the hand of the Father' though
he may intend to set us wondering as we contemplate the two
statements so that they lead us to anticipate what emerges in
10:30. The movement of Johannine thought is always forward and
it never provides subsequent explanations but always new insights.
10:30 is not an explanation; it takes us to a new level of insight.
The exception to this rule is inclusions like 1:2 or 5:30,
integrative literary devices whose function is to fix clearly the
significance of a unit of teaching. This integrative movement in
John's writing stands in a close but subtle relation to its
contemplative dynamics. The Passion narrative for instance is
given a contemplative dimension by the reapparition of Mary and
Nicodemus from the beginning of the Gospel and by the creation of
that inspired theological fiction, the beloved disciple, to
accompany the events as our guide. Why these devices have such
effect is a question for the literary critic. Is the use of
John 10:30 to combat Arianism based on a misunderstanding? This
much can be said for it: the reductive explanation of the verse
in terms of a mere unity of will would make it a truistic anti-
climax and its curious syntax does seem to point to a unity so
profound that, if one must use 'metaphysical' language to describe
it, it is probable that unity of being is a nearer equivalent than
unity of will. Efforts to overcome the metaphysical horizon in
theology fail if they merely revive one of the heretical alternative
also conceived within that horizon. What the Johannine text
suggests is that there is a horizon which is more fundamental than
the metaphysical one and which can never be reduced to its terms.
Johannine language, in its poetic discretion of reference to its
transcendental background - if that phrase be not misleading -
baffles all attempts to categorise or fix the figure of the God
who reveals himself in history.

John 10:34-36 gives an argument of Jesus against the Jews
based on the text 'I said, Ye are gods' (Ps 82:6), an argument
which the Evangelist no doubt picked up in his environment and
enshrined in his own style by introducing the phrase, 'whom the
Father sanctified and sent into the world'. Hilary sees the

argument as justifying the use of the phrase 'Son of God' even
for the Human nature of Jesus - 'omnis enim hic de homine
responsio est' - and while this distinction is not in John's
mind it does seem that these verses are a low-key presentation
of the meaning of 'Son of God' (DT VII 26). In 10:37-38 Jesus
once again appeals to the witness of his works and interprets the
inner meaning of them in the words 'that you may know and understand
that the Father is in me and I in the Father'. This utterance also
takes us *inside* 10:30, to which it appears to provide a structural
parallel. Unfortunately Hilary seems to identify the sense of the
two statements: 'Insunt sibi invicem dum...Deus ex Deo manens non
est aliunde quod Deus est' (VII 31). The mutual indwelling which
is surely of the order of knowledge and love is liable to be
interpreted in almost materialistic terms when stress is laid on
identity of substance and when such metaphors as those of VII 28-30
are invoked, however reluctantly (e.g. images of fire, light).
John 10:38 raises the theme of 10:15 to a new power in the light of
10:30 and yet the perspective still remains clearly an economic
rather than a transcendental one. Hilary's wordplay on this
text anticipates later developments of the theology of 'circuminces-
sion': 'Invicem autem sunt cum unus ex uno est, quia neque unus uni
aliud per generationem quam quod suum est dedit, neque unus ab uno
aliud per nativitatem obtinet quam unius' (VII 32). One may wonder
whether this way of thinking the containment of Father and Son
within the unity of one nature (still primarily the Father's in
Hilary, rather than the impersonal common essence of later Latin
theology) is quite licensed by the Nicene consubstantial which was
hardly formulated with such refinements in view. They may overstep
a limit in our speech about God. Still greater are the misgivings
occasioned by the following: 'spiritalis virtutis hoc opus est,nihil
differro ecce et inesse: inesse autem non aliud in alio ut corpus
in corpore,sed ita esse ac subsistere ut in subsistente insit;
ita vereo inesse ut et ipse subsistat' (VII 41). Here mutual
indwelling has become a topological paradox. The Johannine saying
eludes logic but it does not wave a red rag to it.

John 14:1-10 is a fine example of the contemplative movement
characteristic of the Fourth Gospel. One of its high points is
14:9, 'He who has seen me has seen the Father', which in its bold
abolition of duality is meant to remain a perpetually bewildering
utterance, one which we should avoid the temptation to explain away.
All the fathers deny immediately that the human form of Jesus is
referred to and most speak of the eyes of faith that discern the
divinity of Jesus through his words and works. Hilary writes:
'Homo Jesus Christus cernitur: et quomodo si ipse cognitus sit,erit

cognitus pater,cum naturae suae,id est,hominis in eo habitum
apostoli recognoscant,et liber a corporali deus carne non in hac
corporalis carnis infirmitate noscendus sit?' (DT VII 34). 14:9
must then point to the 'divinity of the paternal nature' in Jesus
(36) In his divine nature the Son is the invisible image of the
Father (37). Now this triple scheme of ascent from the human
form of Jesus to his divine being as the Image of the Father and
thus to the Father Himself is an extreme example of how metaphysical
schemes can interfere with the direction of John's text which is
the exact reverse. Jesus begins by speaking of a way to the Father,
goes on to identify the way with himself and finally identifies
himself with the Father - in the sense that the way and the goal
indiscernibly coincide. In each case Jesus is referring to his own
human presence - not of course as something to be viewed externally
but in the dynamism of its filiality.

        Christology is one possible leading-theme that can be followed
in an attempt to reconstruct the history of faith, and is certainly
a more promising one than that of eschatology on which so much
weight is put by some theologians and at least one historian of
dogma, but I should like to indicate another theme which might be
an even better guide, for it coincides more neatly with the content
of revelation and undergoes more significant epochal variations: the
notion of truth. At the end of his 'La vérité dans saint Jean'
(Rome 1977) Ignace de la Potterie takes Walter Kasper to task for
suggesting that 'the truth of dogma must be determined afresh
starting from the biblical concept of truth'. It is a suggestion
that I would fault, as de la Potterie does, for implying that there
is a univocal biblical concept of truth and also for its ungrounded
acceptance of the biblical concept(s) as a yardstick for measuring
everything else, forgetting that modern concepts of truth can be
applied to Scripture itself with critical effect. But I feel that
de la Potterie's reaction, his claim that Kasper's proposal would
undermine the truth-claims of the Church and that, however
Platonists like Origen and Augustine may have lost the Johannine
sense of truth incarnate, the biblical concept has 'remained in use
in the official texts of the tradition' (example: Leo XIII:
'Catholica doctrina quae sola est veritas'!) and in such theologians
as Tertullian, is most unsatisfactory. Clearly what is called for
is a history of Christian truth which will take into account the
ever-varying horizons in which the question of truth arises. This
paper has played with the contrast between two different domains
of truth operative in theology, that of contemplation and that of
dogma, and no doubt within these domains many further differentia-
tions of the kinds of truth sought would have to be made. If in

the logic of metaphysical deduction truth is transcendentally one,
in empirical and historical awareness it is more the pluralism of
its manifestations that demands our attention. A more attentive
reading of John can help us recover the many dimensions of
religious truth and thus provide dogmatic theology with a new
breathing-space, free from the constrictions of a narrow
rationalism or dogmatism.

Vincent Taylor and the Messianic Secret in Mark's Gospel

Brian G. Powley,
Methodist Chaplain,
University of Birmingham,
Edgbaston Park Road,
Edgbaston, Birmingham B15 2TU.

I.   Vincent Taylor's considered views on the messianic secret
in Mark are set out in his commentary, where a section of the
introduction is devoted to the question.   Like the majority of
British scholars before him, Taylor believes that it was Jesus' own
particular understanding of his Messianship which required him to
impose silence.   "To Him it was not primarily a matter of status
but of action.   In His own estimation Jesus is Messiah in His works
of healing, His exorcisms, His victory over Satanic powers, His
suffering, dying, rising, and coming with the clouds of heaven.
Messiahship is a destiny; it is that which He does, that which the
Father is pleased to accomplish in Him and which He fulfils in
filial love.   It is for this reason that He silences the demoniacs
and commands His disciples to tell no man His secret till after the
Resurrection.   The Messiah already, He would not be the Messiah
until His destiny was fulfilled " /1/.   Jesus was "Messias
absconditus" and, above all, "Messias passurus".   There is, then,
a doctrine of the messianic secret, but the doctrine is Jesus' own.

And yet more than once in the body of the commentary Taylor
empties the theme of the dogmatic content with which he has filled
it in the introduction.   On 1:44, for example, his first suggestion
is that the command to silence must not be isolated from the order
to the leper to show himself to the priest.   "The man is to make
this duty his first concern" /2/.   But Taylor then goes on to say
that "it may be questioned whether Mark understood the injunction
in this way, and, in this case, the hypothesis of the 'Messianic
Secret' is overstressed" /3/.   This is puzzling.   Taylor gives no
hint in the introduction that the doctrine of the messianic secret
is anything else than Jesus' own, but here he implies that Mark
has intruded it.   Then, to confuse the situation further, he says
a few pages later that the injunction "is naturally explained by

the withdrawal of Jesus from Capernaum and His desire to devote
Himself to a preaching ministry" /4/. But this "explanation" is
complete in itself. The same is true of Taylor's comment on 7:24,
where Jesus' reason for seeking privacy is probably that "He
desired to reflect upon the scope and course of His ministry" /5/.
In these instances Taylor in effect explains the messianic secret
away.

Taylor is confronted by acute difficulties when he comes to
discuss the injunctions to silence in 5:43, 7:36 and 8:26. However,
in his comments on 5:43 he still feels able to argue that Jesus
"sought for a time at least to avoid the embarrassments of
publicity" /6/. On 7:36 he remarks that whether or not the verse
is a Markan addition depends on one's view of the messianic secret.
The implication here is that Taylor recognizes the historical
problem (how could the cure possibly be concealed?), but he over-
comes it with the lame explanation that "reluctance to have the
fame of the cure noised abroad might be felt and expressed even if
the injunction was sure to be disobeyed" /7/. 8:26 presents the
acutest difficulty of all. Even here Taylor would like to suggest
that the prohibition was temporary, but he is forced to admit that
more probably it is editorial, "reflecting the Evangelist's
interest in the idea of the Messianic secret" /8/.

II. I draw two conclusions from the discussion so far. First,
the account of the messianic secret which is sketched in his
introduction is not substantiated by Taylor's detailed comments on
particular texts. Secondly, Taylor will allow the presence of
editorial activity only as a last resort. The question is worth
asking: If the secret really did belong to the history of Jesus,
why should there be editorial activity at all? But if there is
editorial activity, it is likely to be more widespread than Taylor
concedes.

Taylor gets things the wrong way round. He starts from a
hypothetical reconstruction of the messianic self-consciousness of
Jesus instead of from the text of Mark. This becomes clear in his
comment on 1:34 (which is similar to his comment, already referred
to, on 7:36): "Whether this detail belongs to the tradition or is
a dogmatic construction on the part of Mark... depends on the
view which is taken of the 'Messianic Secret'" /9/. What Taylor
ought to say is that the view which is taken of the messianic
secret depends on the interpretation of evidence such as 1:34.

1:34, as it happens, is part of the "residuum of truth" which
A.E.J. Rawlinson was prepared to concede to Wrede in his discussion

of *Das Messiasgeheimnis in den Evangelien* /10/. But Taylor is
less generous. Rawlinson had admitted that Mark had a theory
about demons and their supernatural knowledge. Taylor remarks
(not in the commentary but in an earlier article), "Doubtless this
admission is justified"; but then he goes on to say that "the
uncanny perceptions of mentally deranged persons are too well
known for us to dismiss Mark's accounts as imaginary" /11/. In
the commentary on 1:21-28 Taylor appears to accept that Jesus did
indeed carry on the reported conversation with the demoniac in the
synagogue. In fact, as Nineham says, "we, if we had been there,
should have heard simply the half-inarticulate cries of a man in
an epileptic seizure" /12/. In reality there was nothing for
Jesus to silence. Surely nothing is more certain than that here
we encounter a theological idea.

I now draw a third conclusion: Taylor will apply a non-
historical explanation to a narrative only when he is left with no
alternative. For example, in his discussion of 8:14-21 he has to
admit that "the stupidity of the disciples is exaggerated", for
here Mark is writing "didactic history" /13/. Taylor is quick to
forestall a possible objection: "If it be asked why such an
explanation is given to this narrative while others in Mark are
accepted more objectively, the answer is that the data call for
this kind of explanation, and that it is mistaken to assume that
Markan narratives are of one stamp" /14/. Many will feel that
the data should require Taylor to make use of "this kind of
explanation" more often than he does. The *first* question Taylor
asks is: "Did this happen?", and he usually answers in the
affirmative.

III. In 1957 there was an interesting exchange of views
between Taylor and T.A. Burkill on the question of the messianic
secret in Mark. Burkill had complained that Taylor's commentary
failed "consistently to recognize that St. Mark's gospel is
essentially a religious document in which history subserves a
doctrine of salvation" /15/. Taylor's reply was unsatisfactory.
He did not face Burkill's detailed criticisms but simply
reaffirmed his earlier position, and, predictably, he even went so
far as to assert: "If, with Dr. Burkill, we think that this Gospel
is essentially a soteriological document in which history is
subservient to theology, we had better cease discussing historical
problems, since the ultimate end is historical nihilism" /16/.
This *non sequitur* was followed by Taylor's endorsement of the
judgment of F.C. Burkitt, pronounced in 1935, that Mark's gospel
"embodies the private reminiscences of Peter, supplemented for the
last week by the reminiscences of young Mark himself" /17/.

Here Taylor only reinforced Burkill's contention that he was
unwilling to abandon a mode of interpretation which was once
universally prevalent but which now impeded the progress of
research.

It was not without significance that the very title of his
next but one book after the commentary, *The Life and Ministry of
Jesus* /18/, was in a measure a gesture of defiance against the view
that a life of Jesus was something that could no longer be
attempted.

Taylor's commentary is implicitly a work of apologetics, in
which two motives predominate. One is to defend the historical
reliability of Mark, the other is to vindicate a modern christology.
Taylor does the former by accepting every vivid detail as evidence
of primitive tradition; he does the latter by explaining away many
of the miracles. Everybody is agreed that the commentary is an
immense deposit of learning, but at the same time it is a memorial
to Taylor's own piety. The apologetic assumptions which he brings
to the text and the apologetic questions he asks of it prevent him
from being able to give a clear statement of "the Gospel according
to St. Mark".

NOTES

/1/   Vincent Taylor, *The Gospel According to St. Mark* (London,
1952), p.123.

/2/   Op.cit., p.186.   /3/   Ibid.

/4/   Op.cit., pp.189f.   /5/   Op.cit., p.349

/6/   Op.cit., p.297.   /7/   Op.cit., pp.355f.

/8/   Op.cit., p.373.   /9/   Op.cit., p.180.

/10/   A.E.J. Rawlinson, *The Gospel According to St. Mark* (London
1925), p.260.

/11/   Vincent Taylor, Unsolved New Testament Problems: The
Messianic Secret in Mark, *The Expository Times*, lix (1947-48),
p.147.

/12/   D.E. Nineham, *Saint Mark* (London, 1963), p.45.

/13/   Taylor, *The Gospel According to St. Mark*, p.364.

/14/   Ibid.

/15/   T.A. Burkill, Concerning St. Mark's Conception of Secrecy,
The Hibbert Journal, lv (1957), p.158.

/16/   Vincent Taylor, The Messianic Secret in Mark: A Rejoinder to
the Rev. Dr. T.A. Burkill, *The Hibbert Journal*, lv (1957), pp.247f.

/17/   Op. cit., p.248.

/18/   London, 1954.

Lessing as Editor of Reimarus' Apologie

J.K. Riches,
Department of Divinity and Biblical Criticism,
The University,
Glasgow G12 8QQ.

In November 1774 Lessing wrote to his brother Karl declaring his distaste for recent developments in the German theatre and mentioning his own plans: 'I would prefer to stage a little play with the theologians, if I had any need of the theatre. And in a sense that is what the material I have promised to send Herr Voss is about. But perhaps just for that reason it is none too acceptable to him, for he perhaps feels he needs to go carefully with Semler and Teller' /1/.

Lessing had been in possession of an unfinished manuscript by Reimarus since 1770 at the latest /2/ and had in 1774 published a first section of it, entitled 'Of the Toleration of Deists' /3/, in the publications of the Wolfenbüttel Library. He now proposed to publish a further selection of this deeply rationalist work on the Bible and Christian doctrine and thereby to instigate a debate with his contemporary theologians, in particular the Neologists, like Semler and Teller /4/.

As can be seen from Lessing's letters /5/ of the period, what primarily concerned him was the inadequacy of contemporary understanding of the positive religions. Rationalists /6/ had argued that many of the central doctrines of Christianity were contrary to reason (e.g., the doctrine of the Trinity) and to morality (e.g., the doctrine of eternal punishments for the damned). Equally they attacked the trustworthiness of the documents which were supposed to contain the divinely revealed truth. On these grounds they rejected Christianity as a corruption of natural religion. Natural religion, founded on necessary truths of reason, was the only true guide for man. The orthodox /8/, by contrast, insisted that Christianity was the revelation of God and must therefore be believed, no matter what criticisms might be levelled against it by man's - corrupt - reason. The Bible was inspired and the truth of the Christian revelation attested by miracles and the fulfilment of prophecy.

Between these two positions the Neologists attempted to find a
via media. They believed that there was much in revealed
religion that was compatible with and analogous to natural
religion and that in this way natural religion could actually
support revealed religion. Revealed religion on the other hand
was not to be identified with the letter of the Bible or of
Christian doctrine, both of which were subject to rational
scrutiny, but was to be found in the profound moral-religious
sense which was the essence of Christianity. Lessing's
revulsion for the Neologists was occasioned by their failure to
define this moral-religious essence /8/ and by the fact that in
practice what they did was to construct an amalgam of natural
and revealed religion which was neither one thing nor the other
but detrimental to both /9/. The question that Lessing wished
to pose was then: is it possible to come to an understanding of
positive religions which is truly rational, which involves no
submission to reason to faith, and yet which does not prematurely
reject positive religion because it fails to conform to
philosophical ways of discovering and expressing the truth?

Lessing did not, I believe, have any final answer to this
question himself, nor did he wish simply to identify himself
with Reimarus' opinion. The 'little play' which he proposed to
stage was an attempt to get his contemporaries to debate it
seriously. In the remarks which he added to the *Fragments* and
in his contributions to the subsequent controversy, Lessing is
therefore more concerned to state sharply certain arguments, to
chastise those who attempt to bluster their way out of difficult
intellectual problems, than he is to state his own views. Hence
we must be careful not to make too quick an identification
between Lessing's statements and his own views. He is a master
of irony who is all too often read as a writer of flat prose
/10/.

But why did Lessing, one of the greatest dramatists of his
age /11/, turn at this point of his career which up to now had
been in developing a national bourgeois theatre, to theology, for
whose practitioners he had a little sympathy? It was not least
because he saw here an important task to be performed for the
emancipation of the German people from the absolutism of the
German princes. In short, he attacked the orthodoxy of his day,
and even more its step-brother Neology, because they were
fundamentally authoritarian, heteronomous, advocating the
submission of reason to authoritative revelation, and as such
providing a powerful reinforcement for the political absolutism
of the princes. At the same time Lessing believed that the

positive religions contained truths which could be important in overthrowing such tyranny /12/.

I would like now to document and develop some of these contentions from the way in which Lessing selected and presented the sections of Reimarus' *Apologie* which he published as *Fragments of an Anonymous Wolffenbüttel Author*.

The first fragment (1774), 'Of the Toleration of Deists', /13/ need not detain us long. It sets out clearly the subject of the debate: that it is about revealed religion and, in particular, the Biblical history - and about questions of tolerance and tyranny.

The second collection of fragments (1777) /14/ is a powerful statement of Deist views worked out with all Reimarus' undoubted philological and logical skill. 'Of the Denunciation of Reason from the Pulpit' attacks the doctrine of the corruption of human reason and its Biblical basis in the Fall story and Paul's dictum about the obedience of faith. 'Of the Impossibility of a Revelation which all could believe in a rational way' shows painstakingly, but convincingly, the truth of that proposition. Few could have adequate grounds for accepting or scrutinizing a revelation contained in ancient writings in foreign languages. 'The Israelites' Crossing of the Red Sea' subjects the logistics of that particular exercise to a detailed investigation and suggests that the miracle would be not so much in the parting of the waters as in getting three million Israelites with their animals, baggage waggons, etc., across in the time. The fourth fragment denies that the books of the Old Testament were written to reveal a religion, on the grounds that they contain no doctrine of immortality. The last attacks the consistency of the Resurrection narratives, comprehensively and with great force.

Lessing's 'counter assertions' /15/ provide a first taste of the dialectical skills which he was to display so dazzlingly in the controversy with Hauptpastor Goeze. Here we can only note two points. Lessing says he has published in order to promote a genuine confrontation between Christianity and its critics and he hopes that the ideal opponent and the ideal defender may soon appear to lift the debate to a more fitting level. The orthodox he accuses of having allowed themselves too often to be drawn out of the bastion of their belief in an authoritative, binding revelation. No matter how men may mock and entice them they must remain within these walls. Reimarus

he considers to come close to the ideal opponent of Christianity;
only in two respects does he fall short: he fails to take account
of the diversity and development of the Christian tradition; and
he fails to press on beyond his refutation of orthodox
interpretations of, for example, the story of the Fall to a
consideration of its correct interpretation. The Neologists are
accused of having attempted to build a ramshackle building out
of incompatible materials, reason and revelation. Secondly,
Lessing concentrates particular attention on the Fragment 'Of
the Denunciation of Reason from the Pulpit'. The very concept
of revelation, he argues, implies *some* captivity of reason, i.e.,
some heteronomy, the notion of an authority which can overrule
our reason and demand absolute obedience - and this is
acknowledged by orthodox and Neologists alike. It is also
evidently unacceptable to Lessing who sees in this the
ideological counterpart of political absolutism. But while
Lessing could never accept a religion which obliged men to
abandon their reason he is fully aware of the vulnerability of
human reason and further /16/ aware that the Judaeo-Christian
tradition had reflected deeply on the subject (certainly more
deeply than either the orthodox or the Neologists). Moses'
'fairy-tale' about the Fall gives an account of that vulnerability
in terms of 'the power of our sensual desires, of our dark
conceivings over all knowledge however clear'/17/. One might
say that what Lessing is looking for is then some account of
the nature of these corrupting powers and also of those powers
within a given religion which assist men in their struggle
against sensual desires and the force of prejudice and the
misuse of myth. His own *The Education of Mankind* /18/ is an
initial essay in this kind of hermeneutic.

        The third selection from the *Apologie* consists simply of
the section 'Of the purpose of Jesus and his disciples'.
Lessing's introductory remarks are brief, largely tactical and
political. He indicates that he has replaced the offence of
the fragment on the Resurrection by the far greater offence of
the present offering /19/. All that has gone before remains
within the bounds of rationalist criticism of positive religions.
The offence of the section on Jesus and his disciples lies above
all in the question which provides the title for the fragment.

        In the first two paragraphs Jesus is portrayed as the
preacher of a - purified - natural religion. Like the Pharisees
he taught the doctrine of immortality. Unlike them he taught
a righteousness purged of outward observance and free of
hypocrisy. But then quite suddenly Reimarus introduces a

question of a quite different kind: 'Just as then there can be
no doubt that Jesus pointed men in his teaching to the true
great purpose of religion, namely eternal blessedness, so then
it remains only to ask what purpose Jesus had for himself in his
teaching and actions' /20/. The question is slipped in almost
as an afterthought - 'it remains only to ask' - as if we are
here present at the moment when the question formed in Reimarus'
mind. It is then followed by an astonishing passage in which
Reimarus lists in rapid succession the literary and historical
problems attendant on such a question. Interestingly in later
versions of the manuscript all this has been systematised, and
the immediacy of the passage thereby forfeited.

The question - as Semler /21/ noticed - is odd. If Jesus
pointed to the true end or purpose of all religion, viz.,
eternal blessedness, then what sense does it make to speak of
Jesus' purpose for himself? Did Jesus operate in two spheres,
the religious and the political? Reimarus' question must be
seen in its historical context. The Alexandrian model of
christology which had dominated Christian thought had led
Protestant orthodoxy to portray Jesus primarily as the - divine -
revealer of new mysteries and rites. Reimarus' question about
Jesus' purpose for himself put Jesus back into the sphere of
human history and asked how his life and teaching was related to
the particular condition of Judaism at the time. The quite
unacceptable answers that Reimarus gave to this question should
not blind us to its significance as a question. It led him to
a detailed consideration of historical fact, *res facti* /22/, in
his search for an understanding of positive religion, to a
consideration of Jesus' place in the religious, social and
political life of his time. Certainly for Reimarus there was
an irreconcilable gulf between his own rationalist understanding
of religion as comprised of necessary truths of reason and the
material with which he was now confronted. But it was Reimarus'
contribution to theology that, rather than therefore neglecting
the historical material, he pressed on to ask his question and to
ask it with a historical will.

For Lessing, Reimarus' enquiry served two purposes. First,
by concentrating attention on Jesus' involvement in contemporary
Jewish movements it showed that in order to understand the
positive religions one would have to be able to offer an account
of historical developments within given religious traditions.
In particular one would have to see how such religions related
to the aspirations, hopes and purposes of men at a given time
and place. Theology, that is, was to be historical and that

meant that it was to be related to the history of man's search
for meaning, truth and happiness /23/.

   Secondly, in thus pressing for an account of Jesus as an
initiator of change within a given religious and political
history, the question would prove a powerful weapon against the
essentially authoritarian myth of Alexandrian christology with
its doctrine of the impersonal manhood of Christ. At the heart
of the Christian religion would then stand a figure whose
humanity was not simply a passive and pliable instrument of the
divine will, but a real source of creativity and change and
initiative. Moreover it might be that an investigation into
Jesus' purposes and involvement in contemporary Judaism would
not only serve to counteract the authoritarian character of
certain Christian myths, but also to reveal the truly creative
and liberating forces which the Christian tradition also
contained. In this way Lessing hoped to make his contribution
to the emancipation of the German people from the tyranny
imposed on them by the unholy alliance of the Orthodox and the
Princes. His questions continue to have a disturbing and
creative force both for our contemporary theology and the church.

NOTES

/1/   *Gotthold Ephraim Lessings Sämtliche Schriften* (ed. K.
Lachmann; 3rd revised and enlarged edition by F. Muncker,
Leipzig, 1907), vol. 18, p.117 (abbrev. SS).
/2/   The final version of the Reimarus manuscript has now been
edited by G. Alexander and published as *Apologie oder
Schutzschrift für die vernünftigen Verehrer Gottes* (Frankfurt a.
Main, 1972). Lessing's manuscript represented a "substantially
earlier stage of the work" (op.cit., p.14) which disappeared
after its confiscation by the Duke of Brunswick on 20th July
1778. For the textual history see G. Alexander's introduction
to the 1972 edition. Lessing had possession of the manuscript
not later than 10th April 1770; see his letter to J.A.H. Reimarus
Reimarus, H.S. Reimarus' son (SS.17 pp.318f.).
/3/   *Lessings Werke* (ed. L. Zscharnack, Leipzig, n.d.), vol.22,
pp.31-49 (abbrev. LW). Lessing had had plans to publish the
whole manuscript in Berlin in 1771, but they foundered on the
theological censor's refusal "to put his *Vidi* on it", i.e. to
give express approval, though he agreed to do nothing to
prevent its printing (see LW 22, p.27). The chance to publish
came when he was granted freedom from censorship to publish
manuscripts from the Wolfenbüttel Library. Lessing's plans to

publish a further selection with Voss (cf. SS 18, p.115) in
Berlin, entitled *An even freer investigation of the Canon of
the Old and New Testament,* came to nothing. The title was a
reference to a work by J.S. Semler, *Treatise of a free
investigation of the Canon* (Halle, 1771-1775). In the end
Lessing published the second selection in the Wolfenbüttel
Library series in 1777, after his journey to Italy with the
Prince; see G. Pons, *Lessing et le Christianisme* (Paris, 1964),
pp.272ff.

/4/   The most thorough treatment of the Neologists is still
K. Aner, *Die Theologie der Lessingzeit* (Halle, 1929), but cf.
too E. Hirsch, *Geschichte der neuern evangelischen Theologie*
(Gütersloh, 1952), vol. 4. For special treatment of J.S. Semler
see H.-E. Hess, *Theologie und Religion bei Johann Salomo Semler*
(Diss. Berlin, 1974) and its excellent bibliography.

/5/   See especially the letters of 9th January 1771 (SS 17,
pp. 364ff.; cf. my article, 'Lessing's Change of Mind', *JTS*
29(1978), pp.121-36), of 2nd February 1774 (SS 18, pp.100ff.)
and the letter quoted above, n.1.

/6/   For good surveys of the material see P. Hazard, *The
European Mind* (Harmondsworth, 1973) and L. Stephens, *History of
English Thought in the Eighteenth Century* (London, 1962),
especially vol. 1.

/7/   An excellent study of Lutheran Orthodoxy is available in
C.H. Ratschow, *Lutherische Dogmatik zwischen Reformation und
Aufklärung* (Gütersloh, 1964).

/8/   See his unpublished fragment, 'Gegen Johann Salomo Semler',
LW 23, p.303.

/9/   SS 18, pp.101f.

/10/ For Lessing's purpose, cf. the comments of M. Claudius and
G. Herder quoted by G. Pons, op.cit., pp.311f. For Lessing's
prose style see F. Schlegel's appreciation in his essay "Über
Lessing", in F. Schlegel, *Schriften zur Literatur* (Munich,
1972), pp.215-249.

/11/ As Director of the Hamburg theatre Lessing had broken away
from the French courtly drama which had dominated Germany and in
Minna von Barnhelm had produced a comedy whose style and subject
matter was truly German and bourgeois. His last play before the
publication of the *Fragments, Emilia Galotti,* contains a clear
attack on political absolutism. Lessing's distaste for Goethe's
Götz von Berlichingen (see the letter quoted in n.1), which
idealises the robber baron, doubtless stemmed from his political
orientation. He remarks in SS 18, p.109: "That Götz von
Berlichingen has found great approval in Berlin does credit, I
fear, neither to the author nor to Berlin." Lessing had long
since lost his taste for the Berlin enlightenment with its

delight in French manners and letters, and the superficiality
of its religious scepticism and its domination by the Court. For
Lessing's contribution to the political thrust of the German
Aufklärung see the work of the East German scholar, P. Rilla,
Lessing und sein Zeitalter (Munich, 1977).

/12/   See SS 17, pp.364ff.
/13/   LW 23, pp.31ff.
/14/   LW 23, pp.50ff.
/15/   LW 23, pp.186ff.
/16/   See again SS 17, pp.364ff.
/17/   LW 23, p.190.
/18/   Quoted by Lessing at the end of the "Counter-assertions".
The text is found in LW 6, pp.61ff.
/19/   LW 23, p.209.
/20/   LW 23, p.212. The translation offered by G.W. Buchanan
in H.S. Reimarus, *The Goal of Jesus and his Disciples* (tr. by
G.W. Buchanan, Leiden, 1970) p.36, completely blurs the
distinction.
/21/   J.S. Semler, *Beantwortung der Fragmente eines Ungenanten
insbesondere vom Zweck Jesu und seiner Jünger,* 2nd improved edn.,
Halle, 1780, pp.15f.
/22/   "We want to know what Jesus' teaching actually was, what
he said and preached; and this is a question of *res facti,* a
question of something that occurred; and therefore something
that has to be drawn out of the reports of those who wrote the
histories" (LW 22, pp.212f.).
/23/   Cf. Reimarus' later version of the passage quoted in n.22:
"All *theologia positiva* is historical and exegetical. What
matters is the *res facti,* what the founders of a new sect said
and wrote, and how their words are to be understood" (H.S.
Reimarus, *Apologie,* vol. 2, p.21).

The Meaning and Significance of 'The Seventh Hour' in John 4:52

B.P. Robinson,
St. Mary's College,
Fenham,
Newcastle-Upon-Tyne, NE4 9YH, England.

We read in John 4:52 that when the servants of the *basilikos*, the royal official or soldier, brought him news of his son's recovery, the father asked at what hour he had felt easier and was told that the fever had left him 'at the seventh hour'. I shall seek first to ascertain whether this means at the seventh hour of the boy's illness or at the seventh hour of the day; next to discover what hour would be meant by the seventh hour of the day (7 a.m., 1 p.m., 7 p.m., 1 a.m. ?); and lastly to see if the term was intended to carry any symbolic overtones.

A small number of scholars have favoured the view that 'the seventh hour', whether in the narrative as it now stands or in a putative source from which it may have been taken, refers to the seventh hour of the patient's illness; this under the influence of Archbishop J.H. Bernard's statement in the International Critical Commentary on John (1928) that 'it was the common belief that the seventh hour of fever was the critical hour' (vol. 1, p. 170). It seems to me, however, quite inconceivable that the Gospel text as we now have it should mean by 'the seventh hour' the seventh hour of the boy's illness. Even if one could believe that the father's question means 'at what hour of his illness' (Pap. Oxyrhynchus VI. 935. 5 can be quoted, as it is by Hoskyns - where, however, the number of the papyrus is wrongly given as 937 - as evidence for taking *kompsoteron eschen* to mean 'did he take a turn for the better'; one might in that case with some justification take the father himself to be thinking of such a gradual improvement as might follow the natural crisis of the illness), the 'seventh hour' occurs in the *reply*, a reply that speaks not of an improvement but of an instantaneous cure ('the fever left him'), and that the hour in question here is the seventh hour of the day is clearly shown by the presence of *echthes*, 'yesterday'. Moreover, I cannot believe that there was an earlier version without the *echthes* in which the hour meant the hour of the fever. This for three reasons:

(i) In the famous Jewish parallel to this miracle story, the account of the telepathic healing of R. Gamaliel's son by Hanina ben Dosa (B. Ber. 34b; J. Ber. 9d), we also have a reference to the hour of healing (Gamaliel's emissaries noted the hour at which Hanina told them that the boy was all right and on their return they discovered that 'at that very hour the fever had left him'), and the hour in this instance must be the hour of the day.

(ii) An examination of Greek medical writers has convinced me that the 'common belief' in the seventh hour of a fever being critical is a modern figment. Greek writers, with the exception of Asclepiades /1/ and Celsus /2/, certainly believed in critical days /3/, of which the seventh was considered the most important, but of the supposed doctrine of critical hours I have been unable to find any trace. I shall later have a suggestion to offer as to how Archbishop Bernard came by the idea.

(iii) If the seventh hour did refer to a critical hour of the illness, the point of the story would presumably be not so much to present Jesus as a miraculous healer as to show him to be expert at foretelling, as Galen was wont to do, when diseases would, by virtue of the *vis medicatrix naturae*, reach a climax. That there was a tradition of seeing Jesus in these terms, I know of no evidence to suggest.

Having eliminated the idea that the hour was the hour of the fever rather than of the day, we must now ask which hour of the day is the seventh.

Both Jews and Romans normally reckoned from sunset and sunrise. According to this system (which most commentators think represents the constant practice of the Fourth Gospel) the seventh hour will be either 1 a.m. or 1 p.m. Since to take it as 1 a.m. one must suppose that the encounter of Jesus and the *basilikos* is represented, rather implausibly, as taking place at night, far the more likely meaning, if the usual system of counting is being employed, will be (as NEB puts it) 'at one in the afternoon' (similarly Phillips; probably Moffatt's 'at one o'clock' will also mean 1 p.m.; E.V. Rieu's 'at noon' also involves counting from sunrise, but a 5 a.m. not a 6 a.m. sunrise). This interpretation, however, is not without difficulty. Why are the servants shown as not arriving until the next day? The distance between Cana and Capernaum (whether Cana is Kefr Kenna or, as is more likely, Khirbet Qana /4/) is not great enough to provide a plausible reason

for the servants to have deferred their journey until the next day
if the boy recovered at 1 p.m. I shall return to this point
shortly.

Westcott /5/ argued for the use here, and throughout John, of
the other system of reckoning sometimes followed by the Romans,
viz. from midnight and noon, which corresponds to our practice
today. He is able to adduce in support of his thesis examples
from Asia Minor, the district with which Church tradition
associates the Fourth Gospel, of reckoning from midnight (in
Smyrna Polycarp was put to death 'at the eighth hour' [*Martyrium
S. Polycarpi*, XXI, H. Musarillo (ed.), *The Acts of the Christian
Martyrs*, 1972, p. 18] and Pionius 'at the tenth hour' [*Martyrium
S. Pionii*, XXIII, Musarillo *op. cit.*, p. 166]) and since there is
some evidence that executions normally took place in the mornings
(e.g. Flaccus is said to have made the morning his preferred time
for massacring Jews: Philo, *In Flaccum*, 85) we may take it that
8 a.m. and 10 a.m. are the times meant) but none, from either Asia
Minor or elsewhere, of reckoning from noon, so Westcott's belief
the the writer means 7 p.m. (so too perhaps Weymouth's *New
Testament in Modern Speech*: 'yesterday, about seven o'clock'), well
though that would fit - it would give an excellent reason for the
servants' deferring their journey - cannot be said to rest on a
firm foundation.

It seems likely, therefore, that the seventh hour will be
either 7 a.m. or, more probably, 1 p.m. The difficulty about the
servants' putting off of their journey till next day is not
insuperable. It seems very possible that the presence of the word
echthes may reflect, on the part of whoever was responsible for it,
an imperfect knowledge of Palestinian geography and the supposition
that the distance between Cana and Capernaum is greater than in
fact it is. Possibly, I would suggest, he confused Cana of
Galilee with the Cana near Tyre (Jos. 19:28), which is 27 miles
from Capernaum. We know that Eusebius fell into the trap of
confusing the two Canas in his *Onomasticon*; others too, including
Jerome, after him (P. de Lagarde, *Onomastica Sacra*, Gottingae,
1870, tom. 1, pp. 271 and 110). Admittedly one could argue that
the evangelist is not likely to have made such a mistake on the
ground that he is generally, though not universally, thought to
have been well informed about the geography of the Holy Land, but
then Eusebius and Jerome also knew Palestine well. Furthermore, I
think there are good grounds for assigning the whole *basilikos*
story to a redactor rather than to the evangelist: the lack of
primary symbolism in the passage (on which Bultmann has pointedly

commented /6/), the negative attitude to signs evinced by 4:48,
and the strangely unJohannine reference to a household conversion
in 4:53, together with an almost total lack of the literary
characteristics of the Fourth Evangelist /7/, all, in my view,
conspire to make this probable.

Of the view of H. Braun, B. Weiss and others, that 'yesterday
at the seventh hour' could, if spoken after dark, mean 'at 1 p.m.
this afternoon', it is sufficient to say that no evidence has ever
been adduced to show that *echtes* could be so used. That the
evening, though technically in Jewish thinking the start of a new
day, was in ordinary usage thought of as the end of the preceding
one, is strongly suggested by John 20:19 ('on the evening *of that
same day*...').

There remains the task of attempting to discover whether a
symbolic significance is likely to have been intended by the
reference to the seventh hour, and if so what. We have noted
above the absence of what I have called primary symbolism from the
pericope, by which I mean that the healing of the boy is not
symbolic of any reality beyond itself in the way that the changing
of the water into wine signifies the arrival of a new dispensation,
the feeding of the five thousand God's gift of the Bread of Life,
and suchlike; but this need not argue the absence of all symbolism
from the passage. That a secondary symbolism attaches to the idea
of the seventh hour is rendered probable, I think, by the fact
that in the Hanina parallel no specific hour is mentioned. I
shall examine five symbolic interpretations that have been
advanced, rejecting three of them and seeking to back up the other
two by arguments and evidence not hitherto adduced in their
support.

(i) A reference to the idea of the seven heavens was
detected by the earliest commentator on the Fourth Gospel,
Heracleon (fl. c. 150), a disciple of Valentinus. 'By the hour',
Heracleon wrote (quoted in Origen, *In Joan.*, tom. XIII. 59: *PG* 14.
516), 'the nature of the man healed is defined'. Heracleon took
the boy to signify the psychic man, the product of the Demiurge
(represented by the boy's father, the *basilikos*), who in
Valentinian thinking dwelt above the seven heavens (Irenaeus, *Adv.
Haer*. I. 5. 2; Hippolytus, *Ref*. VI. 32. 7). Since Heracleon was
clearly imposing a Gnostic reading on a text that was saying
something quite different, and since the idea of the seven heavens
is totally absent from the text of John 4, we need delay no longer
on this interpretation.

(ii) An allusion to the idea of the sabbath rest was found in the 'seventh hour' by Origen (*In Joan.*, tom. XIII. 58: *PG* 14. 512) /8/. Sabbath symbolism would not be unparalleled in the Fourth Gospel (it is clearly present in John 5), but nothing in the context points to its presence here. I would like to suggest, however, before passing on, that Origen's use of the term *anapausis* ('not arbitrarily', he wrote, did the fever leave him at the seventh hour: it is the number of *anapausis*'), by which he meant sabbath rest, may have been mistakenly thought by J.H. Bernard to refer to medical respite and relief (although in point of fact the medical writers appear not to have used the word in this sense) and have given rise to his idea of the critical seventh hour. Knowing that the medical writers held that the seventh day of a disease was critical, he saw in Origen's statement evidence that there was also a doctrine of the critical seventh hour.

(iii) Bede (*In S. Joannis ev. expos.*, IV: *PL* 92. 690) saw in the seventh hour a reference to the seven gifts of the Spirit. He also suggested that we ought to see in the number seven a symbol of the Trinity and the world (the latter being represented by the number four because of the four elements, the four seasons, etc.). Once again, there is nothing in the context to lend any plausibility to such notions.

Coming down to modern times, I note two suggestions made by J.E. Bruns /9/, which both seem plausible; in fact they have more to be said for them than Bruns actually claims. They are not mutually exclusive.

(iv) Bruns suggests first that 'seven, the perfect number, is appropriate for a miracle of healing' (p. 288). He offers no evidence to show that the number was in fact thought apt for such a context, but I should like to suggest that support is given to his theory by the following bizarre passage from the Talmud which very clearly links the number seven (whether or not because it is a perfect number) with the cure for a fever:

> R. Huna said: (As a remedy) for a tertian fever one should
> procure seven prickles from seven palm trees, seven chips
> from seven beams, seven pegs from seven bridges, seven
> (heaps) of ashes from seven ovens, seven (mounds of)
> earth from under seven door sockets, seven specimens of
> pitch from seven ships, seven handfuls of cummin, and
> seven hairs from the beard of an old dog, and tie them
> in the nape of the neck with a white twisted thread.
> (B. Shabbath 67a, Soncino transl.)

(v)   Bruns, who believes that 'the Evangelist uses time
throughout his Gospel for its symbolic value' (p. 290), has a
further suggestion, namely that the seventh hour in this story is
to be contrasted with the sixth hour in the preceding narrative
of the Samaritan woman, and that both are to be seen in terms of
the pervasive light/darkness motif of the Fourth Gospel:

> Perhaps we may ... see in the first hour after noon the
> beginning of a decline, a decline which progresses till
> it reaches its climax at xiii. 30 ['it was night']. The
> king's officer seeks Jesus out not to hear what Jesus has
> to say about eternal life, but to have his son cured, and
> Jesus himself reproves this kind of interest in him with
> the words, 'Unless you see signs and wonders' (iv. 48),
> even though he grants the man's plea... Yet the man and
> his whole household believe as a consequence (iv. 53);
> the light is still high in the sky, though not at its
> peak as it was earlier in the chapter [verse 6 'it was
> about noon'] when faith followed upon hearing, not upon
> seeing (p. 288).

In support of this interesting suggestion, I would offer the
following supplementary observations. There are excellent grounds
for thinking that the *basilikos* story comes from a written source
which contained also the first Cana sign. The two Cana stories
are described, in the Gospel as we have it, as being respectively
Jesus' first (2:11) and second (4:54) sign, despite the fact that
in 2:23 other signs are recounted as happening between the 'first'
and the 'second'. Since it would be gratuitous to suppose 2:23 to
be redactional, we must postulate the existence of a written
document narrating the two Cana signs but making no reference to
the intervening signs worked in Jerusalem (the signs of 2:23, the
mention of which will be the work of the Evangelist).

Now 2:12 ('After this Jesus went down to Capernaum...') will
also come from this written source, and will have been the bridge
between the wedding-feast sign and the second sign, which in its
original version will have been located at Capernaum, not at Cana.
As it stands in the Gospel at present, 2:12 describes a journey
from Cana to Capernaum which has no purpose, for only one verse
later, without any mention of anything having been achieved in
Capernaum, Jesus moves south again. John 2:12 'obviously formed
the introduction to the "second" sign' (Bultmann; similarly
Boismard, Fortna, Schnackenburg, Schweizer). The source evidently
had Jesus perform his first sign in Cana, then travel to Capernaum
(without, as in the Gospel, visiting Jerusalem) to perform the

second.

Why, then, has 2:12 become detached from 4:46-52? Why has
the healing of the son of the *basilikos* been inserted into a
different context from its original one, namely a visit to Galilee
which included the wedding-feast sign? Bruns' suggestion surely
solves this problem (to which he does not advert) very
satisfactorily. The placing of the pericope immediately after
that of the Samaritan woman invites the reader to see the
conversion of the *basilikos'* household as similar to the
collective conversion of the Samaritans but as less noble than the
latter to the extent that it depended on experience of a sign.
The person who placed the pericope in its present position (the
Evangelist in Bruns' view, a redactor in mine) wished to say that
the faith of the Samaritans shone more brightly than that of the
household of the *basilikos*, just as the sun shines more brightly
at its zenith, midday, the sixth hour, than in the afternoon /10/.

I conclude that the seventh hour means probably 1 p.m., and
that the number seven was probably significant for the writer in
two ways, firstly in that Jewish tradition saw that number as
particularly appropriate in respect of healing fever patients, and
secondly in that the seventh hour suggested a contrast with the
sixth hour of the Samaritan woman story.

NOTES

/1/   See Galen, *On the Natural Faculties* I. xiv. 47 (Loeb ed., tr.
A.J. Brock, 1916, pp. 72-75): 'Asclepiades ... showed no scruples
in opposing plain fact; he joins issue ... not merely with all
physicians, but with everyone else, and maintains that there is no
such thing as a crisis, or a critical day'.
/2/   Celsus, *De Medicina* III. 4. 11-15 (Loeb ed., tr. W.G.
Spencer, 1935, I, pp. 236-41).
/3/   The Hippocratic corpus contains two tracts on the subject,
entitled respectively *Crises* and *Critical Days*; Galen wrote a tract
about critical days, and mentioned the subject also in ch. 10 of
his *On Prognosis*. 'The doctrine of critical days', in fact,
'developed into a complete system, which long held its own, the
most important day being the seventh' (M. Neuberger, *History of
Medicine*, 1909, I, p. 261). See also A.J. Brock, *Greek Medicine*,
1929, X, p. 215 and E.D. Phillips, *Greek Medicine*, 1973, pp. 65,
131. John Marsh (*Saint Joan*, 1968, p.241) seems to be under the
impression that the medical writers thought of the seventh hour *of
the day* as a critical time for fevers. I can only suppose that he
has misunderstood Bernard (who, in his turn, was, I shall argue,

misunderstanding Origen).

/4/   Kefr Kenna, the 'traditional' site, is 4 miles NE of
Nazareth; Khirbet Qana, the site favoured by most scholars, is 9
miles N. of Nazareth.

/5/   B.F. Westcott, *The Gospel According to St John*, new impr.,
1908, p. 282.

/6/   This sign, thinks Bultmann, stands apart from the others in
that all the rest (save, he says, the healing of the lame man: but
is this really an exception?) are 'pictures, symbols' and have
'specific symbolic meaning', while this story is a sign only in
the general sense that it points to the Revealer's work as being
of a life-promoting kind (*Theology of the New Testament,* tr. K.
Grobel, 5th impr., 1970, II, p. 44).

/7/   The pericope, as Schnackenburg says (*The Gospel According to
St John,* tr. K. Smyth, 1968, I, p. 470) 'contains hardly any
characteristics of Johannine style'. The word *palin,* which ocurs
in 4:46, 54, though far from being peculiar to John, is, it is
true, especially common in the Fourth Gospel (E.A. Abbott,
Johannine Vocabulary, 1905, section 1707, notes 43 occurrences in
John as against 28 in Mk, 17 in Matt. and 3 in Luke). A more
markedly Johannine characteristic is the use of *oun historicum*
(4:46, 48, 52, 53). The pericope has, however, fewer of the
features typical of the Fourth Evangelist than most passages of
comparable length in the Gospel, certainly too few, in my view, to
prove the author to be the Evangelist rather than a redactor
influenced by, or affecting, his manner of writing.

/8/   It may be noted that Hippolytus, *Ref*. VI. 32. 8, says that
the Valentinians called the human soul '*hebdomas* and rest' because
it is mortal. Perhaps the idea will be that the cessation of work
on the sabbath day symbolizes the cessation of life that awaits
all human beings. Such a notion, as well as that of the seven
heavens, could have been in Heracleon's mind when he commented as
he did on John 4:52.

/9/   J.E. Bruns, 'The Use of Time in the Fourth Gospel', *New
Testament Studies* 13 (1966), pp. 285-90.

/10/   That the *basilikos* story should be compared and contrasted
with that of the Samaritan woman is a suggestion at least as old
as Bede, who contrasted the lesser faith of the *basilikos,* which
depended on seeing signs and seeing the Son of Man performing them,
with that of the Samaritans who believed 'solo sermone, id est
praedicatione apostolica' (*In S. Joannis ev. expos.*, IV: *PL* 92.
690). Bede's further suggestion that there is a contrast also
implied between the multitude of the Samaritans who believed and
the single household of the *basilikos,* is perhaps less compelling
(had the writer wished to point such a contrast he would surely
not have included the word *hole*, and that in an emphatic position,
in verse 53).

Studia Biblica 1978: II, 263-300

The Canaanite Woman and the Gospels
(Mt 15. 2-28; cf. Mk 7.24-30)

E.A. Russell,
14 Cadogan Park,
Belfast BT9 6HG.

What we propose to do is to examine critically the view
that Matthew uses Mark here. Then we ask questions about the
omission of the pericope by Lk and Jn and attempt to show what
kind of parallels there may be in these Gospels to what is being
being said in this pericope /1/.

It is assumed by most scholars that Matthew uses Mark's
story of the Syrophenician woman /2/. Yet Held recognised that
the matter of their relationship was still a problem /3/. When
we examine carefully the parallel sections, we find that the
pericope in both Gospels is approximately the same length,
Matthew with 139 words and Mark with 130. They are however
quite dissimilar in much of their vocabulary. We can find
parallels in only 41 words, yet even these are organised often
quite differently. In the introductory verse we have ἐκεῖθεν
and Τυροῦ (Mt 15:21; Mk 7:24). Then we have γυνή (Mt 15:22;
Mk 7:25,26) ἐλθοῦσα (Mt 15:25; Mk 7:25) /4/. Though the
illness in both is attributed to demon-activity, it is
described differently. Mt has κακῶς δαιμονίζεται (15:22) and
Mk εἶχεν...πνεῦμα ἀκαθαρτόν (7:25). Both Mt and Mk have θυγατήρ
(Mt 15:22,28; Mk 7:26,29) but Mk has, in addition, two
diminutives θυγάτριον (7.25) and παιδίον (7.30).

It is not surprising that the one point where the
similarity is striking both in vocabulary and order of words is
the definitive saying of Jesus: οὐκ ἔστιν καλὸν λαβεῖν τὸν ἄρτον
τῶν τεκνῶν καὶ τοῖς κυναρίοις βαλεῖν, Mk inserts a γάρ in view
of what precedes: ἄφες πρῶτον χορτασθῆναι τὰ τέκνα. If we
take the structure as:

οὐκ ἔστιν καλὸν
λαβεῖν τὸν ἄρτον τῶν τεκνῶν
καὶ βαλεῖν τοῖς κυναρίοις

with λαβεῖν parallel to βαλεῖν (is the metathesis here a
deliberate ploy to help memorising?), then Mk's form would spoil

the parallelism. Does Matthew reflect better the Aramaic form
of Jesus and therefore is to be preferred as the more original?
Or with a liturgical or catechetical motive has he created the
parallelism? Or going back beyond Mt, do we find the Aramaic
form of Jesus who, it has been claimed, sought to instruct his
disciples as the bearers of the holy tradition /5/? The τεκνῶν
is thus suitably parallel to the diminutive κυναρίοις.

Is it possible to see this saying as part of oral
tradition, a floating saying like many of those we find in the
Gospels without any kind of context? It would then presumably
be necessary to give it a context to make it meaningful?
Burkill, for example, suggests what is not unlikely that 'this
saying could have been proverbial, somewhat corresponding to the
the English aphorism "Charity begins at home" /6/. In this
context however the saying is placed alongside the reply of the
woman and in this saying the similarity is only less striking
than that of the first saying and we may inquire about the
possible significance of the differences:

Mt 15.27	Mk 7.28
ναί, κύριε	ναί, κύριε
Καὶ (γὰρ) τὰ κυνάρια	καὶ τὰ κυνάρια (ὑποκάτω) τῆς τραπέζης
ἐσθίει ἀπὸ τῶν ψιχίων (τῶν πιπτόντων ἀπὸ) τῆς τραπέζης	ἐσθίουσιν ἀπο τῶν ψιχίων τῶν παιδίων

In both cases we have the 'Yes, Lord'. It is the only
point where Mk uses the conjunction of 'Ναί' and 'Κύριε'. Mt
on the other hand has the conjunction also in the story of the
blind men. In response to Jesus' question as to whether they
believe he can heal them, they reply - and it is in effect a
confession of faith - 'Yes, Lord' (9.28).

The woman addresses Jesus as 'Κύριε'. This is usually
taken as 'Sir' /7/, though in the context of a church that
confesses 'Jesus is Lord', it can often take on a fuller
Christological content. It is only in Matthew that we get a
further use of 'κύριος'. The little dogs have 'masters', and
they are represented as eating the crumbs that fall from their
masters' tables. It is difficult to imagine that Matthew if he
had a form of tradition like that in Mark could have given it
such extensive alteration. Does he have an independent
tradition which was more rigorous than that of Mark and which
he preferred? Whatever may be the explanation, the woman
addresses Jesus as 'Κύριε' but in relationship to him and her

concern for her daughter, she speaks of sharing as a Gentile in whatever falls from the tables of their masters. Are we to leave it as a simple play on 'little dogs' from which is deduced 'their masters'? If the plural 'masters' is used, it is natural after the plural 'little dogs'. She addresses Jesus as 'Sir' or 'Lord' and then proceeds to underline that relationship by a further use of 'κύριος' where by analogy she too is humble enough to recognise her position and yet at the same time to suggest a deeper relationship. Thus she first of of all shows she consents to what Jesus says - the 'Ναί' expresses such agreement /8/. In addition to taking up Jesus' term, she uses the diminutive 'ψίχιον' i.e. a little bit. Thus she makes little or no claim, just a tiny morsel of bread for which the 'masters' have little or no use. We can interpret in terms of sheer grace i.e. that the woman felt she had absolutely no claim. It is not even the scraps that are given by the masters but it is those that fall in the course of the meal. The net result is that the humility of the woman is brought out in a most striking way /9/.

If the members of the Jewish people of God are represented as 'lords', this makes it more offensive than the parallel saying in Mark. The latter makes no mention of 'masters' but merely of 'children' and the small crumbs that would more readily fall from the children's table whose eating habits would not be as well organised as those of the 'masters'. The introductory sentence in Mark ('Let the children first be fed') makes the latter form of the saying more appropriate and implies that the Gentiles are to be given a share later. It is difficult if not impossible to imagine Mark writing to a mixed church at Rome the kind of things that are said in Matthew. If he had a form of the tradition like that in Matthew before him, he could well be compelled to alter it to make it less offensive. Is there a possibility that Matthew might see the saying of Jesus, 'I was sent only to the lost sheep of the house of Israel', as a justified insertion in the light of 'let the children first be fed', whereby he makes it clear that as far as Jesus' own lifetime was concerned he concentrated only on Jews. Later, i.e. after Jesus' lifetime, the mission to the nations would begin. If Matthew is concerned to emphasize the Jewishness of Jesus over against those who accuse him of being otherwise, then the rigorist shape he (or the tradition he uses) uses) gives it, can be understood.

Whatever may be the explanation of the different forms of the sayings present in the two pericopae, the saying of Jesus

and that of the woman are complimentary and would be helpful in
breaking down Jewish prejudice against the Gentile mission.   Mt.
would show this by emphasizing how firm Jesus was on the Jewish
mission and reassure those orthodox Jewish-Christians who were
afraid of what too ready and free acceptance of Gentiles might
mean for the church.   Even in Mark's church, which is probably
that at Rome, and where the prejudice would not be as tough, we
find from Paul's letter to the Romans that the prejudice still
persists and Paul directs his polemic against the works of the
law including circumcision and particular meats, indicating
that Jew and Gentile are alike in having sinned and that there
is only one way of acceptance for Jew and non-Jew.

      Among those who insist that Matthew uses Mark we select
one recent attempt to illustrate the kind of things that are
claimed on the basis of this procedure.   This is the 1974
publication *Jahwebund und Kirche Christi* by Hubert Frankemölle
/10/.   The basic thesis is that Matthew is a deliberate
literary work, written after the church had broken with the
synagogue.   Matthew makes use of the Old Testament to introduce
into the Gentile-Christian church the theological concept of
the Covenant as it is represented by the Chronicler and the
Deuteronomist.   The problem as Matthew sees it is how to
maintain that God is faithful to his covenant promises if
Israel has rejected the Gospel.   The reply Matthew gives is
that the Christian church has become the heir of the Old
Testament promises and in itself provides the confirmation of
God's promises.   The section on the Canaanite woman comes under
the general heading of 'Church Members as disciples' with a
second chapter dealing with 'Individual and personal ideas in
Matthaean Ecclesiology' (114-115, 135-137)".

      Frankemölle holds with Held that Matthew uses Mark and has
reshaped it by substituting the statement of the woman's faith
for a mere record of the cure, i.e. 'O woman, great is your
faith.   Let it be as you wish' (Mt 15.27,28; Mk 7.29,30) /12/.
The woman in Matthew addresses Jesus as 'Lord, Son of David'.
Frankemölle believes that implicit in this (vs 22) is the
contrast between the believing Gentile woman, using the term
'κύριε', and the mission of Jesus to Israel, as expressed in
the Messianic title 'Son of David'.   Thus this is merely a
double-pronged confession, put on the lips of the woman by the
reactor.   Frankemölle follows Heald in claiming that the real
intention of the passage as presented by the evangelist is to
bring out the woman's faith which he regards as the high point,
quoting Held with approval: 'This last sentence has a majestic

note about it' /13/.

     With regard to 15.24 ('I have not been sent except to the
lost sheep of the house of Israel'), it is seen to be
redactional. It is parallel to the redactional insertion of
Matthew 8.11f in the Q pericope of the centurion's servant:
'I tell you, many will come from east and west and sit at table
with Abraham, Isaac and Jacob in the kingdom of heaven while
the sons of the kingdom will be thrown into outer darkness;
there men will weep and gnash their teeth.' Both of these
sayings are the deliberate creation, Frankemölle claims, of the
evangelist. The situation thus becomes dehistoricized and we
are brought to the theological problem behind it. In 15.21-28
Frankemölle claims that the Gentile mission is already assumed
and presents no problem. In this he accepts the position of
Held while rejecting that of Strecker /14/. According to
Frankemölle - and it is related to the thesis he is
constructing - Matthew has the problem of the Israel-Gentile
church chiefly in mind, which is basically a matter of faith
in the mission of Jesus. Matthew sharpens the drift of the
passage and brings us to the essential alternative. He cannot
accept that Israel is first in a succession of two in the
mission of Jesus. To him, Frankemölle insists, Jesus is only
the promised Messiah of Israel and, on the basis of the Old
Testament promises, he can be sent only to Israel. The
Messiah is sent by Yahweh to the one and only chosen people of
the Covenant. There can be no 'first' for the Jews for as yet
no conversion has taken place and if Matthew eliminates the
'first' of Mark, it suits his insertion of the words 'I have
been sent only to the lost sheep of the house of Israel'. If
Matthew makes these modifications, it is to suit his theology
which asserts that Jesus was sent only to Israel who rejected
him but the Gentiles on the other hand by reason of faith are
admitted. Thus we see what the function of faith is in
Matthaean theology.

     There is no doubt this thesis of Frankemölle is thorough
and impressive in its presentation based on the assumption that
Matthew uses Mark. What Matthew does then in this pericope
which he finds in Mark is to add on the saying on faith, to put
the confession 'Lord, Son of David' on the woman's lips instead
of the mere 'Lord' of Mark. In such a confession Matthew
indicates the Israel-Gentile contrast. The emphasis on Israel
is in the Messianic confession 'Son of David' and in Jesus'
declaration of mission only to Israel. With all this emphasis
on Israel, the main thrust of the passage is to bring out the

the faith of the Gentile woman.

Supposing however we were, in connection with this
pericope, to suggest that Matthew's Gospel was prior merely
for the purposes of discussion, what could be said? /15/ While
isolating the pericope, it must be acknowledged that the
similarity in contextual order between Mark and Matthew, while
it could go back to oral tradition of instruction or lectionary
use, more probably does imply some documentary interdependence,
whether Mark on Matthew or vice versa. We propose however to
concentrate on the data given us by the two accounts of the
story.

The description of the woman is Χαναναία in Matthew (22)
and Ἑλληνίς, Συροφοινίσσα in Mark (26). What is the
explanation of this difference? As far back as 1896, Bernard
Weiss explained Matthew's Χαναναία 'als eine von den Einwohnern
Canaans stammende Heiden' /16/. Later McNeile speaks of
Matthew's 'biblical and archaic interest' in using this term
/17/. It is true that the term 'Phoenicia' was first used by
the Greeks to refer to the country of the Canaanites with whom
they had commercial transactions and as early as 1200 B.C. we
find the two descriptions "Phoenicians" and 'Canaanites' inter-
changeable terms. The term 'Canaanites' however was the
familiar term in the Old Testament for 'non-Israelites' and
Matthew, by using it, is said to show that the Gentiles are
distinct from the people of God /18/. So the Old Testament
contrast 'Israel-Canaan' now becomes 'Israel-Pagans' /19/.

It is difficult to see, however, how 'Canaanite' conveys
more clearly than 'a Greek, Syrophenician by race' that the
woman is a Gentile. If it had been Ἑλληνίς by itself we could
possibly have thought of her as speaking Greek but the addition
of 'Syrophenician' makes it clear she is not a Jewess. Matthew
by his fondness for Old Testament quotations fulfilled in Jesus
can of course be said to have a 'biblical interest' but can we
say he has an 'archaic interest'? When we compare for example
the place-names that occur in Mark with the parallel passages
in Matthew to find confirmation if possible of this 'archaic
interest', we find little support for this claim /20/.
Matthew tends to have fewer place names than Mark and the usual
way of interpreting this is to say Matthew condenses Mark and
the omission of some place-names can show this. On one
occasion, however, the contrary is the case (Mt 19.1 and Mk 10.
1) and on other occasions he is content to leave them as they

are /21/. On the other hand if Mark has expansive tendencies
and adds in extra detail as Apocryphal writers do, then the
additional names could perhaps be explained. It is difficult
however to support an 'archaic interest' from such evidence.
'Tyre and Sidon' are an ancient combination which Matthew
prefers here in this pericope. He does however prefer to omit
the twofold description where Mark on two occasions retains it
(Mk 3.8 and Mt 4.25; Mk 10.1 and Mt 19.1). In the former case
he adds the more modern description 'Decapolis' /21/.

    If Matthew then does not display an 'archaic' interest but
reflects the tradition of the Jewish-Christian church where, in
narrating this story, it sought to make quite clear it had to
do with Gentiles, he could readily take it over as meaningful
for the church of his time (though it would hardly suit a
Gentile church). If the tradition inherited by Mark had its
roots in Jewish-Christian tradition, then it could well be
that 'Canaanite' had become linked with this pericope. It
would mean little to the Gentile-Christians in the mixed church
at Rome. To give it edge, Mark (or the church tradition)
preferred to make it clear 1. that the woman was of Greek
culture and perhaps language /22/; and 2. that she was a
Gentile. It does appear that the term Συροφοινίσσα is hardly
likely to have been used in a Palestinian milieu by the
primitive church /23/. Indeed the feminine adjective is found
only here in the whole of Greek literature /24/. As for the
masculine form Συροφοῖνιξ, it is to be found only in Lucian, in
the *Deorum Concilium* in the second century A.D. There it is
used of a wholesale merchant with a slight nuance of
depreciation. In the Latin Satires of Juvenal, the masculine
form is found on two occasions /25/. It is linked up with
rather shady circumstances whether of unscrupulous profit or
moral decadence. We may illustrate by quoting the passage:

   But when it is his pleasure to go and spend the whole night
   At the taverns, a Syrophenician ever damp with amomum
   Hastens before him, a Syrophenician living in an Idumaean
                                                         port
   And salutes him with the cordiality of a host, with the
   Greeting 'master' or 'king'. Cyanus also comes, scantily
                                                         clad
   To sell him a 'bottle'.

It may be that the term is an invention of the Romans who used
it to express their disdain for those who came from the near
East /26/.

The connections of the adjective Συροφοινίσσα can give
rise to speculation. Is the woman of doubtful reputation,
perhaps even a prostitute? No father is mentioned. It is this
lack of information that can tempt some copyists to supply the
missing details. We have for example in the Sinaiticus
Syriac - and the connection with Syria of this manuscript make
it possible - which replaces the word Ελληνίς by the word χῆρα
(widow) (latin: vidua) /27/. If Jesus is harsh to the woman -
and a number claim this - is it because she is a woman of
doubtful character with little sense of shame? Jesus'
attitude to those who were prostitutes or ostracised from
society was merciful.   But how merciful would he be if there
was no indication of any desire to repent (cf. e.g. his
attitude to the Pharisaic scribes as a group)? Does Jesus
discern a wrong approach, a view of him as being some sort of
sorcerer, one practised in the magic arts? Mark does not give
us any hint of the description being used with a depreciatory
nuance. Was he the first to use it as a term well-known in
Roman circles with its sordid associations? It may imply an
ill-reputation for the woman and he prefers it to the '
'Canaanite' of the oral tradition? Does 'Syrophenician'
suggest the woman came from the Syrian ports? /28/ If this is
the case then the term would not be unsuited to a woman of
doubtful reputation, but we cannot in the nature of the
evidence be certain. The description Συροφοινίσσα with its
unsavoury associations is chosen by Mark or his source. It
belongs to familiar or colloquial language. If Mark
deliberately cultivates a colloquial style as that which can
communicate much as colloquial Arabic writing can communicate
in modern Lebanon, it is what we would expect. Here then is
not only a Gentile woman but one of doubtful reputation and
she is admitted by faith and receives the response of Jesus.
It serves to bring out more clearly the sheer grace of Jesus.

As part of the argument for the priority of Mark, we have
the familiar claim that Matthew and Luke improve Mark's Greek
/29/. Thus the paratactical style of Mark with its numerous
introductory καί's, is often improved by Matthew who replaces
the καί with a δέ /30/. Mark then prefers καί to δέ. At the
start of this unit we find an unusual situation. Matthew begins
begins with καί and Mark uses δέ. It is possible to explain
Matthew's καί as follows: It may relate to his ending to the
discussion on 'clean and unclean' where he alone has τὸ δὲ
ἀνίπτοῖς χερσὶν φαγεῖν οὐ κοινοῖ τὸν ἄνθρωπον (Mt 15.20).
This is an adversative δέ, i.e. Jesus says it is what comes out
of a man that makes him unclean *but not* eating with unwashed

hands. Matthew then proceeds, Καὶ ἐκεῖθεν ὁ'Ιησοῦς ἀνεχώρησεν εἰς τὰ μέρη Τύρου καὶ Σιδῶνος. Perhaps the insertion of another δέ might have taken away from the impact of the concluding δέ and does the καί suggest that, on the basis of what he believes, Jesus proceeds to Tyre and Sidon? δέ, of course, is used often merely as a link particle without any adversative sense, though someone with a Semitic background might find it difficult to employ. But what about Mark's use of δέ here? An examination of all the possible form units up until this passage would suggest they begin invariably with καί /31/. The δέ of 1.32 could be an exception but it can be taken, as often δέ in Mark, in an adversative sense /32/. The δέ of 1.14 can perhaps not easily be regarded as introducing a form-unit, but it may suggest an occasional use of the particle as marking an important point in the narrative, here the beginning of Jesus' ministry /33/. Whatever may be the explanation, by using δέ here Mark is going against his regular practice. It makes us ask whether he takes this from his usual source (where the repeated καί could suggest a Semitic origin?) or whether we have material that does not belong to that source. Has some hand come in and polished up the material? The evidence for an answer is absent. It still remains however that, contrary to what we might expect, Mark has a δέ over against the καί of Matthew.

Again both Matthew and Mark use ἐκεῖθεν. Who is more likely to use the term? Matthew has more occurrences of the word than all the other Gospels put together /34/. While Mark uses the word on five occasions, three of these are absent from Matthew /35/. On the other hand, while one is omitted probably as redundant, the other two are expanded and explained. In Matthew 10.14 the ἐκεῖθεν becomes ἔξω τῆς οἰκίας ἢ τῆς πόλεως ἐκείνης (cf. Mk 6.11): in 19.1 it becomes ἀπὸ τῆς Γαλιλαίας (Mk 10.1). Matthew tends to condense Mark on occasions, e.g. the story of the Gadarene demoniac (Mk 5.1-20; Mt 8.28-34) or that of Jairus daughter and the woman with the haemorrhage (Mk 5.21-43; Mt 9.18.26). In Matthew 10.14 however we can understand why Matthew expands it in this way. The parallel in Q has ἀπὸ τῆς πόλεως ἐκείνης (Lk 9.5). Matthew has given us a saying in antithetic parallelism about a house which accepts the disciples on mission or rejects them, following on a saying about a city or village which accepts them. So he takes the opportunity to bring these two together, i.e. city and house, and to replace the ἐκεῖθεν. It makes his presentation clearer and more orderly. The other instance where where Matthew replaces the ἐκεῖθεν with ἀπὸ τῆς Γαλιλαίας

(Mt 19.1; Mk 10.1) follows on the group of sayings in Ch. 18.
After the sayings in Ch. 10 and in Ch. 13 Matthew says of Jesus
μετέβην ἐκεῖθεν (11.1) or μετῆρεν ἐκεῖθεν (13.53). But in 19.1
Jesus is moving from Galilee to Judaea. It is a pivotal point
and later, following this, we are told 'Jesus was going up to
Jerusalem' (20.17). The last mention of a place was Capernaum
(17.24), but this is some distance away, and Matthew thus
clarifies or announces precisely the movement from Galilee on
the road to Jerusalem. Whatever may be the explanation, on two
occasion Mk's ἐκεῖθεν is shorter. He is as likely to use
ἐκεῖθεν as Matthew and the matter of redactional preference
must be left open. There is no reason why either should alter
the ἐκεῖθεν and so it is retained.

We may note next that Matthew says Jesus went to the
'parts' (μέρη) of Tyre and Sidon whereas Mark uses the word
ὅρια. The frequency of usage shows that Matthew uses μέρη on
four occasions to one of Mark /36/ and ὅρια on six occasions to
Mark's five /37/, and, it would appear, with little difference
in meaning. Both agree in the use of ὅρια in the story of the
Gadarene demoniac where Jesus is asked to leave the country
(Mt 8.34; Mk 5.17); and the entrance of Jesus to the region of
Judaea on his way to Jerusalem (Mt 19.1; Mk 10.1). In Mark
there are three occurrences of ὅρια and not one of them is
reproduced in Matthew (Mk 7.24,31[2]). Mark however uses μέρη
once: 'Jesus came into the regions of Dalmanutha' (8.10) where
Matthew has ὅρια (15.39). It would appear that the evidence is
indeterminate. One evangelist is equally likely to use either
term as the other.

In Mark it is said that Jesus entered a house (οἰκία) and
would not have anyone know it, but he could not be hid (7.24).
It is notable that in Mark the terms οἶκος (3) and οἰκία (3)
are used for a situation of privacy where either the disciples
or Jesus can consult and inquire of each other /38/. Four out
of six uses show this private consultation (9.33; 10.10; 7.17;
9.28). Are we to assume that there is a private gathering in
this house? Has it to do with the possibilities of a Gentile
mission by implication, i.e. a serious decision in which the
church has to be involved? Mark however does not mention
disciples, though they are found in Matthew, and that not in a
happy portrayal - the kind of thing we could well find in Mark
/39/. What about Matthew and these private consultations in
a house? On one occasion he shows it is a private conversation
(17.19), using κατ' ἰδίαν (cf. Mk 9.28). All the other

occasions in Mark are left out. It is clear that it is part of
Mark's purpose and interest to stress the number of private
consultations that Jesus has with his disciples as part of
Jesus' general concern not to court publicity. Even here in
the district of Tyre where it was not likely he would be known,
there is still the hiddenness of Jesus' person represented in
his entry into a house. Elsewhere in Mark, we have the same
thought (οὐδένα ἤθελεν γνῶναι) expressed with a slight
difference in wording (οὐκ ἤθελεν ἵνα τις γνοῖ: Mk 9.30). If
Matthew were to present the story on his own account, it is
probable then that he would not, even if he knew, be inclined to
make much use of the 'house', especially if Jesus is in Gentile
territory, and such a presentation might prejudice the rather
strict Jewish portrait of Jesus in this pericope. On the other
hand, Mark's theological purpose includes an emphasis on the
hiddenness of the person of Jesus and consultations with the
initiated group in a private house. If he had the account of
Matthew in front of him, would he not reshape it to suit his
theological purpose? At the same time it is possible to
explain why Matthew does not mention a 'house'. The setting of
Mark 9.33 is probably transferred to Matthew 17.24 and in the
transfer of 'Capernaum', 'house' may be implied but Matthew
could see it as redundant. 'Capernaum' implies Jesus
headquarters. The mention of 'house' is probably felt to be
unnecessary in 19.8(Mk 10.10) though Mark, if he uses Matthew,
could equally well insert the circumstances of a house in
keeping with his theological purpose. A similar argument can
be used in relation to Mark 7.17 and Matthew 15.12 and to Mark
9.28 (where 'house' may come strangely at the foot of the
Transfiguration Mount) and Matthew 17.19 (where Matthew does
use κάτ ἰδίαν) /40/.

     We may note the introductory participle used by both
Matthew and Mark. The verb used by Matthew is ἐξέρχομαι,
common in Matthew /43/ and in Mark /39/. Proportionately then
Mark uses the verb more frequently. In this verse however Mark
uses the introductory ἀναστάς and the type of use we have here
is found on only one occasion elsewhere in Mark, i.e. 10.1 'He
left there and went to the region of Judaea'. In neither of
these two instances of ἀναστάς is Mark followed by Matthew.
Both uses occur when Jesus moves from one location to another.
Strictly neither is necessary and in this use of the redundant
participle, Mark follows the style of Luke (15.18,20; 17.19).
If Matthew uses Mark he does not make use of the interesting
variation of participle in ἀναστάς - an idiomatic use - but
prefers his own form of redundant participle . Ἐξελθών is

equally unnecessary. We cannot see any improvement on Mark's
Greek here if Mark is used by Matthew. One point should not
perhaps be overlooked. In Matthew when the participle is used
with ἐκεῖθεν, it invariably precedes the ἐκεῖθεν /41/. But this
is also true of Mark (6.1,10,11). What we can say then is that
either participle is appropriate to each evangelist's style and
from this it would be impossible to say which uses which.

     The verbs used for Jesus' departure are different, Matthew
using ἀναχωρέω and Mark ἀπέρχομαι. The former is a favourite
use of Matthew /42/ and the latter is common in both /43/. If
Matthew uses Mark, and replaces ἀπέρχομαι with ἀναχωρέω, this
would not be out of place, but if frequency of use is any guide,
he would be even more likely to use Mark's term. But perhaps it
is the meaning of ἀναχωρέω that is determinative. While it can
simply mean 'depart', it can also suggest 'withdraw', i.e. from
some threat. This too would be suitable enough. Jesus has said
some scathing things in the discussion on what was clean and
unclean in the preceding pericope and he could be withdrawing
from the menace of the Pharisees. Indeed Matthew's term could
have implicit in it the foreshadowing of the Passion. It is
used of Jesus' action after we are told the Pharisees were
plotting to destroy him (12.15 = Mk 3.6,7), after the death of
the Baptist (14.13) and the discussion with the Pharisees and
scribes on what is unclean (15.21). It is possible to claim that
it is used in Ch.2 at every point in relation to escape from
danger (2.12,13,14,22; but cf. 9.24; 27.5) or in the face of
unbelief /44/. There is no reason why Matthew should not have
composed the pericope from a tradition of his own. The language
is the kind of language he (or his tradition) would use though
it is possible the ἀναχωρέω could take into consideration the
phrase 'He did not want anyone to know of it' (Mk 7.24). On the
other hand, Mark could well have reshaped as we have noted the
tradition of Matthew to suit his own theological point of view
on the hiddenness of Jesus. The difference in wording between
Mt 15.21 and Mark 7.24 is not easy to explain.

     Matthew gives us the double description 'Tyre and Sidon'
while Mark prefers 'Tyre'. Is Mark not the more accurate?
According to Jeremias /45/, the territories of Tyre and Sidon
stretched for some distance to the East over Lake Huleh. Sidon
was further north and reached as far as Damascus. If this is
so, and Jesus is on his way to Caesarea-Philippi, then Jesus
would only touch the territory of Tyre. Here then it could be
argued - though geographical locations in the Gospels can be
speculative - that Mark preserves a more accurate tradition than

that of Matthew. If the story developed within a Jewish-Christian
setting perhaps in Syria, it is possible that, before it was
committed to writing, the traditional description 'Tyre and
Sidon' was used, encouraged no doubt by the saying attributed
to Jesus, 'If the mighty works done in you (i.e. Chorazin and
Bethsaida) had been done in Tyre and Sidon' (11.21). Tyre on
the borders of Israel was a more formidable opponent and the
prophecies of doom levelled against it by Isaiah (23.1-17) and
Jeremiah (25.22) were related to this fact. The mention of both
names would suggest more clearly a non-Jewish region and make
an appropriate setting for the story. There is no reason why we
cannot accept it as an historic encounter though the details
in the course of transmission may vary, and the hand of the
redactor can be discerned. Since the admittance of the Gentiles
was such a crucial issue, any rare encounter would be remembered
all the more clearly and if the church later opened the door to
the Gentiles, it would be naturally, if possible, patterned on
Jesus' example. On the other hand, those who prefer to think
it is created by the church, will relate it to the necessity
for getting a basis for the Gentile mission /45/. The point we
are trying to make relates to the Mark-Matthew relationship,
and if Mark comes later, then he corrects Matthew. It is of
course possible to argue that Matthew is concerned with
teaching /46/ and to make his points clear. In this case if
the tradition is developed by him from 'Tyre' to 'Tyre and
Sidon' this emphasizes the Gentile setting and, over against it,
serves to make the declaration of the faith of the woman more
impressive.

Mt 15.22-24 are sharply contrasted with vs. 25 of Mark.
In vs. 25 we are told that the woman heard at once (εὐθύς)
about Jesus. This is the kind of thing we expect of Marcan
style /47/. Matthew has a rather condensed style and this
affects the way he tells the story. Mark tells us she 'heard'
where Matthew is content to imply it /48/. Matthew, however,
as in the story of the woman with the haemorrhage (see note
48), makes the reader sit up by an introductory Καὶ ἰδού (Mt
9.20; 15.22) /49/. The phrase is biblical style, used often
by Matthew, in which Mark is scarcely interested, and therefore
could well reshape a sentence into a more colloquial style of
story-telling more suited to the people he has in mind. Matthew
thinks of a Jewish-Christian audience who like the Biblical

idiom and for whom it can have rich associations.

The description of the demon-possession varies. Mark has
his characteristic 'unclean spirit' (πνεῦμα ἀκαθαρτόν)
(2/11/6/-). Of Matthew's two examples one appears to be from
Q(12.43; Lk 11.24) and one from Mark (10.1; Mk 6.7). He does not
then appear to have any objection to using πνεῦμα ἀκαθαρτόν and
we may ask, if Matthew uses Mark who has εἶχον...πνεῦμα ἀκαθαρτόν,
why should he change it to κακῶς δαιμονίζεται? It is a more
emphatic expression than that in Mark, suggesting it is a serious
case of possession. It is the only example of κακῶς with
δαιμονίζεται in Matthew. Does he use it to show that Jesus,
whose mission was only to Israel, will only act in a case of
serious demon-possession and this would be part of the whole
picture that compels the Gentile mission? And even though
compassion seems remote from the rigorous description of Jesus
here, does it not emerge at this point? Whatever may be the
explanation, all the other instances of κακῶς occur with ἔχω
where it means simply 'to be ill'. Does this imply that κακῶς
δαιμονίζεται need not be taken as emphatic? If so, then the
previous argument does not hold. In Mark we have four instances
of κακῶς and all of them with ἔχω (1.32,34; 2.17; 6.55). In
view of the fact that there is no further mention of demon-
possession in the Matthaean account, is there a possibility of
interpreting the phrase κακῶς δαιμονίζεται as a kind of bridge
phrase between a clear case of illness (κακῶς ἔχω) and one which
lies between illness and demon-possession which is unmistakable?
Whatever may be the explanation, the phrase κακῶς δαιμονίζεται
is unique in the New Testament and in the Septuagint, i.e. it
is a *hapax biblicon*. Have we here an independent oral tradition?
We have no way in any case of determining from this evidence
whether Matthew or Mark is prior.

In Mark, the only address of the woman to Jesus is Κύριε
(vs. 28). In Matthew we have Κύριε repeated (15.22,27) and
the additional address 'Son of David' /51/. All that Matthew
would have needed to construct such an address would have been
an oral tradition of the saying which would likely be familiar
with its preface Ναί Κύριε. Matthew uses 'Son of David' more
often than the other evangelists /52/ and it fits into his
christological presentation within the royal Gospel of Jesus,
'King of the Jews', who preaches the kingdom of the heavens.
The family line is that of the 'Son of David' and the structure
of the genealogy may represent an enumeration of the names of
14 built on the numerical value in Hebrew of the consonants of
the name 'David' (daleth, waw and daleth). The combination

'Lord, Son of David' is unique in Matthew (cf. 20.30,31) /53/.
In all three Gospels we have the cry, 'Have mercy on me', linked
with the address 'Son of David' /54/. The father of the
epileptic boy expresses his plea only in Matthew as 'Lord
(Κύριε), have mercy on my son' (17.15). Matthew appears to have
an interest in recording confessions of faith, e.g. he is the
only one to record that the disciples said after the incident
of walking on the water, 'You are really God's Son' (14.33);
similarly he is the only one to record that the multitudes
'glorified the God of Israel' (15.31) at the healings. The
form of confession here could well be thought of as proleptic,
anticipating the commendation of the faith which was present at
the moment of appeal and which forms the climax of the Matthaean
account (Mt 15.28). It could well represent a blend between
the confession of non-Jew (κύριε) and the Jew (Son of David)
/55/. It is evident that the plea for mercy linked up with the
title 'Son of David' is something common to the general
tradition, yet in Matthew it assumes a more penetrating thrust.
It is he alone who says, 'Blessed are the merciful' (5.7), or
quotes on two occasions, 'I will have mercy and not sacrifice'
(9.13; 12.7), in relation to table fellowship and to the
understanding of the Sabbath. It is Matthew alone who tells
us of the merciless servant and the judgment on him (18.23-35)
and depicts for us the drama of the day of judgment when the
basis of entry into the kingdom will be mercy ('Inasmuch as you
did it to one of the least of these', Mt 25.40). Matthew uses
the phrase 'Son of David' of the Messiah (cf. 1.1). 'The
Davidic sonship of Jesus is of special significance, for on
this ground he can show the synagogue that Jesus is the Messiah
of Israel' /56/. Thus he introduces the title into many stories
that tell of the saving work of Jesus /57/. If the Gospel is
to be used in teaching and liturgical practice, there is no
reason why this should not be done. In the same way, Matthew
would ask how best to apply the story to the needs of the
congregation and if we find the emphasis on faith from time to
time /58/, this does not exclude his awareness of the needs of
the congregation for instruction and worship. Thus if Matthew
makes use of an independent tradition of the pericope of the
Cannanite woman, he builds it up into an edifying account for
the strengthening of the church. The links with Mark at this
point are quite tenuous if we recognise the saying (15.26) as
part of a floating tradition independent of Mark.

If we have expansion here in Matthew, it is part of a
process which, if Mark is regarded as base, is remarkably free.
The Markan outline in vs. 25f is simple: the woman heard about

him immediately. Her daughter had an unclean spirit. She came
and fell at his feet and asked him to cast the demon out of her
daughter. Matthew expands this in a number of ways. He brings
in the disciples and portrays them in a way that is reminiscent
of Mark and may belong to tradition. He gives us the wording of
the woman's appeal (22), the refusal of Jesus to answer (23),
the introduction of the disciples who ask Jesus to send her away
and from whom we get the information that she keeps crying after
them (23) and then the reply peculiar to Matthew, 'I have not
been sent except to the lost sheep of the house of Israel' (24).
Thus we have a conversation between Jesus and the disciples and
the woman. Such an expansion by Matthew whether in relation to
Mark or oral tradition is quite characteristic of Matthew /59/.
Matthew often prefers the direct style to the indirect, e.g.
Peter said, 'Explain this parable to us' (Mt 15.15), where Mark
has 'His disciples asked him about the parable' (7.17); or
Peter began to rebuke him, 'God forbid, Lord, this will not
happen to you' (Mt 16.22), while Mark has 'Peter began to rebuke
him' (8.32) /60/. This freedom on the part of Matthew cannot
be closely related to the Marcan account and is difficult to
explain from it.

Matthew introduces the mention of disciples. He quite
frequently introduces the word μαθηταί in order to spell out
what is not explicit in Mark /61/. He may substitute μαθηταί
as a group instead of one or more members of the group (21.20
[Peter]; 24.3 [for Peter, James, John and Andrew]). There is
only one place in addition to the pericope of the Canaanite
woman where we find a tradition additional to that of Mark or
Luke. This is the story of the Transfiguration where the
disciples are said to fall on their face and be frightened when
they hear the heavenly voice. Jesus then comes, touches them
and says, 'Arise and do not be afraid' (17.6,7). Has Matthew
created this tradition or is it part of the oral tradition from
which he draws for material different from the sources we know?
He does it so sparingly and he supplements μαθηταί only where
the context, as far as tradition in Mark gives, lends
justification, we must assume that in the additional information
about the disciples here, Matthew could be drawing on oral
tradition. Again Matthew does not tend to give us an
unfavourable view of the disciples on his own account but where
his tradition warrants it, he can do so. It also suits his
purpose, which is to draw out the reluctance of Jesus and the
disciples to engage upon the Gentile mission. The unresponsive
attitude of Jesus and the uncompromising declaration of his
mission could give us a harsh portrait. Yet by so doing Matthew

serves to bring out the faith which he is always interested in
emphasizing /62/ (Mt 8.10,13; 9.28f; 17.20 [Lk 17.6]; 21.21).
If Mark's purpose is to lay stress on the healing, then the
condensing of any kind of dialogue except the definitive sayings
is explicable. This would take away from the climax he aims
at. Mark does not mention faith though it may be implicit in
the story. He is concerned only with the miracle of grace done
to the daughter of the Canaanite woman. Matthew, whose purpose
(or that of his source) is to bring out the importance of faith
in the admission of the Gentiles, expands the story for this
purpose. Bonnard (ad loc.) tends to minimize the place of the
address ('Lord, Son of David') in the story, stressing the
faith and the humble approach of the woman. It would seem that
for the purpose Matthew had in mind both are important. Faith
makes its own confession of faith and there is the recognition
of Jesus as the Jewish Messiah in it and that by a pagan woman.

There is the possibility that this special material of
Matthew has some links with the Q source. In Q, Jesus declares,
'Ask and keep on asking (the αἰτέω is present imperative) and
you will receive, keep on seeking and you will find, keep on
knocking and it will be opened for you' (Mt 7.7; Lk 11.9). In
Luke's special material we have this illustrated in the parable
of the friend at midnight who for the very barefacedness of
his persistence gets all he wants (Lk 11.5-8), and again
'whatever you ask in prayer, you will receive if you have faith'
(21.22). Elements in our pericope bring out the sheer refusal
of the mother to give up. She begins by asking Jesus to have
mercy on her (Ελέησόν με, κύριε, υἱὸς Δαυί̈δ), not on her
daughter. Later she says again 'Help me'. 'Ausserdem ist
nach altertümlichen Empfinden die Tochter schon in der Mutter
gegenwärtig da'zumal es sich um ein jüngeres Kind handelt, 'das
noch nicht für sich selbst bitten kann' /63/. The implication
is that she is so identified, however, with her daughter's
need that there can be no distinction made. On the other hand
it is the faith of the Canaanite woman that is to be commended.
She believes for the sake of her daughter. Therefore it is
appropriate that she speaks of 'me' /64/.

We are told, 'She kept on crying' (ἔκραζεν: imperfect).
Then there is the offputting silence of Jesus, the first test
of her faith and her genuineness. The second hurdle is the
attitude of the disciples, in whom is mirrored the attitude of
the church of the time. The woman 'keeps crying' (κράζει) after
them and the disciples 'kept on asking' (ἠρώτων) Jesus

'Απόλυσον, i.e. send her away /65/. The concentration of
interest is not on the disciples but, as often, on Jesus. It
is Jesus who is the person of authority and to whom the
disciples are necessarily subject. It is only on his direction
that the woman can be sent away. Or is it because she is a
Gentile woman and they are such hidebound Jews that they wait for
Jesus to act? The disciples say, 'she keeps on crying after
us'. Does the 'us' include Jesus or is the church represented
as doing the wrong thing and cherishing the wrong attitude,
as becomes clear by the end of the story? A third difficulty
which could well turn the woman away is Jesus' declaration of
his mission 'I have been sent only to the lost sheep of the
house of Israel'. To persist after all this serves of course
to bring out the extremity of the woman's position and her
patience and humility. She is not put off. Again she says
simply and briefly, 'Lord, help me'. Through it all there is
still the address Κύριε which in a church context, must have
christological overtones. The final challenge comes in the
saying about the keeping of the bread for the children and not
for the pet animals of the house. All this she surmounts and
receives an exceptional tribute to her faith, not unlike that
given to the centurion, and as immediate a cure expressed in
Matthaean language: 'from that moment' (8.13; 15.28; cf. 9.22;
17.18). The skilful presentation of the material and its sharp
contrast to the story given in Mark in material and thrust
would suggest an independence of Matthew from Mark. On the
other hand, bearing in mind Mark's simple account of a healing,
it is not impossible that Mark may have used Matthew though the
use of an oral tradition of the healing story appears more
probable.

There is a contrast between Matthew and Mark in the
portrait that is given us of Jesus. In Mark it is stated that
Jesus did not want people to know of his visit to the house in
the vicinity of Tyre but he found this impossible. The woman
comes at once and asks him to cast the demon from her daughter.
Jesus' gentle insistence on the priority of his mission to the
Jews is not pushed. The woman recognizes this but still
insists on her need. Then comes the healing because of the
nature of her reply. She recognized the position of Israel in
salvation history. There is a double emphasis, both on the
saying of Jesus and on the fact of the healing which is
explained as an exorcism and is suitable to the emphasis we
find in Mark of Jesus' triumph over demonic forces. In Matthew,
on the other hand, we are shown a Jesus who does not reply to
the woman's importunate cry, the Jesus who often could penetrate

behind people's facade to the real situation underneath. We
have this portrait reflected in the church where the disciples
find it in keeping with their prejudices to interpret the
silence of Jesus as indicating he does not want the woman to
bother him. Indeed if we fitted Jesus' desire not to be known
in Mark to this silence of Jesus, it would make more sense.
The complaint of the disciples is: 'She keeps crying after us'.
It is the picture of a church which does not want to be bothered,
which is lacking in compassion, and is calling upon its Lord to
take the problem of the Gentile demand away from them. Then we
have the saying peculiar to Matthew among the Gospels: 'I have
been sent only to the lost sheep of the house of Israel'. This
is a Jesus we really do not see in Matthew. The Jesus we see
is one who insists on mercy in a way other Gospels do not,
mercy to one another and to the outcasts and despised of society
and who insists that the essence of the law is love to God and
love to one's neighbour (7.12: 22.40). It is not enough to
say that this has to do with Gentiles and that therefore the
situation is changed. In the case of the centurion's servant,
an account found in Q, there is no hint of any reluctance on the
part of Jesus.

We are tempted to say that this is a story which has been
shaped in a rigorous judaistic direction. If the real thrust is
to bring out the faith of the woman and Jesus' reluctance is to
bring out such faith and put her to a severe test, it does not
alter the fact that the depiction of Jesus is quite extreme.
Of course we can interpret the rebuff as showing an awareness
of there being artificial types of faith which give up at any
kind of obstacle. The writer too is asking what can the church
do when the Gentiles are so importunate. Even though Jesus'
mission is concerned with the lost sheep of the house of Israel,
and even though his image is to be protected over against the
Jews as a strict Jew, any thoughtful Jew would recognize the
real urgency of the situation. If we think Jesus is harsh here,
we must remember that Matthew has already spoken of the
compassion of Jesus (9.36; 14.14; 15.32) and of his mercy (9.27;
15.22; 9.13; 12.7) /66/. The story then may be interpreted in
the light of the total presentation. If there is mercy, there
must also be obedience. If Jesus had opened wide the door to
the Gentiles in his lifetime, his mission to his own people
would have been seriously jeopardized. This is the Jesus who
insists on keeping the law and who, with all his compassion and
love for the outcast, is conscious of where his prior task lies.
If Matthew (or his tradition) is responsible for the sharpening
of the issues, it could be in keeping with his didactic purpose.

No one could escape the impact of what is taught. The real
tension within the Jewish-Christian community at the admission
of the Gentiles could scarcely be more starkly put. Matthew
uses a tradition where the sayings of Jesus and the woman have
been reshaped. He has introduced a tradition of the disciples
in vss. 22-24 and the vs. 24 /67/ could also be part of a
floating tradition (cf. 10.5b, 6). The problem of the literary
and traditional relations between Matthew and Mark is not by
any means solved and should call into serious question any too
confident assumption that Matthew uses Mark as we have it.

     We turn now to attempt to draw some kind of relationship
between the presence of the pericope on the Canaanite woman in
Matthew and Mark and its omission in Luke and John. Luke's
concern to show the merciful attitude to women who often had
little claim on mercy would have made him interested in the
story /68/. It is usually and probably rightly claimed that
the description 'dog' was too offensive for him. On the other
hand, the term could mean 'little dog', i.e. little dogs which
could be tolerated in the house /69/. If this is the case and
Luke understood it in this way, then he could have inserted the
story. It was however probably open to misunderstandings which
he could not risk in addressing his twofold work to the Graeco-
Roman world. Mark on the other hand tends to be frank and blunt
and even if he is writing in a Roman setting where there was a
mixed church of Gentiles and Jews, he is not afraid to use the
story. We must not exclude the possibility that the Jews had
set such a high quality of life that even Gentiles could
recognize honestly and fairly that their pagan way of life
really merited such a description by way of comparison. Indeed
it might be that the blunt description could shock them into
thinking about their situation as pagans, and Mark does not
exclude them from a possible place in the household of salvation.
The children must first be fed, i.e. the time of the Gentiles
has now come when Mark writes.

     Luke, on the other hand, shows from the dedication of his
twofold work to Theophilus binding both parts together, that
he appears to have his eye on the literary world and especially
the Roman authorities /70/. It is especially evident in Acts
that he wants his work to be a *captatio benevolentiae* and this
is why he tends to soften the portrait of the Roman authorities.
Related to this is his defending of the church against the
charge of hostility to the state /71/. If Luke writes to
convert unbelievers, then his Gospel represents a simplification
and this may be part of the explanation why he tends to make

salvation a matter of repentance and forgiveness (Lk 15; 18.
9-14; Acts 2.38) - what has been called the Rabbinic doctrine
of salvation /72/.

The essential problem in the story of the Canaanite woman
is that it is a saying of Jesus that is involved. Luke tends
to reproduce the sayings of the Baptist or of Jesus with care
(Lk 3.16-18 and parr. Lk 11.9-10) /73/. At times the tradition
he has may differ from that of Matthew or Mark or he may feel
free to adapt the saying without altering its essential drift.
But this very fidelity would present him with problems in the
Marcan narrative and more acutely in the Matthaean. The form
of the proverb appears to be 'It is not good to take the
children's bread and fling it to the dogs'. It is a piece of
commonsense counsel. The children should not be allowed to
starve while the animals are fed. Either Matthew reproduces
Mark's wording with one slight alteration in order or else it
is a saying so familiar that it would be quoted accurately
without reference to any document. If this is the basic saying,
Mark adds, 'Let the children first be fed' /74/. There is no
reason why it should not be a saying of Jesus and if Paul has
a kind of refrain, 'to the Jew first and also to the Greek'
(Rom. 1.16; 2.9,10), it could reflect a saying of Jesus. On
the other hand, Mark does show signs of Pauline influence /75/
and it may be reflected here, though this does not necessarily
tell against its origin in Jesus. The proverb, then, set in
the context of the encounter with the Canaanite woman, gives us
a programme that Luke follows in Acts, i.e. the disciples are
to be witnesses in Jerusalem, in all Judaea and Samaria and to
the ends of the earth (Acts 1.8).

In Luke's Gospel, the prospect of mission to the Gentiles
is present from the very beginning. The child in the Temple
is described by Simeon as one who would be 'a light to the
Gentile' (φῶς εἰς ἀποκάλυψιν ἐθνῶν; 2.32). In the opening of
Jesus' ministry as it is given us in Luke, Jesus' vocation is
implicitly linked up with the Gentiles. The fulfilment of Isa.
61.1ff takes place in Jesus. Jesus says 'Today this Scripture
has been fulfilled in your hearing' (4.21). He goes on to
speak of the rejection by his own people who might well say,
'Physician, heal yourself' (4.23). Then he points out to the
Jews in the Synagogue that, although there were many widows in
Israel in the days of Elijah, to none of them was Elijah sent.
He was sent to a widow in Zarephath, in the land of Sidon
(1 Kings 17.8ff). In the case of Elisha, although there were
many lepers in Israel, it was only the Syrian Naaman who was

cleansed (4.25-27; cf. 2 Kings 5.1-14). Here in the synagogue
at Nazareth, Jesus is rejected by his own people and, since
they spurn the opportunity, the door to the Gentiles will soon
open. Even within the Gospel, the pattern of the mission in
Acts is emerging /76/. As Jesus sets out on his last journey
to Jerusalem, he sends his disciples to a Samaritan village but
they are rejected (9.51ff). He sends out the seventy, a sending
which suggests the mission to the Gentiles (10.1ff) and is
patterned on the mission to Israel (9.1ff) (though one may be
a doublet of the other). It is interesting that Luke has only
one story of Jesus' mission to a Gentile (7.1-10) /77/.

But if Luke would find the saying of Jesus in Mark
difficult and, in relation to his purpose, difficult to use, the
saying peculiar to Matthew would be even more difficult: 'I
have been sent only to the lost sheep of the house of Israel'.
It is the kind of saying that could well have fitted into the
mission of the Twelve in Luke 9: 'Go only to the lost sheep of
the house of Israel'. Strecker considers that the saying could
have arisen from the application of a familiar Old Testament
motive /78/, e.g., 'We had all gone astray like sheep, each
taking his own way' (Isa. 53.6); 'My flock is straying this
way and that... my flock has been scattered over all the country;
no one bothers about them and no one looks for them' (Ezek.
34.2ff) /79/. It is interesting that the notion of someone
'lost', expressed by the intransitive perfect participle
ἀπολωλός, is not found in Mark. Indeed if we are to look for
an expansion of the thought of seeking for the lost, it is to
be found in Luke 15. There in the context of the Pharisees
and the scribes on the one hand and tax-gatherers and sinners
on the other, we are told on two occasions of the sheep that
was 'lost' (ἀπολωλός, 4,6) and on two occasions of the son who
was lost (24,32). The other occasion of the use of the perfect
participle intransitive is in Luke 19.10 where Jesus declares
what his mission is concerned with: 'The Son of Man came to
seek and to save that which was lost'; and where the one who
is described as 'lost', is the chief of the taxgatherers. The
implication appears to be that the Pharisees and scribes belong
to the ninety-nine just people who need no repentance and are
represented in the elder brother. Are we to take the
description 'righteous' as ironical (cf. the parable of the
Pharisee and the taxgatherer) and are we to say that the
expression 'elder son', who possesses all that the father has,
is not to be applied to Pharisees? Or are we to say that the
sheep are all the concern of the shepherd but it is only those
in particular need and distress that require urgent attention?

Whatever may be the explanation, it is clear that in Luke, we do not have the words 'lost' qualified by the addition 'of Israel' and yet these stories on what is lost belong to the tradition as much as the particularistic saying in Matthew 15.24. The one thing that distinguishes Jesus among his Jewish contemporaries is his concern for the outcast or lost and this is underlined by recent Jewish writing on the subject of Jesus /80/. In connection with the Matthaean saying, Jeremias's contention that the words 'of the house of Israel' are epexegetic (i.e. that 'lost sheep' = Israel) /81/ has been followed by a number of scholars, e.g. Bonnard, Gaechter, Strecker, Frankemölle, Schweizer. Can there be any suggestion that the leaders have already adopted a hostile attitude and therefore, as such, cannot be the objects of mission? The disciples for example are to shake the dust off from their feet of people or villages that reject them (Mt 10.14; pars). And is the description 'lost' for those sheep without a shepherd who are 'harassed and helpless' (Mt 9.36)? Luke insists on repentance and in the parable of the Pharisee and the taxgatherer (Lk 18. 9-14) it is the latter who repents. The representation of the Pharisee - even if overdrawn for emphasis - does show a type which, however religious and sacrificial, is not 'justified', i.e. it does not receive forgiveness. On numerous occasions in Luke, Jesus comes to present his claims and they are turned aside /82/. Thus on the one hand the authorities stand against him, while the taxgatherers and despised people, the 'lost', are found responding. But even if the Gentile mission comes out in a striking way in Luke, we could say with Jeremias that, as far as Jesus is concerned, he is sent only to the lost sheep of the house of Israel. It may be different for Luke in the case of the disciples, i.e. if we accept the mission of the seventy as for Gentiles, but this does not, as we have seen, alter Jesus' general approach. He concentrates on Israel /83/.

If however Luke avoids the particularistic way Matthew puts it, it is in keeping with his general practice. If one way of putting it is to say that Matthew rejudaizes the tradition /84/, we may accept that the tradition as such is not judaistic (though this is by no means certain). On the other hand, if Matthew is prior, we can say for example that Luke dejudaizes the tradition, i.e. by setting one Gospel presentation over against the other and assuming that at least one knows the other. It is an interesting point in this connection that Luke does not use the adjective formed on ἔθνος, i.e. ἐθνικός (Gentile). He does use ἔθνος more frequently than any other Gospel writer (15/6/13/5) but not always in the contrast 'Jewish/Gentile' /85/.

In the Matthaean use of the adjective, there is a note of
depreciation in all three occurrences of ἐθνικοί, viz. it is
like Gentiles to salute only your brethren (5.47), or to 'heap
up empty phrases' (6.7); an offender who will not listen to the
church is to be treated as a Gentile and as a tax-collector
(18.17). Luke retains only the first of these. Presumably if
he knew of them, he would not consider them to be helpful in
the Graeco-Roman situation he is addressing. The term 'Gentile'
appears in Mt 5.47 to be set in contrast with those who keep
the law and here Luke prefers to substitute 'sinner' as more
meaningful than 'Gentile' (6.32). Thus in the one case where
we can attempt to judge, Luke shows his concern about the
relevance of what he writes for the church and the people of his
time. Matthew, on the other hand, either retains these sayings
as reflecting Jesus' own attitude as a strict Jew or is
concerned to show to the stricter Jewish-Christians he addresses
the conservative attitude of Jesus to the law.

Thus in conclusion to this section on Luke, we have
attempted to explain why Luke omitted this pericope and to
discuss whether his reasons were justified or not in relation
to the purpose of his twofold work. There would be the problem
of the use of 'dog', of the particularistic saying of Jesus
which with his respect for the sayings of Jesus he would find
awkward to handle. Yet withal he does generally confine the
mission of Jesus to Israel (though not the mission of the
disciples) and when he speaks of the 'lost', he refers to members
of Israel. He does however on the whole avoid any offensive
terms that come from a Jewish (or Jewish Christian) milieu.

The traditions at the back of the Fourth Gospel, insofar
as they can be discerned, give no indication of knowing such a
narrative as this. Whatever parallels have been noted between
the story of the healing of the official's son and that of the
Canaanite woman are slight and there is really no true
comparison /86/. In the prologue however we find significant
words: 'He came to his own home, and his own people received
him not. But to all who received him, who believed in his name,
he gave authority to become children of God' (1.11,12). In a
way we could use the story of the Canaanite woman to expound
these verses. It was Jesus who made his way to Tyre - he took
the initiative. Was it because his own people had turned him
down? Was it to prepare in meditation for the final rejection;
for very soon the predictions of the Passion were to be made?
This is the one whom the Father sent; this is the one who is
the expression of the great love of God, God's gift; he did not

want anyone to be ill or to waste away or to perish; all who
believe on him, whether it be a Roman centurion or a Gentile
woman, find the way of healing, of life, of restoration. The
Canaanite woman received him, believed in his healing power,
and through her vicarious faith, her daughter was healed. Thus
we have the initiative of Jesus - he came. We have his
rejection - his own people would not have him. To all however
who received him he gave authority to become children of God.
The Canaanite woman responded to Jesus objection, 'It is not
right to take the children's bread and give it to the little
dogs', with her own declaration of faith, 'The dogs under the
table eat of the children's crumbs'. Thus faith opened a door
to the family of God and to the meals shared together where all
had enough /87/.

But in John's Gospel we get the impression that, just as
judgment and life are brought into the present, so in the Son
we have the manifestation of the divine glory /88/ and over
against it, we find the 'Jews', often a description of the
Jewish authorities /89/, in opposition almost from the very
start. It is one of the problems of the Fourth Gospel that the
'Jews" are presented emphatically in so many places in an
unfavourable light. We have to line them up with others who
as darkness oppose light, and as falsehood oppose truth and as
the world oppose God /90/, as suits the kind of dualism in the
Gospel. Not that the Jews are always seen in an unfavourable
light /91/. Jesus here is involved in disputes or discussions
with Jews so that in a way we could consent to the view that
they become a commentary on the saying, 'I have been sent only
to the lost sheep of the house of Israel'; but we would
immediately have to qualify it. Here is a Jesus who from the
start is acknowledged as the Messiah, the Son of God, the King
of Israel (1.41,49). Here is a Jesus who reveals his divine
glory in the first 'sign' of the water become wine (2.11).
Here in effect God confronts men with his total light. The
judgment κρίσις is in the here and now. It is put in this way:
'On these grounds is sentence pronounced: that though the light
has come into the world, men have shown they prefer darkness to
light because their deeds were evil' (3.19). No doubt at times
they are said to believe in him (8.31), and yet it would appear
these very Jews later take up stones to throw at him (8.59).
At other times they become divided over him (6.52; 9.16).

How could these in their hostility and aggressiveness in
any way resemble sheep that are lost? In the saying in Matthew
15.24 Jesus expresses himself in the passive: 'I have been sent'.

The passive has latent in it the action of God. Jesus could
have put it in another way: 'My father has sent me'. Bultmann
had suggested the influence of the Johannine idiom in Matthew
15.24 and that ἀπεστάλην is typical of the terminology of a
later time /92/. On these grounds he denies the saying is
authentic. Jeremias however rightly points out that at no point
in the Fourth Gospel is the passive of ἀποστέλλω used, but
throughout the Gospel the active is regularly used in the sending
of Jesus, e.g. ἀπέστειλεν ὁ θεὸς τὸν υἱόν (3.17) /93/. Rather
the passive ἀπεστάλην to avoid using the name of God is
characteristic of the early tradition. While this is true, we
may well ask if there is no possibility of the saying developing
in an active direction. The passive of ἀποστέλλω in the Gospels
is rare but nowhere else is it used for Jesus' coming except in
this passage /94/. The parallel verb πέμπω in the Fourth Gospel
is invariably in the active where the phrase ὁ πέμψάς με is more
frequent /95/.

We thus find the Jews set over generally in opposition to
Jesus in the Gospel, and no doubt this reflects the situation
in which the Gospel was written. Jews who dare to make
confession of Jesus are to be excommunicated (9.-2; 12.42;
16.2). This is the law of official Judaism. Is it strange
then if we get the impression that their opportunity generally
is forfeited and that they move over into the area of darkness
and the world which is essentially hostile to God? Jesus,
presented in all the glory of his divinity shows up their sin
all the more. It is an interesting point that ἀπολωλός does
not occur in this perfect middle form. Indeed in the sense of
'lose' the word is usually in John used of the disciples. Here
Jesus tells us that it is the Father's will that he should
lose nothing of all the Father gives him (6.39). The Father
gives Jesus the sheep and they shall never be lost or perish
(10.28). Again in the high-priestly prayer, Jesus can say that
he has lost none of them but the son of perdition and if he
is lost, it is to fulfil Scripture (17.12f; cf. also 18.19).
What we are being told here is that the number of the elect
determined by the Father's choice and their response in faith -
though it might appear that even this response is predetermined
/96/ - is never diminished. If the Son of Man came to seek and
save what was lost (Lk 19.10), this is what has been achieved.
Such a task has to do with the earthly Jesus, but it can also
be seen from the standpoint of the end time when those whom the
Father gives Jesus will be safely gathered and it will include
those who are not of this fold. There is still the right of
individual choice. They can 'receive' (1.11) and 'believe'

(1.11), and then at the same time the Father bestows the power
or authority to become sons of God, to enter his family through
a new birth and never be lost to the family of God.

In Matthew, however, it is not the 'lost of the house of
Judaism' but the lost of the 'house of *Israel*'. This is
important for John's Gospel where 'Israel' which occurs on only
four occasions (1.31,50; 3.10; 12.13) is used invariably in a
good sense and associated in some way with Jesus. The Baptist
came to manifest Jesus to Israel (1.31). Nathanael's confession
of faith includes 'You are...the king of Israel' (1.51).
Nicodemus, the ruler of the Jews, sympathetic to Jesus, is
addressed by Jesus, 'Are you a teacher of Israel?'. The term
refers to the (Jewish) people of God /97/. It can stand for the
people of God whether past or present almost 'as a supernatural
entity' /98/. It is not used for the new people of God. Yet
within it, there are those who, like Nathanael, are 'truly
Israelite' /99/. Since the term is linked in John with those
from Israel who are sympathetic to Jesus, it can mean that the
true people of God are defined by their response to Jesus and,
in some sense anticipate their membership of the new Israel. It
should be noted that the phrase 'house of God' does not occur
in John. The Temple is called the 'house of my Father' (2.16)
but there is no suggestion of the 'household of God'. Would
this have been suggestive of an institution for John who prefers
to talk in symbols or images?

Does John envisage a Gentile mission in his Gospel?
Jeremias insists that none of the Gospel writers indicates that
Jesus in his lifetime directed his mission to Gentiles /100/.
The 'Greeks' who through Philip ask to see Jesus would be
representative of the Gentiles /101/. We are not told however
that they met Jesus and the request is left hanging in the air
(12.20ff.) /102/. It anticipates the point, pivotal in the
Gospel, where Jesus announces the hour when he is to be
glorified /12.23). This glorification includes the Cross,
resurrection and ascension /103/. In the discourse on the
Shepherd and the sheep, Jesus mentions the 'other sheep' whom
he must bring and here the Gentiles are clearly implied. The
point, however, when they will be brought is when Jesus is
crucified and exalted: 'I, when I am lifted up from the earth,
will draw all men to myself' (12.32). If the Fourth Gospel
has, as part of its purpose, the encouragement of the Gentiles
/104/, we can understand why any kind of particularist expression
falls into the background. Those whom God seeks to worship him,
whether Jew or Samaritan, are to worship him in spirit and in

truth (4.24). The place where the worship is centred is no
longer a matter of primary importance. In Jesus vital contact
between heaven and earth has been inaugurated (1.51) - this is
the important fact. In addition God's love is directed to the
world. The Samaritans in the apprehension of faith recognise
Jesus as 'the Saviour of the world' (4.42).

It is notable that John does not use the plural ἔθνη
(Gentiles) at all. He uses the singular ἔθνος and applies it
to the Jewish nation, for whom, according to Caiaphas, Jesus
was to die (11.51), and to gather in one the children of God
who were scattered abroad (11.52). The phrase 'children (τέκνα)
of God' occurs only once elsewhere in the Gospel (1.12). There
we are given a definition of the τέκνα θεοῦ, those who have a
right to this description. It is those who receive him, who
believe on his name. 'Children of God...is a way of expressing
the privilege of the 'Chosen People' in a universal way without
the old limitation to Jews' /105/. The description 'scatter
abroad' has Old Testament links which remind us again of Jesus'
concern for lost sheep. Ezekiel, for example, writes of God:
'As a shepherd seeks out his flock when some of his sheep have
been scattered abroad, so will I seek out my sheep' (34.12).
It is probable that John knows the application of Zechariah
13.7 to Jesus: 'Strike the shepherd, that the sheep may be
scattered' (cf. Mt 26.31; Mk 14.27). Even if it is a kind of
apologetic for the disciples' desertion /106/, Jesus still has
to gather again the scattered disciples who have become, as it
were, lost through the events of the Passion. Precisely at the
point of desertion, failure and weakness the gathering again of
the people of God begins. As it is expressed in the Fourth
Gospel, God has given them to Jesus and none of them is to be
lost.

To sum up: our discussion on the Fourth Gospel shows that
there is no sign of any ancient tradition such as we find in the
story of the Canaanite woman. Jesus, seen primarily in his
divine glory, confronts 'Jews' who, in general, with all other
hostile forces in the Johannine dualism, reject him and
judgment, as salvation for others, becomes 'realised' for them.
The church is made up of the elect whose number is predetermined
to such an extent that human choice seems almost but not
completely eliminated. While Jesus does not himself engage in
the mission to Gentiles, such a mission is clearly implicit,
not only in the sayings but some of the incidents in the Gospel.

NOTES

/1/   In addition to commentaries, for recent articles see
T.A. Burkill, *New Light on the earliest Gospel*, London, 1972,
48-120 (earlier in NovT, 1967, 161ff.; and in ZNW, 1966, 23-37);
B. Flammer, *Syrophenician Woman,* ThQ, 1968, 463-478;
A. Dermience, *La syrophenicienne,* Marc 7. 24-30, RevThLouv,
1977, 15-29. Cf. also G. Baumbach, *Die Mission im Mt-Evangelium,*
TL, 1967, 88ff.; S. Brown, *The two-fold representation of mission
in Matthew's Gospel,* StTh, 1977, 21-32. Cf. also G. Strecker,
Der Weg der Gerechtigkeit, Göttingen, 1962, 107-108; G. Bornkamm,
G. Barth, H.J. Held, *Tradition and Interpretation in Matthew*
(ET), London, 1963, esp. 197-200; W. Trilling, *Das wahre Israel,*
Munich, 1964, 99-105; R. Walker, *Die Heilsgeschichte im ersten
Evangelium,* Göttingen, 1967, 60-63; H. Frankemölle, *Jahwebund
und Kirche Christi,* 114-115, 135-137.
/2/   Among recent commentators, e.g. P. Bonnard, Neuchatel,
1963, rev. 1970; J.C. Fenton, London, 1963; W. Grundmann,
Berlin, 1968; D. Hill, London, 1972; H.B. Green, Oxford, 1975;
E. Schweizer, London (ET), 1976.
/3/   Op.cit., p. 198.
/4/   We may note the number of participles which are compounds
of ἔρχομαι in the pericopae of both Gospels: ἐξελθών (Mt 15.21),
εἰσελθών (Mk 7.24), ἐξελθοῦσα (Mt 15.22), ἀπελθοῦσα (Mk 7.30).
Cf. Dermience, op.cit., p.17, noting the double participles
ἀκούσασα...ἐλθοῦσα (Mk. 7.25; 5.27, 33), writes: 'On peut
remarquer de part et d'autre la tournure marcienne du double
participe sans coordination'. Matthew too has a doubling of
the participle in this pericope but the second follows the verb
and is a verb of saying, e.g. ἐξελθοῦσα...λέγουσα (22),
προσελθόντες...λέγοντες (23), ἐλθοῦσα...λέγουσα (25). But both
Mt (9.20; 11.2; 13.46; 14.19(3); 16.1; 20.29; 25.16,20,24,25;
26.44) and Mk (3.5; 5.27,30,33; 6.41; 7.25; 8.23; 12.28; 14.22,
23,45,67; 15.36) have examples of uncoordinated participles.
Of the 13 instances of Mark, only two are found in Mt (Two
feedings: 6.41; 14.22 and two others with the addition of 'and'
(14.23; 15.36).
/5/   Cf. H. Riesenfeld, *The Gospel Tradition and its
beginnings,* London, 1961^2, 27f.; B. Gerhardsson, *Memory and
Manuscript,* Lund, 1964^2, 324-335.
/6/   Cf. Burkill, op. cit., p.118. If the saying is proverbial
then it could lend itself to varying interpretations which could
develop orally in the two directions represented in Matthew and
Mark especially in relation to their situation, e.g. that of
Jewish-Christian for Matthew and that of a (mainly) Gentile
setting at Rome for Mark. We may well ask if it is impossible

that such a proverb had a Christian application. We have a
tradition of Jesus saying not to cast one's pearls before swine
(Mt 7.6 - the only Gospel to mention μαργαριται; cf. Mt 13.45),
i.e. the disciples are to be realistic in a situation of
rejection. When the disciples are sent out on mission, all the
synoptic accounts speak of the disciples being commanded to
leave those who will not receive them and to shake the dust off
their feet from that place (Mk 6.11; Mt 10.14; Lk 9.5) 'for a
witness to them' (only Mk 3.11 and Lk 9.5). Further, while most
of the references to τέκνα have to do with the situation in the
family (Mk 10.29,30; 12.19; 13.12), Jesus uses it on two
occasions in address, first to the paralysed man who is
pronounced forgiven and on the other occasion to the disciples
as a whole (Mk 2.5; 10.24). It is possible that the first is
a recognition that this man, on the ground of his faith which
he shares with those who carry him (Mk 2.5 and pars) is part
of the family of God. Here is one who is given to know the
mystery of the kingdom (Mk 4.11). Similarly, the disciples are
addressed as τέκνα before Jesus lets them into the mystery of
the place of riches in the kingdom of God and in a context
which deals with the sacrifices they make in leaving their
families including their own τέκνα (Mk 10.29). Is there then
implicit in the address τέκνα, the concept of the family of
God, that of the bread of the family of faith and of its not
being available for those who fail to respond? If the saying
has eucharistic overtones (cf. discussion in Q. Quesnell, *The
Mind of Mark*, Rome, 1969, 10ff.) in a wider context which
includes two feedings, then it is even clearer that the
fellowship of the church can be meant. Even if this is the
only clear address of τέκνα to the disciples, taking the
pericope of sayings about sacrifice of family, it is obvious
it prepares for the mention of the family and implies the
family of God over against those who are not of the family.
We have further confirmation of what constitutes membership of
the family elsewhere, i.e. those who do the will of God in a
setting where Jesus' own family along with the authorities
are placed in opposition to the reign of God and in danger of
the unpardonable sin. It is noticeable that Jesus does not
appear to have consented to see them (cf. 3.13-19 and 3.21,22;
3.31-35). Mt and Lk agree in omitting the sentence which
includes the τέκνα, assuming they use Mk. Mk, on the other,
if he expands in a redundant style, deliberately inserts the
τέκνα (10.24; cf. Mt 19.23f.; Lk 18.24f.). The pattern of
salvation and judgment, of acceptance and rejection, of
obedience and rebellion, is something that belongs to the
experience of the OT prophets. It would always be something of

a mystery that God can harden some as an expression of refusal and accept others. In the light of the contrast between the pagan ethic and that of Judaism, it is little wonder if, alongside the food-laws, the attitude to the Gentiles developed as it did. Would it not help to shape the attitude of the church in its thought about those who refuse Jesus as the bearer of salvation?

/7/   Cf. W. Foerster, *TDNT,* Vol.3, Art. κύριος, 1086, 1092; O. Cullmann, *The Christology of the New Testament,* London, 1959, 196.

/8/   W.F. Arndt, F.W. Gingrich, *A Greek-English Lexicon of the NT,* Cambridge, 1957, 534, where Ναί, Κυριε can be an assent to Jesus' statement ('Certainly, Lord'), while the καὶ γάρ (strictly (strictly 'not yet') can mean 'an urgent repetition of the request'.

/9/   Cf. Bonnard, op.cit., ad loc., where he claims that it is not the woman's address of 'Son of David' that brings out her faith but her humble insistence on the help of Jesus. It is not necessary probably to distinguish. Both contribute to the total portrait of the woman with her faith and her humility.

/10/   Münster, 1974, Cf. S. Brown, op. cit., on the tension of Jewish-Gentile mission.

/11/   'Individuell-personale Begriffe in der mt Ekklesiologie', (84-190), and 'Die Gemeindemitglieder als Jünger (Jesu)' (84-158); cf. G. Baumbach, op.cit., on the distinctiveness of Mt's mission.

/12/   Op.cit., 114.

/13/   'diesen lezten, geradezu feierlich klingenden Satz', op. cit., 114. Cf. Held, (ET), p.199.

/14/   Op.cit., 114, n.164.

/15/   Cf. W.R. Farmer, *The Synoptic Problem,* London, 1964, 233, who claims that 'it is possible to explain the history of the Synoptic tradition more adequately on the Griesbach hypothesis than on any hypothesis which posits the priority of Mark'. Among some of his more significant points are; (1) Mk leaves out the Sermon on the Mount because it does not suit his theological purpose. (2) It is not possible to explain the number of changes from καί to δέ in Mt and Lk on the basis of chance; they might have worked on an improved copy of Mk or Mk may have used them both. (3) How is it Mt and Lk agree on omitting the number of the swine (Mk 5.13 pars), or of the cost of the bread (6.37 and pars) or of the ointment (14.5)? Or does Mk have the same expansive tendencies of the Apocryphal tradition? (4) How is it Mt follows Mk's order when Lk deserts it and vice versa? It is better explained if Mk uses both. (5) Is the phrase 'At evening when the sun set'

an instance of Marcan redundancy or of Mk's conflation of Mt
and Lk? (6) If most of Mk is in Mt and a good part in Lk is
this not better explained if Mk makes use of them both? (7)
If Mk has vulgarisms, these are found in Apocryphal literature
and are features of a deliberately cultivated homely style. It
is evident that here in Farmer we have a vigorous challenge
to the theory of Marcan priority. Cf. also E.P. Sanders, *The
Tendencies of the Synoptic Tradition,* Cambridge, 1969, Appendix
II 'Suggested exceptions to the priority of Mark' (290); H-H.
Stoldt, *Geschichte und Kritik d. Markus-Hypothese, Göttingen*
1977.
/16/ B. Weiss, *Das Matthäusevangelium,* Halle, 1896, ad loc.
/17/ A.H. McNeile, *Matthew,* London, 1915, followed by
Klostermann, *Das Matthäusevangelium,* HNT, Tübingen, 1927. Cf.
also P. Gaechter, *Das Matthäusevangelium,* 1962, ad loc.;
Grundmann, op.cit., Bonnard, op.cit.
/18/ Schweizer, op.cit., ad loc.
/19/ Grundmann, op.cit., ad loc.
/20/ Place-names are mentioned at Mk 1.9 (Mt 3.13 omits
Nazareth); Mk 1.14 (= Mt 4.12); Mk 2.1 (Mt 9.1 where Mt replaces
'Capernaum' with 'his own city'); Mk 3.8 (Mt 4.25 omits Idumaea,
Tyre and Sidon but adds Decapolis); Mk 6.45 (Mt 14.32 omits
Bethsaida); Mk 6.53 (Mt 14.32); Mk 7.31 (Mt 15.29 omits Tyre,
Sidon and Decapolis but retains 'Galilee'); Mk 8.27 (= Mt 16.13);
Mk 9.30 (= Mt 17.22); Mt 9.33 (Mt 18.1 omits Capernaum); Mk 10.1
(Mt 19.1 where Mt adds 'Galilee'); Mk 10.46 (= Mt 20.29); Mk 11.1
(Mt 21.1 omits Bethany); Mk 11.12 (Mt 21.18 omits 'Bethany').
/21/ Mt's interest of course in 4.25 is to give as wide a
setting as possible for the sermon on the Mount and he brings
in Decapolis from elsewhere. As for Mk 10.1 and Mt 19.1 it
depends on how we interpret their relationship, i.e. does Mk
expand or Mt reduce?
/22/ Cf. Acts 17.12, the only other place where the term occurs
in the N.T. (τῶν Ἑλληνίδων γυναικῶν τῶν εὐσχημόνων καὶ ἀνδρῶν
οὐκ ὀλίγοι).
/23/ Cf. A. Dermience, op.cit., 23.
/24/ Liddell and Scott refer it only to this passage. It is
not mentioned in G.W.H. Lampe (ed.), *A Patristic Lexicon,*
Oxford, 1968, Fascicle V.
/25/ D. Junius Juvenalis, *Satires,* 8, 158-162. The Latin text
is: "Sed, cum pervigiles placet instaurare popinas
        obvius adsiduo Syrophoenix unctus amomo
        currit, Idymaeae Syrophoenix incola portae,
        hospitis adfectu dominum regemque salutat,
        et cum venali Cyane succincta lagona."
Cf. C.T. Lewis and C. Short, *A Latin Dictionary,* Oxford 1966,

s.v. 'Syrophoenix'.
/26/ Dermience, op.cit., 22.
/27/ For other variants, e.g. 'Aramaean' or 'Gentile' cf.
S.C.E. Legg, *Novum Testamentum Graece*, Evangelium secundum
Marcum, Oxford, 1935, ad loc.; cf. also the variations,
indicative of scribal misgivings, in the spelling of
Συροφοινίσσα in some Greek mss. This would be understandable
if the word was unknown.
/28/ Cf. G.D. Kilpatrick, *The Origins of the Gospel according
to St. Matthew*, Oxford 1946, 132, who, on the basis that Mt
used Mk, argues that Συροφοινίσσα would suggest she came from
the Syrian ports while 'Canaanite' would apply to inland Semitic
villages.
/29/ See note 15.
/30/ For a discussion, see J.C. Hawkins, *Horae Synopticae*,
Oxford, 1909[2], 150-153.
/31/ The list is lengthy: 1.9, 12, 16, 21, 23, 40; 2.1, 13, 18,
27; 3.1, 13, 20, 37; 4.1, 10, 13, 21, 24, 26, 30, 35; 5.1, 21;
6.1, 14, 30, 45, 53; 7.1, 24.
/32/ The following are possible adversative uses of δέ: 1.14,
30, 32, 45; 2.6, 10, 18, 20, 21, 22; 3.4, 29; 4.11, (15), 29,
34; 5.(11), 33, 40; 6.15[2], 16, 19; 6.49, 50; 7.11. Other uses
of δέ are in dialogue: 5.34; 6.37, 38; 7.6; but these too have
a slightly adversative effect, i.e. one speaker over against
another. In this unit (7.24-30) the δέ of vs. 26 is probably
adversative, i.e. she falls at his feet *but* she was a
Syrophenician, i.e. this is what presents the problem; in vs.
28 it occurs in the course of the dialogue.
/33/ The difficulty is that we have no clear parallel to this
except perhaps 10.32, which is different from the other passion
predictions (8.31; 9.31) in that it takes place as they are
going up to Jerusalem, the importance of which is underlined
by the repetition of the fact (10.32,33).
/34/ The occurrences in the Gospels are 12/5/3/2.
/35/ Viz. Mk 6.1, 10, 11; 7.24; 10.1. Mt uses ἐκεῖθεν in the
parallels to 6.1 and 7.24; omits probably as redundant in 6.10;
and expands 6.11 and 10.1.
/36/ Mt. 2.22; 15.21; 16.13; 24.51; Mk 8.10. In Mk it is εἰς
τὰ μέρη Δαλμανουθα while the parallel in Mt (15.39) has εἰς τὰ
ὅρια Μαγαδαν.
/37/ Mt 2.16; 4.13; 8.34 (= Mk 5.17); 15.22 (cf. Mk 7.24), 39
(see note 36); 19.1 (= Mk 10.1). Also Mk 7.31[2].
/38/ Cf. U. Luz, ZNW, 1965, 1ff. on *'Das Geheimnismotiv u. d.
mark. Christologie'*, who deals with the possible implications
of this fact.
/39/ Cf. W.G. Kümmel, *Introduction to the N.T.* (ET), London,

1966, 76, for evidence that MT tended to idealize the disciples but did not proceed consistently in this though the inconsistency may belong to the tradition MT took over.

/40/ Mt may see the incongruity of the mention of a 'house' and substitute for this κατ' ἰδιαν. On the other hand Mk's over-riding purpose may make him refuse to see such incongruity. The theological implication of 'house' was decisive?

/41/ Mt 4.21; 9.9,27; 12.9; 15.21,29. But this also applies to any verbal form, viz. 5.26; 11.1; 12.15; 13.53; 14.13; 19.15. It also applies to Mk (6.1,10,11) except when used with ἀναστάς (7.24; 10.1), and two of these are used with the verb ἐξέρχομαι (6.1,10) and one with ἐκπορεύομαι (6.11).

/42/ The distribution in the Gospels is 10/1/-/1.

/43/ In the Gospels 35/23/19/21.

/44/ So J.C. Fenton, *St Matthew,* London 1963, on Mt 2.14. He suggests that Mt's use of the term is due to the first occurrence of the term in the LXX: 'Moses fled (ἀνεχώρησεν) from Pharaoh, and stayed in the land of Midian' (Exod. 2.15). Cf. P. Gaechter, *Das Matthäusevangelium* on 15.21 where he speaks of the deliberate withdrawal of Jesus in 12.15; 14.13 and here.

/45/ Cf. R. Bultmann, *History of the Synoptic Tradition* (ET), Oxford, 1963, 163; Trilling, op. cit., 101ff.; Walker, op. cit., p.63; Hare, op. cit., 146 note 1; Strecker, op. cit., on 15.24: 'es wird in den Debatten der Urgemeinde um die Heidenmission einen (den ersten?) "Sitz im Leben" gehabt haben' (107); Kilpatrick, op. cit., 119. All of these assume that Matthew uses Mark of course.

/46/ Walker, op. cit., 148, denies that Mt is a catechetical handbook, a new Torah (W.D. Davies, *The Setting of the Sermon on the Mount,* Cambridge, 1964, 93) or liturgical lectionary (Kilpatrick, op. cit., 59). Rather the situation is more complex and he prefers to call it a 'Kerygma-Geschichts-buch' (149).

/47/ Mark has 42 uses of εὐθύς of which only seven are used by Matthew (3.16 (1.10); 13.20 (4.16); 13.21 (4.17); 14.27 (6.50); 21.2 (11.2); 21.3 (11.3); 26.74 (14.72).

/48/ Precisely the same thing happens in the pericope on the woman with the haemorrhage (Mk 5.27; Mt 9.20).

/49/ The phrase is Biblical, e.g. Gen 1.31; 15.17; 24.15; 29.2; etc. Matthew cultivates the Biblical idiom in which Mk is not much interested, e.g. Matthew uses ἰδού on 62 occasions compared with Mark's seven.

/50/ There is however one exception: Mt 21.41.

/51/ Cf. J.M. Gibbs, *Purpose and Pattern in Matthew's Use of 'Son of David',* NTS, 1964, 446ff.

/52/ The statistics are 9/3/3/-.

/53/   Cf. however Luke 18.38 where we have 'Jesus, Son of David'.
/54/   Mk 10.47,48 (Blind man); Lk 18.38,39 (Blind man): Mt 20.
30,31; 9.27 (all blind men. Mt has them in twos unlike the
others).
/55/   Cf. Frankemölle, op. cit., 114.
/56/   Cf. E. Lohse, TDNT, VIII, 486.
/57/   Lohse, op. cit.
/58/   Cf. Held, op. cit., followed by Frankemölle, op. cit.
/59/   Cf. Mgr de Solages, *La composition des Evangiles,* Leiden,
1973, 119ff.
/60/   Mark also can turn indirect style into direct: Solages,
op. cit., 117f. (Lk or Mt). As an example of a direct style
where it is absent in Matthew, cf. 4.35: 'He said to them, "Let
us pass to the other side"' (Mt 8.18: 'He told them to cross to
the other side'); cf. also 6.23 (Mt 14.7); 10.35 (Mt 20.20);
10.52 (Mt 20.34); 13.1 (Mt 24.1).
/61/   Cf. Mt 8.2 (Mk 4.36); Mt 9.19 (Mk 5.24); (Mt 9.35; Lk 10.
2); Mt 16.5 (Mk 8.14); Mt 16.20 (Mk 8.30); Mt 16.21 (Mk 8.31);
Mt 17.6(-); Mt 17.10 (Mk 9.11); Mt 17.12 (Mk 9.13); Mt 18.1 (Mk
9.33); Mt 19.25 (Mk 10.26); Mt 21.6 (Mk 11.4); Mt 21.20 (Mk 11.
21 for 'Peter'); Mt 23.1 (Mk 12.37b); Mt 24.3 (Mk 13.3); Mt
26.1(-); Mt 26.8 (Mk 14.4); Mt 26.20 (Mk 14.17); Mt 26.26 (Mk
14.22); Mt 26.35 (Mk 14.31); Mt 26.40 (Q) (Mk 14.37); Mt 26.45
(Mk 14.41).
/62/   Matthew is the only Gospel writer to describe the disciples
as ὀλιγόπιστοι (6.30; 8.26; 14.31; 16.8) except Luke (only one
occasion: 12.28).
/63/   So M. Lehmann, *Synoptische Quellenanalyse u.d. Frage nach
dem historischen Jesus,* Berlin, 1970, 38, quoting E. Hirsch,
Frühgeschichte des Evangeliums, 1951.
/64/   Other well-known examples of vicarious faith are Mt 9.2
and pars; it is out of character that Mt should omit tradition
of the Marcan kind where the father of the epileptic boy can
say πιστεύω: βοήθει μου τῇ ἀπιστίᾳ (Mk 9.24), but it suits his
purpose of condensing.
/65/   ἀπόλυσον can mean 'set free', and this does appear to fit
in better with what Jesus proceeds to say: 'I cannot set her
free. My mission is to Israel'.
/66/   A point stressed by R.V.G. Tasker, *Matthew,* London, 1961,
ad loc.
/68/   This attitude made Jesus the object of Pharisaic hostility.
Cf. C.H. Talbert, *Literary patterns, theological themes and the
genre of Luke-Acts,* Missoula, 1974, 20.
/67/   Bultmann, op. cit., 155, is suspicious of this type of
'I-saying'. He writes, 'All these sayings which speak of the
θέλειν of Jesus, are also under suspicion of being church
products because this terminology seems to be the means of

looking back to the historical appearance of Jesus as a whole':
cf. also P. Bonnard, op. cit., ad loc. Bonnard discusses the
question as to whether the saying came from Judaizing circles
of primitive Christianity and points out rightly that the
dialogue would be judaizing only if it imposed Jewish legal
conditions on the woman, e.g. purifications, proselyte baptism,
confession of faith, etc.

/69/ O. Michel, TDNT, III, 1104.

/70/ A generally accepted view of Luke's purpose is not to be
found and often contradictory views are held. See Kummel, op.
cit., 99,115.

/71/ Cf. Acts 17,6,7; 24.5; 25.8. On Roman officials proving
Christians are innocent: 16.39; 18.15f; 19.37; 23.29; 25.25;
26.31. Cf. also 28.30f.

/72/ Cf. G.F. Moore, *Judaism*, I, Oxford, 1962[9], 515.

/73/ Other examples may be cited, e.g. Mt 3.7-10 and Lk 3.7-9;
or Lk 19.45-46 and Mt 21.13.

/74/ Cf. Strecker, op. cit., 107, where he suggests the πρῶτον
sentence may not belong to the earliest tradition.

/75/ Eg. in his use of εὐαγγέλιον and his emphasis in the
structure of his Gospel on the Cross and the vicarious death
of Jesus.

/76/ Cf. W. Radl, *Paulus und Jesus im lukanischen Doppelwerk*,
Berne, 1975, inquires into the parallel motives in Luke and
Acts. He draws a parallel between the opening ministry of
Jesus in the synagogue with that of Paul in Acts 13.14-52:
(1) They are both in the synagogue on the Sabbath. (2) Jesus
is invited to read the Scripture while Paul is invited to speak
after the reading of the Scripture (13.15). (3) We have the
effect of the preaching ('astonished by the words of "grace")
(Lk 16.22); Paul & Barnabas urge the converts to 'remain faithful
to the grace God had given them' (Ac. 13.43)). (4) Then the
hostile reaction (Lk 4.28-30: Ac 13.50-52). (5) The rejection
shows that salvation is for the Gentiles (Lk 4.25-27; Ac 13.46).
(6) It is no mere rejection but anger (Lk 4.29; Ac 13.50).
(7) Both Jesus and Paul leave the place of persecution for
another locality (Lk:Capernaum; Paul:Iconium).

/77/ Cf. J. Jeremias, *Jesus' Promise to the Nations*, London,
1959[2], 34.

/78/ Op. cit., 107, note 6.

/79/ Other references are Ps. 119. 176; Isa. 11.12; Jer. 27.6;
26.17; 1 Kings 22.17 (LXX).

/80/ D. Flusser, *Jesus*, New York, 1969, 91; G. Vermes, *Jesus
the Jew*, London, 1973,58; cf. W. Jacob, *Christianity through
Jewish Eyes*, New York, 1974, 104 (Montefiore).

/81/ Op. cit., 26, note 3.

/82/ 4.29; 5.21,30; 6.2,7,11; 7.39; 10.13,15; 11.29.39-54; 13.34; 16.14,15; 9.51-56; 19.41,42,47; 20.19 (cf. also Acts): i.e., in all his sources, Mk, Q and L.

/83/ Jeremias argues for Mt 15.24 as an authentic saying of Jesus, op. cit., 26, note 2; cf. also Hare, op. cit., 94, note 6.

/84/ Strecker, op. cit., 108; S. Brown, op. cit., 26, where mission to Jews is traditional and that to Gentiles redactional.

/85/ = Gentiles (2.32; 18.32; 21.24; 22.25); = Nations (12.30; 21.24; 21.25; 24.47).

/86/ R.E. Brown, *St. John*, I, London, 1971, ad loc.

/87/ Grundmann, op. cit., emphasizes the concept of the family of God in this pericope.

/88/ Cf. E. Käsemann, *The Testament of Jesus* (ET), London, 1968, 6, claims that the phrase 'we beheld his glory' sums up the content of the Fourth Gospel.

/89/ Probably the following refer to 'Jews' as the authorities: 1.19; 5.10,18; 6.41,52; 7.11,35; 8.48; 9.18,24; 10.19,24,31.

/90/ Cf. O. Böcher, *Der johannische Dualismus im Zusammenhang des nachbiblischen Judentums*, Gütersloh, 1965, 26: 'Der Gegensatz zwischen Jesus und den Juden ist ein Gegensatz zwischen 'oben' und 'unten'; der vom Himmel Kommende ist zugleich der von oben Kommende (ὁ ἄνωθεν ἐρχόμενος, Joh. 3.31). Die Juden sind 'von dieser Welt' and damit ἐν τῷ κάτω, während Jesus von sich sagt: Ἐγὼ ἐκ τῶν ἄνω εἰμί (Joh. 8.23)'.

/91/ Cf. 2.6,13,18; 3.1; 4.9,22,52 (dispute among Jews); 7.15; 8.31 (Jews who believe in him); 11.19 (Jews who console Martha and Mary), 11.31,33,36,45; 12.9,11).

/92/ Op. cit., 155f.

/93/ Op. cit., 27.

/94/ Cf. however Mt 23.37; Lk 1.19,26; 13.34; John 1.6,24,28.

/95/ Of 32 uses of the verb, 25 are found in this phrase ὁ πέμψας με in John.

/96/ Cf. S. Schulz, *Die Stunde der Botschaft*, Zurich, 1970[2]: 'die Zugehörigkeit zur Gemeinde ist als absolutes Gnadengeschenk verstanden.' (6.44;17.3; 12.32) (356); E. Schweizer, *Church Order in the New Testament* (ET) London, 1961, where he can say: 'The openness of Jesus' circle of disciples has vanished...such predestination excludes all development within the church' (11e,fg).

/97/ W. Gutbrod, TDNT, III, 385f.

/98/ Op. cit.

/99/ Ἰσραηλίτης' only here in John (1.48). It suggests Nathanael is of pure Jewish stock, the devout Jew ('In whom is no guile'), 'whom the Christian may hope to convert by a reasonable exposition of the Messianic claims of Jesus' (Lindars,

op. cit., ad loc.).
/100/   Op. cit., 37.
/101/   Cf. Lindars, ad loc., who thinks of 'devout Gentiles'; cf.
R. Schnackenburg, *Das Johannesevangelium*, II,Basel, 1971, 478.
/102/   R.E. Brown, op.cit., ad loc., is possibly correct when he
explains that it is more important theologically to the writer
to speak of the *coming* of the Gentiles. He is concerned to spell
out that they reached Jesus. Or, we may add, is he not implying
the Gentiles do not gain admission until after the glorification?
/103/   Schnackenburg, op. cit., ad loc. By 'glorification' he
means the fullness of power for salvation given to him to draw
all men to himself.
/104/   Cf. R.E. Brown, op. cit., II, 442.
/105/   Lindars, op. cit., ad loc.
/106/   Op. cit.

Matthew 25:1-13. A Summary of Matthaean Eschatology?

J. M. Sherriff,
Department of Philosophy and Religious Studies,
University of Stirling,
Stirling, FK9 4LA,
Scotland.

Despite obvious idiosyncrasies, J. Massingberd-Ford's
discussion of the story of the Ten Maidens (at Matthew 25:1-13) /1/,
serves our purpose as a methodological and, to a certain extent,
interpretative paradigm for a number of studies which have dealt
with this pericope in recent years /2/. Analyzing the story's
main elements against an essentially Jewish background, she argues
that the maidens symbolize Jewish scholars, their lamps symbolize
the Torah, and the oil good deeds. Ford believes that Jesus told
the parable against the hypocrisy of the Jewish leaders. Viewed in
this light, the foolish scholars, who simply studied the Torah and
did not practise good deeds (unlike the wise scholars), are refused
admittance to the Chamber of Instruction (the bridal chamber) /3/.

Although much that Ford has to offer is called into question
by her use of late rabbinic sources, she clearly demonstrates that
the pericope does lend itself quite neatly to an allegorical
reading. However, we would wish to draw attention to the fact
that invariably two initial stages of interpretation are omitted
when an allegorical understanding is sought. It is our view that
these two stages provide weighty support for any such analysis.
Hence, in this paper we concern ourselves with:

i) A consideration of the plot of the narrative. An analysis of
the story in terms of its plot reveals via its main features what
is important for the story itself.
ii) A consideration of the setting of the pericope. The story
under discussion forms part of Matthew's eschatological discourse
(chapters 24 and 25). Unless it can be shown that the story is
incompatible with its surrounding material, its setting surely
provides us with concrete grounds for interpretation.

THE PLOT

An investigation of the narrative quickly establishes that
feature which is central to the plot. This is seen to be the
delay of the bridegroom (v.5, χρονίζοντος δὲ τοῦ νυμφίου) /4/.
Several reasons support this observation:

i) The groom's delay causes the true situation of the foolish to be
discovered. It is only because the groom is a long time in coming
that the foolish ones run out of oil. Hence, the groom's delay is
the true cause of the division wise/foolish /5/.

ii) The foolish fall from their appointed duty of greeting the
groom as they are absent, purchasing more oil, when he arrives.
His delay is the cause of their absence.

iii) Those who remained unaffected by the groom's delay, and were
ready to greet him on his arrival, enter with him into the feast
(γάμος).   Those affected by his delay are excluded.

The story seems to counsel preparedness in the performance of one's
allotted duty, in the face of a delay.

THE SETTING

Turning to a consideration of the setting of 25:1-13 within
Matthew's eschatological discourse, it is evident that a deliberate
grouping of pericopes has occurred within the section 24:37-25:30
/6/.   The story of the maidens is placed fourth in this sequence
of five pericopes which all labour under the common theme of the
arrival of a certain person or event. This arrangement is
singularly Matthaean.

Several features can be identified as running throughout this
section /7/. For instance, in *four out of five pericopes* occur
the themes of the suddenness and unpredictability of events (24:39,
50, 25:6, and 19), and warnings of coming judgements and division
(24:40-41, 51, 25:11-12, and 19ff.). *Three out of the five*
pericopes under discussion contain a demand for proper performance
of duties (24:45-51, 25:1-13 and 14-30) and exhibit a note of delay
which is integral to the plot of the story (24:48, 25:5 and 19).
Finally, *two pericopes* contain an exhortation to watch (24:42-44
and 25:13). It seems to be rather significant that all five of
these elements are identifiable within 25:1-13:

a) The groom's arrival is sudden and unpredictable (v.6).

b) The maidens are divided into two groups (vv.2, 12).

c) Abandonment of one's duty results in exclusion, while
    proper performance guarantees inclusion (vv.10-12).

d) The story concludes with an exhortation to watch (v.13).

e) The delay of the groom is an integral feature of the plot (v.5).

So, Matthew himself provides us with an adequate starting
point for interpretation. Not only has the pericope a setting in
his eschatological discourse, but it can be seen that certain
points of teaching evidenced within the whole of the section
24:37-25:30 are included within this one story. In its own
right the story of the Ten Maidens serves as an apt summary statement of this section.

The plot of the narrative suggested that its most significant
feature is the delay of the groom. As we saw from the story's
setting within the discourse as a whole, and particularly within
this section of teaching, Matthew includes a "delay" at three
points. In the material over 24:37-25:30 which Matthew and Luke
share, Luke exhibits the feature of "delay" at one point only
(Lk.12:45, parallel to Mt.24:48). Mark, in his comparable
material, does not include this feature. Therefore, Matthew has
two occasions peculiar to his gospel in which a note of delay
occurs (25:5, and 19). If this story is a Matthaean creation /8/,
then the stress on the delay may indicate something of Matthew's
own situation and concerns. The question remains, however, as
to why Matthew should want to create a story with this particular
emphasis. An answer is perhaps provided by a brief examination of
the situation to which the eschatological discourse as a whole is
addressed.

The discourse (chapters 24 and 25, parallel to Mark 13) is
concerned with an interim period, the time before the coming of
the Son of Man and the end of the age. It warns against being
misled by false messiahs and prophets (24:5f., 11, and 23), and
contains teaching aimed at cooling eschatological fervour (24:8, 14).
While the signs of the Son of Man's arrival will be unmistakable
(24:28), the time at which he comes is known only to the Father
(24:36). To be sure, much of what is said here is merely an
expansion and re-arrangement of the Marcan text. On the whole
Matthew's redaction does not evidence a drastic theological
re-interpretation of Mark. Hence, it is all the more surprising

to find such an emphasis placed on a delay at three points in
Matthew's teaching. The situation to which 25:1-13 is addressed
remains consistent with that of the discourse as a whole. The
note of "delay" is the new feature.

So, against the background of the entire discourse, what
Matthew appears to be doing is offering exhortation to his
community: "do not fall from your duty in the interim". The
delay of the groom (which in this situation presumably refers
to the parousia) is to be understood as a further point of
endurance for which they are to prepare themselves. Understood
theologically, the delay becomes a point of testing.

In conclusion then, we venture to suggest that this story
attempts to answer problems felt to be pressing on Matthew's
community regarding the duration of the interim (its end is
definite, although unpredictable), and the activity of
Christians within it. In this sense also, 25:1-13 can be viewed
as a summary of Matthaean eschatology /9/.

NOTES

/1/   "The Parable of the Foolish Scholars", *Novum Testamentum*, 9,
April 1967, pp.107-123.
/2/   J.D.M. Derrett, "La Parabola delle vergini stolte", *Studies
in the New Testament,* Vol.1, Leiden, 1977, pp.128-142; K.P.
Donfried, "The Allegory of the Ten Virgins (Matt.25:1-13) as a
Summary of Matthean Theology", *Journal of Biblical Literature*, 93,
1974, pp.415-428; F.A. Strobel, "Zum Verständnis von Mt.XXV, 1-13",
Novum Testamentum, 2, 1958, pp.199-227.
/3/   Ford, *op.cit.,* pp.115-117.
/4/   This observation is not new. Günther Bornkamm, "Die
Verzögerung der Parusie", *Geschichte und Glaube,* Vol.1, München,
1968, pp.49f., argues that the delay of the groom belongs firmly
to the substance of the parable and acts as its interpretative
key. In his view the parable presupposes the expectation of the
parousia of the later community. This interpretation is followed,
in the main, by E. Grässer in his book *Das Problem der
Parusieverzögerung in den synoptischen Evangelien und in der
Apostelgeschichte,* BZNW 22, Berlin, 1957, see especially pp.119ff.
and 123ff.
    A recent tendency among scholars has been to play down the

importance of the groom's delay within the plot of the
narrative, and to assert that the oil (ἔλαιον) is the central
feature of the whole episode. Cf. Derrett, *op.cit.*; Donfried,
op.cit.; and J.F. Walvoord, "Christ's Olivet Discourse on the
End of the Age, The Parable of the Ten Virgins", *Bibliotheca
Sacra,* 129, 1972, pp.99-105. This assertion is made on the
grounds that it is on the basis of insufficient oil that the
foolish maidens are ultimately refused entry to the feast.
While this fact may be admitted, it is seen that the feature
which determines the insufficiency of the oil is the long delay
of the groom.
/5/   The division of the maidens into wise and foolish is made at
an early point in the story, 25:2. However, the reason for this
division is not readily apparent, even though we note that the
wise maidens were the ones who took extra oil with them. The
significance of this fact is revealed by the delay of the groom
(25:5, 7).
/6/   The pericopes we include in this section are:
24:37-41   Story of the Flood.
24:42-44   Injunctions to Watch.
24:45-51   The Good/Wicked Servant.
25:1-13   The Ten Maidens.
25:14-30   The Talents.
/7/   Compare Donfried, *op.cit.*, pp.420-21.
/8/   See Jeremias, *The Parables of Jesus,* Third Revised Edition,
London, 1972, pp.52-3, and contrast Donfried, *op.cit.*, p.428.
/9/   At the time of writing (April 1978), the following articles
were unavailable to me: H. Hamann, "The Ten Virgins: An Exegetical-
Homiletical Study", *Lutheran Theological Journal,* 11, 1977,
pp.68-72; I. Maisch, "Das Gleichnis von den klugen und torichten
Jungfrauen, Auslegung von Mt.25:1-13", *Bibel und Leben,* 11, 1970,
pp.247-259; D. Wenthe, "The Parable of the Ten Bridesmaids",
Springfielder, 40, 1976, pp.9-16.

I wish to express my thanks to the various students and
members of staff in the Department of Philosophy and Religious
Studies, Stirling, with whom I have discussed aspects of this
communication.

Satan in the Fourth Gospel

Mrs. Wendy E. Sproston,
238 Westbourne Avenue West,
Hull, North Humberside HU5 3JD,
England.

The references which the author of the Fourth Gospel makes to
the devil are few. The devil is referred to by his name, Satan,
only once, and this is at the scene of the Last Supper in chapter
13 where we are told that Satan entered into Judas Iscariot.
As 'the devil' (ὁ διάβολος) he is described in chapter 8 as father
to the murderous Jews and in chapter 13 as Judas Iscariot's
seducer. In three further references (12:31; 14:30; 16:11) John
designates him 'the ruler of this world' (ὁ ἄρχων τοῦ κόσμου
τούτου). As such he is the antagonist of Christ, seen as
responsible for the events culminating in Christ's death which,
paradoxically, will bring about his own overthrow. Finally, if we
assume a masculine rendering of the Greek τοῦ πονηροῦ in John
17:15, then the devil is again referred to, this time as ὁ πονηρός,
'the evil one'.

But these few references are significant, for the power of
the devil is by no means under-estimated in the thought of the
fourth evangelist. Although John makes no reference to Satan's
coterie of evil spirits familiar to us from the Synoptic accounts,
nevertheless Satan is seen to carry out his plans not only through
the agency of 'the Jews' who in their rejection of Jesus have
become the devil's children, but, most notably, in the person of
his willing henchman Judas Iscariot. Indeed, so close is the
identification of Judas with Satan in this gospel that in his
commentary J.H. Bernard is prompted to suggest the possibility that
John had a special animus against Judas /1/. Is this sufficient
to explain this gospel's portrait of Judas as a malevolent
influence, or could it be that this figure has some specialized
role to play in the Johannine drama? This communication is an
attempt to define the significance of the figure of Judas in
relation to Satan in Johannine thought.

No gospel paints a blacker portrait of Judas Iscariot than the
Fourth Gospel. In each reference to Judas we find his character

even more tarnished than in the Synoptic accounts.

The first of these references is at the end of John 6. The passage 6:66-71 is usually regarded as the Johannine counterpart to the Synoptic account of the confession of Peter at Caesarea Philippi. Here John, like Luke, omits the identification of Peter with Satan contained in Mark and Matthew. However, whereas Luke merely omits the tradition, it seems that in John it has been adapted in such a way that the designation of Peter as Satan in the earlier records is here transferred to Judas. Thus, in the Johannine account, it is Judas whom Jesus accuses of being a devil (6:70).

In chapter 12 we find the Johannine account of the anointing of Jesus. In the Marcan version the complaint about the waste of ointment is attributed to some of the bystanders (14:4), and in Matthew merely to 'the disciples' (26:8). But in John it is Judas who complains (12:4-5), after which the evangelist adds an explanatory note pointing out that this remark was not made by Judas out of concern for the poor but because Judas was a thief, accustomed to stealing from the money-box which was in his possession (12:6).

In John Judas is the tool of Satan. Judas' betrayal of Jesus is attributed directly to his susceptibility to Satanic influence. Here John shows special links with the Lucan narrative since Luke also indicates Satanic influence over Judas, but describes the entering of Satan into Judas before the meal (Lk. 22:3). John, however, makes two references to this. The first is at the beginning of chapter 13 where we are told that the devil had already put into the heart of Judas to betray Jesus. The second is during the scene of the Last Supper. At this point Satan actually enters into Judas, after which Judas goes to betray Jesus. That John informs us that Judas goes out into the 'night' (13:30) which signals the onset of the Passion (cf. 9:4; 11:10) is undoubtedly significant of Judas' choice for evil.

We hear no more of Judas' activities until chapter 18 when he arrives in Gethsemane at the head of the party sent from the Jewish authorities to arrest Jesus. But Judas' arrival is by no means unexpected. At the end of chapter 14 Jesus has already warned his disciples that 'the ruler of this world' is coming (14:30). There can be little doubt that Jesus is referring at this point to Judas when he uses the devil's title, 'the ruler of this world'. This is made clear if we compare the Synoptic parallels. The Johannine passage ends with the words, 'Rise, let

us go hence' (14:31). Where the same exhortation occurs in Mark
and Matthew we see that in each case it is accompanied by the
remark, 'My betrayer is at hand' (Mk. 14:42; Matt. 26:46) and,
moreover, that this is immediately before the arrival of Judas.
Thus we may conclude that for the fourth evangelist the presence
of Judas is synonymous with the presence of the devil.

It seems that from this brief survey that it would be more
accurate to describe Judas in this gospel as a symbol of evil
rather than a common betrayer. Bultmann, commenting on Satan's
possession of Judas during the Last Supper, writes, 'It is not a
man who is acting here, but Satan himself, the antagonist of God
and the Revealer' /2/.

But what has motivated John to present Judas in this light?
As a dramatist, John prefers to use his characters symbolically.
What role, then, in the Johannine scheme has Judas been singled
out to play?

In chapter 17 John gives us a vital clue. In verse 12 Jesus
states that he has guarded all those given him by the Father; all,
that is, except one, whom he describes as 'the son of perdition'
(ὁ υἱὸς τῆς ἀπωλείας) - undoubtedly a reference to Judas Iscariot.

What is the significance for John of the phrase ὁ υἱὸς τῆς
ἀπωλείας? C.K. Barrett informs us that in the New Testament
ἀπώλεια commonly means eschatological perdition or damnation /3/.
It seems, too, that its use in the Septuagint carries the same
meaning /4/. Moreover, we find the Hebrew equivalent of the
Johannine phrase occurring in the Dead Sea Scrolls. In the Manual
of Discipline eternal perdition (שחת) is part of the lot of one
who walks in the spirit of deceit (1QS 4,12), and members of the
sect are instructed not to argue with the 'men of perdition' (1QS
9,17), but nevertheless to regard them with hatred (1QS 9,22).
Similarly, in the Damascus Rule, those of the Covenant must
separate themselves from the 'sons of perdition', and have as
little contact with them as possible (CD 6,15; 13,14). From these
references we may gather that in this Semitic phrase John is
referring to Judas as one who is outside the circle of disciples and
and as such is a man destined for damnation. Judas is the man for
whom Jesus does not pray, and as such is destined to suffer the
fate of one who does not believe in Jesus (see 3:16) and whom
Christ does not have in his keeping (see 10:28).

But there remains one New Testament passage which surely
makes the most significant contribution of all to our understanding

of John's designation of Judas as 'the son of perdition'. In II
Thessalonians 2:3 precisely the same title is used in Paul's
description of the final enemy whose appearance is the signal for
the ultimate onslaught of evil before the Parousia. This
eschatological figure Paul describes as 'the man of lawlessness...
the son of perdition'. Moreover, we see that this 'man of
lawlessness' is not Satan himself but one who executes Satan's
work, who is subject to Satan's will, and whose downfall will
signify the final collapse of the devil's schemes (II Thess.
2:8-9).

For Paul this Antichrist (as he is later termed in the
Johannine Epistles) has not yet come. Can we say, however, that
for John this 'son of perdition' has already appeared in the
person of Judas Iscariot? If we can, then John's reference to
Judas as 'the son of perdition' has become the key to our understanding of his harsh and uncompromising treatment of the
character. In Johannine realized eschatology the figure of Judas
Iscariot has acquired the significance of Antichrist, the 'son of
perdition'. Referring to the Pauline text, C.K. Barrett comments
on John 17:12, 'It seems probable that John saw in Judas this
eschatological character who must appear before the manifestation
of the glory of Christ' /5/. It follows, therefore, that John
treats any statement Judas might make with the utmost suspicion;
and also that Judas, although distinct from Satan, may be accused
by the Johannine Christ of being 'a devil' and referred to by
him as 'the ruler of this world'. In the Fourth Gospel, the
portrait of Judas cannot be treated mercifully for, as the
destined 'man of lawlessness' in the Johannine scheme, Judas'
susceptibility to the will of Satan was a foregone conclusion.

Whereas for Paul the glorious Parousia could not take place
unless the Satanically inspired 'son of perdition' had first
worked the ultimate evil, for the fourth evangelist, to whom the
crucifixion of Christ was synonymous with his glorification, it
is the figure of Judas which symbolizes the final apostasy.

NOTES

/1/   J.H. Bernard, *The Gospel According to St. John*, 2 vols.
(Oxford, 1922), vol. I, p.224.
/2/   R. Bultmann, *The Gospel of John*, Eng. Tr. G.R. Beasley-
Murray (Oxford, 1971), p.482.
/3/   C.K. Barrett, *The Gospel According to St. John* (London,
1955), p.424.

/4/   See B. Lindars, *The Gospel of John*, New Century Bible 16
(London, 1972), p.526; A. Schlatter, *Der Evangelist Johannes*,
Dritte Auflage (Stuttgart, 1960), p.322.
/5/   Barrett, op. cit., p.424.

Studia Biblica 1978: II, 313-327

The Alleged Eyewitness Material in the Fourth Gospel

R.L. Sturch,
London Bible College,
Green Lane,
Northwood, Middlesex HA6 2UW.

In a celebrated section of the introduction to his "Speaker's Commentary" on John /1/, Westcott argued in succession that the author of the fourth Gospel must have been a Jew, a Palestinian, an eyewitness of the scenes he described, an Apostle, and, finally, John the son of Zebedee. It is the quite crucial third step, the alleged presence of eyewitness material in the Gospel, that I wish to concentrate on. Westcott's kind of argument has lost much of its popularity since his day. Barrett, for instance, dismisses it (after quoting a few alleged examples) with the words, "Such features are precisely what a writer adds to his work in order to give it verisimilitude"/2/. Even more conservative scholars seem on the whole to avoid it: Tasker's Tyndale commentary does not use it, nor does Bishop Robinson support his case for an early dating of the Gospel by citing it. Dodd, indeed, does have an appreciative word for it: "the case stated by Westcott remains impressive, though far from conclusive"; yet this is only a kind of counterbalance to an earlier remark that "it would be naive in us at this date to take (such details) at their face value" /3/. The only serious attempt to restate Westcott's argument that I know of is that of Canon Morris in his "Studies in the Fourth Gospel" /4/.

Now the main point that I hope to discuss is the question, How can an item appear to be eyewitness material without actually being such? Those who criticize the "eyewitness" argument are apt to dismiss it without giving proper consideration to this question, and those who defend the argument are apt not to consider it at all; yet it is surely important. I hope to be able to show that there are in fact several ways in which such details can appear in a narrative without being in reality eyewitness material at all, and to look at some of the alleged eyewitness details in John to see how these ways are exemplified in it. This should benefit both sides to the debate, the more sceptical by showing how

scepticism might be justified, the more conservative by offering
the hope of finding evidence which would be immune to attack along
any of my lines of approach. But before I proceed to the main
body of this paper I should like to clear away two preliminary
confusions.

The first is the argument advanced (for instance) by Nineham
in a well-known series of articles in the *Journal of Theological
Studies* about twenty years ago /5/. "John's motives for his
reformulation of the tradition were essentially theological...
He will have had no need of recourse to eyewitnesses; despite his
narrative form, his was not the *kind* of reformulation that needed
fresh eyewitness testimony as its basis." This is, I think,
fundamentally correct. But it does not touch Westcott's position.
Nineham was criticizing those who thought the existence of
eyewitnesses during the period of oral transmission would have
acted as a check on historically inaccurate reformulation of that
tradition. But Westcott's belief was that John, whether
reformulating or not, was not dependent on tradition but more or
less automatically used his own eyewitness knowledge of what he
described.

The second is what I might call the "argument from
authenticity"; it is a favourite with Canon Morris. Such-and-such
a detail or story is likely to be historical, not invented; such-
and-such a saying is surely dominical: therefore - and here comes
the leap - it can be cited as eyewitness material. This leap is
clearly illegitimate. No doubt a genuinely authentic item must go
back ultimately to someone present when it happened, but its
authenticity does not guarantee that the *writer* was present, or
even that his immediate informant was. And this applies, I fear,
to a good deal of the evidence which Morris cites in support of
his case.

Having said this, we may proceed to ask our main question:
How can an item appear to be eyewitness material without actually
being such? On what principles, if any, are we entitled to reject
the considerable body of material collected by scholars like
Westcott and Morris?

We may look for our principles under two main headings: the
principle of the *internal cause* and that of the *external control*.
That is to say, there may be cases in which we can see a reason
for the appearance of a particular item which derives from the
internal logic of the Evangelist's work; and there may be cases
where we have external evidence to show that an item need not, or

even could not, be derived from close contact or identity with an eyewitness. Let us amplify these headings, and cite possible examples for clarification.

Among internal causes the most obvious is what we may call *symbolic* or *theological motivation*. If a detail might have been added for discernible theological reasons, we cannot be sure that it derives from an eyewitness (though of course it *may*). For instance, Bultmann regarded the reference to the "tenth hour" in 1:39 (cited in support of their case by both Westcott and Morris) as symbolic; the tenth hour is the hour of fulfilment. If this is correct (which I admit I personally doubt), this detail must be set aside as inconclusive.

I should, however, note one exception to this rule. That is 19:34-5, the passage about the blood and water from Christ's side. This is explicitly claimed to be based on eyewitness evidence, and we cannot use the "internal cause" argument to set it aside. John is either recording for its theological significance an event which he really did get from an eyewitness or deliberately pretending to do so. I hope to discuss this particular point later.

A second internal cause is what we may call the *stock epithet* or *inferred detail*. (The two are often hard to distinguish.) By these terms I mean details that would appear in many people's mental images of a story, or be a natural inference from some element in that story. There is an instructive example in Taylor's *Formation of the Gospel Tradition* /6/. He describes an experiment to see how a story might change in the course of oral transmission. The story concerned a Rabbi who ended up walking along the seashore at night. Now most "transmitters", as expected, curtailed the original; but some details were *added*. In some versions, the Rabbi came to be described as "old", and his walk as "by moonlight". For Gentiles probably feel that a Rabbi ought to be old and venerable, and night by the sea naturally suggests moonlight on the waves; and the imagination affects the wording.

Thirdly, we may note the existence of *emphasizing* detail, intended to stress some feature of a story. In a fragment of the *Gospel according to the Hebrews,* the (second) rich man, told to give all his wealth to the poor, "scratched his head" in perplexity; the cruciality of his decision is thereby emphasized. (This kind of detail can of course overlap with the previous one.)

Fourthly, there is novelistic detail. A modern novelist may

describe, say, people and places with invented detail in order to
make the reader feel part of the action; I imagine this is what
Barrett had in mind with his remarks about "verisimilitude". It
is not characteristic even of fiction in ancient literature, and I
do not think it is found anywhere in the Gospels, but it is a
theoretical possibility. It really needs to be done on a large
scale to work.

Fifthly, there is detail which *satisfies curiosity*. It is
sometimes said (e.g. by Nineham in the articles referred to) /7/
that the apocryphal gospels have far more "eyewitness material"
than the canonical. This is, as far as I can judge, true
primarily of this "curiosity-satisfying" detail. What was Jesus
like as a boy? What happened to him during the Descent into Hell?
What were the names of his grandparents? It is sometimes
suggested /8/ that John's use of names not otherwise recorded is
an example of this.

And sixthly, there is detail caused by *literary style*. For
instance, Morris quotes 10:31 as part of his evidence, where the
Jews, it is said, ἐβάστασαν stones to throw at Christ; this, he
suggests, means "brought", not "picked up", and reflects the fact
that stones were not readily available in the Portico /9/. But
the attached adverb πάλιν shows that this verb is simply a
variation on ἦραν in 8:59. John has, as often, avoided using the
same word twice where a synonym will do (a habit of which Morris
himself has a lengthy discussion elsewhere in his book).

There is of course a theoretical seventh - the deliberate lie,
intended to give the impression of eyewitness backing where no
such backing was present. But whatever else John was up to, it
was not this. His narrative in general is not controlled by any
passionate desire to have it accepted as an eyewitness account
(again excepting 19:34-5), and there is no reason to suppose that
his occasional details were either. Six is our limit.

What then of external controls? There are, I think, three.
First, a detail which also *appears in a Synoptic account* cannot
be relied upon to be eyewitness material. This is not to say it
is unreliable as truth; the double attestation clearly makes it
more likely to be true, not less: but it clearly was preserved in
the Church's tradition, and we cannot therefore be sure that that
was not how John received it. The most obvious instance is that
of the five loaves and two fishes in Jn. 6:9, which is in fact
cited by Westcott (though of course he realized it could carry no

weight by itself).

Secondly, there is the *inaccurate detail*. Luke's phrase, τοῦ ἡλίου ἐκλιπόντος (Lk. 23:45), would be a Synoptic example, assuming, as is natural, that it means "the sun was eclipsed". Some have seen Jn. 2:20 ("It took forty-six years to build this temple") as a Johannine example. I am not convinced of this myself; but 19:39 (the weight of spices) would probably do as well.

And thirdly, there is the *inaccessible detail*: one which may indeed be true, but which the writer could not have known to be true (e.g. because the only witness died before describing it). The statement in Jn. 12:6 that Judas pilfered from the money entrusted to him is a case in point: if anyone had known at the time, Judas would surely have left the Twelve sooner than he did, and certainly no one audited his books afterwards!

We have, then, six ways in which an apparent eyewitness detail may arise from internal causes, and three checks by which apparent eyewitness details may have to be passed over on external grounds. There is no space here to go through every piece of evidence adduced by Westcott or Morris; I shall limit myself to an examination of three passages supposed to be particularly rich in eyewitness details, and to some remarks (a) about the personal names peculiar to John and (b) about his Passion-narrative. (Possible treatments of other passages are indicated in an appendix.) It is to be remembered that the classification of an item under one of my headings does not (except with the last two, "inaccurate" and "inaccessible") imply that the item is untrue, nor even that it is not in fact eyewitness material; only that we cannot *show* that it is such.

The first passage is Jn. 4:6ff. - the episode of the Woman of Samaria. This opens with three promising-looking touches: Jesus was "tired from his journey"; he "sat down beside the well"; and it was "about the sixth hour". Then in verse 20 we have the striking reference by the woman to "this mountain", and in verse 27 the description of the disciples' thoughts (which does not advance the story at all, and can hardly have survived oral transmission).

Of these, the first two clearly could arise from our second "internal cause", the "inferred detail". John's mental picture of the episode must obviously have included Jesus waiting by the well before the woman arrived; that he was sitting would be a natural inference, and that he was tired almost as natural, especially as

he was evidently thirsty. The disciples' thoughts in verse 27
could also be "inferred detail". Bultmann indeed seems to take
them to be theologically motivated, our first "internal cause":
"The Redeemer encounters individual people, whether men or woman,
often to the surprise of his disciples, who cannot understand why
it should be this particular man or woman with whom he speaks; it
is however not permissible to ask why this is so" /10/. But this
seems very doubtful; it is not Jesus' talking to this particular
woman that surprises the disciples, but his talking to any woman
at all (not regarded as suitable for a Jewish teacher, as Bultmann
himself notes). But given that unsuitability, the Evangelist (or
a source) could well have inferred the disciples' reaction, though
I admit it is a little odd that he should have bothered to record
it unless there was some sort of theological motive behind his
doing so, or unless he had more than inference to go on.

        This leaves us with two details to account for. The note of
time could have been emphasizing detail (our third class) if there
had been any reference to the heat; but there isn't. Still it
could be a kind of second-level inference. Jesus is already
pictured as tired and thirsty; it is natural enough to think of
him as hot as well, and so to place the episode at noon. But I am
not altogether convinced by my own argument here, and should be
glad of an alternative explanation. (One possible one, of course,
it that it is a genuine reminiscence.)

        The phrase "this mountain" seems to me much the most stubborn
item here. The natural thing in an orally transmitted story, or
an invented one, would be to say "Mount Gerizim". The only
explanation I can think of which avoids regarding the phrase as
derived fairly directly from an eyewitness would be to suppose
that John was well acquainted with the site of the conversation
that it was his automatic reaction to refer to Gerizim (in this
context) as "this mountain" - his, and not the woman's. It then
becomes, so to speak, a genuine eyewitness detail, but from an
eyewitness of the scene of the episode, not of the episode itself.
(In fact, of course, there *were* no eyewitnesses of the episode
itself; but this does not make the whole thing "inaccessible
detail", as we are told that it became common gossip almost at
once. If the detail *is* eyewitness material, it comes from this
gossip, not from the woman's original speech.)

        The second passage to be considered is 6:5-9, the Feeding of
the Five Thousand. There are again several points in these verses
that have been supposed eyewitness evidence: the numbers (five
loaves, two fishes, five thousand assembled, two hundred denarii),

the names (Philip and Andrew), the "barley" of which the loaves
were made, and the "lad" who brought them. Of these the numbers
can be discounted at once, for they are all to be found in the
Synoptists; even if they do derive directly from someone present
at the time, there is no way of checking this. The "barley" could
come under our first heading, symbolic detail; for barley is what
the loaves were made of in the similar miracle of Elisha (II
Kgs. 4:42) and John or his source could have brought it in with
the suggestion that "a greater than Elisha is here". Barrett
indeed ascribes reference to the "lad" (παιδάριον) to the same
cause. This is much less likely. A servant is indeed mentioned
in the II Kings passage, but he is not called a παιδάριον in the
LXX (though one in the previous verse is), and, perhaps more
important, he does not produce the loaves; he only helps pass
them round, thus corresponding to the disciples rather than to the
"lad". The "lad" is not symbolic; but as he only occurs in a
speech ascribed to Andrew, it is to the appearance of Andrew and
Philip that we must turn before we can decide about the "lad".

Commentators have tended to feel doubtful about these two
disciples. "The individualizing of actors in a story is often,
though not always", says Dodd, "a sign of 'legendary'
developments". This suggestion is related to our category of
"curiosity-satisfying" detail: it would please someone who wanted
to know more about these disciples, or perhaps someone who wanted
to know who it was who mentioned the two hundred denarii and the
loaves and fishes (that *someone* had was of course implied by the
tradition found in the Synoptists). Lindars, on the other hand,
takes the dialogue to have been adapted for theological reasons,
to introduce John's "favourite theme of misunderstanding". This
last is unlikely, for, as Bultmann notes /12/, "the Johannine
'misunderstandings' have nothing to do with πειράζειν, while on
the other hand we miss here the ambiguity which goes with such
'misunderstandings'". I think theological adaptation is unlikely;
certainly it did not generate the names. But "legendary"
development is more promising. Its chief difficulty is the odd
way in which John introduces names in one place and not in another.
If he were seeking to satisfy curiosity, or depended on sources
which sought to do so, it is a little surprising that this is the
only passage in the first ten chapters of the Gospel (apart from
the calling-narratives) in which any disciple other than Peter and
Judas is named, although "the disciples" are mentioned many times,
several of which afford obvious chances to do so (e.g. 4:31,33 or
9:2; cf. 11:8,12; 16:17,29; and 20:25).

In fact, John only names six of the Twelve (unless Nathanael

be a seventh), which suggests that satisfying his readers'
curiosity about them was not a major object for him; indeed, would
anyone who felt curious about Judas "not Iscariot" feel satisfied
after reading Jn. 14:22? It remains, however, possible that
John's sources were responsible for the names in this passage;
Andrew, after all, does figure in one Synoptic passage apart from
his call, namely Mk. 13:3, so there is a precedent for his name's
being preserved in (or inserted into) a Gospel source. Philip,
however, does not so appear; nor of course do Thomas or Judas
"not Iscariot": the tradition seems to have concentrated on the
two pairs of brothers, Peter, Andrew, James and John. I must
admit to feeling that we may well have material close to an eyewitness source here (Bernard's point, that Philip and Andrew both
came from Bethsaida, possibly near the site of the miracle, could
be relevant, especially as John seems unaware of any possible
significance in this); in which case the παιδάριον may point the
same way.

     The third passage for consideration is the story of Peter's
denials (Jn. 18:15-18, 25-27). Dodd /13/ describes this as
"either the product of a remarkable dramatic flair, or [resting]
on superior information". This description is borne out by a
series of vivid details: the "disciple known to the High Priest"
and his part in getting Peter admitted; the explanation of the
fire (taken for granted by Mark, stated but not explained by Luke,
and omitted by Matthew); the identification of two of Peter's
challengers as "the portress" and a relation of Malchus. The
sheer concentration of details might itself seem some evidence
for its being genuinely such, as such details might well occur
together in an episode vividly remembered, whereas there is no
particular reasons why pseudo-eyewitness material should be
collected together in this way. But what happens when we pass
them under closer scrutiny?

     The fire is weakened as eyewitness testimony (though not of
course as accurate history) by the fact that it is in Mark and
Luke as well; and the lighting of the fire (in Luke too) and the
cold that led to it are natural inferences from its existence.
We cannot base anything on the fire. The "disciple known to the
High Priest" is more interesting. His going in with Jesus and his
re-emergence to get Peter admitted are wholly unnecessary to the
action. Even if John felt a need to explain how Peter got into
Annas' palace (which none of the Synoptists felt) and "inferred"
that a friend had arranged it, he could hardly have "inferred" the
friend's disappearance and return. I am not at all sure that I
can think of a plausible explanation for this detail unless the

Evangelist had it from someone there.

What about the identification of Peter's questioners? All
four Evangelists agree that the first was a maidservant. John
specifies her position more exactly, as the portress, which could
be to satisfy readers' curiosity (unlikely, as he does no such
thing with the second questioner) or could just possibly be
inferred; he has just been thinking about Peter's admission
through the gate, and the first person to challenge him might
reasonably be the servant in charge of it. After her, the
Evangelists part company. The second challenger was the same maid
(Mark), a different one (Matthew), a man (Luke), or just "they"
(presumably the slaves and officers of Jn. 18:18) (John). The
third was "bystanders" (Matthew and Mark), "another man" (Luke),
a relative of Malchus (John). All four, of course, agree on the
three-fold denial; that is deeply rooted in the tradition.

Matthew's second maid we can surely discount, as having
appeared because it seemed unlikely the first would have persisted
after Peter's denial; and similarly with Luke's first "man" (Lk.
22:58). The third challenge too looks very much as if it had no
certain details given in tradition: Matthew this time keeps Mark's
version, but Luke has not bothered to make the challenge plural,
and simply says ἄλλος. The reference to Peter's being a Galilean
may be traditional, but hardly convinces; there must have been
hundreds of Galileans in Jerusalem at the time, and not all of
them followers of Jesus! Appearances suggest that the basic
tradition said little more than that there were three denials and
that the first was in response to a maidservant.

John agrees about the maid, and is even vaguer than the
Synoptists about the second challenge. But the third is suddenly
specific again: "a relative of the man whose ear Peter had cut
off". This must either be a very neat piece of literary cross-
referencing (as Lindars calls it) or historical; and surely John
did not take so much literary trouble over Denial 3 with no
obvious motive, and yet leave Denial 2 hanging in the air. (It
has, however, been suggested to me that the motive was to make
Peter's last denial inexcusable - he'd been *seen*; an "emphasizing
detail". This could be so, though the man's challenge was a
question, not an assertion.) If it is historical, the link with
the name "Malchus" suggests a source close to Malchus himself. I
suspect that while no Evangelist had full details of the Denials,
John had access to some source or sources (the "disciple known to the
the High Priest" is an obvious candidate) which was not simply
current tradition but stood much closer to the original events.

But this links up with both our remaining topics, the names
peculiar to John, and his Passion-narrative; for "Malchus" is one
of the former, and the whole Denials episode part of the latter.

There are five or six names peculiar to John. The sixth,
doubtful one is "Cephas" (1:42), which is confined to John as far
as the Gospels are concerned, but is of course testified to by St.
Paul (I Cor. 1:12,etc.; Gal. 1:18, etc.). It is interesting that
the only other N.T. writer to use this name should be one who knew
St. Peter personally, but it may not be significant.

Of the others, "Nathanael" (1:45ff. and 21:2) could be
traditional. Names were clearly preserved in or attached to "call"
stories, and Nathanael's first appearance is of course of this
type (though more elaborate than any other). 21:2 is different,
of course, but the complications of that chapter would take too
long for the present discussion. "Nicodemus" might be a
"stylistic" detail. His role in chapter 3 almost cries out for a
name to be given: to describe him by some circumlocution throughout
would be very clumsy (though John does this with the man born blind
in ch.9), and his reappearances in chs. 7 and 19 could perhaps be
based on this one. "Lazarus" is linked with Mary and Martha, and
since their names were certainly preserved in the tradition Luke
drew on, there is no reason why their brother's could not have been
preserved in the same way.

This leaves two. "Simon Iscariot" (6:71; cf.12:4; 13:2,26)
and "Malchus" (18:10). The names of some of the Apostles' fathers
were preserved in the Synoptists, so we cannot put to much reliance
on the former as "eyewitness material", though it could be argued
that Judas dropped out of the Twelve too early for his patronymic
to have been much in use except among his actual associates. But
"Malchus" is another matter, not so much because of anything very
striking about the name itself (though Bultmann suggested it was
Arab and could well be that of a slave) as because of three factors.
One is the link with the third of Peter's denials, which we have
already noticed. The second is the great improbability of
tradition's having ever contained the name of this man, neither a
public figure nor an associate of Christ's. So far as this point
is concerned, the name could be pure invention (curiosity-
satisfying, perhaps); but the way John brings it in makes this, I
think, rather unlikely. When an inventor wants to supply a name,
he normally tags it on to the description of the character, or
substitutes it for that. There are many examples in the apocryphal
gospels and the "Acts of Pilate": "a chief priest named Levi",
"Annas the scribe", and so on - usually pretty obvious names. But

I do not recall a single case where the writer tells his story,
however brief, and then adds, "His name was X", as John does in
18:20. On the other hand, this is surely just what someone who
was closely acquainted with the actual facts would very naturally
do - tell his story and then remember an interesting detail.

I turn, then, to some very brief remarks on the Passion-
narrative. Dodd pointed out once /14/ that there is very little
Johannine theologizing in this part of the Gospel. But no one as
far as I know has noted what to me seems a very remarkable
peculiarity of John's Passion. The Synoptic accounts follow Jesus
from the arrest onwards like a hand-held cine-camera; except for
Peter's denials, Jesus is always in the centre of the picture, and
we never lose sight of him. In John's, on the other hand, we
see only from a few viewpoints: the house of Annas, inside and
outside the Praetorium, and Golgotha itself. Our cine-cameras
are at fixed points. And in some of the scenes Jesus is not himself present: apart from the Denials, there are two points where
only Pilate and the Jewish leaders are present. Moreover, this
discontinuity leads to peculiar omissions. Jesus is taken off to
Caiaphas's house, and is seen coming from it to the Praetorium,
yet we see nothing of what went on inside. We lose sight of Jesus
again as he leaves the Praetorium carrying his cross, and pick him
up again on Golgotha being nailed to it; Simon of Cyrene (and for
that matter the Daughters of Jerusalem) is missing. I am aware
of course that various explanations have been offered for these
omissions. But it seems to me that the simplest is this: John
has compiled his Passion-narrative, not from a general and well-
shaped tradition, but from a very few sources close to the actual
events. One can surely be identified, as we have seen, with the
"disciple known to the High Priest". One, or possibly two, must
have been at the Praetorium (the number depends on how reliable
one thinks the accounts of what went on inside that building).
And one at least was present on Golgotha.

It will, I hope, be clear by now that when I speak of
"eyewitness detail" I do not mean (as Westcott and Morris do)
"detail of which the Evangelist or his immediate or almost
immediate source was an eyewitness". It is in fact rather
difficult to pick out individual details on Westcott lines from
the Passion-narrative. It contains a number of aspects in which
I think it is superior to the Synoptic accounts; but, as I said
earlier, accuracy is not enough to prove eyewitness testimony. It
may help to confirm it if there is other reason to believe in it;
that is all. And in fact only eight or nine items are cited by
either Westcott himself or Morris from chs. 18 and 19, apart from

the Denials story, and most of these come under one or other of
the headings I have described, or are merely cases of apparent
accuracy. The strongest is perhaps the incident of the breaking
of the robbers' legs in 19:31ff. Lindars indeed takes this to be
what I have called "inferred detail", but this is hard to believe.
It would require that John should calculate (a) that the robbers
were unlikely to die before nightfall; (b) that they *were* likely to
die before the *next* nightfall; (c) that this would mean that their
bodies could not be removed; (d) that this would infringe Dt. 21:
22f; and (e) that the Romans therefore would probably break their
legs in order to hasten death: all this in ignorance of what
actually happened. Theological motivation would be more plausible;
but while this might explain why Christ's legs were *not* broken, it
could hardly produce the notion that the robbers' *were*.

But of course just after this, in Jn. 19:35, we have an
explicit claim to eyewitness authority. And I may say at once
that I can make sense of the language of this verse only on the
assumption that the witness referred to is the Evangelist himself,
and that he is either telling the truth or deliberately setting
out to mislead. Given time, I should be happy to defend this
position. But if it is in fact correct, it bears out to some
extent what I said earlier about the Passion-narrative in general.
The Evangelist was actually present on Golgotha, and he says so;
but he does not say that he witnessed any of the other scenes.
(Indeed he can hardly have seen both what went on inside the
Praetorium and what went on outside it!)

I should conclude that it is quite definitely possible to
explain a great many of the alleged eyewitness details in John
as arising from some cause internal to the Evangelist, and to
justify disregarding others on the basis of external controls.   I
think, however, that both in the areas we have examined in this
paper and in the rest of the Gospel there is a residue of items
which resist either sort of elimination; and this may suggest that
eyewitness evidence could also lie behind some of the details where
it cannot be proved. Nevertheless, I would venture to say that
Westcott's original purpose, to show that the Evangelist was
himself an eyewitness of nearly all that he reported, and so to
prepare a way for demonstrating his identity with the Apostle John
the son of Zebedee, cannot in fact be achieved.

NOTES

/1/   Westcott, B.F., *The Gospel according to St. John* (repr.,

London, 1958), pp.v-xxv.
/2/   Barrett, C.K., *The Gospel according to St. John* (London, 1956),p.104.
/3/   Dodd, C.H., *Historical Tradition in the Fourth Gospel* (Cambridge, 1963), p.14.
/4/   Morris, L., *Studies in the Fourth Gospel* (Exeter, 1969), pp.134-213.
/5/   Nineham, D., "Eyewitness Testimony and the Gospel Tradition", *JTS*, n.s. ix (1958) and xi (1960), esp. ix, pp.245ff.
/6/   Taylor, V., *The Formation of the Gospel Tradition* (London, 1935), pp.202ff.
/7/   Nineham, *op.cit.*, *JTS* ix, p.22.
/8/   E.g. by Barrett, *op.cit.*, pp.104, 228.
/9/   Morris, *op.cit.*, p.166.
/10/ Bultmann, R., *The Gospel of John* (E.T., Oxford, 1971), p.193.
/11/ Dodd, *op.cit.*, p.206.
/12/ Bultmann, *op.cit.*, p.212 n.5.
/13/ Dodd, *op.cit.*, p.86.
/14/ Dodd, C.H., *The Interpretation of the Fourth Gospel* (Cambridge, 1953), pp.423ff.

APPENDIX

CLASSIFIED LIST OF SOME ALLEGED CASES OF EYEWITNESS MATERIAL

A. Cases where John may well be accurate, but need not depend on
    eyewitnesses:

1:46-9	Nathanael's salutation of Jesus as King.
2:17,22	The disciples' reactions to the Cleansing of the Temple and the subsequent dialogue.
3:3,5	Use of the term "Kingdom".
5:19	Subordination of the Son.
7:15	Jesus "unlettered".
7:23-7	"Rabbinic" arguments.
7:37	Untraceable "quotation".
13:13	Role of Annas (but see above on Passion-narrative generally).
13:25	Peter's question via the Beloved Disciple.
19:23	The seamless robe (could also be "B").

B. Cases where detail may have symbolic or theological motivation:

(1:19 etc.)	The "first week".
3:2	"By night".
5:5	"Thirty-eight years".
7:20	Bewilderment at reference to a plot.

C. Cases of possibly inferred detail:

2:13,23	Passover.
2:24-5	Jesus' knowledge of minds.
(4:52)	"The seventh hour".
6:16	The disciples' boat.
6:19	"25 or 30 stades".
6:22	The crowd's actions.
7:28	"Cried out".
7:45-52	Debate among Councillors.
10:23	"Winter".
11:30	Jesus "not yet in village".
11:56	The Jews' questionings.
13:11	Jesus' knowledge of Judas.
13:30	Disciples' ideas about Judas's exit.
13:30	"Night" (could also be "B").
18:3	Lanterns.
18:28	Refusal to enter Praetorium.
19:23	Parted garments (could also be "B").

D. Possible "emphasizing details";

2:6	Six jars.
11:6	"Two days longer".
11:17	"Four days".
12:3	"House filled with the scent".
12:5	"Three hundred denarii".

E. Details possibly meant to satisfy curiosity:

(4:40)	"Two days".

F. Details possibly a matter of style:

3:1	Use of name "Nicodemus".
7:40	Impact on crowds.
10:31	"Took up/brought stones".

G. Details of a kind paralleled in the Synoptists:

2:2	"His" disciples.
3:23	"Aenon": the Synoptists too give place-names. So also with e.g. 5:14; 6:59; 7:14; (8:20); 10:23,40; 11:54.

H. Inaccurate details:

(2.20)	"Forty-six years".
19:39	Weight of spices.

I. Inaccessible details:

12:6	Judas' dishonesty.

   I have not included passages discussed in detail in the main
text, nor ones from the Resurrection-narrative, which I think
requires separate treatment. References in brackets are to cases
where I think a strong case can be made out for *doubting* this
classification.

J. Cases where none of the above seem applicable:

1:39	"The tenth hour".
2:12	The visit to Capernaum.
4:46	References to Cana and Capernaum.
8:40	Use of ἄνθρωπον.
14:22	Judas's question.

Mark 11:25 and the Gospel of Matthew

Charles A. Wanamaker,
Abbey House,
Palace Green,
Durham, England.

Mark 11:25 has often provoked comments that it reflects knowledge of the Lord's Prayer by the evangelist Mark /1/. Recently, however, several scholars have maintained that Mark 11:25 shows various signs of literary dependence on the Gospel of Matthew /2/. Some have even taken this conception a step further, arguing, against all known manuscript evidence, that Mark 11:25 is an interpolation based on Matthew /3/. The leading exponent of the interpolation hypothesis, Dr. H.F.D. Sparks, avers, "A scribe with the Sermon on the Mount running in his mind, and with 'prayer' as a stitch-word, added vs. 25, concluding with words almost identical with Matt. 6:14" /4/.

It is my contention that the present strong support for the literary dependency view, in whatever form it takes, but especially the interpolation hypothesis, is unsupported by the evidence. The most compelling case for the literary dependence of Mark 11:25 on Matthew has been presented by Dr. Sparks in his arguments for the interpolation hypothesis. It is thus possible to examine both the interpolation theory and the more limited claims of literary dependence by carefully considering his position. As Dr. Sparks' position is examined, notice will be taken of others who use similar arguments in their varying claims, but it is unnecessary to treat them separately.

In support of the interpolation theory, Dr. Sparks presents four arguments which he thinks, *when taken cumulatively,* render Mark 11:25 every bit as textually uncertain as 11:26, even though no textual evidence exists for its absence from Mark. In the first place, he maintains that Mark 11:25 and 26 obviously belong together: they both refer to forgiveness, have similar phraseology, and have parallels found in the adjacent verses of Matt. 6:14 and

15. He therefore asserts, "If any suspicion is raised about the
genuineness of one of them, that suspicion is bound in some
measure to be communicated to the other". He finds this suspicion
well-founded because in Matt. 21:20-27 "the whole of the material
in Mark 11:20-33 is reproduced verse by verse, with only minor
variations, except for the two verses Mark 11:25, 26". This, he
argues, tends to indicate that both verses were absent from
Matthew's text of Mark /5/. The internal evidence of Mark 11:20-25
further strengthens the doubts concerning the genuineness of Mark
11:25. Through v.24 the subject under discussion is faith, but in
v.25 it becomes forgiveness; thus, according to Dr. Sparks, "We are,
in fact, left with the impression that the end of verse 24 is the
natural end of the section, to which something else has been added
as an afterthought". Finally, he maintains, "The style of verse 25
is very definitely Matthean not Markan". In support of this claim
he isolates several Matthean characteristics. The expression "your
Father who is in heaven" is a favourite phrase of Matthew's; Mark,
however, only uses it in 11:25-26. The word παραπτώματα is not
found elsewhere in the Gospels except in two passages in Matthew
(6:14-15 and 18:35). The phrase ἔχειν τι κατά τινος is found in
Matt. 5:23, but nowhere else in Mark; and lastly, the Jewish custom
of standing for prayer is mentioned in Matt. 6:5, but is not
mentioned elsewhere in Mark.

It is now necessary to examine the evidence presented by Dr.
Sparks for the interpolation hypothesis in order to assess the
strength of his case. Since those who argue for a less specific
form of literary dependence base their conclusions almost
exclusively on Dr. Sparks' fourth argument, particular attention
must be given to the details of this argument /6/.

The first argument of Dr. Sparks draws on the doubts concerning
v.26. These, he asserts, must invariably affect our view of v.25
because the two are obviously connected together. No one
seriously doubts that v.26 is an interpolation which originated as
a gloss based on Matt. 6:15; there is no logical reason, however,
ipso facto why the dubiousness of v.26 should be transferred to
v.25 when absolutely no manuscript evidence favours such doubt /7/.
It is not difficult to account for the interpolation of v.26 given
the obvious similarity of v.25b with Matt. 6:14. But the case of
v.25 is different. It is especially difficult to explain the
origins of v.25 as an interpolation, if, as Dr. Sparks suggests
in his third argument, there is a pronounced disjunction between
vv.24 and 25. Is it reasonable that a copyist should create a

saying from various bits and pieces of Matthew's Sermon on the
Mount /8/, and then put it in an inappropriate context, simply
using "prayer" as a stitch-word, as Dr. Sparks maintains? A
scribe capable of the gratuitous insertion of a composite,
Matthean-like saying after Mark 11:24, in all probability, would
have left other traces of his free style of transcription.

With respect to Dr. Sparks' third argument, careful
examination of vv.22-25 suggests the whole saying is a composite
unit /9/. Mark 11:20-25 forms the sequel to the cursing of the
fig tree in Mark 11:12-14. But vv.22-25 may easily be detached
from vv.20-21 which seem to provide a loose framework for the
saying of Jesus concerning faith. For this reason, Matthew has
noticeably tightened up the connection in his Gospel (cf. Matt.
21:20-22). The independence of vv.22-25 from the miracle story
of the cursing of the fig tree is supported by the complete
absence of reference to the fig tree in them. The focus of
attention is placed instead on the mountain mentioned in v.23:
"Whoever says to this mountain, 'Be taken up and cast into the
sea', and does not doubt in his heart, but believes what he says
will come to pass, it will be done for him". The phrase ἀμὴν λέγω
ὑμῖν ὅτι at the beginning of v.23 links the whole of v.23 with v.22
/10/; nevertheless, the connection is abrupt: "Have faith in God
(v.22). Truly, I say to you, whoever says..." This weakness in
the connection between vv.22 and 23 has led E. Haenchen to posit
that v.22 may be a redactional formulation of Mark to get from the
fig tree to the sayings about faith /11/. The shift from the
address of the disciples with the second person plural in v.22 to
the generalized address of v.23 (ὅς) is inappropriate to the
context of the inner circle of disciples and thus provides further
support for the independence of v.23 from v.22. Moreover, even
the content of v.23 is somewhat at variance with v.22. In v.22
Jesus instructs the disciples to "have faith in God", but in v.23
he gives a general command to believe what is asked will come to
pass /12/.

In its present connection v.24 is intended to interpret the
statement in v.23 by referring it to prayer that is accompanied
by faith. The reason a person is to believe what he says will
come to pass (v.23) is that he has asked it in prayer (v.24). It
is possible, however, for vv.23 and 24 to stand alone, and they
very well may have stood alone, since once again there is a change
of address from the generalized "whoever" of v.23 to the disciples
themselves (second person plural) in v.24. This observation is
strengthened by the fact that v.24 is joined to v.23 by the phrase

διὰ τοῦτο λέγω ὑμῖν which looks like another linking phrase /13/.

When vv.24 and 25 are isolated from v.23, the disparity between them is reduced considerably. Both deal with prayer, and both are addressed to the disciples in the second person plural. It is possible, but unprovable, that vv.24 and 25 were brought together prior to the bringing together of vv.23 and 24. At any rate, it is not impossible that v.25, dealing with prayer and the need to forgive, was brought together with v.24, dealing with faith in prayer, by Mark, if not by his sources. This possibility is at least as probable, if not more so, than Dr. Sparks' hypothesis about the composition and insertion of v.25 into the passage.

This still leaves the important problem raised not only by Dr. Sparks, but also by F.C. Grant, of why Mark 11:25 is not found in Matt.21:20-22. The answer is to be sought in redactional considerations.

On a number of occasions Matthew has excluded material from his Marcan source where Luke has not. Two examples will confirm this. Matt. 9:3 reads, "And behold, some of the scribes said to themselves, 'This man is blaspheming!'" Matthew's Marcan source reads, "Why does this man speak thus? It is blasphemy! Who can forgive sins but God alone?" (Mark 2:7; cf. Luke 5:21). A similar exclusion has occurred in Matt. 12:10 which asks, "Is it lawful to heal on the sabbath?" The Marcan version reads, "Is it lawful on the sabbath to do good or to do harm, to save life or to kill?" (Mark 3:4, cf. Luke 6:9). In both of these instances where Matthew has excised material, he also has altered the context to suit his own purposes. The same is true of Matt. 21:20-22 where he unifies and sharpens his Marcan source. When it is remembered that the idea of Mark 11:25 has been included already by Matthew in Matt. 6:14, where it is used to underscore and amplify the fifth petition of the Lord's Prayer, and that a similar thought occurs in 18:35 at the conclusion of the parable of the unforgiving servant, its absence from Matt. 21:20-22 is not totally surprising. Matthew probably realized that he had already preserved two traditions closely related to Mark 11:25 (three, if the fifth petition of the Lord's Prayer is counted), and that Mark 11:25 was somewhat loosely related to its present context. Therefore, he removed it from the faith saying of 21:20-22 when he reworked the material from Mark 11:20-25.

The final claim of Dr. Sparks, that the style of Mark 11:25 is Matthean in character, is the most widely supported of all his

arguments. For Dr. Sparks this is the final proof of an
interpolation based on Matthew's Gospel in general and upon Matt.
6:14 in particular. Others, as we have mentioned, such as
S.E. Johnson and H. Anderson, are more cautious, but see the
influence of Matthew on Mark, although it has left no textual
aberrations. Once again, however, the case is less straightforward
than is often thought. The features which are pointed to as
being Matthean are not necessarily so.

The assertion that παραπτώματα is Matthean is clearly
unsupportable. The word occurs twice in Matt. 6:14-15 (v.15 being
the negative form of v.14), but nowhere else in the best texts of
Matthew. Dr. Sparks' reference to Matt. 18:35 is unacceptable
(he himself places a question mark by it), since it does not occur
in the best early manuscripts, but only in the manuscripts of
C,W, and the *Koine* group. The interpolation of παραπτώματα into
Matt. 18:35 undoubtedly occurred as an expansion based on Matt.
6:14-15 since both deal with the need to forgive others. Thus we
are left with a word which is found twice in Matthew in back to
back verses, and once in Mark. Such a word can hardly be called
Matthean.

The case for the supposed Matthean character of ἔχειν τι κατά
τινος is no sounder since Matthew employs it only in 5:23 /14/.
This is also true of the reference to the Jewish custom of standing
for prayer in Matt. 6:5 (cf. Luke 18:11). In both of these instances,
as with the word παραπτώματα, it is incorrect to describe them as
Matthean. In theory it is just as possible that Matthew has been
influenced by Mark in his usage; though, in actuality, Matt. 5:23
and 6:5 are probably totally unrelated to Mark 11:25.

The derivation of the expression ὁ πατὴρ ὑμῶν ὁ ἐν τοῖς οὐρανοῖς
in Mark 11:25 from Matthew is crucial for anyone wishing to maintain
the theory of the literary dependence of Mark 11:25 on Matthew.
The specific designation of God as "your Father who is in the
heavens" is found in Matthew several times (cf. 5:16, 45; 6:1;
7:11) and with certain variation on a number of occasions (cf.
5:48; 6:4, 6, 8, 9, 14, 15, 18, 26, 32; 7:21, etc.). Mark uses
the word "Father" for God in relation to Jesus on three occasions
(8:38; 13:32; and 14:36), but 11:25 is the only place where God
is described as "*your* Father" and as "who is in the heavens". The
"your Father" designation occurs in Luke (cf. 6:36; 12:30, 32) and
cannot therefore be said to be unique to Matthew. Doubtless it
formed part of the common Gospel tradition originating in Jesus'
instruction to his disciples. This being the case, there is no

reason why Mark may not have found "your Father" in the Gospel
tradition and used the designation with respect to God. The
argument then would seem to focus on whether the phrase ἐν τοῖς
οὐρανοῖς belonged only to Matthew. However, Mark does know the
expression ἐν τοῖς οὐρανοῖς and employs it with respect to the
angels in 12:25 (ἄγγελοι ἐν τοῖς οὐρανοῖς; cf. 13:32), and the
powers in heaven in 13:25 (αἱ δυνάμεις αἱ ἐν τοῖς οὐρανοῖς).

So the question becomes whether Mark could have known and
therefore used the combination of ὁ πατηρ ὑμῶν and ὁ ἐν τοῖς
οὐρανοῖς αἱ ἐν τοῖς οὐρανοῖς). The answer seems to be yes.
Although Luke does not use the expression ὁ πατηρ ὑμῶν ὁ ἐν τοῖς
οὐρανοῖς. The answer seems to be yes. Although Luke does not
use the espression ὁ πατὴρ ὑμῶν ὁ ἐν τοῖς οὐρανοῖς, he does
have a Hellenized form, ὁ πατὴρ [ὁ] ἐξ οὐρανοῦ, in Luke 11:13
/15/. This a Q-saying in which the corresponding passage in
Matthew has ὁ πατὴρ ὑμῶν ὁ ἐν τοῖς οὐρανοῖς. The ὑμῶν is
probably a Matthean addition /16/, but the fact that Luke has
who is in the heavens" existed in the pre-Matthean Gospel
traditions /17/. The fact that the "Father in the heavens"
tradition is pre-Matthean means that it could have been available
to Mark when he wrote his Gospel, and therefore, little reason
exists to attribute its use in Mark 11:25 to the influence of
Matthew.

The position that Mark 11:25 reveals Matthean stylistic
influence is simply indefensible upon close examination. Not one
of the features normally pointed to as being Matthean need be so.
Several of the stylistic features put forward by Dr. Sparks,
notably his references to παραπτώματα, ἔχειν τι κατά τινος, and
the mention of standing for prayer, are incontestably no more
Matthean than Marcan. The question of the expression ὁ πατὴρ ὑμῶν
ὁ ἐν τοῖς οὐρανοῖς is more complex, but, as I have shown, there
is sufficient evidence to suggest that Mark could have used it in
complete independence from Matthew.

The above examination reveals the inadequacies of Dr. Sparks'
interpolation theory of Mark 11:25. Serious objections have been
raised with each point in his argument. He himself maintained his
interpolation hypothesis was defensible only when his four
arguments were taken cumulatively. The failure of all four of his
arguments to carry conviction must, of necessity, lead to the
rejection of the interpolation hypothesis. The inadequacy of each
point in his fourth argument regarding the presence of Matthean

stylistic features is also fatal for the less specific literary
dependence theory. In all probability, Mark 11:25 was an
independent Gospel logion which was brought together with 11:24
in the pre-Marcan period because of their common theme of
prayer /18/. When Mark 11:24 was joined with the saying about
moving mountains (11:23), in order to interpret it, 11:25 came
to look somewhat out of place. Matthew, in editing his Marcan
source, realized this and therefore dropped it from his sequence
in 21:20-22. His use of the tradition (or similar traditions)
elsewhere in his Gospel made the exclusion of Mark 11:25 an
obvious move in ordering the disjointed Marcan version of the
cursing of the fig tree.

NOTES

/1/   Cf. A.E.J. Rawlinson, *St. Mark* (London, 1925), pp. 158-59;
A.W.F. Blunt, *The Gospel according to St. Mark* (London, 1929),
p. 228; V. Taylor, *The Gospel according to St. Mark* (London, 1952),
p. 467; E. Lohmeyer, *Das Evangelium des Markus,* Meyer Kommentar 2
(Göttingen, 1951), p. 239; and W.L. Lane, *The Gospel according to
Mark* (Grand Rapids, 1974), p. 411.
/2/   Cf. S.E. Johnson, *A Commentary on the Gospel according to
St. Mark* (London,1960), p. 193; D.E. Nineham, *The Gospel of St.
Mark* (London, 1968[2]), p. 305, though he is sympathetic to the
interpolation hypothesis; and H. Anderson, *The Gospel of Mark*
(London, 1976), p. 269.
/3/   F.C. Grant, "The Gospel according to St. Mark", *The
Interpreter's Bible,* Vol. 7 (New York, 1951), p. 833; H.F.D.
Sparks, "The Doctrine of the Divine Fatherhood in the Gospels",
Studies in the Gospels. Essays in Memory of R.H. Lightfoot, ed.
by D.E. Nineham (Oxford, 1955), pp. 244-46; and R. Bultmann,
The History of the Synoptic Tradition, ET (Oxford, 1963), pp. 25,
61, though he does not attribute the interpolation specifically
to the influence of the Gospel of Matthew.
/4/   Sparks, "Divine Fatherhood", p. 245. His essay is directed
towards proving the thesis that divine Fatherhood in the Gospels
is never universalized. It has reference either to Jesus'
Messianic sonship or to the sonship of his disciples. This is
certainly correct, *contra* H.W. Montefiore, "God as Father in the
Synoptic Gospels", *NTS,* 3 (1956-57), pp. 31-46, who argues
unconvincingly that Jesus taught the universal Fatherhood of God.
The contention of Dr. Sparks that Mark knew only of the Messianic
Fatherhood of God hinges on whether Mark 11:25 should be excluded

from Mark or not.

/5/   Prior to Dr. Sparks, though Dr. Sparks does not seem to be
aware of the fact, Grant, *Interpreter's Bible,* 7, p. 833, argued
that Mark 11:25-26 was an interpolation based on its absence from
Matt. 21:20-27.

/6/   The style argument is primary to all who maintain literary
dependence. Grant, *ibid.*, p. 833, argues that "*your Father... who
is in heaven* and *forgive you your trespasses*" are Matthean
expressions. Johnson, *Mark*, p. 193, says, "The words *your Father
who is in the heavens* and *wrongdoings* are in Matthew's style, not
Mark's, and the text here may be influenced by Matthew 6:14-15;
the original form was perhaps 'that you also may be forgiven.'"
The style argument would also appear to lie behind the claim of
Nineham, *Mark*, p. 305, that Mark 11:25 is an insertion or at
least "much influenced, by Matthew 6", and the view of Anderson,
Mark, p. 269, that v. 25b reveals "the influence of Matt. 6:14".

/7/   Grant, *Interpreter's Bible,* 7, p. 833, maintains, "The
fact that the Syriac (sy^s) contains vs. 25 may afford a clue to the
way in which the interpolation took place; again and again this
MS reflects the powerful influence of the text of Matthew upon
that of Mark during the period down to, say, A.D. 325. Its
influence was limited mainly to insertions, and did little to
remold the Marcan text". This explanation begs the whole
question. The issue is not why Mark 11:25 is in sy^s, but why it is
not absent from other early reliable witnesses. On the basis of
the available manuscript evidence, it is hardly surprising that
Mark 11:25 is found in sy^s.

/8/   Namely, Matt. 5:23; 6:5 and 14.

/9/   Cf. E. Haenchen, *Der Weg Jesu* (Berlin, 1968^2), p. 391; Lane,
Mark, p. 409; and Bultmann, *Tradition*, p. 25.

/10/   Mark uses the phrase "truly I say to you" to join several
independent sayings to their current contexts. Cf. Mark 3:28;
9:1; 10:15; and 13:30.

/11/   Haenchen, *Der Weg*, p.391.

/12/   Further support for the independence of Mark 11:23 from its
present context may be provided by Matt. 17:20. This verse
preserves a saying about moving mountains by faith which is similar
to Mark 11:23; but there is no correspondence between the two
contexts. This may indicate the saying regarding the moving of
mountains by faith originally circulated without a narrative
framework. On the other hand, the differences between Mark 11:23
and Matt. 17:20 make it conceivable that these two verses
represent two independent sayings from the teaching traditions
of Jesus. Luke 17:6 adds further confusion to the situation. It
is similar to Matt. 17:20, but not to Mark 11:23. It speaks of a

sycamine tree instead of a mountain. From this it would be
possible to argue that Matt. 17:20 originally referred to the
sycamine tree but was subsequently influenced by Mark 11:23, or
its oral progenitor, so that the reference to the sycamine tree
was replaced by the mountain.

/13/ διὰ τοῦτο λέγω ὑμῖν is only used here in Mark, but it
does occur in Matt. 6:25 (cf. Luke 12:22); 12:31; and 21:43. In
the first two instances it appears to link independent material
with a larger discourse.

/14/ Elsewhere in the New Testament, Col. 3:13 has a very
similar phrase, τις πρός τινα ἔχειν, and interestingly enough,
it occurs in an exhortation to forgive others.

/15/ J. Jeremias, *The Prayers of Jesus*, ET (London, 1967),
pp. 38-39 says of this phrase in Luke, "One would expect ἐν rather
than ἐξ. This ἐξ is an instance of the attraction of a preposition
as the result of the presence of δώσει; it is a classical usage...
The flourish - and it is no more - does not in any way justify our
taking the phrase ἐξ οὐρανοῦ with the verb (δώσει)."

/16/ See *ibid.*, p. 37 where Jeremias argues, following A.T. Cadoux,
that this saying was originally addressed to the opponents of
Jesus, and so the ὑμῶν was not part of the saying. Luke thus has
preserved the more original form at this point. See also Jeremias,
The Parables of Jesus, ET (London, 1963), pp. 144-145.

/17/ G. Schrenk, "πατήρ", *TDNT*, vol. 5 (Grand Rapids, 1967),
pp. 985-86, is correct when he maintains, "It is obvious that Lk.
sometimes cuts down the longer 'Father in the heavens' as a Jewish
expression. Suspect is Lk. 6:35 where Mt. 5:45 has: υἱοὶ τοῦ
πατρὸς ὑμῶν τοῦ ἐν οὐρανοῖς... It is probable that Lk. made
changes consonant with his purpose of writing for the Greek world".

/18/ Although it cannot be treated at present, the claim that
Mark 11:25 reflects knowledge of the Lord's Prayer is no more sound
than the view of literary dependence. The frequent commands to
forgive in the early Christian traditions, the main link between
Mark 11:25 and the Lord's Prayer, renders this view unnecessary
(cf. Mark 11:25 with Matt. 5:23-24; 6:14-15; 18:35; Col. 3:13 and
Eph. 4:32).

Studia Biblica 1978: II, 339-350

Cultic Elements in the Fourth Gospel

J.T. Williams
United Theological College,
Aberystwyth

The title of this brief communication may appear to be a
little unusual. As far as I have gathered over a number of years,
the term "cultic" has not been employed very often with specific
reference to elements in the Fourth Gospel. Indeed, Bultmann
once remarked that there were hardly any specifically cultic
traits in the Johannine writings /1/. Nevertheless, I have
recently discovered that the German scholar, Franz Mussner, had
already used the term with reference to John's Gospel in his
article, "'Kultische' Aspekte im Johanneischen Christusbild" /2/
and that Elisabeth Schüssler Fiorenza has written recently on
"Cultic Language in Qumran and in the New Testament" /3/. I may
be allowed to add that my own views on the subject were formulated
long before I saw their work.

First of all it is necessary to define the term "cultic" as
it will be used in this paper, for it can be employed with
reference to a wide field of ideas. Ernst Lohmeyer claimed that
it includes "well-known words like priest, temple, sacrifice;
cultic concepts such as forgiveness of sins and holiness; ritual
stipulations such as those about purity and impurity; and
ecclesiastical practices such as observance of the Sabbath and
fasting" /4/. In this discussion we shall confine ourselves to
some of those cultic terms and ideas directly connected with the
sacrifices, the priesthood, the Temple, and the feasts of Judaism,
and with the ritual cleanliness practised by the Jews /5/.

Before proceeding we should also note that confusion can
arise concerning the use of the term "cultic" with reference to
the worshipping community of the early Christians. Thus we must
differentiate between our use of the word to denote Jewish worship
and practices, which appear to form part of the evangelist's
background, and "cultic" (or "liturgical") as used with reference
to the early Christian community, which also forms part of the

Gospel's background, but which will not be discussed in this paper /6/.

Of the cultic terms significant for the ritual of the Old Testament and reproduced in the LXX very few are not found in the New Testament /7/, and of those found a number appear in the Fourth Gospel. John /8/ does not seem to want to avoid using such language, especially, as we shall suggest, when he wishes to draw out the contrast between Jewish cultic practices and Christianity.

A contrast is often drawn between the sacrificial language in the First Epistle of John, which is used to describe the work of Christ (1:7,9 - καθαρίζειν; 2:1-2; 4:10 - ἱλασμός) and its comparative absence from the Gospel /9/. Whilst admitting that there is a greater emphasis upon the expiatory aspect of Christ's death in the Epistle, I would submit that sacrificial language is by no means eschewed by the Evangelist either. This is so with respect to Jn. 1:29 (36): "Behold the Lamb of God who takes away the sin of the world" /10/. Admittedly there is no lamb in the Old Testament which bears sin vicariously and thereby expiates it, and it would appear that the Passover Lamb was not an expiatory sacrifice /11/. Yet it was clearly a sacrifice /12/. Similarly in Isa. 53:10 the Suffering Servant is called an אָשָׁם ('āšām) (a guilt-offering), which the LXX renders here as περὶ ἁμαρτίας /13/. Thus, whatever choice is made between these two possible sources for John the Baptist's statement about Jesus, both are very much bound up with sacrificial ideas /14/. Although one's personal preference is for the figure of the Paschal Lamb, that does not necessarily mean that one should exclude entirely the influence of the Suffering Servant concept on the statement of Jn. 1:29(36).

As has often been argued, the Evangelist can be shown to have presented Jesus as the New Testament fulfilment of the Old Testament paschal lamb. This may be demonstrated by his timing of the crucifixion to coincide with the slaughtering of the paschal lambs in the Jerusalem Temple (Jn. 19:14). In this way he draws out the contrast between them and Jesus, the true Paschal Lamb. The Old Testament quotation in Jn. 19:36 is, I believe, also dependent upon Pentateuchal texts concerning the Paschal Lamb (Exod. 12:10 [LXX only], 46; Num. 9:12) rather than upon Ps.34(33): 20. Likewise there are other indications of the Evangelist's interest in paschal features in his Passion narrative (e.g. the hyssop of 19:29) and indeed elsewhere in the Gospel. Regrettably there is no opportunity for considering these any further here in this brief communication. For the same reason the whole question of the relation of the Passover and the other Jewish feasts to the structure and theology of the Gospel must be left aside.

The vicarious aspect of Christ's death is conveyed by John's use of the preposition ὑπέρ (Jn. 10:11,15; 11:50-2; 15:13; 17:19; 18:14; cf. I Jn. 3:16). In this respect he echoes the primitive Christian view that Jesus' death is a death ὑπέρ (Mk. 14:24; I Cor. 15:3; II Cor. 5:21; Gal. 3:13; Heb. 2:9, etc.), and it is especially connected with the verb διδόναι (Gal. 1:4; 2:20; Rom. 8:32; Eph. 5:2; Tit. 2:14; Lk. 22:19). In fact τιφέναι and διδόναι are synonymous, as the textual variants at Jn. 10:11,15 further indicate /15/. In addition to being depicted as the Good Shepherd who lays down his life for the sheep (10:1-18) /16/, Jesus is also described as the door (θύρα) of the sheepfold (Jn. 10:7,9) through which the sheep enter (cf. also 10:1-2), and θύρα also may symbolize Jesus' sacrificial death /17/. Further sacrificial significance can be discerned in Jn. 3:16 ("He gave his only-begotten son") where ἔδωκεν has the double meaning of sending (cf. I Jn. 4:9) and of committing to death (cf. Rom. 8:32 - παρέδωκεν) /18/.

Sacrificial language is, therefore, clearly employed in the Fourth Gospel to describe the meaning of the death of Christ /19/, but it is delineated mainly as a vicarious self-sacrifice and it is its voluntary nature which is particularly emphasized (Jn. 10:15, 17,18,21; and also 17:19) /20/. Nevertheless, its expiatory character is not entirely neglected as 1:29 and 11:50-2 appear to indicate /21/, this aspect having been added as a gloss by the Evangelist /22/.

In Jn. 6:51c, "And the bread which I shall give is my flesh on behalf of (ὑπέρ) the life of the world (cf. Lk.22:19b; I Cor. 11:24), we have a clear reference to the sacrificial death of Christ, for "to give up" to death means "to be sacrificed" /23/. When the Johannine Christ proceeds in the same discourse to talk of his flesh (σάρξ) and blood (αἷμα), he is in this context using terms from the language of sacrifice, for in the Old Testament בשׁר (bāśār) and דם (dām) describe the two component parts of the body, especially of a sacrificial victim, which were separated when it was killed (Gen. 9:4; Lev. 17:11,14; Deut. 12:23; Ezek. 39:17-18; cf. Heb. 13:11) /24/. In other words, Jesus is described here again as a sacrifice.

A connection may also be discerned in this chapter with the feast of Passover. There is a note at verse 4 that the feast was near. May there not be a connection between this fact and John's comparison of Jesus to the Paschal Lamb? /25/ Indeed, it has been

claimed that Jesus's words in Jn. 6 provide in a Johannine form
the words of institution of the Last Supper /26/, and it appears
likely from the Synoptic accounts of this event that Jesus compared
himself to the Paschal Lamb during the meal /27/.

In the LXX the verb ἁγιάζω frequently renders קָדַשׁ (qiddēš)
(Piel) and הִקְדִּישׁ (hiqdîš) (Hiphil) so that it is always a case of
cultic situations /28/. In the New Testament it is only in the
Fourth Gospel that the verb is applied to Jesus: ὃν ὁ πατηρ ἡγίασεν
(10:36) implies that the Father set him apart for his divine
purpose. It is not necessary to refer solely to a sacrificial
background here, but rather to a more general one including the
consecration and choice of prophets as well as of priests (cf.
Jer. 1:5; Ecclus. 45:4; 49:7). In Jn. 17:17a; "Sanctify (ἁγίασον)
them in the truth", and 17:19; "And for their sake (ὑπὲρ αὐτῶν) I
santify myself (ἁγιάζω ἐμαυτόν) that they also may be sanctified
(ἡγιασμένοι) in truth", Spicq has discerned a reference to the
consecration of Aaron and his sons to be priests in the service of
Yahweh: cf. ἁγιάσεις αὐτοὺς ἵνα ἱερατεύωσίν μοι (Exod. 28:41) /29/.
However, one would be in danger of reading too much of later
Christian thought into these verses if one were to regard the
disciples as priests here. The disciples are sanctified "in
truth": this means either in contrast to the old dispensation /30/,
or, more probably, in an ethical sense through knowledge of the
truth /31/. In verse 19 again we have sacrificial language in the
reference to Jesus' sanctifying himself "for their sake" (ὑπὲρ
αὐτῶν) /32/.

The view that Jesus is portrayed as High Priest in Jn. 17
("the high-priestly prayer" /33/) is really dependent upon two
things: (a) the verb ἁγιάζω; and (b) the general character of the
chapter. We have already indicated the close cultic connections
of ἁγιάζω: "The language", says Barrett, "is equally appropriate to
to the preparation of a priest and the preparation of a sacrifice;
it is therefore doubly appropriate to Christ" /34/. It has thus
been claimed that Jesus consecrates himself both as priest and as
victim /35/. Yet apart from pointing in this way to the
sacrificial associations of the word ἁγιάζω, I would not wish to ꜱ
go further and suggest that it leads inevitably to a high-priestly
Christology either in this chapter or in the Gospel as a whole.
It is rather in the general character of chapter 17 that we may
discern certain priestly traits for here Jesus is portrayed as one
praying on behalf of his disciples, interceding for them before
God (Jn. 17:9,15,20; cf. also 14:16; 16:26) /36/.

The reference in Jn. 19:23 to the seamless robe (χιτών) of

Jesus reminds us immediately of the Jewish high-priest's robe
(χιτών) /37/ described by Josephus (*Ant.iii*.7.4) /38/. χιτών is also
used by the LXX to render the Hebrew כְּתֹנֶת (kethōneth) (cf. also
כֻּתֹּנֶת) (kuttōneth) in descriptions of the high-priest's apparel at
Lev. 16:4 and Exod. 28:39: indeed the two words correspond
etymologically as well as in usage /39/. These facts appear to
indicate the Evangelist's desire to compare Jesus with the high
priest at this point. This may reflect a controversy about his
high-priesthood - a factor which is, of course, much more
significant for the Epistle to the Hebrews /40/. Nevertheless, the
Fourth Evangelist does not appear to have any theological reasons
for pursuing this interest in the high-priesthood of Christ any
further. Nor does the appelation ὁ Ἅγιος τοῦ θεοῦ (Jn.6:69) -
although possibly a Messianic title for Jesus /41/ - have any
connection with the priestly Messiah of Qumran /42/, where to my
knowledge this title from the Messiah of Aaron has not been
discovered /43/. Its basic meaning here is to describe Jesus'
particular relationship with God (cf. 10:36) /44/, and it also
hints at his consecration of himself as a sacrifice for the world
/45/.

A comparison of the Christologies of the Fourth Gospel and
the Epistle to the Hebrews shows that whereas that of the Epistle
is clearly orientated towards underlining the full humanity of
Jesus in order to support its argument concerning the adequacy of
his high-priesthood, the Gospel does not appear to be concerned
with such a high-priestly doctrine in its presentation of Jesus'
humanity. Again, despite frequent parallels between the two
writings with respect to the divinity of Christ (especially as
they are drawn out by Westcott and Spicq) /46/ there is no
specifically priestly aspect as regards the Johannine contribution.

The Christ of the Fourth Gospel is depicted cleansing the
Temple at the Feast of Passover (2:13ff.) at the beginning of his
ministry, and he proceeds to relate this action to the destruction
of the Temple (ναός) and also to the raising of it again within
three days. These statements are explained by the Evangelist, as
a member of the post-Resurrection Church, as corresponding to
Jesus' death and resurrection.

In a subsequent discourse (4:21ff.) it is explained that
worship is to be confined neither to Jerusalem nor to Mount
Gerizim; it is rather to be a worship of the Father in Spirit and
in truth: "In place of the Jerusalem Temple-worship comes that
worship in which the crucified and risen One assumes the central
place which the Temple holds in Jewish worship", says Cullmann,

and he refers to Jn. 1:14,51 /47/. With the replacement of the
old order by the new we are now to recognize the tabernacling
presence (Shekinah) of God in the Word made flesh (1:14). The
Greek σκηνοῦν corresponds to the Hebrew שָׁכֵן (šākēn), and it can
hardly be fortuitous that their consonants are similar /48/. It
is often pointed out that the LXX does not regularly translate שׁכן
(saken) by σκηνοῦν or κατασκηνοῦν /49/. This may be conceded, but
I suggest that the significant fact is this: when שָׁכֵן (šākēn)
describes the dwelling of God among his people Israel - and this
happens some 26 times in the Old Testament - the LXX renders the
Hebrew verb by κατασκηνοῦν 17 times and by σκηνοῦν once /50/.
Thus in this significant context the connection between the Hebrew
and the Greek verbs is unmistakable.

In Jn. 1:51, "You will see heaven opened and the angels of
God ascending and descending on the Son of man", Christ is seen as
the new and only mediator between God and man, replacing the holy
place sacred to the Jews /51/. Moreover, Odeberg pointed to the
appearance of the δόξα of Christ in this episode too /52/, thus
indicating another point of contact with the Shekinah.

So the view that the Temple is abolished and replaced by
Christ is very much to the fore in the Fourth Gospel and can be
traced in a number of places within it /53/. This theological
position differs radically from that of the Qumran sect in its
opposition to the Jerusalem Temple and its ritual /54/.

It may rightly be claimed that of the Gospels it is John's
which gives the greatest prominence to the symbolism of water /55/
(1:25-33; 2:1-10; 3:1-15,22f.; 4:1-26; 5:1-9; 7:38; 9:1-15;
13:1-16; 19:34). In Jn.2:6 and 3:25 the term καθαρισμός is used
in a cultic sense /56/. In 2:6 a contrast is implied between the
rites of Jewish purification which are ineffectual and Jesus'
miraculous power. It is, however, unlikely that further symbolism
is to be discerned in the mention of the six jars of water for the
Jewish rites, although the number six is only one short of the
seven which symbolizes perfection /57/. In 3:25 a dispute is
recorded between some of John the Baptist's disciples and a Jew
(or Jews, according to the text followed) about purification.
Clearly the Baptist saw the Jewish rites to be inadequate /58/,
but so was his own baptism recognized by him as being incomplete
(Jn. 1:33) /59/. Jn. 3:25 may refer back to 2:6 /60/, although
clearly in the latter there is no dispute about John's baptism.
These passages, therefore, indicate a contrast between Jesus'
purification and that both of the Jews and of John the Baptist
/61/.

I have suggested in this paper the the Fourth Gospel is
dependent in part upon the sacrificial system of Judaism for its
imagery and that sacrificial language concerning the death of
Christ is more prominent in the Gospel than has often been
recognised. Sacrificial language has also been detected in
relation to some of the titles given to Jesus in the Gospel,
notably the Lamb of God (1:29,36), the Shepherd and the Door (10:
1ff.), and possibly the Holy One of God (6:69). The Jerusalem
Temple and its worship, which was so significant in Judaism up to
70 A.D., is seen by the Evangelist to have been replaced by Jesus
himself, and his death and resurrection have made possible the
worship of the community formed as a consequence of these events.
God's tabernacling presence, the Shekinah, which was associated
with the Temple in Judaism, was now seen to rest on Jesus. The
paschal lambs of the Jewish ritual were now replaced by the
decisive death of Jesus, the Lamb of God. The Jewish rites of
purification are seen to be transcended by the life-giving water
brought by Jesus (4:10ff.; 7:37-9). These features of the theology
of the Fourth Gospel point clearly to the theme of the
spiritualization of the cult /62/ and of the terms associated with
it, and they indicate the Evangelist's firm belief that Judaism
has been replaced by Christ.

There is a general consensus today that Jewish influences
were considerable in the community where the Johannine tradition
was formed /63/, and the Evangelist may well have been addressing
himself to a Jewish audience (and this need not necessarily mean
a Palestinian Jewish audience, for the ceremonial of the Temple was
just as significant for Diaspora Jews) /64/. After all he often
draws a contrast between Jesus and Christianity, on the one hand,
and features of Judaism, on the other, and depicts Jesus as the
fulfilment of elements, including cultic elements, in Judaism.

NOTES

/1/   R. Bultmann, "Die Bedeutung der neuerschlossenen mandäischen
und manichäischen Quellen für das Verständis des
Johannesevangeliums", *Z.N.W.*, xxiv (1925), p.103.
/2/   Originally published in *Liturgisches Jahrbuch,* xiv (1964),
pp.185-200 (and reproduced in *Praesentia Salutis. Gesammelte
Studien zu Fragen und Themen des Neuen Testament* (Düsseldorf, 1967),
pp.133-45.
/3/   *C.B.Q.*, xxxviii (1976), pp.159-77.
/4/   *Lord of the Temple* (E.T. Edinburgh, 1961), p.24; cf. also

p.52, and his remarks about cultic references in Mark's Gospel on
p.5.
/5/   Cf. J. Jeremias' definition of cultic expressions: "terms
that are at home in the language of sacrifice" ("'This is My
Body'...", *Exp.T.*, lxxxiii (1971/2), p.202).
/6/   This latter usage with regard to John's Gospel is that set
forth by W.H. Raney, *The Relation of the Fourth Gospel to the
Christian Cultus* (Giessen, 1933), O. Cullmann, *Early Christian
Worship* (E.T. London, 1959); and A. Hamman, "Lignes maîtresses de
la prière johannique", in *The Gospels Reconsidered (Studia
Evangelica*, Oxford, 1960), pp.78-89.
/7/   They are ὁλοκαύτωσις (burnt-offering), σωτήριον (peace-
offering), σπονδή (drink-offering), and πλημμελ(ε)ία (guilt-
offering).
/8/   The use of the name "John" implies no particular view
regarding the authorship of the Fourth Gospel.
/9/   See e.g. C.H. Dodd, *The Johannine Epistles* (M.N.T.C., London,
1946), p.liv.
/10/   M. Barth, *Was Christ's Death a Sacrifice?* (Edinburgh, 1961),
pp.35-6, states that "four sacrificial interpretations of this
statement seem irreconcilably to confront two non-sacrificial
explanations". The former he lists as the Passover Lamb, the
second goat of the ritual of Atonement Day, the ram substituted for
Isaac, and the (daily) *Tamid*-offering in the Temple, while the
latter consist of the Suffering Servant of Isa.53:7 and C.H. Dodd's
suggestion that the idea of the Lamb of God has been derived from
Jewish apocalyptic (cf. *The Interpretation of the Fourth Gospel*
[Cambridge, 1953], pp.232,236-7).
/11/   Although T.C. Vriezen, *An Outline of Old Testament Theology*
(E.T. Oxford, 1958), p.27, can claim that "the idea of the
expiatory sacrifice was originally bound up with the Passover-
offering even in pre-Mosaic times".
/12/   G.B. Gray, *Sacrifice in the Old Testament* (Oxford, 1925),
pp.352-3. Cf. H.H. Rowley, *The Unity of the Bible* (London, 1968),
p.41: "It is true that the Passover was unlike other sacrifices,
but it was certainly regarded as a sacrifice". Cf. also Jeremias,
The Eucharistic Words of Jesus (E.T., London, 1966), p.225; R. de
Vaux, *Ancient Israel: Its Life and Institutions* (E.T. London, 1968),
p.441.
/13/   Contrast N.H. Snaith, *Mercy and Sacrifice* (London, 1953), p.
59, who held that "אָשָׁם (ʾāšām) in Isa. 53:10 has no connection
whatsoever with the guilt-offering of the Priestly Code and the
Second Temple". See, however, M. Burrows, *An Outline of Biblical
Theology* (Philadelphia, 1946), p.88; C.R. North, *The Suffering
Servant in Deutero-Isaiah* (London, 1956), p.126; Rowley, *The Faith
of Israel* (London, 1961), pp.46,97-8; and *The Unity of the Bible*,

pp,55-8; de Vaux, *Studies in Old Testament Sacrifice* (Cardiff, 1964), p.112, n.66; Dodd, *According to the Scriptures* (London, 1965), p.125; D. Kellermann, אשם (*'āšām*), in *T.D.O.T.*, i (E.T., 1974), p.435.

/14/ V. Taylor, *Jesus and His Sacrifice* (London, 1937), pp.226-7; Barth, *op.cit.*, p.9, n.1.

/15/ Cf. K. Romaniuk, "L'origine des formules pauliennes 'Le Christ s'est livré pour nous', 'Le Christ nous a aimés et s'est livré pour nous'", *Nov.Test.*, v (1962), p.70. Moreover, the expression τιθέναι τὴν ψυχήν (Jn.10:11,15,17,18) may well refer back to Isa. 53:10 (M.T.) (12, Aramaic) (Cf. Jeremias, *The Servant of God* [E.T. London, 1957], p.96). This supports further the sacrificial significance of the phrase in view of the cultic associations already noted of אשם (*'āšām*) in Isa.53:10.

/16/ Dodd commented that this section "provides the evangelist with the clearest and most explicit statement he has yet permitted himself upon the Passion of Christ as a voluntary and vicarious self-sacrifice" (*Interpretation*, p.360).

/17/ L.S. Thornton, *The Common Life in the Body of Christ* (London, 1941), p.417; P.W. Meyer, "A Note on John 10.1-18", *J.B.L.*, lxxv (1956), p.234; W.A. Meeks, *The Prophet-King: Moses Traditions and the Johannine Christology* (Leiden, 1967), p.68,n 2.

/18/ Cullmann, "Der johanneische Gebrauch doppeldeutiger Ausdrücke als Schlüssel zum Verständis des vierten Evangeliums", *Th.Z.*, iv (1948), p.366; R.H. Lightfoot, *St. John's Gospel*, ed. C.F. Evans (Oxford, 1960), p.259, n.1.

/19/ Cf. J. Denney, *The Death of Christ* (London, 1902), pp.254-63; Taylor, *The Atonement in New Testament Teaching* (London, 1940), p.201; W.H. Rigg, "The Atonement in the Johannine Writings", in *The Atonement in History and in Life*, ed. L.W. Grensted (London, 1929), p.158; Cullmann, *The Christology of the New Testament* (E.T., London, 1963), p.70.

/20/ See the remarks of Dodd quoted above in n.16.

/21/ A.E. Brooke, *The Johannine Epistles* (I.C.C., Edinburgh, 1912), pp.xxi-xxii.

/22/ According to Lightfoot, *op.cit.*, pp.96-7, a reference to the work of Christ in removing the sin of the world was added to the paschal symbolism. With regard to 11:50-2, Dodd, *More New Testament Studies* (Manchester,1968), p.63, claimed that the λύτρον-concept found here came to the Evangelist from a Jewish-Christian circle.

/23/ Denney, *op.cit.*, p.258; G.H.C. MacGregor, *The Gospel of John* (M.N.T.C., London, 1928), pp.152-3; D. Mollat, "The Sixth Chapter of Saint John", in *The Eucharist in the New Testament* (E.T. London, 1964), p.146.

/24/ Rabbinic examples in Jeremias, *Eucharistic Words*, p.221,

n.10. Generally, of course, the words together refer to man's
living body compounded of flesh and blood (cf. Strack-Billerbeck,
i, pp.730-1).
/25/ So, for example, E.C. Hoskyns, *The Fourth Gospel,* ed. F.N.
Davey (London, 1940), pp.315,335; J.M. Creed, "Sacraments in the
Fourth Gospel", *The Modern Churchman,* xvi (1926), p.372; J.K.
Howard, "Passover and Eucharist in the Fourth Gospel", *S.J.T.,*xx
(1967), pp.334-5.
/26/ J.H. Bernard, *The Gospel According to St. John* (I.C.C.,
Edinburgh, 1928), p.clxx.
/27/ Jeremias, *Eucharistic Words,* p.223.
/28/ O. Procksch, ἁγιάζω, *T.W.N.T.,* i,p.112 (E.T., p.111).
/29/ C. Spicq, *L'Épître aux Hébreux,* i (Paris, 1952), p.122; cf.
also "Priestly Virtues in the New Testament", *Scripture,* x (1958),
pp.10-11.
/30/ Cf. W. Heitmüller, *Das Johannes-Evangelium* (Göttingen,
1918), p.165; A. Loisy, *Le Quatrième Évangile* (Paris, 1921),
p.448; Hoskyns, *op.cit.,* p.598.
/31/ E.D. Freed, "The Meaning of Worship in John 4:23f.", in
Search the Scriptures, ed. J.M. Myers et al.(Leiden, 1969), pp.
37-8, denies any real connection between truth in this passage
and truth in 4:23f., which he in fact interprets in an ethical
sense *(ibid.,* pp.34-5, 46-8).
/32/ F.-M. Braun, *Jean le Théologien,* ii (Paris, 1964), p.83,
believes the verb ἁγιάζω has been intentionally used by the
Evangelist, who wishes to relegate the Israelite cult to the
remains of an economy which has been surpassed and to point out
that Jesus is to be identified with the new Temple and that his
superiority over the ancient schema was signified by the
excellence of the consecration which has been stamped upon him. I
fail to see the contrast implied in connection with this verb,
although below I shall suggest a contrast between the old Temple
and Christ as the new Temple.
/33/ This particular description is in fact no older than the
sixteenth century when Chytraeus, a Protestant theologian, first
used it and it has been in general use ever since. In fact Clement
of Alexandria had recognized Jesus as High Priest here long before
that (*P.G.* lxxiv. 505).
/34/ C.K. Barrett, *The Gospel According to St. John* (London,
1958), p.426; cf. also W. Bauer, *Das Johannes-Evangelium* (H.B.N.T.,
Tübingen, 1925), p.199.
/35/ Bernard, *op.cit.,* p.575.
/.36/ Cf. G.B. Caird, "The Will of God: In the Fourth Gospel",
Exp.T., lxxii (1960/1), p.117. According to A. Richardson, *An
Introduction to the Theology of the New Testament* (London, 1958),
p.200, when the Johannine Christ claims to be the Way (14:6), there

is a reference to his work as priest through whom we have access
to God. Cf. also Spicq, *Hébreux*, i, pp.123-4. There is, however,
a danger here lest one should read the ideas of the Epistle to the
Hebrews about Jesus as "the new and living way" (10:20), who by
his sacrificial death opens the way, into the exegesis of the
Johannine statement.

/37/ So, for example, B.F. Westcott, *The Gospel According to
St. John* (London, 1894), p.275; Loisy, *op.cit.*, p.485; Hoskyns,
op.cit., p.636; F.-M. Braun, *Jean le Théologien*, iii (Paris, 1966),
p.166, n.3; Barrett, *op.cit.*, p.457.

/38/ Cf. also *B.J.* v.5.7.

/39/ Strack-Billerbeck, i, pp.343,565-6; Barrett, *op.cit.*, p.457.

/40/ B. Lindars, *New Testament Apologetic* (London, 1961), pp.91-2.

/41/ Taylor, *The Names of Jesus* (London, 1953), p.80; Barrett,
op.cit., pp.59, 253; P. Ricca, *Die Eschatologie des Vierten
Evangeliums* (Zurich, 1966), p.77, n.189; J.N. Sanders, *The Gospel
According to St. John*, ed. B.A. Mastin (B.N.T.C., London, 1968),
p.199. Contrast Bultmann, *Das Evangelium des Johannes* (Göttingen,
1959), p.344 (E.T. Oxford, 1971, p.449).

/42/ *Pace* G. Friedrich, "Beobachtungen zur messianischen
Hohepriestererwartung in den Synoptikern", *Z.T.K.*, liii (1956),
p.293.

/43/ Cf. H. Braun, "Qumran und das Neue Testament", *Th.R.*,
xxviii (1962), p.215.

/44/ Cf. Bultmann, *op.cit.*, p.345 (E.T., p.450); J. Gnilka,
"Die Erwartung des messianischen Hohenpriesters in den Schriften
von Qumran und im Neuen Testament", *R.Q.*, ii (1960), p.423.

/45/ See the following verses (6:70-1) with their reference to
the betrayal, and so ultimately the Passion; cf. Bultmann, *op.cit.*,
p.345 (E.T., p.450).

/46/ Westcott, *The Epistle to the Hebrews* (London, 1889), pp.
424-6; Spicq, *op.cit.*, i, pp.113,287-91.

/47/ *Early Christian Worship*, p.73; cf. also "L'opposition contre
le Temple de Jérusalem, motif commun de la théologie johannique
et du monde ambiant", *N.T.S.*, v (1958/9), p.170; and "L'Évangile
johannique et l'histoire du salut", *N.T.S.*, xi (1964/5), p.118.
Spicq, *op.cit.*, i, pp.106-7, may be exaggerating when he claims to
recognize a contrast between the animals sacrificed in the Temple
and the Christ sacrificed in the new "cult". Yet in view of the
festal occasion, the Passover, there may be implied here a
contrast between these sacrificial animals and the true Paschal
Lamb because of the undoubted prominence of paschal symbolism in
this Gospel.

/48/ Both Delitzsch and the version of Ginsburg and Salkinson use
the Hebrew word שׁכן in translating Jn. 1:14: cf. T.F. Glasson,
Moses in the Fourth Gospel (London, 1963), p.65.

/49/ By, for example, Barrett, *op.cit.*, p.138; and Gnilka, *art. cit.*, p.422.

/50/ H.B. Swete's text of the LXX was used in this assessment of the evidence.

/51/ Cf. Y. Congar, *The Mystery of the Temple* (E.T., London, 1962), p.134; B. Gärtner, *The Temple and the Community in Qumran and the New Testament* (Cambridge, 1965), p.118; R.J. McKelvey, *The New Temple* (Oxford, 1969), p.77.

/52/ H. Odeberg, *The Fourth Gospel* (Uppsala, 1929), p.36.

/53/ Cullmann, *art.cit.*, *N.T.S.*, v,p.168.

/54/ Cf. Schüssler Fiorenza, *art.cit.*, pp.159-77.

/55/ Cf. F.-M. Braun, "L'arrière-fond judaïque du Quatrième Évangile et le Communauté de l'Alliance", *R.B.*, lxii (1955), p.23; R.E. Brown, "The Qumran Scrolls and the Johannine Gospel and Epistles", in *The Scrolls and the New Testament,* ed. K. Stendahl (London, 1958), p.202; Sanders, *op.cit.*, p.91, n.2.

/56/ F. Hauck, καθαρισμός, *T.W.N.T.*, iii, p.433 (E.T., p.429).

/57/ This is proposed by J. Marsh, *The Gospel of Saint John* (Harmondsworth, 1968), pp.58-9; cf. also Barrett, *op.cit.*, p.160.

/58/ Marsh, *op.cit.*, p.145.

/59/ Cf. Dodd, *Interpretation*, pp.310-12.

/60/ Marsh, *op.cit.*, p.199.

/61/ In fact, the concept of purity is prominent in the Gospel: cf. 3:25; 13:10-11; 15:2-3). See Hauck, καθαρός, *T.W.N.T.*, iii,p. 430 (E.T., p.426). Contrast H. Braun, *art.cit.*, p.196, who says it is peripheral for John. I cannot agree with L. Mowry, "The Dead Sea Scrolls and the Background for the Gospel of John", *B.A.*, xvii (1954), p.90, that there is definite polemic against the Qumran sect in Jn. 2:1-11 regarding ritual washing.

/62/ What is the correct term to use in this context? Is it to be "spiritualization" or, as G. Klinzing, *Die Umdeutung des Kultus in der Qumrangemeinde und im Neuen Testament* (Göttingen, 1971), suggests, "re-interpretation"? According to Schüssler Fiorenza, *art.cit.*, p.162, n.12, "the New Testament writers do not so much re-interpret cultic institutions and terminology but express a new reality in cultic language".

/63/ "Were the major ideas and symbols of Johannine Christianity derived from Judaism? An impressively broad consensus exists today that this question must be answered in the affirmative" (W.A. Meeks, "'Am I a Jew?' Johannine Christianity and Judaism", in *Christianity, Judaism and Other Greco-Roman Cults*, ed. J. Neusner, i (Leiden, 1975), p.167).

/64/ Cf. W.D. Davies, *Paul and Rabbinic Judaism* (London, 1956), p.231.